2020

University of Pennsylvania
Stuart Weitzman School of Design
Department of Architecture

212 Meyerson Hall
210 S. 34th Street
Philadelphia, PA 19104-6311

19

Weitzman
SCHOOL OF DESIGN
UNIVERSITY *of* PENNSYLVANIA

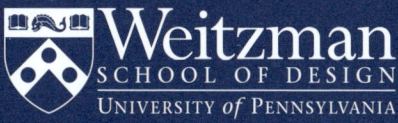

215.898.5728
www.design.upenn.edu/architecture/graduate/info
archdept@design.upenn.edu

20

INTRODUCTION

Looking back, this was a special and difficult year, a year in which we taught half of the spring semester online due to COVID-19, and we were challenged to change the way we think, operate, and communicate. It was also a year in which we learned valuable lessons and often got closer to each other. We held final reviews, a commencement, and celebrated a graduation party all virtually. The Year End Show went online as well, and was featured for the first time with its own website: https://www.design.upenn.edu/yes2020.

Knowing that internships and employment were not easy to obtain this summer, the Department of Architecture and *Surface Magazine* launched a unique and free Summer School at Penn with a phenomenal, diverse list of speakers that included furniture designers, graphic designers, architects, and doctors. The theme for the competition was inspired by our Weitzman students' recent involvement in the 3D-printing of nearly 1,000 face shields for Penn Medicine first responders, guided by Associate Professor Franca Trubiano, Director of Operations Karl Wellman, and Fabrication Lab Manager Dennis Pierattini. For the Summer School, the 75 participating students were charged with designing a mobile medical testing station. It was also a competition; seven winning proposals received awards and were published on our website, by *Surface Magazine*, and by Penn Today. While most proposals were developed by a team, the impressive winning proposal was just a single student: Hanqing Yao, with her proposal FLIP IT.

OPEN SOURCE

This year Pressing Matters 9 was completely reimagined. We focused on sharing; and changed the concept and layout to more clearly represent how in recent years we have integrated expertise and content from our Technology, History & Theory, Professional Practice, and Visual Studies courses into our Design Studios. This follows our concept of design-research, an integral approach of critical thinking, rigorous research, and a deep understanding of the complex layers of architecture, to better prepare our students for the challenges ahead.

NEW PROGRAM

We also launched the one-year MSD-RAS program, directed by Assistant Professor Robert Stuart-Smith. The Master of Science in Design: Robotics and Autonomous Systems aims to critically develop novel approaches to the design, manufacturing, construction, use, and lifecycle of architecture through creative engagement with robotics, material systems, and design-computation. Students will develop skills in advanced forms of robotic fabrication, simulation, and artificial intelligence, in order to develop methods for design that harness production or live adaptation as a creative opportunity. This is an excellent addition to our already existing MSD programs: the MSD-EBD directed by Professor Bill Braham and the MSD-AAD directed by Professor Ali Rahim.

AWARDS

Established in 2017 by a generous gift from alumna Lori Kanter Tritsch and Penn Trustee and Wharton alumnus William P. Lauder, the Kanter Tritsch Prize is awarded annually to a second-year Master of Architecture student in the form of a $50,000 scholarship, and a medal to a practicing architect or architects for leadership in energy and architectural innovation. This year's Student Prize was awarded to Patrick Danahy (MArch'20) and this year's medal was awarded to alumnus and New York-based architect A. Eugene Kohn, FAIA RIBA JIA, Founder and Chairman of Kohn Pedersen Fox Associates.

We are proud that Professor David Leatherbarrow was named as the 2020 recipient of the AIA/ACSA Topaz Medallion for Excellence in Architectural Education. The Topaz Medallion honors an individual who has been intensely involved in architecture education for more than a decade and whose teaching has influenced a broad range of students. Assistant Professor for Architectural History and Theory Sophie Hochhäusl was appointed the Princeton Mellon Fellow in Architecture, Urbanism, and the Humanities for the 2020-2021 academic year, and she was also the recipient of the Provost Grant in Excellence through Diversity. Assistant Professor Masoud Akbarzadeh received Silver A' Design Award by the International Design Academy, and also received the National Science Foundation CAREER Award. Our students were also recognized: former student Portia Malik was one of five winners in the London Festival of Architecture's contest to design a series of benches across the Royal Docks in London's East End. Portia's project, Peekaboo, is located at the dock edge in front of The Crystal.

NEW FACULTY

This fall we are joined by Billie Faircloth as adjunct professor. Billie is a partner at KieranTimberlake, where she leads transdisciplinary research, design, and problem-solving processes across fields including environmental management, chemical physics, materials science, and architecture. In January 2021 we look forward to welcoming Ferda Kolatan as associate professor in architecture on tenure track and Laia Mogas-Soldevila as assistant professor on tenure track to our standing faculty. Laia is a licensed architect and experienced researcher interested in biological material systems and novel material practices in design. She completed her PhD at Tufts University's Biomedical Engineering SilkLab, and worked at the MIT Media Lab with Neri Oxman.

This summer we witnessed protests supporting Black Lives Matter worldwide. We recognize our profound obligation as a school to support diversity, equity, and inclusion in the Weitzman community and the professions we help sustain. We will continue our focus on promoting diversity, equality, social equity, excellence in design, and rigorous research. We created a DEI committee for the Department of Architecture, and a study plan that elaborates on the expanded role of the architect, beyond that of the designer, where the architect is considered an expert, a rigorous researcher, and a team leader.

In this time of food and water scarcity and environmental and climate challenges, we train our students to be active participants in the global discourse towards a better, safer, and cleaner world. We pride ourselves on the inclusion of diverse external experts, not only in our design studios, but also through annual symposia, weekly lectures, and regular design reviews. Our vast group of visiting critics add to our own dedicated and talented faculty, that every year challenge us to think harder, move faster, and create a better world.

Pressing Matters is published by ORO Editions and designed by WSDIA. It is also available as an e-book. We hope you enjoy our latest publication and that you will visit us in the near future.

> Winka Dubbeldam, MSAAD
> Miller Professor and Chair
> Department of Architecture
> Weitzman School of Design
> University of Pennsylvania

CONTENTS

INTRODUCTION	4
RESEARCH LABS	10–13
FOUNDATION 501	
	14–64
CURIOUS CABINETS	65–73
FOUNDATION 502	
	74–124
EVENTS	112–113
CORE 601	
	126–180
EVENTS	181
CORE 602	
	182–236
FALL NEWS	237–241

ADVANCED 701
COVID-19

242–324
325

ADVANCED 704
EVENTS

326–396
397–401

MSD–AAD

402–409

MSD–EBD

410–423

IPD

424–427

DOCTORAL DEGREE
SPRING NEWS

428–431
432–437

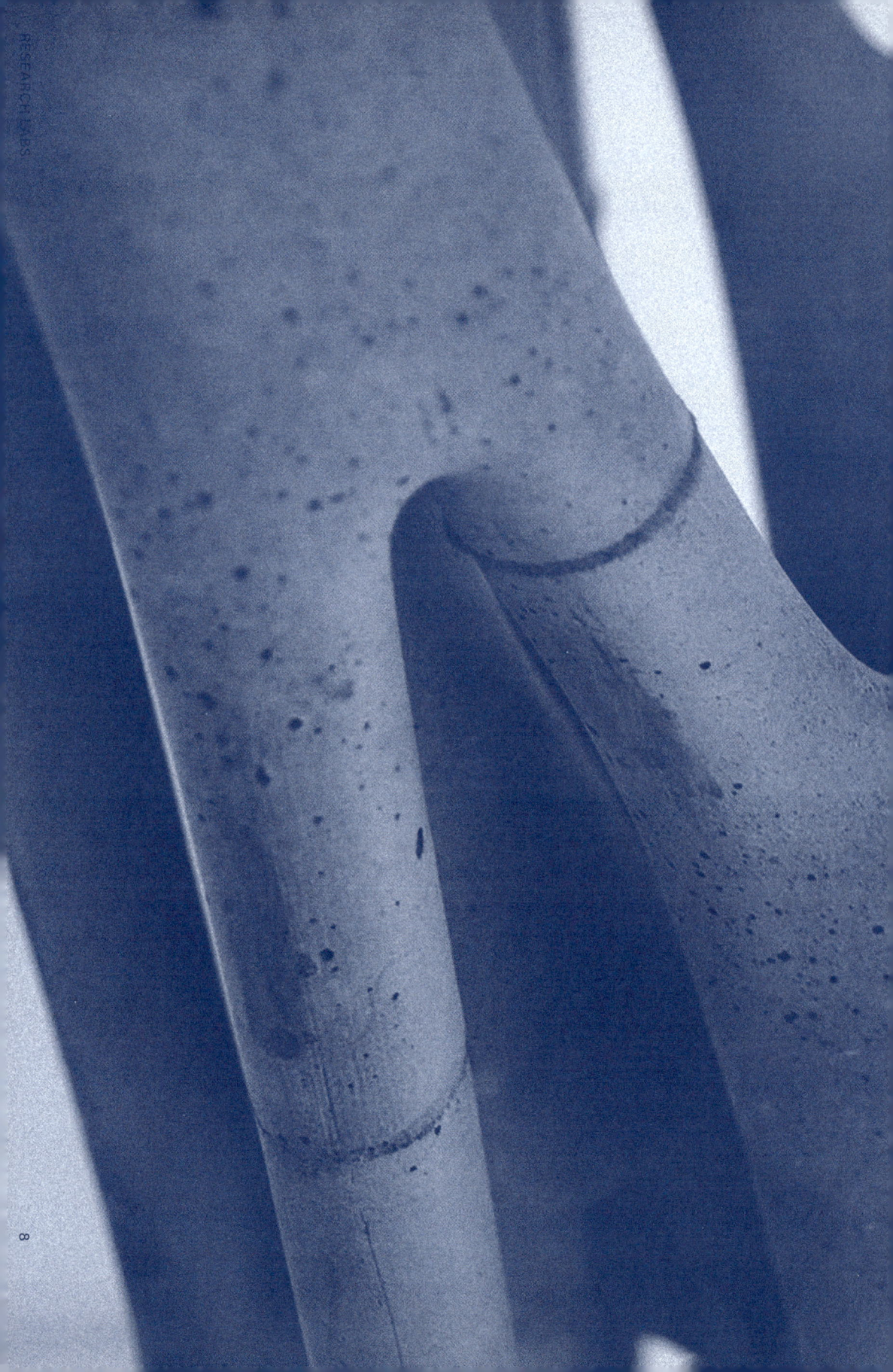

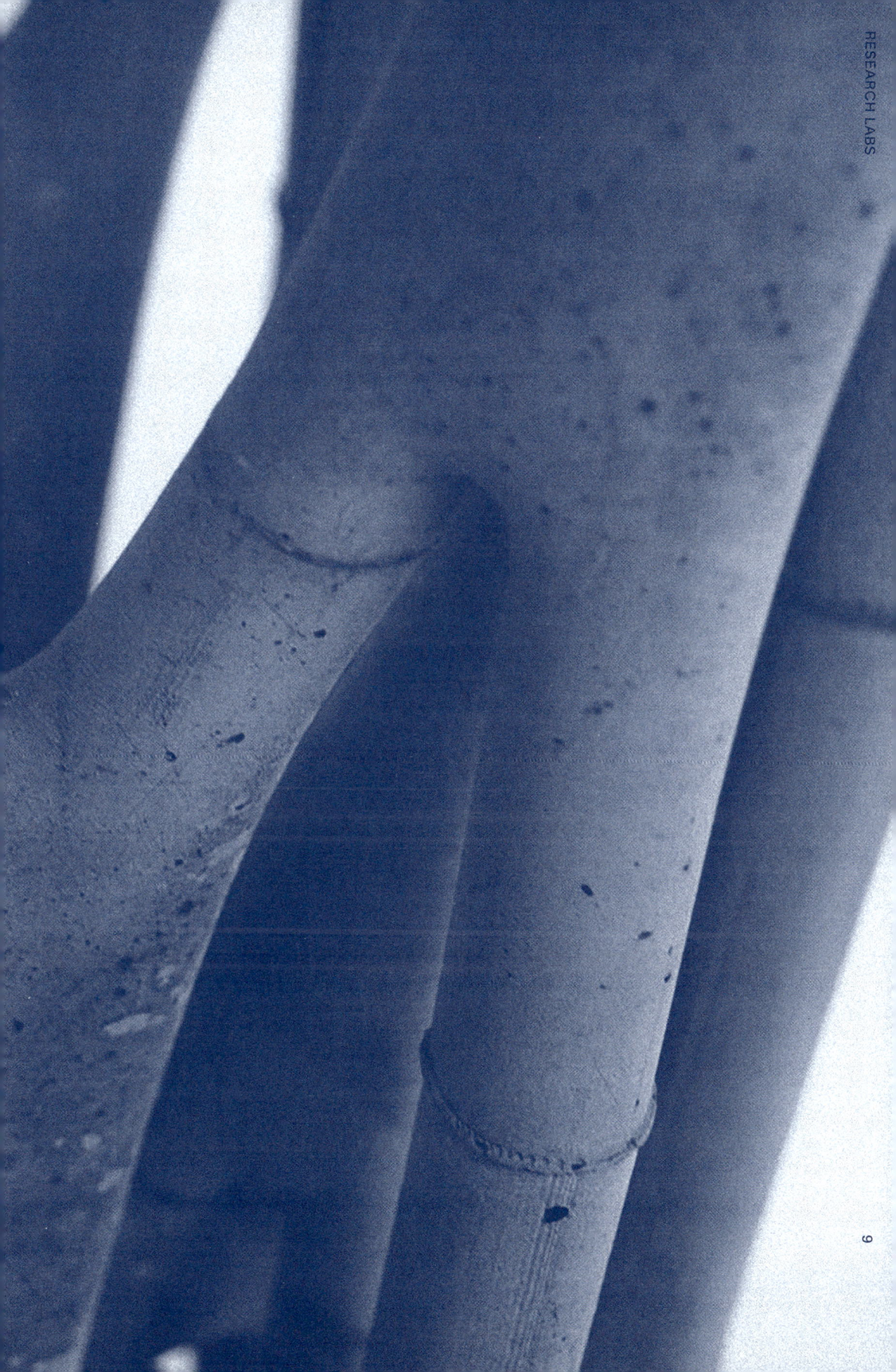

AUTONOMOUS MANUFACTURING LAB
Robert Stuart-Smith, Director

The Autonomous Manufacturing Lab (AML) explores the integration of design and production within robotic processes of building manufacturing. The economic and environmental cost of building is able to be reduced through increases in the intricacy and complexity of design and engineering solutions. This, however, is dependent on the design possibilities and production efficiencies of building manufacturing processes. Beyond industrial automation, autonomous and semi-autonomous manufacturing are able to provide embodied forms of decision making, providing new opportunities for bespoke fabrication where adaptive processes can actively engage with the formation and physical manipulation of materials in novel ways. The interdisciplinary AML lab aims to develop innovative methods of manufacturing that leverage real-time robotics, computation, sensor and computer vision technologies within generative design processes, in order to expand the creative and practical possibilities of design through a direct engagement with the physical world of manufacturing. AML is part of Weitzman's Advanced Research and Innovation Lab (ARI).

Robert Stuart-Smith is the Director of Penn's Autonomous Manufacturing Lab (AML-PENN), Assistant Professor of Architecture, and Program Director for Penn's new Masters of Science in Design in Robotics and Autonomous Systems (MSD-RAS). Stuart-Smith's research explores architecture through robotic manufacturing and generative design, specializing in multi-agent systems and behavior-based computation. He also co-directs AML-PENN's sister lab, AML-UCL, in the

Bespoke Fabrication

Robotic Manufacturing has enabled industry to advance from mass-production to mass-customization (Post-Fordist production). Flexible technologies relatively agnostic of specific designs, allow for greater diversity and experimentation within the design fields. Design potentials however, remain limited to the material processes and manufacturing techniques utilized. Through the development of novel techniques of manufacture, the AML seeks to provide customized, tailored responses to design and production that integrate material processes of formation with novel methods of robotic programming.

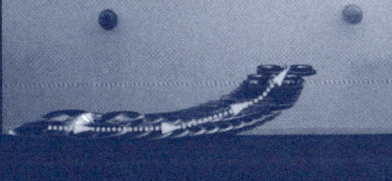

Generative Design Computation

Robotic manufacturing enables an increase in the complexity and intricacy of building designs, which in turn, presents challenges to how designs are developed and evaluated. Generative Design Computation exploits the creative potential of computing, to develop novel solutions to relatively complex problems. The AML develops computational processes that address various pragmatic, performative, and creative design concerns. These methodologies aim to incorporate bespoke manufacturing logistics whilst creating qualitative design affects that arise through various material processes of production.

Behavior-Based Robotics

Sensor and computer vision technologies enable robotic systems to operate with feedback from their environment, providing "situated" awareness to actions. While most robotic fabrication involves explicitly described (preprogrammed) tasks, the lab's research also develops event-based decision making capabilities that enable bespoke manufacturing processes to be adaptive to various physical and computational circumstances.

Department of Computer Science at University College of London, where he is currently undertaking funded research into autonomous multi-robot construction.
Patrick Danahy [Research Assistant] is a third year MArch student and recipient of the 2019 Kanter Tritsch Prize in Energy and Architectural Innovation. **Mariana Righi** [Research Assistant] is a lab-operator for Penn's ARI Robotics Lab, and Adjunct Professor at Northeastern University. Mariana holds a Masters in Advanced Architectural Design from Penn's Weitzman School of Design.

POLYHEDRAL STRUCTURES LAB
Dr. Masoud Akbarzadeh, Director

Background

Polyhedral Structures Lab (PSL) is a research unit concentrating on advancing structural geometry and construction technologies within the Advanced Research & Innovation Lab (ARI) at the School of Design, University of Pennsylvania. ARI is led by Professor and Chair of Architecture Winka Dubbeldam and comprises a wide variety of research groups: the Autonomous Manufacturing Lab (Assistant Professor of Architecture Robert Stuart-Smith), the Polyhedral Structures Lab or PSL (Assistant Professor of Architecture Masoud Akbarzadeh), and the Baroque Topologies Lab (Associate Professor of Architecture Andrew Saunders), with additional initiatives in development.

Interdisciplinary collaborations

PSL is an interdisciplinary research lab connecting architecture, structural engineering, computer science, mathematics and material science to enrich architectural geometry and to reconcile function, form, and technology. PSL aims to bridge the gap between architecture and structural design using geometry, which is considered the common language between these two inextricable disciplines. At PSL we intend to push the boundaries of research in the field of architectural technology, and we are continually looking for teams and individuals to interact with across various academic disciplines.

Professional/Industrial Collaborations

PSL is highly interested in collaborating with professional practices and industrial partners to apply the innovative research in practice and construction industries. Some of the current companies and industrial partners include SOM, Summum, Sika, Quarra Stone, and 3M.

Research Interests

The research interests of the lab include but are not limited to innovative construction techniques, robotic fabrication, computational design, 2D/3D graphic statics, geometry-based structural design techniques, form-finding techniques, lightweight structures, spatial structures, structural details, and much more.

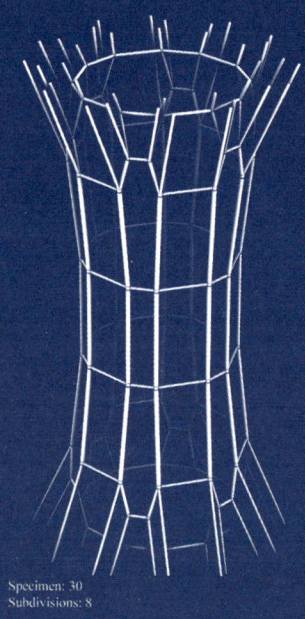

Specimen: 30
Subdivisions: 8

Geometric Structural Design Methods

One of the main concentrations of the lab is to research and contribute to the geometry-based structural design methods for its intuitive characteristic and apply them in the design and fabrication of efficient, elegant, and non-conventional structural forms. Geometry-based structural design methods have a history as early as the sixteenth century, and they continue to be

Dr. Masoud Akbarzadeh is a designer with a unique academic background and experience in architectural design, computation, and structural engineering. He is an Assistant Professor of Architecture in Structures and Advanced Technologies and the Director of the Polyhedral Structures Laboratory (PSL). He holds a D.Sc. from the Institute of Technology in Architecture, ETH Zurich, where he was a Research Assistant in the Block Research Group. He holds two degrees from MIT: a Master of Science in Architecture Studies (Computation) and a MArch, the thesis

used and developed until today. Graphic statics is a renowned method that has been developed and practiced by many researchers, engineers, and architects since 1864. Masoud's Ph.D. research, 3D Graphic Statics using Reciprocal Polyhedral Diagrams, has started a new direction in the development of the existing methods of graphic statics in three dimensions based on a historic proposition by Rankine in Philosophical Magazine in 1864.

Robotic/Innovative Fabrication Research

The state-of-the-art robotic facilities at Weitzman allow pushing the boundaries of conventional construction methods and develop new fabrication techniques for challenging geometries and structural systems.

Material Design

We are interested in revisiting the conventional construction materials and detailing and devise innovative techniques to go beyond the existing construction/assembly methods.

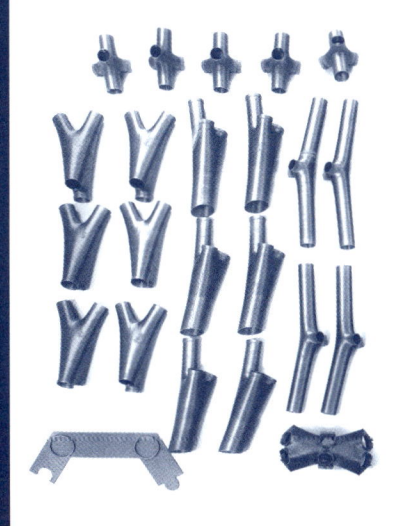

Computational Design

Computational methods are at the core of our research projects from theory to construction. We consistently develop computational tools and methods relevant to our research. We borrow concepts and from mathematics, geometry, and computer science and adapt them for design research applications.

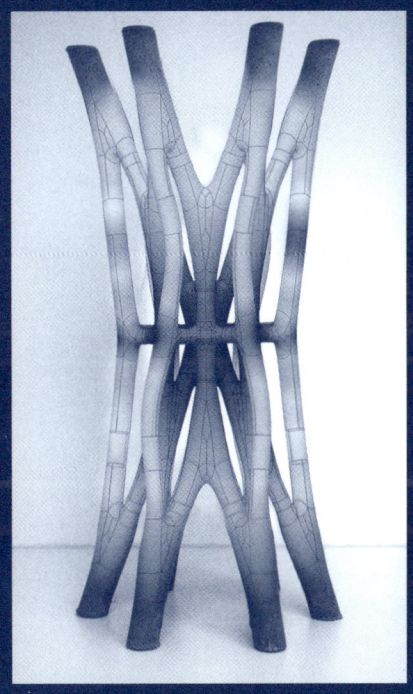

which earned him the renowned SOM award. He also has a degree in Earthquake Engineering and Dynamics of Structures from the Iran University of Science and Technology and a BS in Civil and Environmental Engineering. His main research topic is Three-Dimensional Graphical Statics, which is a novel geometric method of structural design in three dimensions. In 2020, he received the National Science Foundation CAREER Award to extend the methods of 3D/Polyhedral Graphic Statics for Education, Design, and Optimization of High-Performance Structures.

FOUNDATION 501

Andrew Saunders, Coordinator
Associate Professor of Architecture

As the initial design studio in the MArch three-year studio sequence, the 501 studio plays a foundational role as an introduction to studio culture at Weitzman Architecture. The semester-long design project revolves around contemporary design questions concerning the role of cultural institutions in society. This year the studio capitalizes on the resources of the greater University of Pennsylvania through a cross-disciplinary collaboration with the Penn Museum, one of the world's finest archaeological and anthropological museums. Currently, the Penn Museum stands at a crossroad. No longer expanding its collection, the studio probes questions of public interface through curation of its collection for the 21st century audience as well as its physical presence in a rapidly expanding university campus.

The semester is divided into three distinct design exercises, beginning with students working in the museum by 3D scanning actual artifacts from all departments of the museum including western and non-western collections. Once digitally scanned, students analyze the artifacts by modeling, drawing, and 3D printing precise replicas. The first design exercise is to design and fabricate containers for the artifacts as curatorial devices. The containers showcase specific material culture attributes of each artifact by revealing, hiding and transposing certain features through specific material and fabrication methods introduced by individual studio critics. Examples include unrolled, developable surfaces, pipe bending, and framing tactics. The container as a project is a beginning analog for the ultimate container—the extension to the museum archive that will contain and curate the artifacts.

The second phase of the studio builds on the container project through the full-scale fabrications of Curious Cabinets to house and curate a range of artifacts. The title Curious Cabinets alludes to the early Renaissance concept of Wunderkammer— "room of wonder" in German—also referred to as a "Cabinet of Curiosities." As precursor to the contemporary museum, aristocratic collections of art, zoological, and geological specimens, as well as archaeological and anthropological finds, were gathered together to form a Wunderkammer. While the term "Cabinet of Curiosities" today is problematic in current museum culture due to colonialist implications as well as its curatorial crudeness (in an age of specialized academic expertise), as a contemporary architectural exhibit, Curious Cabinets emphasizes the wonderment of the design of the "room" or "cabinet" itself.

Students work for four weeks in groups of four to design, fabricate, and install Curious Cabinets as a public exhibition in the museum entrance courtyard. Each team works in the school's fabrication lab to expand on specific material and fabrication techniques to construct a full-scale assemblage to house the four originally scanned and 3D printed museum artifacts.

For the final project, each student designs an Archive and Research Extension to the Penn Museum to house research artifacts similar to those analyzed previously. The clear set of spatial material and tectonic principles established in the previous Curious Cabinets exercise continue to evolve through a full engagement of architectural criteria including, site, context, enclosure, program, circulation, lighting, materiality, space, and form.

DEEP HISTORIES & STRONG FIGURES

Andrew Saunders (ASSOCIATE PROFESSOR OF ARCHITECTURE)
Paul Germaine McCoy (TA)

Andrew Saunders (Associate Professor of Architecture, Director of Baroque Topologies)**:** Principal of Andrew Saunders Architecture + Design (2004) — Received an M.Arch from Harvard GSD with Distinction for work of clearly exceptional merit. (2004) — B.Arch from Fay Jones School of Architecture, University of Arkansas (1998) — Winner of The Robert S. Brown '52 Fellows Program (2013)

As contemporary designers operating in the current post-digital paradigm of 2019 (one defined by a fatigue of purely digital innovation–characterizing a majority of the last thirty years of progressive architecture) we re-examine the land art movement and their similar reaction to the aesthetic fatigue of the avant-garde obsession with abstract expressionism in the late 1960s. Influenced by Kubler, Robert Smithson, a key figure of the land art movement, sought to break free of the confines of the museum as an institution by developing epic projects that explored and alluded to larger scales and scopes of time and history—including terraforming and archeological swaths. Beginning exterior to the museum within the Stoner Courtyard, the Curious Cabinets act as analog studies for the final project, an extension of the Penn Museum archives. The expanded scale and scope of the land art movement offers compelling tactics to compete with the rapid monumental growth of the surrounding Penn Museum context currently consuming its physical presence. Due to the disciplined Euclidean principles that guided the construction of the new volumetric figures echoing the signature profiles of the artifacts they contain; each surface of the figure is developable (able to be unrolled to a planar surface). Employing sartorial techniques of a tailor, each surface of the Curious Cabinets is templated two-dimensionally from planar wood veneer and re-rolled to constitute the full three-dimensional figure.

1 MONUMENTAL MEMORIES
Elisabeth Machielse

Seeing the shapes of famous pieces of ancient architecture evokes memories and associations that one has learned over the years. Students learn about these structures in history class, audiences see references to them in movies and books, and patrons can learn about them while exploring museums. These experiences turn into memories that shift when one sees the shapes of such structures, calling forth everything that they may already know and, even more importantly, the awareness of what they don't know about those places. In the new extension to the Penn Museum, these immense blocks establish subtle associations with ancient monuments of history, such as Stonehenge and the Moai of Easter Island. By emulating the weight and regularity of these historic examples, the new addition to the archive encourages exploration and the search for connections between the past, present, and future. Each section is made to be reminiscent of those great stone figures, with an emphasis on structure through the use of Euclidean geometry. Furthermore, referencing the form of these ancient figures in a new way allows the building to become a space for reinterpretation of artifacts without redefining them—visitors can ask how the present-day events relate to the historical events connected to these objects.

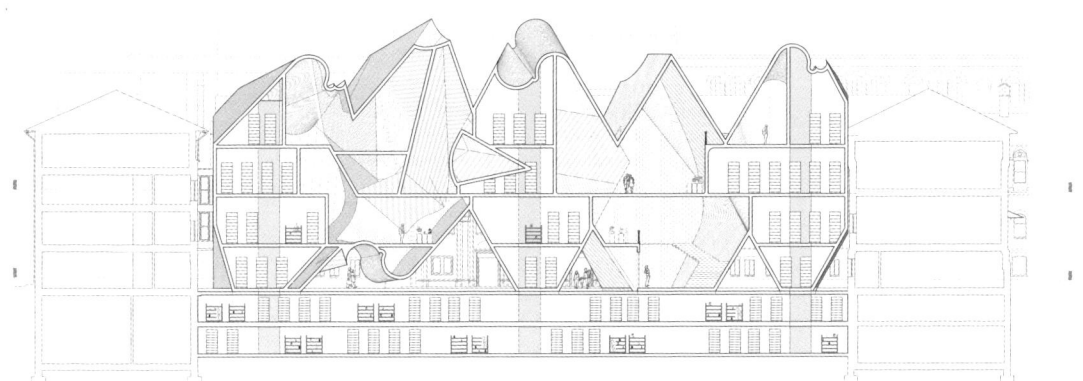

2

1 – *Monumental Memories*, Elisabeth Machielse, Project Description
2 – *Monumental Memories*, Elisabeth Machielse, Section Longitudinal

Establishing strong connections between history and the present emphasizes the importance of exploring what is in the archives, understanding how the objects connect to one another, and encourages the preservation of such objects for years to come.

The new extension also addresses some of the logistical concerns present in the museum today by making artifacts in the archives more accessible to the public, while also ensuring security and the ability for conservators to do their work easily. In the basement of the extension is the main archive, where there is plenty of space for conservation efforts. Extending from that space, three cores connect the main archives in the basement to the galleries and classrooms above: each core consists of a set of stairs, a secure elevator, and more archive storage. This archive section is largely visible to the patrons of the museum through large windows, allowing them to see more artifacts that are usually hidden away in the basement, but are only accessible by museum staff. Furthermore, each of these archive sections are connected to a classroom or presentation space, allowing the artifacts to be easily moved in and out and allowing more groups of students to work with them. Such a configuration further emphasizes the importance of preserving history and connecting it to how we live today.

3

4

3 – *Monumental Memories* by Elisabeth Machielse, Rendering, Courtyard
4 – Studio Review

5 – Andrew Saunders in Studio Review

ENTWINED TANGENTS
Jamaica Reese-Julien

The project creates a new gateway into the Penn Museum, which engages visitors to explore the collection and the building itself. The form is created from the synthesis of curves derived from profiles found in ancient civilization. The building encloses the courtyard by creating a fourth wall and adds a new presence for the museum on south street. As one enters the site, two-dimensional curves are interpolated into a three-dimensional space, at moments both revealing and concealing their strong profiles. As these lines morph, an undulating surface is created overhead, at times coming to the surface to create openings for light to enter the mass.

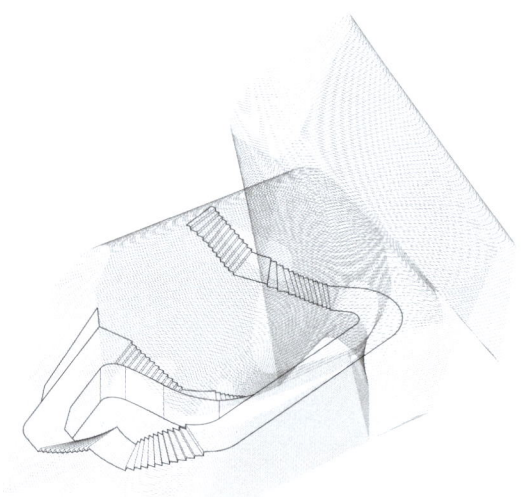

The lines on the exterior facade of the building represent projected geometries of interior spaces and their tangent lines. These lines operate as both a graphic and a formula for modifying the shape of the building and the landscape. The building describes itself visually. The texture or "patina" breaks down the mass as it touches the ground. Acting organically, it follows the main public spaces and entrances, mimicking how the building might naturally wear with time.

5

The interior space comprises of two main voids. One is circumscribed by circulation, while the other is for entry and pause. The voids introduce light from above and come together at the ground level to create a gallery space and entrance lobby. Flexible educational spaces branch off these voids on the upper levels. While in dialogue with its context, this project is representative of the collection it holds. The carved, vault-like spaces are monumental, but not in the neoclassical tradition that surrounds it. This space invites exploration and discovery, and uses the built form as a medium for reassessing the artifacts within the museum.

6

7

5 – *Entwined Tangents* by Jamaica Reese-Julien, Stair Diagram

6 – *Entwined Tangents* by Jamaica Reese-Julien, Interior View

7 – *Entwined Tangents* by Jamaica Reese-Julien, Courtyard View

BREAKING BOUNDARIES
Madison Tousaw

The existing Penn Museum is withering away into the increasingly dense urban fabric of the university. The main entrance fades into obscurity as its courtyard wall keeps it hidden from the street. The new design utilizes historical references to create both its formal construction and materiality. The overall form reinterprets prime figures of monumental structures across history, transcending the original volumes through manipulation of scale and orientation to create a new modern form. This new form becomes a new gateway for the museum. The materiality of the building references the patina of an artifact contained in the museum itself. The building becomes a signal of historical significance of the museum and the importance of the objects within. While not immediately obvious of the artifact it emerged from, the material pattern removes automization of the structure, slowing down visitor's perception of the massing evoking a sense of curiosity. Visitors are drawn up through the slippages between the figures, bringing back a sense of excitement and discovery into the museum. Moments present themselves to visitors throughout the building creating vertical courtyards. By elevating these social spaces, it reframes the inward nature of the existing museum to a more outward and forward view.

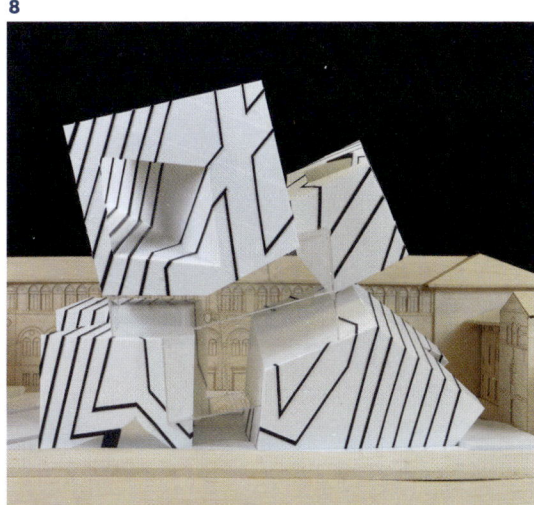

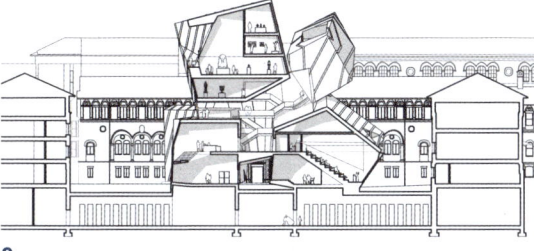

8 – *Breaking Boundaries* by Madison Tousaw, Render Gallery
9 – *Breaking Boundaries* by Madison Tousaw, Drawing Section
10 – *Breaking Boundaries* by Madison Tousaw, Model
11 – *Breaking Boundaries* by Madison Tousaw, Render Street

FLATLESS

Maya Alam (LECTURER)
Megan York (TA)

Maya Alam (Lecturer) – Founding Partner A/P Practice –
Dipl. Ing. Peter Behrens School of Architecture, Düsseldorf –
M.Arch with distinction from Southern California Institute
of Architecture (SciArc)

This studio is focusing on new media applications and its effects on our perception and understanding of space and materiality as it relates to third-dimensionality and flatness. While *flatlessness* is understood formally as well as it applies to socio-political conditions, the putative non-hierarchical flatness of our contemporary, multilayered environments is challenged via a constant loop between physical and digital processes. Students are asked to look closely at the world we are constructing via new imaging technologies in order to not simply accept but to find ways to become an active participant. Therefore, the studio utilizes scanned data, point clouds and images from the Penn Museum courtyard not as singular representations of truth but as multivalent virtual casts with the potential to have more than one single reading.

Considering the different technological and political forces at play in the site and program these casts become embodiments of the Image and begin to investigate how we define the space and form. What is made visible through the machinic eye is seen equally as important as the invisible.

1

DIGITAL INTERFERENCE
Beikel Rivas

The project began with a reinterpretation of the digital scan of the Penn Museum which allows for new types of spatial operations that begin to blend what is digital and what is physical. The physical characteristics of the project consist of a game of volumes that are designed to fit together as puzzle pieces to create structural stability while the digital interpretation of the site or 3D scan begins to interfere with the physical space. The program is organized in three areas: education, museum archive, and gallery spaces. As archives become more and more interested in how to better present their artifacts, spaces for digital exhibits become key for the spatial organization of the project. In addition to this, the project elevates from the ground to allow for pedestrian activity by allowing the different geometries to connect to create a balance of forces.

2

1 – *Digital Interference* by Beikel Rivas, Model Photos
2 – *Digital Interference* by Beikel Rivas, Courtyard

The body of the image in the context of the museum is an interesting one: In the age of digitization, what constitutes an authorized image and how is it shared, challenges traditional protocols inside of institutions. In order to redraw established boundaries of the existing collection and archive, the program speculates on a scenario where 3D scanned artifacts are made publicly available to reach an audience that is more and more part of an ubiquitous image-making culture. The feedback loop between digital and physical challenges existing formats of preservation while aiming to reclaim new territories for museums and architecture alike.

AN INSTANCE OF THE IMMATERIAL
Yuxuan Xiong

One of the main breakthroughs in the digital age is the shift from the 2D perspectival representation of spaces to the 3D scanning and modeling of them.

Extending from the original building, the archive stands at the intersection of multiple receptor planes from which the facades, the Stoner Courtyard and the sky are reflected, captured and digitalized into their pixelated forms, just as how an artifact is filmed and analyzed with photogrammetry.

The new archive extension serves as means to resist the irreversible corrosion, decay or accidental damage of these artifacts over time by recording the 3D instance of each artifact at a set time interval and storing the instances in an open-source database. The archive takes online requests by the museum visitors to print any altered or unaltered 3D models of the artifacts which upon finish will be circulated around the museum, fostering a collective understanding of the origin as an everchanging, temporal instance that safeguards something of much greater importance.

3 – *An Instance of the Immaterial* by Yuxuan Xiong
4 – *An Instance of the Immaterial* by Yuxuan Xiong, Site Plan
5 – *An Instance of the Immaterial* by Yuxuan Xiong, Courtyard

6 – Maya Alam in Studio Review

SHIFTED FRACTIONS
Anabella Fabiola Gilbert

As three-dimensional scanning technologies continue to advance, individuals are starting to perceive digitized geometric forms that nearly replicate their original copies. In architecture, we can take these perceptions and visualize them as mediums for designing spaces. Hito Steyerl, author of *Ripping reality: Blind spots and wrecked data in 3D,* introduces the concept of fractional space and states, *"Fractional space is a transitional space that allows people to enter and exit images, to freeze or become images and then leave the state of flatness again and go somewhere else or missing"* (Steyerl, 3).

Shifted Fractions aims to guide its visitors through a series of galleries that exhibit physical artifacts and digital archives. Its design was derived from photogrammetry scans of the existing Penn Museum site. Throughout this process, each scan produced unique fractional spaces that were then interpreted to create the building's forms. Its interior oscillates between these solid forms, figural voids and their complementing interstitial spaces. Finally, Shifted Fractions is completed by the use of textured seams that slightly shift the building's overall form. These shifts bring light into the interior and give visitors a chance to transition between views of the existing site and the building's archives.

1

2

3

4

1 – *Shifted Fractions* By Anabella Fabiola Gilbert, Museum Extension, Model Photo
2 – *Shifted Fractions* By Anabella Fabiola Gilbert, Museum Extension Exterior Perspective
3 – *Shifted Fractions* By Anabella Fabiola Gilbert, Studies
4 – *Shifted Fractions* By Anabella Fabiola Gilbert, Museum Extension Elevation

INTERPOLATED RESIDUALS
Danny Ortega

More than ever, objects and artifacts are continually scanned to translate parts of the physical world into digital data. This manifested data creates a new image of these objects, normally in the form of point clouds, which then can be shared, multiplied, and projected through any means of contemporary media. Subsequently, this process of digitizing artifacts creates questions on how museums and archives should be designed to accommodate the new age of digitalization, causing us to wonder how we can begin to create formal spaces that start to publicly exhibit and share access of knowledge to these new forms of data.

Interpolated Residue is an investigational project that seeks to find answers to these new understandings by creating a methodological approach through form-finding, layering programmatic spaces, creating spatial relationships with solids and voids, and by applying new manifestations of materials through digital translations.

5 – *Interpolated Residuals* by Danny Ortega, Model
6 – *Interpolated Residuals* by Danny Ortega, Elevation
7 – *Interpolated Residuals* by Danny Ortega, Render

FOURTH FRAME

Daniel Markiewicz (LECTURER)
Madison Green (TA)

Daniel Markiewicz (Lecturer) **:** Partner of FORMA Architects PLLC, Co-Editor of the architecture journal: PROJECT, Partner of Aether Images, Formerly an Associate at Diller Scofidio + Renfro, M.Arch from the Yale School of Architecture, B.S.E. in Civil Engineering/Architecture from Princeton University

The studio was an investigation into the Frame as both a conceptual and physical organizing device. Frame (and framework) acts as both a structural system to which enclosure is applied—space-frame, balloon frame, A-frame—but also as metaphorical "lens" through which discursive positions are constructed—"frame of view," "frame the argument." The final project for the studio—an archive extension to the Penn Museum —is an institution that itself grapples with these concepts when deciding how to "frame" their collection as a whole (conceptually) and in what "frames" individual objects are displayed (physically). Ultimately students were asked to respond to these prompts through the design of the "fourth wall" of the Stoner Courtyard at the Penn Museum.

Students began their investigations by designing a "container" for a small scale museum artifact using tube framework inspired by Marcel Breuer's Wassily Chair. Building on this understanding of tube framing students developed large scale

its appearance of disconnect above ground. The form itself developed upon a strict grid of thirty degrees and a sense of slippage and suspense that foster framed views that conceal and reveal the existing museum. Disconnected Continuity establishes a new gate to the Stoner Courtyard, illustrating the rebranding and modernization of the museum, while also paying homage to existing museum and its rich history; a classic case of the future meets the past.

2

1   DISCONNECTED CONTINUITY
                     Lisa Knust

In reimagining an archive extension to the Penn Museum, Disconnected Continuity looks at the potential of the "fourth wall" and completing the remaining side of the Stoner Courtyard. This "fourth wall" is established through a meeting of three points of extension, one from the east wing of the courtyard, the second from the west, and finally, upward from underground. The result is a continuous loop around the courtyard, despite

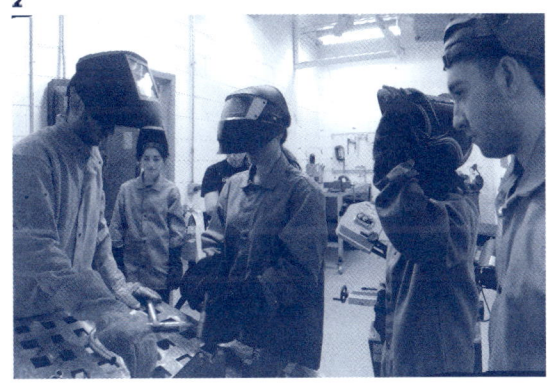

3

fabrications with bent steel tube and a combination of cold connections and MIG welding. Eventually the studio asked students to develop their own approach to the design of an archive extension based on the concepts established in these early studies, essentially

1 - *Disconnected Continuity* by Lisa Knust, Container Project Model

2 - *Disconnected Continuity* by Lisa Knust, Courtyard Render
3 - Studio Metal Workshop

to formulate their own set of questions and then defend that through design. Some questions that were raised over the course of the studio's explorations included:

• How can vehicular, pedestrian and other active movement flows influence the form of a building?

• How can the "fourth wall" of the courtyard be articulated as both a horizontal and vertical extension of the existing wings of the museum?

• How can large scale building movement activate museum programming and areas of the museum beyond the Stoner Courtyard?

Students were asked to develop their ideas through Plan, Section, Perspective and Model. Color was excluded from consideration.

4   VIEWS BEYOND
Dario Sabidussi

In this three-part assignment, this project uses experimentation of spatial engagement as well as framing as a tool to explore architectural opportunities and experiences beyond the existing Penn Museum. The Museum is, in many ways, currently being treated as an artifact itself. It serves as an architectural relic with its own history, its own story. Tucked away and engulfed by the vertically modernized developments, the museum and the views created by the museum are entirely hidden like the artifacts in museum archives, stored and kept away from public engagement. Ultimately, the formal dialogue between the existing and the beyond is non-existent. This project explores the relationship between the new extension and the existing urban context of Philadelphia surrounding it. The new system serves as an initiator for the many dialogues between urban space and architecture itself by blending both historical and modern design into one cohesive structure. It acknowledges not only the views available to the museum, but abstractly reinvents the museum to be a view in its own way. It directly competes with the vertical construction surrounding the museum, offering a new architectural experience both within and beyond the museum. The extension questions what is beyond the existing and explores how architecture can engage with the artifacts kept within the museum. Through the exploration of floating space and vertical development, the extension attempts to expand above the existing and exploit the new and beyond.

4 – *Views Beyond* by Dario Sabidussi

5 – *Views Beyond* by Dario Sabidussi, Render
6 – *The Force of Flow* by Hongbang Chen, Studio Review

7 – Daniel Markiewicz in Studio Review

THE FORCE OF FLOW
Hongbang Chen

This project is aiming to create the "fourth wall" of the Penn Museum, which is the extension of archive space with education and exhibition space. The location of this project made it both the interfaces of the existing museum courtyard and nearby urban space. Therefore, the design is driven by its unique site condition. The project began with generating the massing by using major circulation axises of the museum. Next, the urban interface was formed by registering the traffic flow next to the museum. The directional force of the traffic flow became the force to manipulate the form and space further. In this way, the project not only echoes the existing primary circulation but also reflects the movement of the adjacent urban space.

The programmatic arrangement is a combination of the formal approach and analysis of the existing museum program. The archive space occupies the west side and connects to the existing museum on all floors. The center volume of the project becomes the education and public space, where it connects to the archive space to provide multipurpose learning spaces. The exhibition space locates on the East side of the project and links to the Penn Museum, and this space sets apart from the rest of the project to form an undisturbed and coherent spatial experience.

The idea of the traffic flow pushing and pulling the form also extends into the interior space. The interior walls and ceiling are designed in a way that, when people inside the building, the sense of flow can be experienced at a more intimated level.

Moreover, the material of the building I use is brick. There are two main reasons that I think the brick is the most suitable material for this project. Firstly it echoes with the existing museum, but most importantly is the nature of constructing the brick wall helps to describe the force applied to the massing subtly.

Last but not least, because I wanted to use opaque volumes to describe the series of formal manipulation. Therefore to increase transparency and lighting conditions inside the project, the skylights are introduced. The form of the skylight also follows the idea of pushing and pulling manipulation from the traffic flow.

8

9

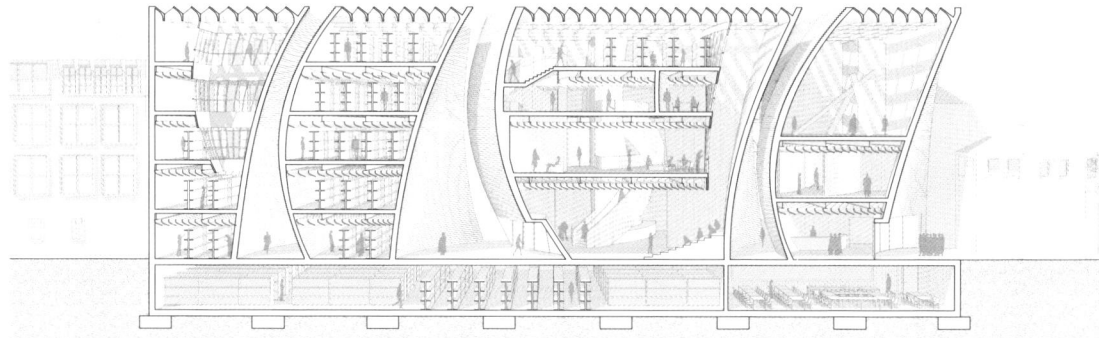

10

8 – *The Force of Flow* by Hongbang Chen, Sectional Perspective

9 – *The Force of Flow* by Hongbang Chen, Render New And Old

10 – *The Force of Flow* by Hongbang Chen, Model

DISTORTION IN LAYERS
Riley James Engelberger

Distortion is heavily manifested in our current reality—most clearly observed through the lenses of social media, economics, and politics. As architecture is in part tasked with representing current realities, the objective of relaying distortion through form, material, and concept finds reason. We can relate the archive and museum itself to distortion as artifacts are artificially displayed in a regularized way, without much regard to their backstory and original interest beyond placing them amongst other objects with associated found geographic location. The story—the true story, of each individual artifact is lost, and its presented story on behalf of the institution is, as a result, also distorted. The archive specifically muddles the goals of the museum, which is meant to show these artifacts to the public, when in fact only a small portion of the institution's collection is on display at any given time. The use of layered glass and the forms that are derived to create the addition to the archive not only represent the distortion, but actively distort even the building itself when viewed from outside and within. This active distortion is revealed through visual overlays of material which obscure that which is beyond and refract light in unpredictable ways with the goal of bringing the understanding of our current societal issues to the forefront of our discourse. The architecture goes beyond simply a critique or representation of the museum and archive and finds its way into the current issues we, as a society find ourselves within, and attempts to inform all who may observe its standing.

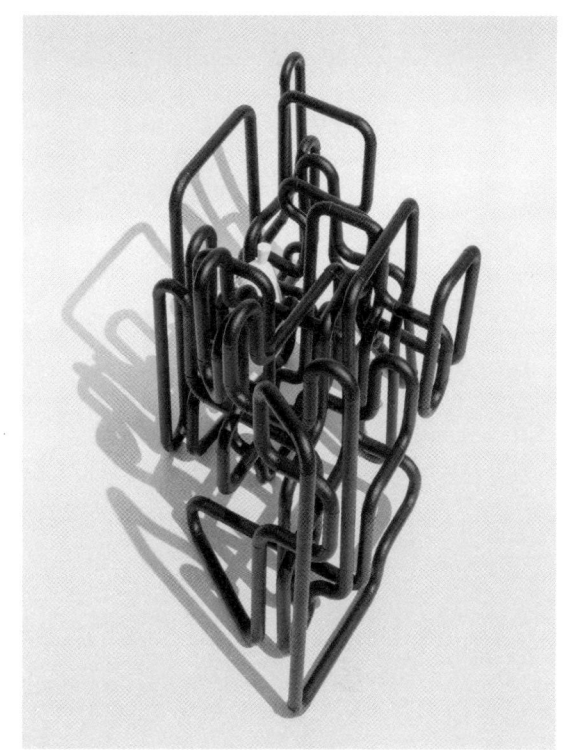

11

12

13

14

11 – *Distortion In Layers* by Riley James Engelberger, Container Project Model
12 – *Distortion In Layers* by Riley James Engelberger, Archive model

13 – *Distortion In Layers* by Riley James Engelberger, Street Render
14 – *Distortion In Layers* by Riley James Engelberger, Cross Section

THE TROJAN DUCK
DECOLONIAL TACTICS FOR THE PENN MUSEUM

Eduardo Rega Calvo (LECTURER)
Marta Llor (TA)

Eduardo Rega Calvo (Lecturer) Founder of Architectures of Refusal. Editor in urbanNext, Actar publishers. M.Sc. in Advanced Architectural Design from Columbia University, GSAPP – M.Arch from Polytechnic University of Madrid, ETSAM – B.Arch from University of Las Palmas de Gran Canaria

1 – Hyperactive Monument. A 'Socially Interactive Machine' By Reem Abi Samra, Front Render

Due to their instrumentality and complicity with colonialism and western imperialism, ethnography, anthropology, archeology and natural history museums have been sites of controversy particularly since the second break up of the European Colonial empires after WWII and until today. Some of these museums, once named after the explorer-collectors that sponsored them, have recently started to question the very principles of collecting and exhibiting still so deeply determined by colonialism. Artifacts (traded, taken or stolen from indigenous peoples) have traditionally been decontextualized, archived, and displayed following western classification systems that disregard the cultures and knowledges to which they belong.

1   HYPERACTIVE MONUMENT.
A "SOCIALLY INTERACTIVE MACHINE"
Reem Abi Samra

The Hyperactive Monument is a reactivating megastructure: it is cooperative with the context, infusing hyperactivity and program while still integrating itself within the site. It activates the ground with suspended activities from above datums, creating various levels of hyperactivity and programatically flexible spaces. It is designed as a scaffolding system within which constant performance and hyperactivity occurs, reactivating the context and offering flexible spaces to exhibit, perform, educate, research, gather, and play.

In this year's collaboration with Penn's Archaeology and Anthropology museum, our studio section will start by collectively and critically studying Penn Museum's history of complicity and instrumentality with colonialism and imperialism. Framed as institutional critiques and in line with this art movement,[a] the various projects of our studio (from containers and curious cabinets to building extensions) will be aimed to be politically conscious, critical and radically imaginative: at once challenging the museum's structures of power and offering spatial visions of aesthetic and spatial decolonizing strategies.

Détournement of the Decorated Duck

DUCKS: "WHERE THE ARCHITECTURAL SYSTEMS OF SPACE, STRUCTURE, AND PROGRAM ARE SUBMERGED AND DISTORTED BY AN OVERALL SYMBOLIC FORM."
— R. Venturi, D. Scott Brown, and S. Izenour, 1972

DECORATED SHEDS: "WHERE SYSTEMS OF SPACE AND STRUCTURE ARE DIRECTLY AT THE SERVICE OF PROGRAM, AND ORNAMENT IS APPLIED INDEPENDENTLY."
— R. Venturi, D. Scott Brown and S. Izenour, 1972

"THE DUCK IS A SPECIAL BUILDING THAT IS A SYMBOL; THE DECORATED SHED IS A CONVENTIONAL SHELTER THAT APPLIES SYMBOLS."[b]
— R. Venturi, D. Scott Brown and S. Izenour, 1972

DECORATED DUCK: "THERE IS NOW A WHOLE FLOCK OF 'DECORATED DUCKS' THAT COMBINE THE WILLFUL MONUMENTALITY OF MODERN ARCHITECTURE WITH THE FAUX-POPULIST ICONICITY OF POSTMODERN DESIGN."[c]
— H. Foster, 2004

DÉTOURNEMENT: "BY INTRODUCING INTO THE THEORETICAL DOMAIN THE SAME TYPE OF VIOLENT SUBVERSION THAT DISRUPTS AND OVERTHROWS EVERY EXISTING ORDER, DÉTOURNEMENT SERVES AS A REMINDER THAT THEORY IS NOTHING IN ITSELF, THAT IT CAN REALIZE ITSELF ONLY THROUGH HISTORICAL ACTION AND THROUGH THE HISTORICAL CORRECTION THAT IS ITS TRUE ALLEGIANCE."[d]
— G. Debord, 1967

Denise Scott Brown, Robert Venturi, and Steven Izenour considered the *Duck* and the *Decorated Shed*, findings from their

---

a – "*Institutional critique* is an artistic practice that reflects critically on its own housing in galleries and museums and on the concept and social function of art itself." *Institutional Critique: An Anthology of Artists' Writings*, edited by Alexander Alberro and Blake Stimson

b – *Learning from Las Vegas*: the forgotten symbolism of architectural form, by Venturi, Scott Brown and Izenour
c – "Image Building" by Hal Foster in *Artforum*
d – The *Society of the Spectacle*, Chapter 8: Negation and Consumption Within Culture, by Guy Debord

Yale studio analysis of commercial strips of Las Vegas, as architectural concepts of late capitalist culture to be embraced, enhanced and celebrated in architecture discourse and practice. Our studio will critically interrogate these concepts to mobilize them through *détournement*, or against that which created them: late capitalism and architecture's corporatization. If *Ducks, Decorated Sheds* and *Decorated Ducks* are semiotic manifestations of architecture at the service of capitalist management systems, *Détournement of Decorated Ducks* are architecture's semiotic and spatial sabotage of these systems.

Back in the Penn Museum, an architecture that integrates decolonial forms of exhibition design should aim to maximize its semiotic and storytelling power through a tactical re-organization of sociospatial relations. We therefore reject the opposition between *Duck* and *Decorated Shed* to pursue a third category, one that combines and exceeds the semiotic characteristics of each: the *Decorated Duck*. According to Hal Foster, the *Decorated Duck* combines "willful monumentality" with "faux-populist iconicity" to produce an architecture mainstream of "building as Pop sign, as media logo" fully subservient to the managerial and market logics of late capitalist corporations (museums, universities, companies, cities, states, etc). The studio will explore subversions (or détournements) of the *Decorated Duck* against the social order that produced it: capitalism in its relation to western imperialism.

As *Trojan Horses*,[e] or rather *Trojan Ducks*, our studio's projects will enter the walls of the Penn Museum, to critique and subvert an institution originally founded as a colonialist tool. The *Détournement of the Decorated Duck* will be a spatial-conceptual avenue for institutional critique that explores an architecture of signs, symbols, scenes and stories telling the hard truths of colonialism and altogether re-imagining spatial and power relations differently.

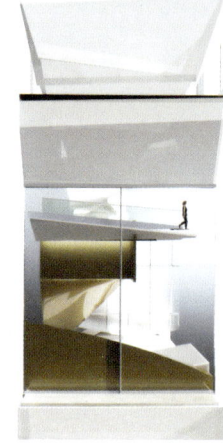

2

STONER VAULTS AND TOMBS
Diego Ramirez

A primary critique of the institution is its inability to properly manage and display their collection. Items go for years in storage due to poor infrastructure and therefore the museum often loses track of information or items. The public directly suffers as information that should be public dissolves in the privacy of the archives. A secondary point of contention is the lack of collaborative spaces for visiting keepers of culture whose genealogy is attached to the items in the museum. The museum should be a prominent civic entity established for education through absolute transparency.

The Stoner Vaults and Tombs is a symbiotic complex that will allow for the correction and exposure of past transgressions while simultaneously allowing for new spaces in discourse. Through operations of the oblique, the bottom tombs will extend the archive into an open exhibit of fragile objects, finally released from archival storage. The ground floors will supplement light for the tombs and split the project into two axes. The top program creates anew. The bottom program redefines.

e – "(in Greek mythology) a hollow wooden statue of a horse in which the Greeks are said to have concealed themselves in order to enter Troy. A person or thing intended to undermine or secretly overthrow an enemy or opponent." Oxford Dictionary

2 – *Stoner Vaults and Tombs* by Diego Ramirez, Slits

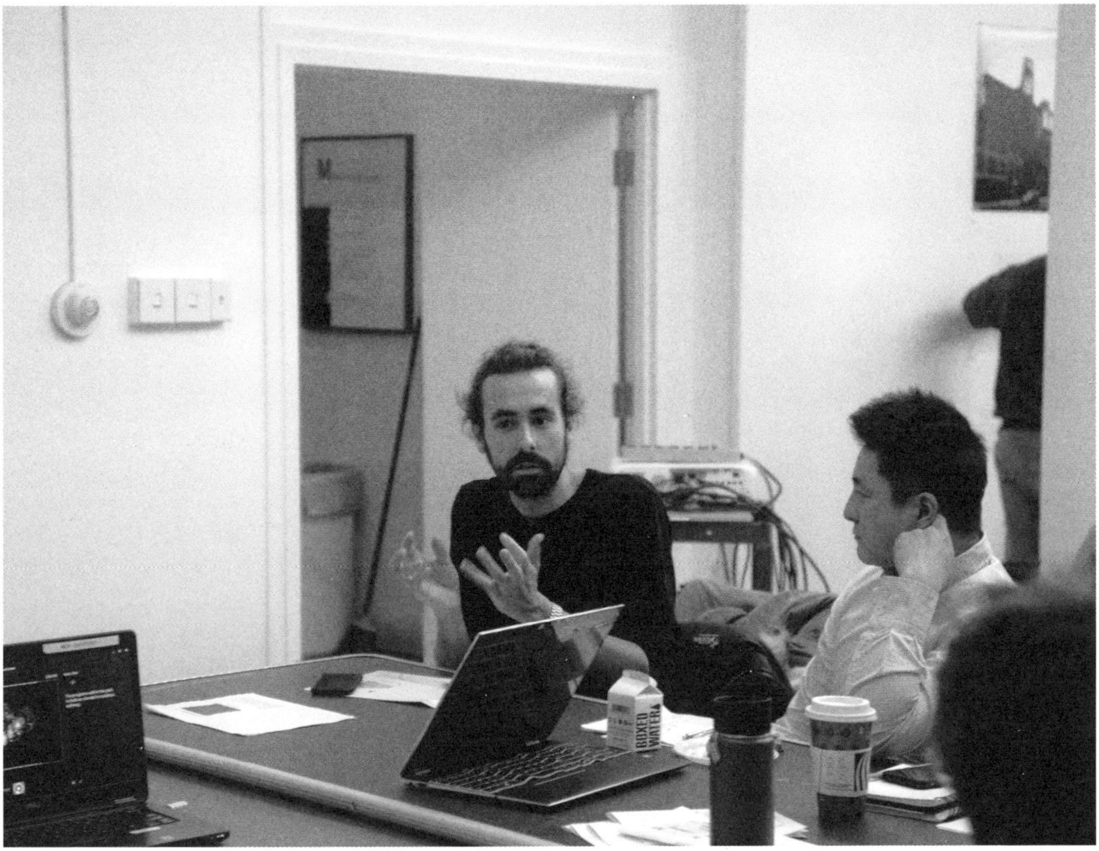

3

4

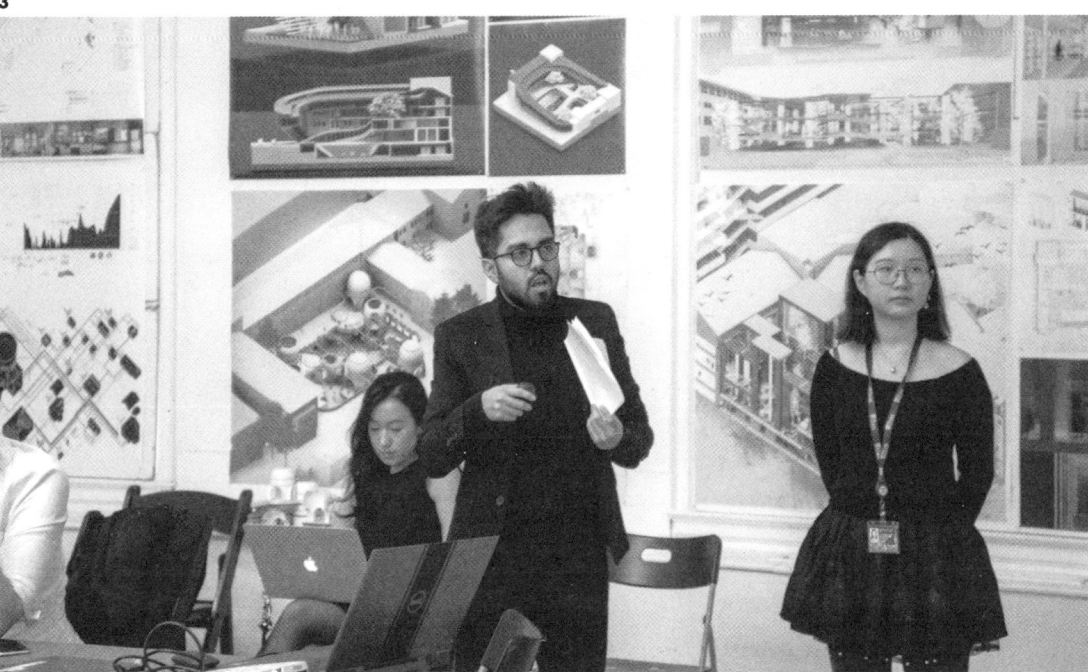

3 – Eduardo Rega Calvo in Studio Review
4 – Studio Review

LIFTING THE VEIL. A NEW DIALECT
Liam Lasting

Studying the museum through the lenses of the Society of the Spectacle, it is apparent that the museum has fabricated an ideology that it hides behind to cover up its involvements in colonial efforts and its expeditions to obtain these collected artifacts. This manifested ideology encourages people to view these objects outside of their troubled pasts or to even idolize trophy-collecting as imperial propaganda. By only focusing on their physical appearances, the museum is concealing how these objects were actually immorally obtained, which creates this spectacle for the world to observe. We are brainwashed consumers of this fabricated image that the museum presents to us. The mass produced reality is projected as one that is noble, but their excess of objects are collected out of greed in an effort for the museum to improve its standing in the institution's game of numbers. It is the Penn Museum's moral responsibility to give the public total transparency, exposing their entire archival collection and giving a glimpse into the inner-workings of the museum through educational opportunities and an expansion of community and global engagement.

5

6

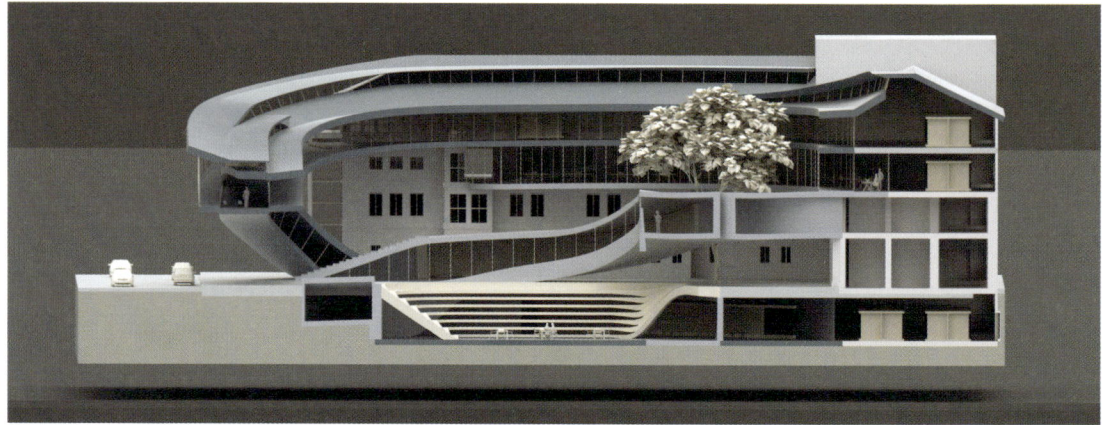

7

5 – *Lifting The Veil. A New Dialect,* by Liam Lasting, Chunk

6 – *Lifting The Veil. A New Dialect,* by Liam Lasting, Experiential Render

7 – *Lifting The Veil. A New Dialect,* by Liam Lasting, Section A

MUSEUM AS URBAN THEATER. RETHINKING THE PENN MUSEUM THROUGH PERFORMANCE.
Tingdong Xiong

Borrowing the type of a giant billboard, the project aims to expose the museum's inner workings literally as performances to an audience. The museum is also reimagined as producer of cultural events, like a theater, that connects its narratives and histories with society. Specifically, the project aims to free the museum from the rigidity of its current function, carefully guiding visitors and non-visitors through statically classified content, and turn it to focus on its capacity to provide a space for cultural events that can communicate the, sometimes painful, histories behind their collection to a broad audience and attempts to inform all who may observe its standing.

8

9

10

8 – *Museum As Urban Theater. Rethinking The Penn Museum Through Performance,* by Tingdong Xiong, Model
9 – *Museum As Urban Theater. Rethinking The Penn Museum Through Performance,* by Tingdong Xiong, Axon 1
10 – *Museum As Urban Theater. Rethinking The Penn Museum Through Performance,* by Tingdong Xiong, One Point Persepective

PROTOMORPHS
EMERGENT ONTOLOGICAL FORMATIONS

Danielle Willems (LECTURER)
Merrick Castillo (TA)

Danielle Willems (Lecturer) Co-Founder of Mæta Design (2008) – Visiting Professor at Pratt University, Brooklyn NY – Earned a MArch from Columbia University, GSAPP (2007)

Our world is increasingly being understood as an emergent outcome of complex systems. Similarly, both analytical and generative tools for the definition of spatial and architectural complex systems have been established within our discipline. These projects incorporate the scanned artifacts from the Penn Museum, through the translation of digital point cloud geometry into views that frame the 3D-printed artifacts exploring the color, texture and custom perspectives.

The museum as an institution is questioned through these projects by rethinking how we view and experience artifacts that cannot be touched. The studio methodology consists of three feedback layers: generative diagram, prototyping model, and video. The generative diagram is the assembly machine to Curious Cabinets. The physical model is method of rapid prototyping, testing the limits of the generative diagram in order to explore the realities of fabrication and the feedback loop between the digital and the physical.

These projects use carbon fiber as a material that tests the limits of lines of structure and the geometry of interior and external vantage points. Across these three projects, there is an exploration of polyhedral Stellation and projective geometry within the tensile structures. There is also a focus on the 2D to 3D textile

1   PENN MUSEUM ARCHIVE EXTENSION
    Meera Toolsidas

The Penn Museum as it exists today represents a building typology trapped in the era in which it was constructed, a museum whose ability to grow and transform in order to meet shifting demands and functions is limited by a sheer lack of space. Drawing from SANAA's concepts of adapting to the challenges of a restrictive site in their design of the New Museum of Contemporary Art in New York City, in designing an extension to the Penn Museum I aspire to create a space that both retains the historic elegance of the existing museum and embraces modern concepts of circulation and viewing.

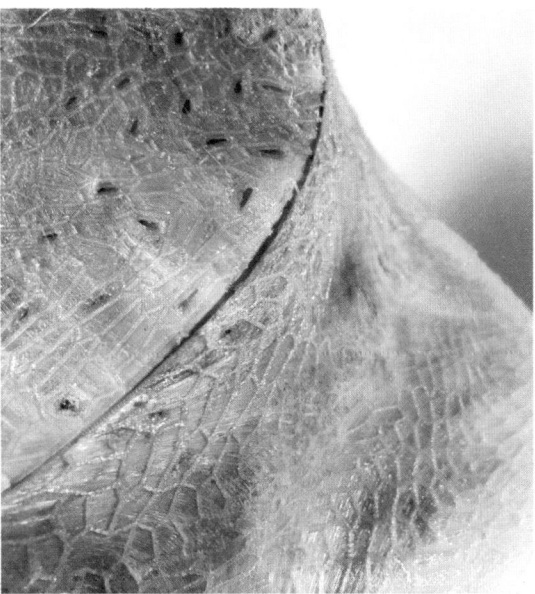
3

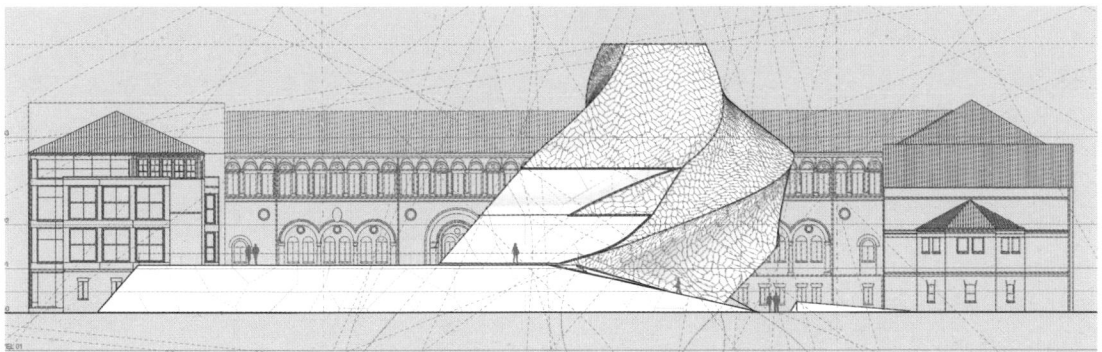
2

1 – *Penn Museum Archive Extension* by Meera Toolsidas, Project Statement

2 – *Penn Museum Archive Extension* by Meera Toolsidas, Elevation

3 – *Penn Museum Archive Extension* by Meera Toolsidas, Project Model

qualities and techniques of woven, loomed and wrapped fibers. This studio explores new mediums of contingency through material experimentation and behavioral systems analysis, looking deeper into the intelligence and complexities that surround our everyday experience.

Emergent Ontological Formations is an investigation into multi-scalar definition of computational constructs and ultimately attempts to merge architecture and composites materials into direct relationships with "artificial materials." The focus of this research in the Curious Cabinets is to develop innovative fabrication techniques using carbon fiber in relationship to the exhibition experience, spaces and objects.

PENN MUSEUM ARCHIVE EXTENSION
Shan Li

Inspired from the cabinet project that, volume and mass can be achieved with a lightweight effect using certain material and structure, which has the potential to create a significant contrast with the existing heavyweight Penn Museum. However, the challenge is how to achieve the floating effect visually and structurally.

This project challenges the conventional museum that is always an open plan enclosed cubic building with rigid structure grid, the objective is using carbon fiber as the rebar to achieve a space with organic shape, meanwhile, by introducing the unified spinal form, an episodic spatial arrangement is created to display items and infuse the public visiting tour with a rhythm.

The overall gesture of the building footprint is a loop in order to simplify the visiting circulation while maintaining the public courtyard. The purpose of the ground relief is to give the above-ground space a vertical variation while creating enclosed archive space within, it also encases the courtyard space in the center with opening directly linking the front street towards the existing entrance of Penn Museum. The project explores different types of tiling patterns and how they interlocked with each other, which could be the connection of individual discrete.

4 – *Penn Museum Archive Extension* by Shan Li, Project Statement
5 – *Penn Museum Archive Extension* by Shan Li, Interior Rendering

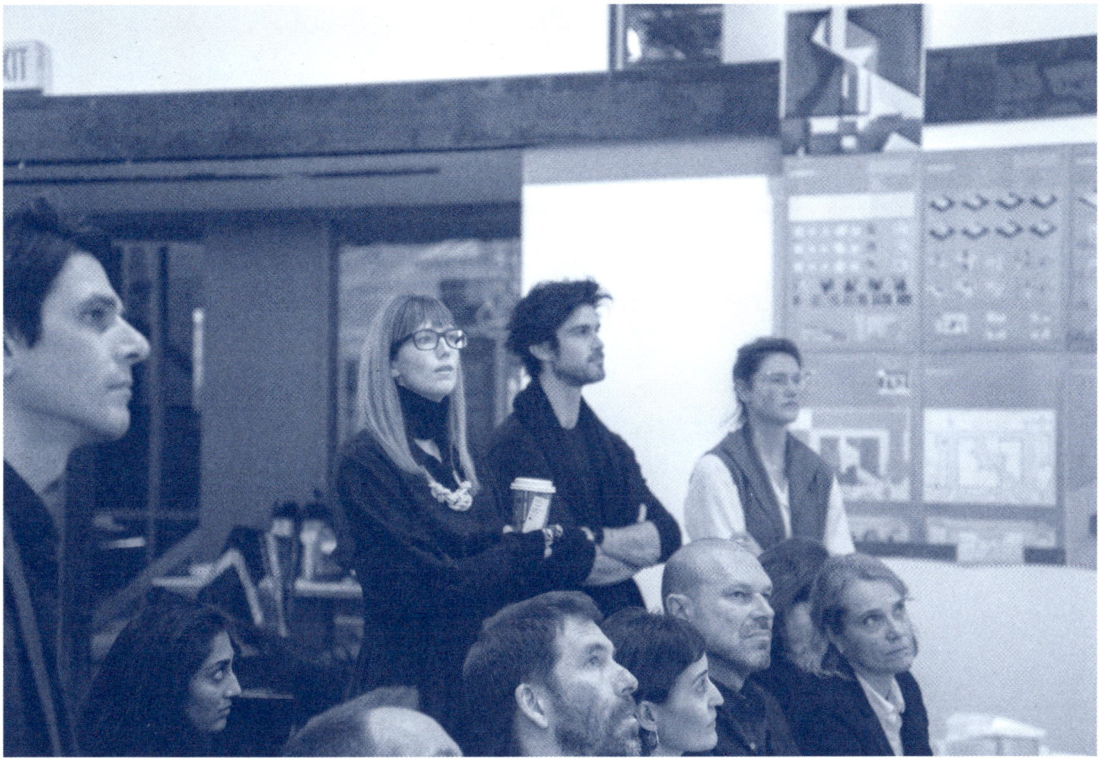

6

7

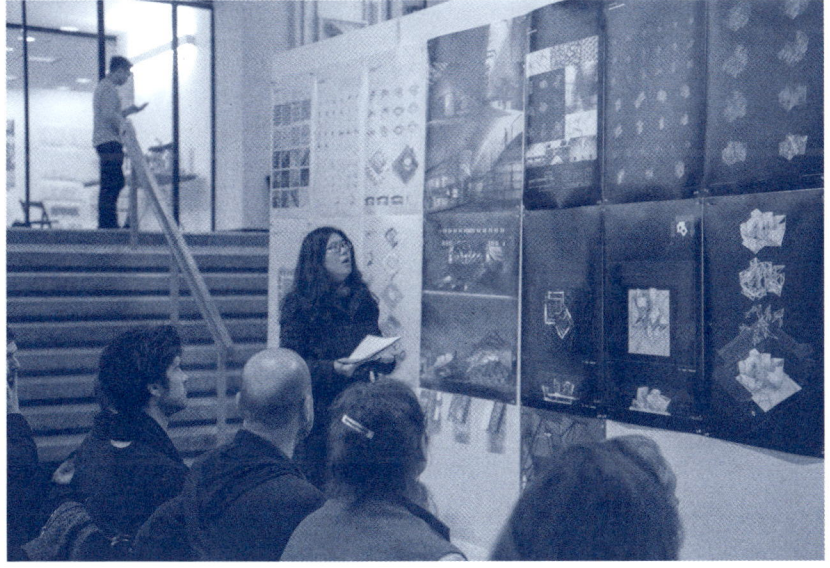

6 – Danielle Willems in Studio Review
7 – Studio Review

PENN MUSEUM ARCHIVE EXPANSION
Bolai Ren

In this Archive Expansion project, the potential of modular design in museum is further researched. The traditional way of museum designing that each function such as exhibition and storage are located and managed separately is challenged. Exhibition space, education space and storage space are considered as a set of interconnected functions in this project, and those are arranged into every single module of the project. In this way, the distance and difficulty of artifacts' transportation process are minimized and restricted inside each module, which means the minimization of possibility that artifacts are damaged and efficiency of educational activities.

Furthermore, the characteristic of carbon fiber is challenged. Generally, the void between the internal massing and external massing are defined by the boundary of massing. The lightness and strongness of carbon fiber are hoped to further blur the boundary of the void and create a new experience in the voids.

8

9

10

8 – *Penn Museum Archive Extension* by Bolai Ren, Model   **9** – *Penn Museum Archive Extension* by Bolai Ren, Render
10 – *Penn Museum Archive Extension* by Bolai Ren, Elevation

PENN MUSEUM ARCHIVE EXPANSION
Kevin Cheung

Movement of materials throughout space to create perception of motion. Carbon fiber is a lightweight form that can creates the sense of motion through projection and shadows. Using dense and porous weaving, one can create different viewing qualities at different moments.

I am interested in using this strategy manipulate one's visual perception of an object. In a way that inherently circulates viewers to certain locations. The Typology I chose is an exhibition space called Yingliang Stone Archive. It's use of viewing from the courtyard with its textile facade is interesting.

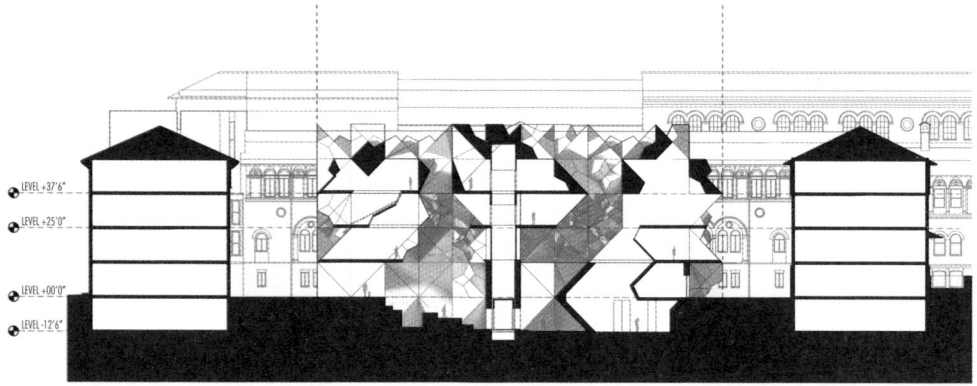

11 – *Penn Museum Archive Extension* by Kevin Cheung, Model

12 – *Penn Museum Archive Extension* by Kevin Cheung, Ortho

13 – *Penn Museum Archive Extension* by Kevin Cheung, Exterior Render

ROUGH FRAMING

Emmett Zeifman (LECTURER)
Peik Shelton (TA)
Zach Jones (TA)

Emmett Zeifman Lecturer, Weitzman School of Design, 2019-present – Principal, Medium Office, 2014-present – Founding Editor, Project: A Journal for Architecture, 2011-present – Adjunct Associate Professor, Columbia GSAPP, 2017-present – Yale Bass Scholar (M.Phil Architecture by Research), University of Cambridge, 2013-14 – M.Arch, Yale School of Architecture, 2008-11 – B.A., McGill University, 2002-06

This studio explores rough framing as a conceptual problem and a literal technique. In some sense, architecture is always a frame, defining the limits of spaces and the difference between inside and outside. Parallel to this, in many contexts, framing remains the predominant technique of architectural construction: it establishes the "rough" spatial and material organization of architecture, with varying degrees of expression in the "finished" building.

Students are tasked with developing frames for the collection of the Penn Museum at the three scales: a container for a single artifact, a cabinet for small group of artifacts, and a new wing of the museum containing numerous artifacts and programs. Students must calibrate the hierarchy of the architectural frame and its contents. In what ways does the architecture express itself, and in what ways does it recede to foreground its contents? Rather than deriving the containers from the artifacts they contain, the studio proposes open, approximate systems for supporting and exhibiting the collection of the Penn Museum. These "rough frames" explore the potential of the architectural container to assert spatial and material qualities that may be prototypical or generic, while not reducing the complex cultural histories and diverse constituencies of the Penn Museum to static architectural symbols.

At the tectonic level, rough timber framing is defined by its simplicity and its capacity to structure diverse forms. It is light, cheap, easy to assemble and renewable. It is rules-based, allowing for the democratization of technical knowledge (anyone can do framing), as well as its automation in contemporary applications. While the traditional craft of joinery has largely been replaced by mass-produced systems of connectors, the studio asks students to consider the material and formal implications of specific methods of connecting one element to another, including material waste, prefabrication, ease of

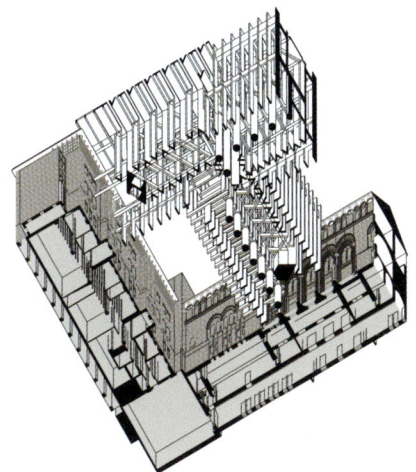

1 EXTENSION TO THE PENN MUSEUM AND ARCHIVE
Tuo Chen

My initial inspiration comes from the play of "Hide and Seek." When people are curious to know something, they actively ponder and act to find things out. Museum archive as a building typology is the space for human curiosity. People come to seek for information of the past, the present and the future. The curiosity raises emotion and emotion finally leads to body motion. Thus, the idea of layering the frameworks is to slightly hide the artifacts in a way that it stimulates and enhances people's curiosity at each moment of experiencing the space. When people walk parallel with the framing layers, they will see the artifacts and exhibitions frame by frame like an animation. The lateral and longitudinal movement with repetitive layering elements will achieve enduring seeking curiosity physically and sensuously.

2

1 – *Extension to the Penn Museum and Archive*
by Tuo Chen, Drawing
2 – *Extension to the Penn Museum and Archive*
by Tuo Chen, Street View Render

construction, and relative expression of the individual element and the aggregated system. And as framing is typically a substrate onto which further architectural effects and systems are layered, in the first exercises of the term, the studio explores paint as a "finish" material that articulates or complicates the formal qualities of the frame, particularly its density, repetition, and order.

EXTENSION TO THE PENN MUSEUM AND ARCHIVE
Eleanor Garside

To expose the frame is to turn established conceptions of a museum on its head. At the Penn Museum, structure is covered by blank walls and ceilings, hiding the skeleton. The archives are similarly suppressed. A new addition exposes the structure and exposes the archives within.

Visitors experience lively interaction throughout the new building amidst layers of serenity in the archives through the framing of a social courtyard. Galleries and archival storage are visible to one another, allowing for spontaneous discovery of the ancient worlds and the ability to see all types of activities. Student collaboration space bridges storage and exhibition. With the shift of function in each space brings the shift of the size of the frame, reacting to clear differentiation of intended level of movement. The facade unifies the shifting program, filtering light into the spaces and offering dynamic moments between the building and the skin to occupy.

Lifting the entire structure off the ground dissolves the barrier between street and museum. What was once a thick masonry gate becomes a field of columns lightly touching the ground. With the new addition, the existing museum is not hidden; however, a new formal identity is revealed. Activities of the Penn Museum are exposed, bringing visitors in and throughout to give life to the obscured museum and all the history it buries.

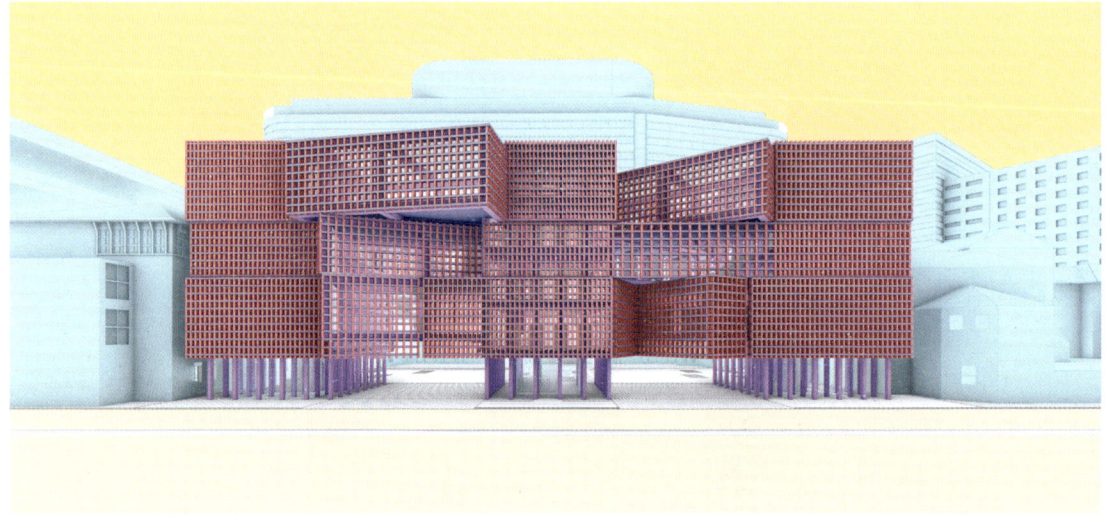

3 – *Extension to the Penn Museum and Archive* by Eleanor Garside
4 – *Extension to the Penn Museum and Archive* by Eleanor Garside, Section Perspective
5 – *Extension to the Penn Museum and Archive* by Eleanor Garside, Elevation Perspective

6 – Emmett Zeifman in Studio Review

EXTENSION TO THE PENN MUSEUM AND ARCHIVE
Weiting Zhang

The Penn Museum is a setting for communication that traverses time and space. Artifacts from past civilizations converse with the visitor in a silent, universal language. The visitor take delight in his exchange with a decorative vessel or a bronze dagger not purely for the beauty of the object but also for the answer it gives to a question of his. A hundred artifacts will evoke a hundred answers and a thousand questions more. An archive on display is a natural space for learning. The extension to the Penn Museum promotes conversations—between stored artifacts and visitors, between museum educators and students, and between fellow visitors, who can share their newly gained insight and curiosity.

At the new Penn Museum, monumental storage towers are juxtaposed against transitory corridors, along which glimpses of carefully curated artifacts lure the visitor to delay his pace. Movement becomes a cinematic progression where the cadence is dictated by the affinity one feels for the artifacts on view. People come and go, always around the towers of artifacts. Corridors twist and turn, and cracks along the wall let in light to illuminate the interior. Where corridors converge the exchange of ideas and reflections happens against the backdrop of the museum archive.

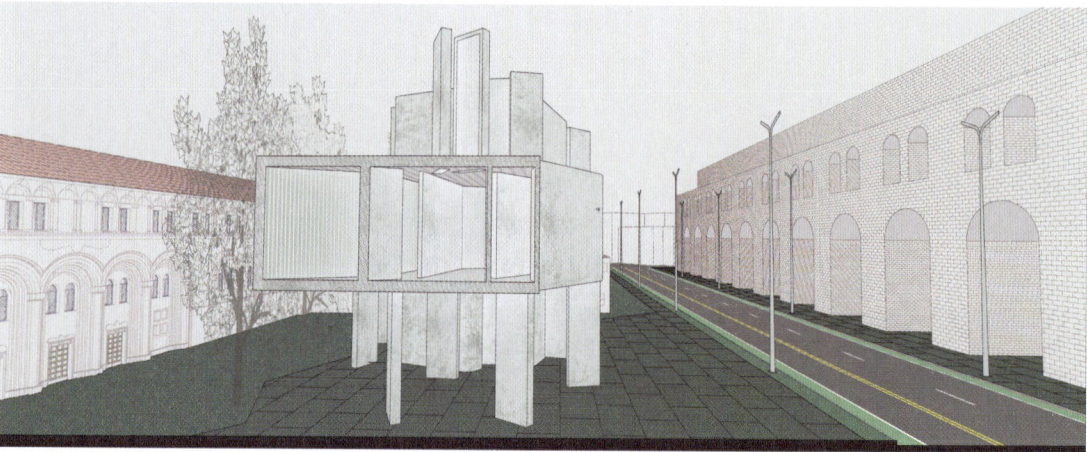

7 – *Extension to the Penn Museum and Archive* by Weiting Zhang, Interior Render

8 – *Extension to the Penn Museum and Archive* by Weiting Zhang, Short Section

9 – *Extension to the Penn Museum and Archive* by Weiting Zhang, Model

EXTENSION TO THE PENN MUSEUM AND ARCHIVE
Yasmine McBride

A theater is a dynamic and lively. It is where we go to be surprised and excited and confront the unexpected.

An artifact archive is stagnant and dead. It is where we go to be somber, and educated, and pretend we know what we are looking at when we really have no idea.

A museum of artifacts could use a dose of theatricality. Since the act of bringing together a series of objects from disparate locations and arbitrarily placing them side by side is an invented phenomenon, it is fair to invent a new one. We steal these places and these pieces, calling them our own and then caging them in glass, naively assigning them significance in place of the value that was lost.

The act of procuring, moving, preserving, and displaying these objects is so foreign to their initial intended use that the act itself is unreal and performative. The new Penn Archive will be a place where this process, alongside the artifacts themselves, will be displayed as performance and therefore critiqued as concepts. Storage will become an auditorium, preservation will become an operating theater, and glass boxes will become black boxes. The Archive will be transparent in every sense of the word, the artifacts will be freed of their false identities, and we will be allowed to have fun in a place that we least expected it.

10

11

12

10 – *Extension to the Penn Museum and Archive* by Yasmine McBride, Exterior Perspective
11 – *Extension to the Penn Museum and Archive* by Yasmine McBride, Ground Plan
12 – *Extension to the Penn Museum and Archive* by Yasmine McBride, Section Perspective

Wednesday, October 2, 2019 — Sunday, October 13, 2019

SPATIAL EFFICIENCY NOW: Work from the Polyhedral Structures Laboratory exhibited at DesignPhiladelphia

For DesignPhiladelphia 2019, this exhibition brings together some of the ongoing design research projects at the Polyhedral Structures Laboratory (PSL) at the University of Pennsylvania Stuart Weitzman School of Design. Each work on display is a unique design response to specific conditions of forces being brought into equilibrium. These examples illustrate an unconventional design method that introduces the inclusion of force equilibrium at the very early stages of design. With this method, a designer can precisely control the geometry of the flow of forces in a three-dimensional space to design architectural structures.

PSL is an interdisciplinary research center working at the intersection of architecture, structural engineering, computer science, mathematics, and material science to bridge the gap between engineering and design. The works in this exhibition were designed using Polyframe Beta, a geometry-based, structural form-finding plugin for Rhinoceros3d, developed by the Weitzman School's Assistant Professor of Architecture Dr. Masoud Akbarzadeh and Dr. Andrei Nejur. PolyFrame Beta allows architects and structural designers to explore a variety of unconventional spatial structural forms, accessing possibilities that they could not discover or design before. PSL is part of the Advanced Research and Innovation Lab in the Department of Architecture.

November 11, 2019

WOMEN [RE]BUILD: STORIES, POLEMICS, FUTURES BOOK LAUNCH

Edited by Associate Professor Franca Trubiano and Weitzman School alumnae Ramona Adlakha (MArch'18) and Ramune Bartuskaite (MArch'18).

Published by Applied Research and Design

The book includes contributions from Senior Lecturer Joan Ockman, Despina Stratigakos, Lori Brown, and Mary McLeod. It also features conversations and position statements from Miller Professor and Chair of Architecture Winka Dubbeldam, Inaugural Kanter Tritsch Medal Recipient Billie Tsien, Jeanne Gang, Graham Chair Professor of Architecture Marion Weiss, and Sadie Morgan.

[ARCH 511] HISTORY AND THEORY
Joan Ockman

ARCH 511 is a global history of modern architecture from the mid-nineteenth to the mid-twentieth century taught in the fall semester and required of all incoming M.Arch. students. Along with ARCH 512, which picks up in the spring with the period after World War II, this lecture course is intended to provide not just wide and deep knowledge of the history of modern architecture but also a critical reflection on the present. Among the large questions taken up in ARCH 511 are the following: How did accelerating processes of industrialization and urbanization transform the practice and profession of architecture? What social and environmental problems attended these transformations, and how did architects endeavor to solve them? What role was played by aesthetic movements, cultural and intellectual discourses, and visionary proposals? How did wars and political upheavals, economic cycles, and ideological cross-currents affect architecture? In what ways did new attitudes toward public and private space, toward identities and popular culture, and toward nature shape architecture and its imaginary? Questions like these have lost none of their resonance as we grapple with unprecedented changes and challenges in today's world. The course goes well beyond the familiar canon of names and isms, aiming to impart knowledge that that can amplify and enrich the education of professional architecture students.

More specifically, ARCH 511 engages with historical episodes and theoretical issues that are implicitly or explicitly relevant to the 501 studio with which it runs parallel. Currently, students in first-semester studio at Penn design and fabricate containers for the display of artifacts in the collection of Penn's Museum of Archaeology and Anthropology. This design problem can be valuably informed by discussions in 511 related to the institutionalization and systematization of forms of knowledge, the history of colonialism, the changing status of the object in the shift from craft to industrial production, the rise of new modes of visuality and spatial perception, modern architecture's relationship to history, the role of representational and symbolic spaces like exhibition pavilions and world's fairs as cultural flashpoints, and many others. These shared thematics offer interesting opportunities for integrating studio and classroom learning, from formal and informal dialogues to collaborative research to joint workshops and reviews.

[ARCH 521] VISUAL STUDIES I
Nate Hume, Brian De Luna

The coursework of Visual Studies will introduce a range of new tools, skills, and strategies useful for the development and representation of design work. Drawing and modeling strategies will be investigated for ways in which they can generate ideas and forms rather than be used solely as production tools. Control and the ability to model in an intentional manner will be highlighted. Likewise, drawing exercises will stress the construction of content over the acceptance of digital defaults in order to more accurately represent a project's ideas. Documents will be produced which strive to build on and question drawing conventions in order to more precisely convey the unique character of each project. The workflow will embrace a range of software to open up possibilities to achieve intended results and resist constraint of a single program's abilities.

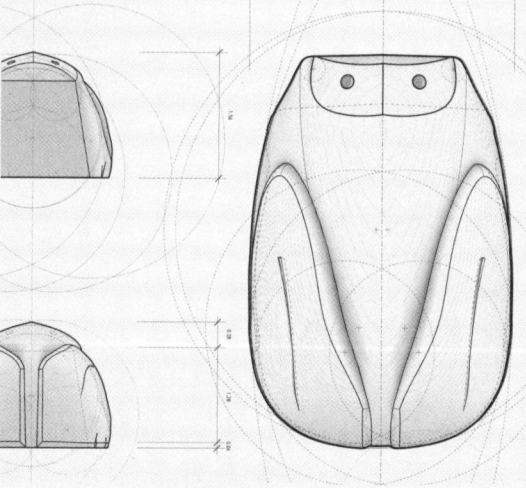

Phase 01 will strengthen drawing and modeling techniques necessary for working with precise controlled geometry. A workflow will be developed to move from photographs and scans of artifacts to controlled digital constructions. These models will then be used to produce a series of drawings conveying and interrogating the qualities of the artifacts. Drawing and modeling techniques will be used to amplify conditions and generate additional features. Layout, notation, projection, and post-production will be explored to fully represent the conceptual and geometric ideas embedded in the work.

Phase 02 will work through orthographic drawing conventions within digital environments. The orthographic set, namely: plan, section, and elevation will be emphasized individually as autonomous entities instead of an interrelated group of drawings to explore the potentials of aesthetics within each disciplinary convention. Existing digital models (501 Pavilion Project) will serve as the test objects to further explore and speculate through the abstraction of planametric, sectional, and elevational line drawings.

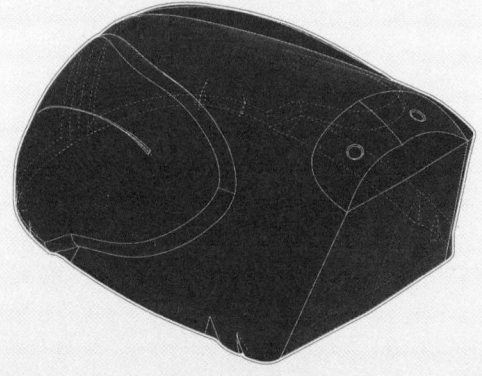

Phase 03 will explore ways of building a conceptual and spatial argument through drawing. Diagrams and analytical drawings are the ways to communicate ideas and design intentions, by

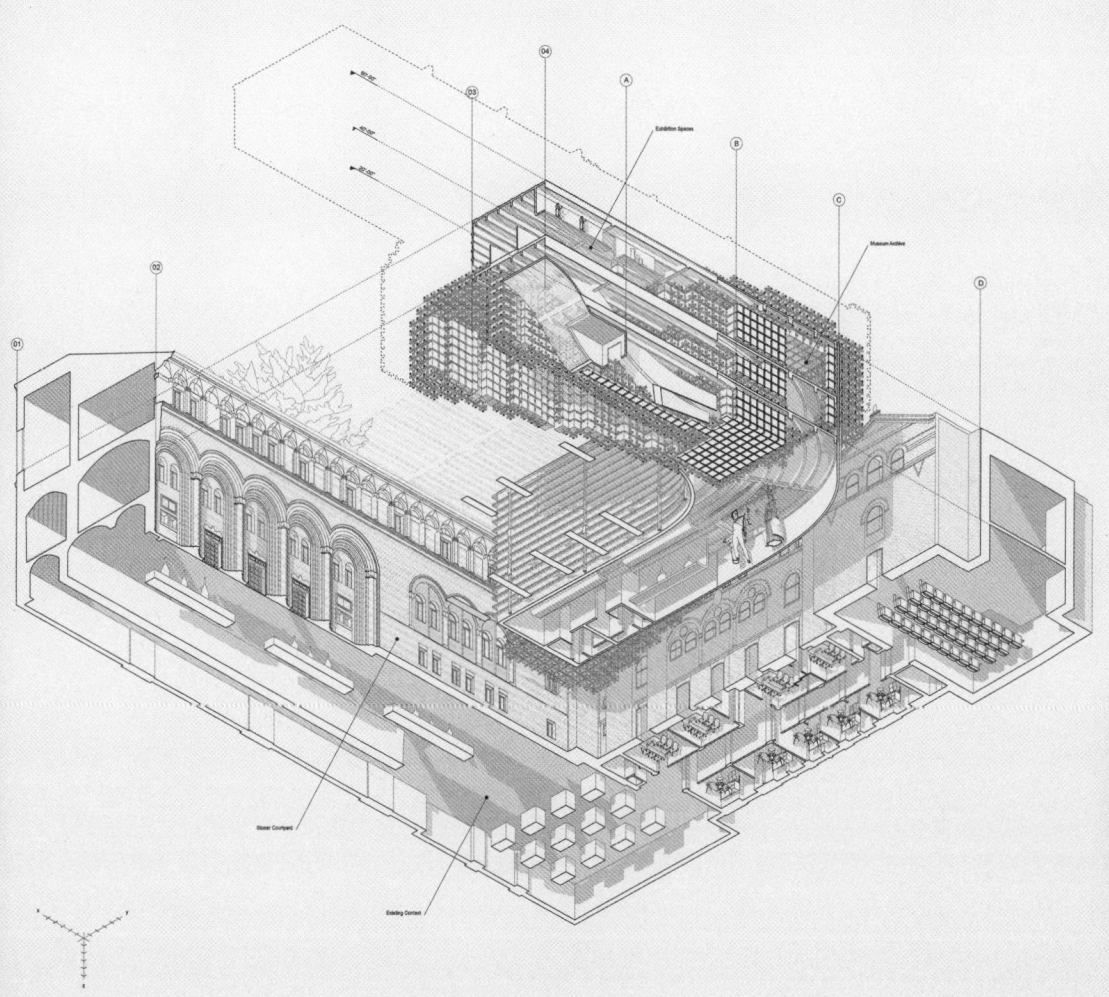

reducing a whole to digestible parts and uncovering unrecognized relationships between these parts. On one hand, an analytical framework defines an armature of measurable constraints and observations; on the other, it is a rhetorical device—a selective re-presentation of the object or site that reveals the architect's attitude toward it. During this phase, parallel projections (multiview, axonometric, and oblique) and descriptive geometry will be used as analytical and generative tools to re-present and explore the individual projects from the concurrent 501 studio.

[ARCH 531] CONSTRUCTION I
Philip Ryan

This is the first of two courses explaining Construction Technology. This course will introduce the student to the relationship of design and construction in the creation of buildings. The early lectures will trace the evolution and innovation of construction technique throughout history. It will then be followed by a primer describing how design and the act of drawing establishes a vocabulary that architects use to describe the construction of buildings. This will look at how

[ARCH 535] STRUCTURES I
Masoud Akbarzadeh, Richard J. Farley

The Structures courses serve multiple purposes within the program. Fundamental structural principles of systems, elements and materials are related to the study of morphology of structure. Methods are taught to develop skills, knowledge, and intuition for the application of structures to architectural design, including form-finding. The students are propelled to apply analytical digital skills directly to architectural design and to pursue structural optimization in subsequent seminars and design studios, carrying out into the profession.

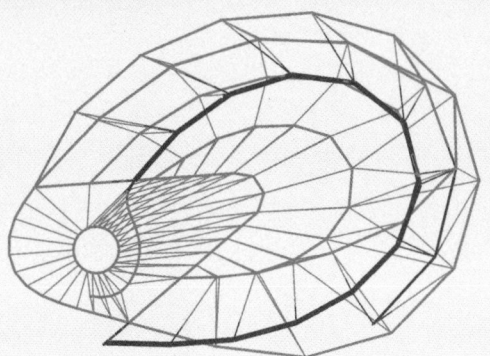

Structures I—the course introduces structural principles, morphology, form-finding and material science, complemented with digital analysis techniques that are verified with standard calculation techniques for selecting and sizing structural elements. This then becomes an increasing resource in the students' architectural design process with particular consideration for physical dimensions, span, materiality, and construction determinants.

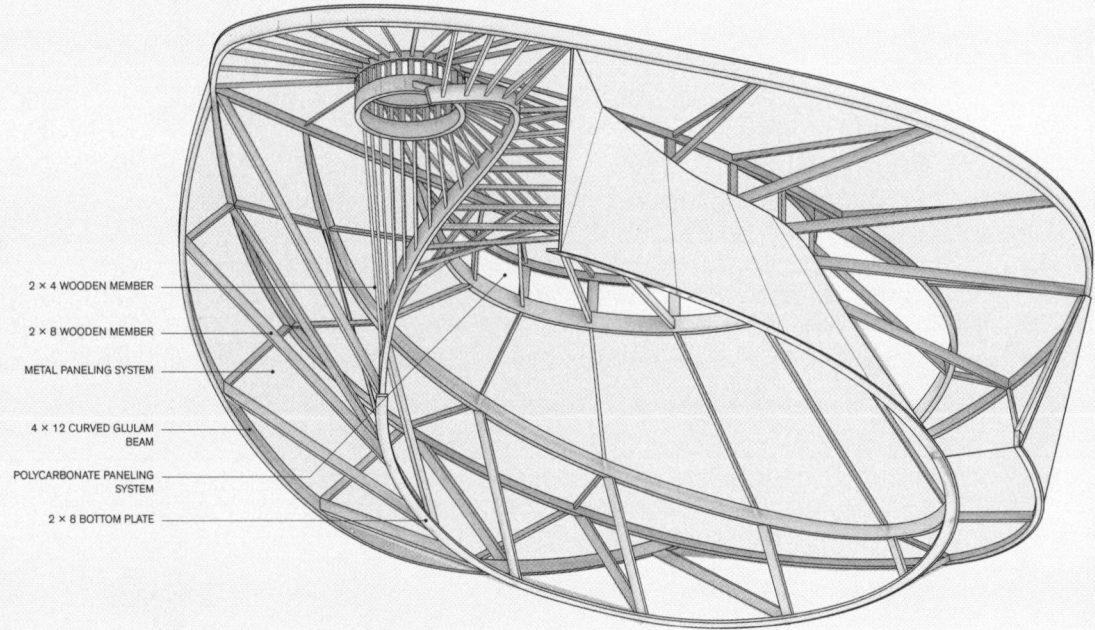

2 × 4 WOODEN MEMBER
2 × 8 WOODEN MEMBER
METAL PANELING SYSTEM
4 × 12 CURVED GLULAM BEAM
POLYCARBONATE PANELING SYSTEM
2 × 8 BOTTOM PLATE

Monumental Memories by Elisabeth Machielse, Street View
Critic: **Andrew Saunders** [p.17]

AMERICA'S
MUSEUM OF
ANCIENT
WORLDS

PENN MUSEUM

Penn Museum Archive Expansion by Kevin Cheung, Exterior Render
Critic: **Danielle Willems** [p.45]

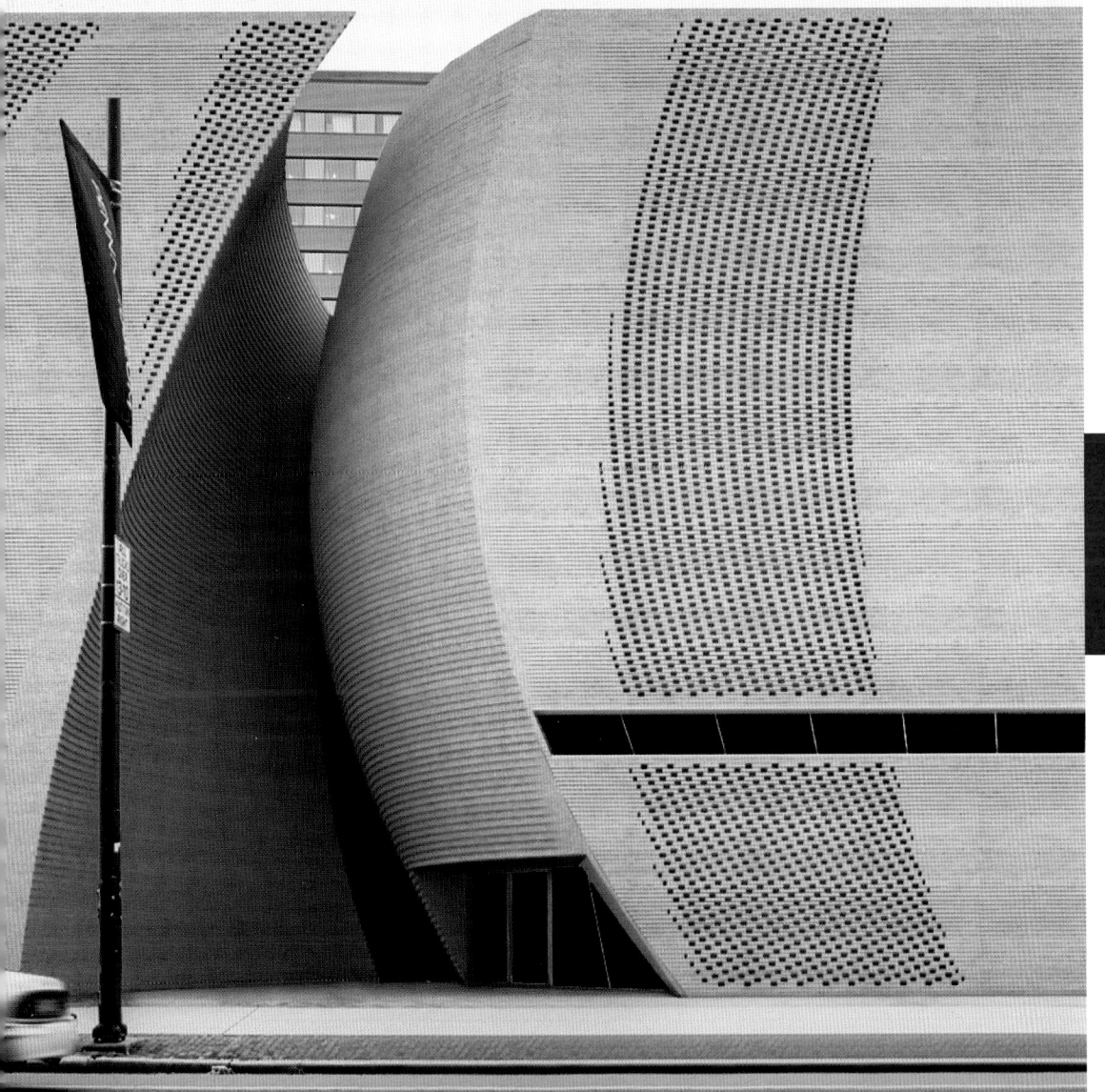

The Force of Flow by Hongbang Chen, front facade render
Critic: **Daniel Markiewicz** [p.32]

Interpolated Residuals by Danny Ortega
Critic: **Maya Alam** (p.27)

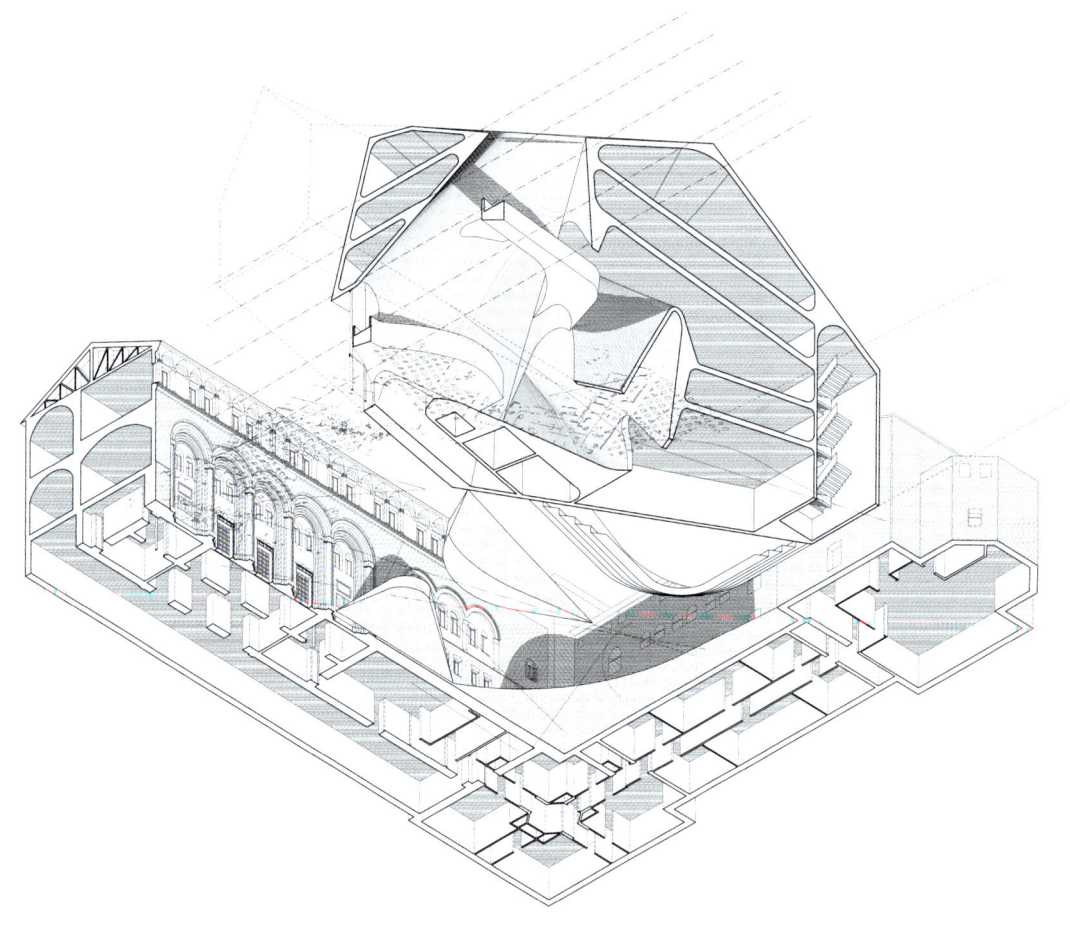

Entwined Tangents by Jamaica Reese-Julien
Critic: **Andrew Saunders** [p.20]

Four Artifacts in Five Colors by Maria Sofia Garcia, Mengdi Jia, Yasmine McBride, David Ka Wai Wong
Critic: **Emmett Zeifman**

Now You See Me by Dongqi Chen, Laura Elliott, Jiacheng Huang, Lisa Kunst
Critic: **Daniel Markiewicz**

Stratigraphic Vestige by Benjamin Hergert, Shiyue Liu, Yifan Shi, Madison Tousaw
Critic: **Andrew Saunders**

CURIOUS CABINETS
AN INSTALLATION BY THE FIRST YEAR GRADUATE ARCHITECTURE STUDIO

Curious Cabinets is an installation project by the Weitzman School of Design first year graduate architecture studio situated in the Stoner Courtyard of the Penn Museum. As an interim project in a semester-long collaboration, the full-scale fabrications of Curious Cabinets house and curate a range of artifacts from across one of the world's great archeology and anthropology research museums. The title *Curious Cabinets* alludes to the early Renaissance concept of *Wunderkammer*—"room of wonder" in German—also referred to as a "Cabinet of Curiosities." As precursor to the contemporary museum, aristocratic collections of art, zoological and geological specimens, as well as archaeological and anthropological finds, were gathered together to form a *Wunderkammer*. While the term "Cabinet of Curiosities" today is problematic in current museum culture due to colonialist implications as well as its curatorial crudeness (in an age of specialized academic expertise), as a contemporary architectural exhibit, *Curious Cabinets* emphasizes the wonderment of the design of the "room" or "cabinet" itself.

Funeral Fire by Valerie Pretto, Penny Peng, Bevy Silanqincuo, Diego Ramirez
Critic: **Eduardo Rega Calvo**

FOUNDATION 502

Annette Fierro, Coordinator
Associate Professor of Architecture, Associate Chair

The second design semester of the first year follows the introduction in the previous semester of properties of objects and lessons of artifacts, conveyed through basic tools and technical skills. In Architecture 502, these foundational precepts are situated and challenged within the plethora of external contingencies which architecture must answer. The semester preoccupies itself with concepts of site, taking students through analytical and speculative methodologies through which the complexities of an urban site are understood, conveyed, and mobilized. The semester also introduces students to the aspirations of program, assigning a large, multifaceted program for students to implement, but also asking students to write for themselves an addition to that program, imparting the affect that program, as a dimension of human activity, has to embodying architectural form. The final component of Architecture 502 is a historical precedent, a figure or seminal idea or reading, chosen yearly for its ability to reflect on a contemporary issue; this year's, for example, is Colin Rowe and Fred Koetter's Collage City, which interrogates and reflects upon the increasing use of graphic techniques of collage which have reappeared in advanced design pedagogies. This topic is taken up in conjunction with the history/theory curriculum of the first year.

The first part of the semester is devoted to research—research of site, research of program and typological precedent, as well as research of representational techniques in conveying urban information and attribute. In exercises which incrementally embrace design, the content of research is embedded into the architectural form which it precipitates. During the first part of the semester, students in sections across the studio meet together bi-weekly for lectures and symposia. This semester hosted Sarah McEaneny, artist and community activist, Francesca Ammon, City and Regional Planning at Weitzman, and Yue Wu of the Philadelphia Chinatown Community Corporation. The studio also worked in conjunction with Richard Farley to explore fundamental ideas of structure. Each section took on a different investigation, from timber construction (Fierro), dome structures (De Luna), concrete construction (Lucia), and others.

This year's program is an urban market, placed in Philadelphia district characterized as a failed urban renewal site of the 1970s, now contested between two identities: the first as a traditional part of Philadelphia's Chinatown, the second as part of a quickly gentrifying arts and residential loft district. Running next to the site is a much-anticipated park development on a disused section of elevated rail—a project that is at the center of the neighborhood's cultural strife. The first intention of the urban market is to explore the potential of this program in particular as a social condenser, overlapping and accommodating the intersection of different agencies and agendas: historically the urban market functioned as the agora, the center of social and civic life, as well as the commercial center of every city and town. While urban markets still function in this capacity to varying degrees around the world, the urban market in the United States can be traced through a series of diminishments. In contemporary America, the cultural centrality of the traditional market has long been suspended, but its traces continue in different forms, scales, and disposition to city morphology. This typology is open to reconsidering—a market is transparent to its local and regional constituency, a market acts as a potent translator of the needs and conditions of site, a mobilizer of economic past and future terms.

FUTURE SUTURES

Annette Fierro (ASSOCIATE PROFESSOR OF ARCHITECTURE, ASSOCIATE CHAIR)
Richard Farley (ADJUNCT PROFESSOR OF ARCHITECTURE, STRUCTURAL ENGINEERING CONSULTANT)
Francesca Ammon (ASSISTANT PROFESSOR OF CITY AND REGIONAL PLANNING)
Saran McEaneny (ARTIST AND COMMUNITY ACTIVIST)
Yue Wu (PHILADELPHIA CHINATOWN COMMUNITY CORPORATION)
Sami Samawi (TA)

Annette Fierro: (Associate Professor of Architecture, Associate Chair) MArch from Rice University (1984) – BS in Civil Engineering from Rice University (1980) – Author of The Glass State: The Technology of the Spectacle/Paris 1981-1998 (MIT Press, 2003)

The identity of the city has always been co-dependent on its representation: from early fantastical maps, to factually surveyed aerial perspectives, to Nolli diagrams of positives and voids, and collages done by early "post-modernists." The latter took on collage as an acknowledgement of the existing city, a rebellious gesture positioned against the autonomous, scientifically ordered modernist city. Here inclusions of photographic evidence of the city represented its ungraspable messiness, its resistance to being taken over and rationalized by over-arching entities. This studio takes as its site of production the capacity of collage: to identify by existing matter outside of drawn representation, to depict ephemera of simultaneity, to incorporate multiple levels of information impossible to convey otherwise. With the many transformative possibilities made available by the original technique, and its digital extensions, the attributes of a given physical site at different scales can be refigured in multiple meaningful ways. What does it mean to graphically characterize and then to follow through the implications of photographic description? What new dynamic conditions can be mobilized when taking conventional 2D collage and finding new ways to express three-dimensional relationships? What does it mean to find and nurture disjunction through graphical method which takes on the additional consequences of social, physical, and economic domains? These techniques will be mined to reimagine how they lie tangential

1   SIPHONOPHORIC MARKETPLACE
                    Liam Lasting

The Callowhill community is a collage of programs, services, and people. All of which are stitched into the identity of this neighborhood and the rich history behind it. The dam created by the Vine Street Expressway has isolated Callowhill from Center City, rendering it as a desert. A place that has been frozen in time, as the city and developers squabble over what is to be done with this land that has fallen through the cracks. In consequence, essentials such as food and housing within the area have been severely neglected as many lots are either languished or converted into parking lots. The lack of these essentials has produced a void that the morphology of this market can fulfill in the form of an oasis to this desert.

Although markets are spaces that provide for the exchange of goods and currencies between parties, they also provoke an infrastructural network, one that is embedded with identity, that can provide additional services and values to the surrounding community. A market can provide a space of accessibility for all income levels as well as cultivate its own goods through the integration of urban farming and building workshops to learn the methods of construction for these petal-like pods. This stitching of housing for the homeless, building workshops, and urban farms into the market produces a Siphonophoric relationship, where each program is designated a specific function to support the operations and growth of this overall being.

The symbiosis which is produced through the coordination of these programs creates more than just a single entity, but a dynamic community. This coalition between a market, food production spaces, and housing units for the homeless will support everyone within Callowhill in one form or another.

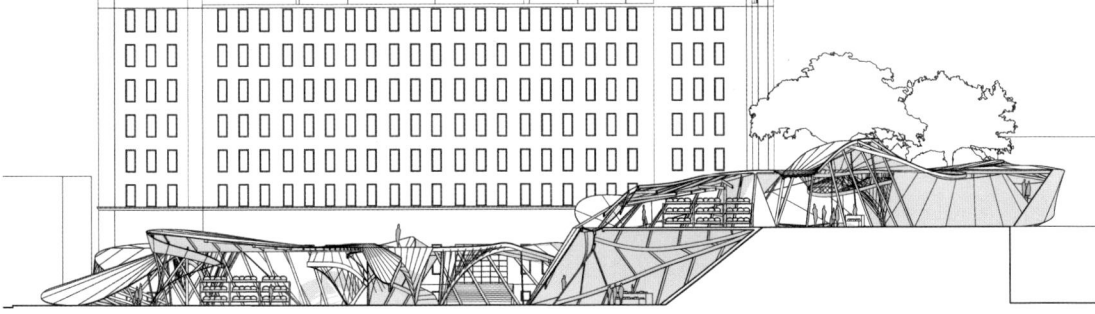

2

1 – *Siphonophoric Marketplace* by Liam Lasting, Project Description

2 – *Siphonophoric Marketplace* by Liam Lasting, Transverse Section

to critical investigation, and then to utilize overlay, morph, collision, to locate newly figured edge or set of points, which will be the loci for finding and releasing the tension of the site. As an entirely different focus, and in conjunction with your structures course, the studio will also investigate the properties of timber construction, in new as well as historical means and methods, to configure these critical intersections/edges. Timber will provide the vehicle—the language, the vocabulary—to manifest prototypes of exchange at moments of critical juncture.

3

4

3 – Studio Travel

4 – *Siphonophoric Marketplace* by Liam Lasting, Transverse Section

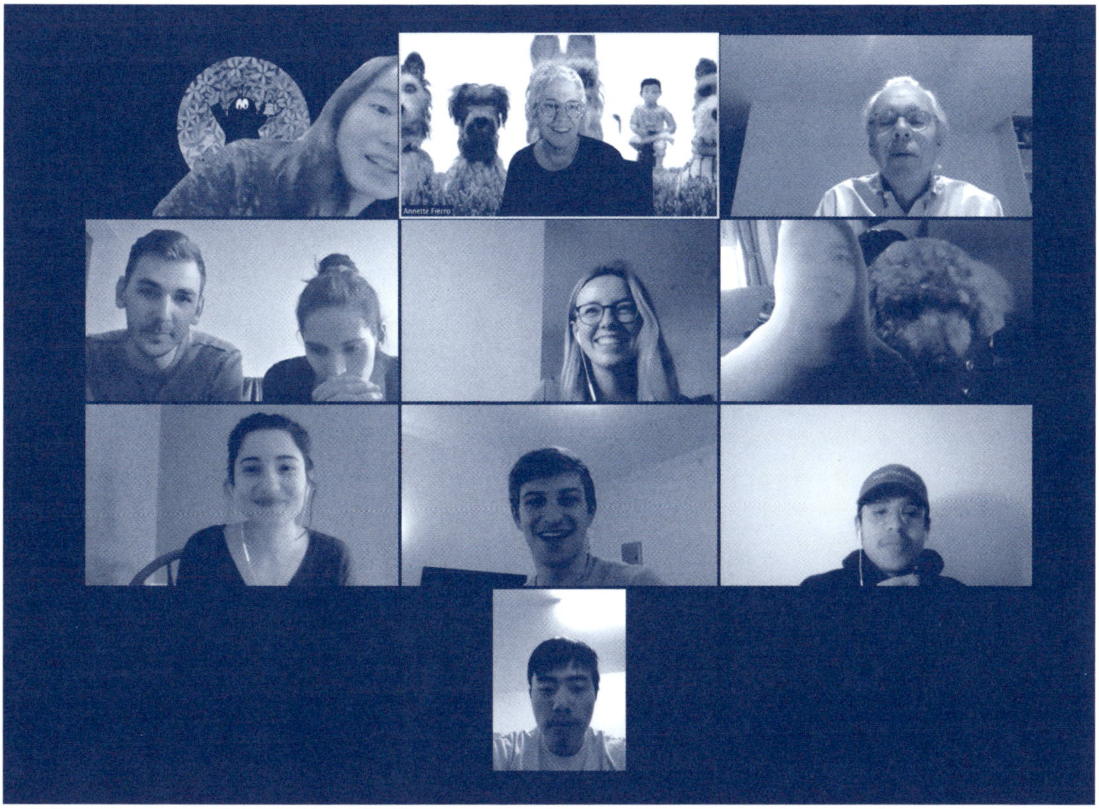

5

6

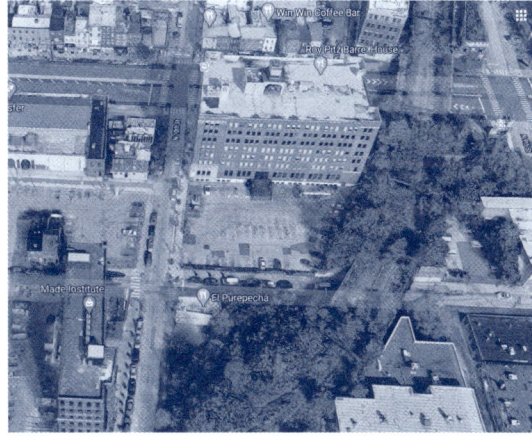

5 – Annette Fierro in Virtual Studio Review

6 – Project Site

APIAN DANCE
Juli Petrillo

This project aims to understand the complex political, artistic, and ideological elements of apian metaphors and implement them into a new marketplace. Visitors of the market will gain a deeper understanding of the symbiotic relationship between architecture, ecology, and the local reviviscent community of Chinatown North.

Bees collect nectar at flowers, then dance from one flower to the next, pollinating and cultivating as they travel. Eventually, they return to their hive to collectively make honey. This collective dance of making drives the program of the marketplace. Humans, animals, insects, and foliage are brought together into a unified system of ecosystems which facilitate the cycle of farming, harvesting, making, learning, and sharing. To achieve this, the structure is woven into the site's existing vegetation and each biome employs sustainable practices. The enclosed spaces' temperatures are passively maintained by allowing air to circulate through the structure similar to how bees allow air to circulate through their hives. Flowering structures grow around the biomes and create an aerial blossoming canopy. While bees circulate above, pollinating the flowers, market visitors can purchase seeds and farming goods below to foster pollination and plant colonization throughout the local community of Chinatown North.

This project invites people to enter the public realm and participate in a celebration of ecological synergy. People can reacclimate themselves to the outdoor environment by exchanging goods and ideas related to urban farming and cultivation. Similar to how the existence of orchids relies on bees, the presence of mycelium enriches plant roots, and the introduction of fish aids in the growth of rice, the market's visitors enter into a mutually beneficial relationship with their natural surroundings.

7

8

9

7 – *Apian Dance* by Juli Petrillo, Plan Axon Combined
8 – *Apian Dance* by Juli Petrillo, Rendering

9 – *Apian Dance* by Juli Petrillo, Collage Image

THROUGH THE ROOF
Danny Ortega

The Callowhill/Chinatown neighborhood has grown into an area that encompasses a complex dichotomy of relationships. Through the extensive research of mapping murals and graffiti in the neighborhood, one might start to digest the complex behavior and their implications that are beyond the understanding that these are solely images on the wall. Through the research and mapping on how the murals and graffiti work on the site reveals issues of class, accessibility, public/private spaces, and the erasure of an urban morphology. For example, murals by the Mural Arts Philadelphia are speculatively used as attractors for urban renewal, however, graffiti within the same vicinity is perhaps used as an antagonist against it. Furthermore, graffiti is created in areas that are inaccessible to the public, whereas murals are used to activate public areas. Finally, murals and graffiti are acting together as a way of populating the vacant lots and open spaces in the area, creating speculative spatial qualities that were once populated by functional buildings.

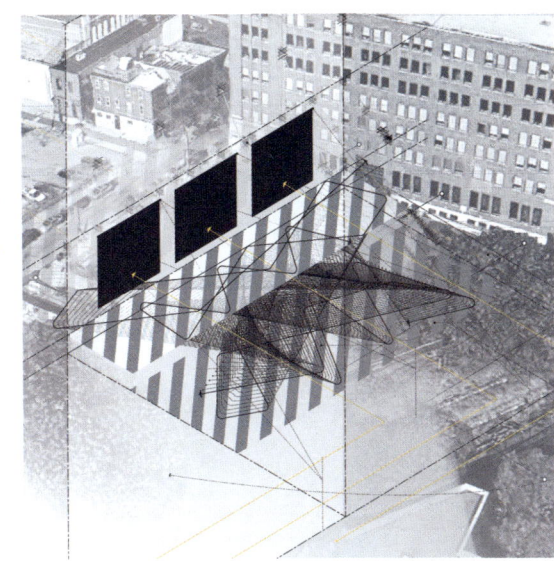

10

With the murals being a perfect precedent to understanding this complex nature, one might start to question how to address these contentious behaviors on the site and how one can rehabilitate an erased urban morphology by observing existing alternative cultural practices like murals and graffiti. By looking beyond these vacant spaces and the images (murals and graffiti) displayed beside them, one can uncover the complexity and dichotic relationships of the neighborhood. It's by virtue of the understanding of these relationships and underlying practices of how murals and graffiti come to fruition that lead to the creation of this project, and for the allowance to create a project that honors these as a form of institution of creative making by interpreting them as architectural form.

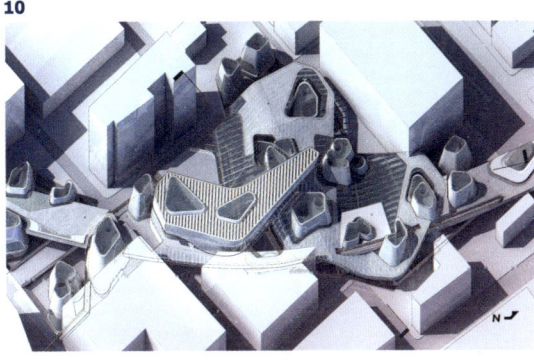

11

12

10 – *Through the Roof* by Danny Ortega, Moment of Exchange Diagrams
11 – *Through the Roof* by Danny Ortega, Site Plan
12 – *Through the Roof* by Danny Ortega, Rendering View

ECCENTRICS OR HOW (NOT) TO FIT IN

Maya Alam (LECTURER)
Megan A. York (TA)

Maya Alam: (Lecturer) Co-founder of Alam/Profeta – Dipl. Ing. Interior Architecture from Peter Behrens School of Arts, Düsseldorf – M.Arch with distinction from Southern California Institute of Architecture, Los Angeles – Inaugural Harry der Boghosian Fellow

This studio is studying how our vision oriented society is affected by new image-making technologies and how understanding architecture through this lens can challenge our ideas of aesthetics, community, and commodifications.

We began with asking some questions: What is considered Normal & and what is considered Weird? What is straight and what is out of shape? What is marketable & what is considered waste? Who decides?

Eccentricity played a role in these questions on aesthetics and power as well as in our approach to site, program and form. An eccentric person or thing is—literally and figuratively off-center. However, who decides what and where this assumed center is located, is always dictated by an existing power structure that claims one single right way for everyone.

Our site, the neighborhood Callowhill, aka *Eraserhood* (named by David Lynch fans, hipsters, and cynics), was designated a so-called Opportunity Zones by

1   URBAN MISPLACEMENT
Dario Sabidussi

Callowhill is a district molded by diverse cultures and people throughout history. The assortment of traditions and people that compose Callowhill creates the "misfit neighborhood." These divisions, or seams, in its urban context allow for a new development that embraces the misalignment of the district's components by combining its cultural and historical elements in a new building form. The exploration of "misfit" through eccentric form and market program enables the reimagination of a city development than can symbolize diversity, and seeming misplacement, of the elements that have created Callowhill. *Urban Misplacement* will emerge as a Construction Debris Recycling Facility, Community Park, and Hardware Supply Market. The integration of industry and community will provide the residents of Callowhill with an understanding of the process of regenerating the materials that once defined the district in building form and will begin to reimagine a future that celebrates the beauty and dynamism of Callowhill.

2

3

1 – *Urban Misplacement* by Dario Sabidussi, Project Description
2 – *Urban Misplacement* by Dario Sabidussi, Oblique Site
3 – *Urban Misplacement* by Dario Sabidussi, West Elevation

the Trump administration in 2019. It is, off-center, cut-off from the city center due to the American urban renewal era.

In order to leverage this site as a space of negotiation, our studio is challenging surveying technology, its data biases and what we understand as real and true. Who controls what we see and how we see it? What is included in our digital (Google) earth but maybe more importantly—what is not? Spherical views, as well as off-center geometric operations were utilized to design these architectural projects.

4

Image – Mining

Students are asked to investigate the site through everyday media. Google Earth, Images, and Social Media are utilized and their fidelity is tested and discussed. Instead of more common analytical drawings of the context, these images become a foreign object that is rigorously studied, drawn, displaced, and recomposed. This incoherent composition became the first proposal for their overall architectural strategy.

Wasted Program

We looked closely at the phenomenon of silicon valley start-ups like Imperfect Produce and its Philadelphia equivalent Misfits Market that understood the interrelationship between our aesthetic ideals and waste culture and are now selling perfectly good produce that would otherwise be trashed because it does not conform to market norms.

Using the case of the ugly fruit as a starting point, students are asked to question what waste is and how it could potentially turn into a cyclical program strategy, by researching a site specific market program and composing a Waste Still Life.

Corona Deliverables

As the semester evolved the students developed tiny planet images of their projects in order to contemplate the future that lies between questions of publicness and our own isolation-islands.

5

4 – *Image-Mining* by Silanqincuo Bevy
5 – *Still Life* by David Ka Wai Wong

6

7

8

6 – *Image-Mining* by Changzhe Xu
7 – *Image-Mining* by Garside Eleanor
8 – Maya Alam in Virtual Studio Review

SHIFTED NOTIONS
Miguel Matos

Geometrically, there was an interest in the exploration of the resulting conditions generated by the clash of primary volumetric shapes. The ability of the resulting object to transition from the clash of two cubes to the absence of spheres allows it to exist between the formal qualities of those two primitive figures while avoiding being categorized as either or.

The project presents itself as an objection to the way that small neighborhoods like Callowhill are misrepresented by big corporations like Google in this digital era. While wealthy neighborhoods are visually represented at the highest resolution possible, other small neighborhoods get relegated to the flatness of a two-dimensional image.

The intervention aims to develop a strategy that creates purposeful misreadings that make a stand against this additional form of gentrification. The extraction of high and low resolution imagery from the site, which reflects how these corporations decide how good or bad a neighborhood is, allowed for the manipulation of the existing textures of Callowhill into a new urban camouflage that blends existing conditions and digital perception.

9

10

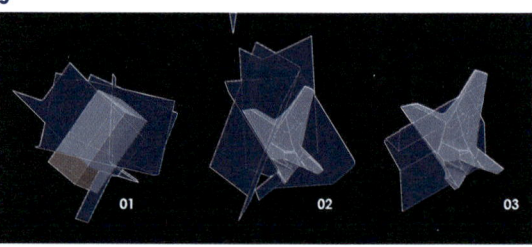
11

12

9 – *Shifted Notions* by Miguel Matos, Render Year
10 – *Shifted Notions* by Miguel Matos, Northwest Elevation
11 – *Shifted Notions* by Miguel Matos, Process Diagrams
12 – *Shifted Notions* by Miguel Matos, Section

LIMINAL FORMATIONS
Jamaica Reese-Julien

Liminal Formations is an exploration of the ability of both form and program to be multiple, often contradictory, elements simultaneously. This project wants to exist in the liminal space between binary conditions, being both flat and volumetric, graphic and spatial, realistic and abstract, decaying and growing. Within this ambiguity, a complex, multi-faceted space emerges. This project is set within the former industrial neighborhood of Callowhill and sits on a brownfield site. The program, distributed across two main forms, holds community spaces—farmers market, dining area, co-working space—and a composting facility that takes food waste generated from local warehouses and nearby Chinatown restaurants. The compost is used to create a series of community gardens and grow hyperaccumulators— plants that absorb toxic metalloids out of the contaminated soil in the neighborhood. After the metals are removed, the soil can be safely resold or used. Liminal formations creates a regenerative marketplace out of the transformative "in-between" space.

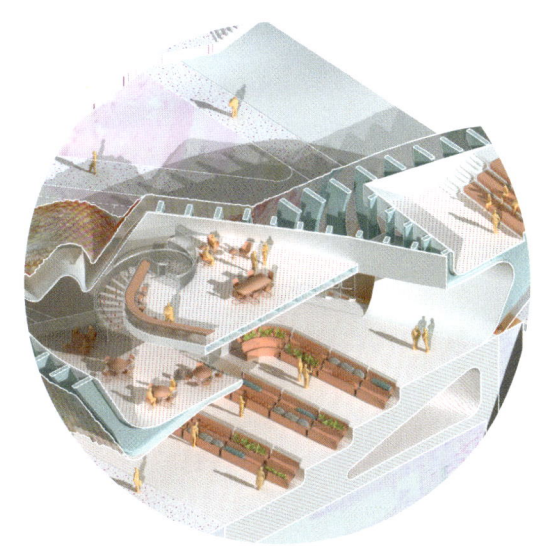

13

 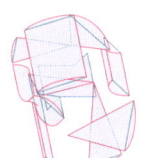 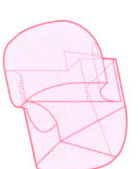 

14

15

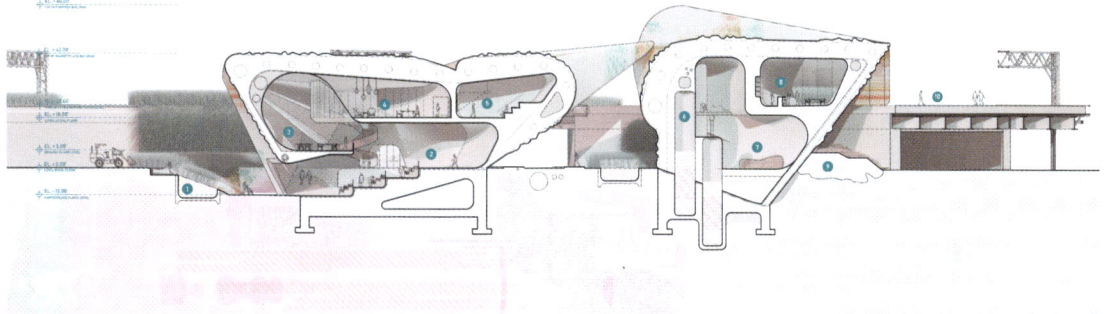

16

13 – *Liminal Formations* by Jamaica Reese-Julien, Chunk Close-up 2
14 – *Liminal Formations* by Jamaica Reese-Julien, Object Investigation
15 – *Liminal Formations* by Jamaica Reese-Julien, 360 Rendering
16 – *Liminal Formations* by Jamaica Reese-Julien, Section

SPOLIA AGENCY

Brian De Luna (LECTURER)
Paul Germaine McCoy (TA)

Brian De Luna: (Lecturer) Founder Studio De Luna – Teaches at Weitzman School of Architecture & Pratt Institute, SOA – MS.AAD. GSAPP Columbia University 2009 – B. Arch. Southern California Institute of Architecture 2006

> "ARCHITECTURE SEEMED INELUCTABLY PARTITIONED INTO BINARY OPPOSITIONS VARIOUSLY LABELED MODERN/POST-MODERN, RATIONALIST/REALIST, EXCLUSIVIST/INCLUSIVIST, NEW YORK/YALE-PENN, WHITE/GRAY, AND THE LIKE."[a]
> – Colin Rowe

Cities, from the unbuilt/theoretical to the existing/developing cities have long been a recurrent subject of intrigue and curiosity for architects throughout history. Analyzing the city is often the basis of opportunity to reflect and theorize on the broader context of architecture, as well as an opportunity for realignment according to various criteria ranging from the pragmatic to the delirious. Besides understanding and cataloging cities into a myriad of different architectural typologies, one can also begin to examine the built environment as a "Holistic design of urban elements."[a] Colin Rowe believed that "Real cities have been shaped by the accumulation of a step by step progress,"[a] that retain and record hidden characteristics and less tangible histories. Rowe believed that modernism strived for unrealistic and unattainable concepts of "Utopia and Tradition"[a] and theorized "That utopias are despotic and lack tolerance."[a] Today as the discipline of architecture seeks to realign itself creates entirely new forms of cultural alignment and expression.

Philadelphia grew from a rigid orthogonal grid connecting east to west along the rivers. Most of the urban development occurred along main transportation systems such as ports and rail road lines. During the 20th century, there was a bloom in urban development due to factories and manufacturing plants. The orthogonality of Philadelphia's initial grid was kept within the old city area, while new neighborhoods were developed in response to manufacturing plants locations. Today, Philadelphia describes a completely different scenario where those factory buildings that were abandoned are now being repurposed. This urbanization can be interpreted as a glitch where the city morphology loses clarity and redefines itself again later.

From an overlay of analytical map studies and an analysis of the features of Art Nouveau, the project seeks to reflect how Philadelphia's grid combines modularity and fluidity. This movement was a new approach to technology and it was described as a redefinition of the industrial movement. This project merges the symmetry and regularity of typical industrial buildings with dynamism and movement inspired by natural forms such as the sinuous curves of plants and flowers. The industrialization left us the buildings, while nature has seized the ruins and evolved them into gardens. Unlike those robust factory ruins, this market works as a machine in function of nature.

> "UTOPIA: DECLINE AND FALL?"
> – Colin Rowe

Cities are extensive systems that contain histories and memories, which go beyond the memories of the built environment. Rowe's criticism of modernists' urbanism stemmed from their lack of understanding of the city. He criticized modernism's belief that cities are

1 – *Crepta* by Ana Celdran, Project Description

2 – *Crepta* by Ana Celdran, Elevation

understood as a construct of unlimited space, with a great emphasis on "Utopian visions"[a] and argued for more spatial diversity with greater variety between space and object, through a process of collaging and layering of parts, objects and space, which can be seen in Rowe's ideal precedent Hadrian's Villa which was the epitome of Roman opulence. Examining urban structure as found objects, Rowe reimagined a new city through a ceaseless operation of fragmentation, collision, superimposition and contamination of what he believed imposed on it by successive generations, to produce new anti-utopic urban forms. Those principles reflect his use of ongoing investigative techniques into the typology of urban elements to produce a less binary partitioned city.

This Studio began with multiple modes of researching and cataloging of selected cities through graphic and symbolic representation. The first exercises studied cartography, texture, data, projection, and topographic types of mapping. We researched and explored how to layer different, various elements and results of the cultural, social, topographic and the built environment. Students selected an artist to be used as a lens or filter to produce a more focused, rich and in depth aesthetic. Themes drawn from certain art tendencies or artists' works were used as a filter for analysis, inspiration, graphics and form finding. The market became a culmination and hybridization of the multiple exercises from 2d and 3d objects and graphics. A selected Architecture precedent and a conceptual theme from Rowe was used to produce a stereo-metric Euclidian object that informed the spatial and programmatic embodiment of the proposed market. This Studio included historic precedents from the Baroque to the Contemporary. The goal of the Studio was to utilize new and existing explorations of cities to produce original architectural scenarios (prototypes) that led to new visual and spatial relationships.

3 The city plan of Philadelphia is a significant creation in American city planning since that it was the first one to provide five public parks for the free enjoyment of the community, and together with other historical sites, they are all connected by a grid pattern featuring streets of varying widths, which have made the transportation system of the city as complicated as a huge urban labyrinth.

Phi-labyrinth starts with the analysis of the grids pattern and the diagonal axis of the city of Philadelphia, as well as visual labyrinth studies by Robert Morris to create a figure-ground map as a filter. Besides the map study, Phi-labyrinth is also related to a case study of the subterranean labyrinth for a gothic house by the French paper architect, Jean Lequeu, who made a very narrative section with a series of primitive shapes.

By using the displacement map as visual guidance, several primitives are selected to flourish the spatial and material composition of the Phi-labyrinth. Multiple mapping and overlapping are developed to multiply the overall complexity of Phi-labyrinth, which is an urban complex consisted of a horizontal park and a vertical market. The former is served as a natural threshold between the huge urban labyrinth and the market, and the latter is served as an observation market to provide citizens a new perspective to overlook the city of Philadelphia and read its labyrinth urban fabric.

3 – *Phi-labyrinth* by Zhongming Fang, Project Description

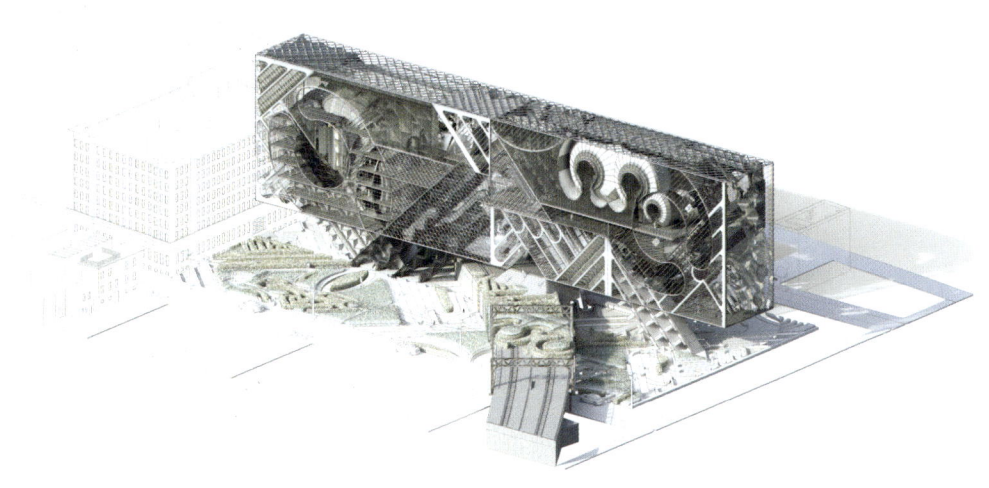

4 – *Phi-labyrinth* by Zhongming Fang, Iso
5 – Brian De Luna in Virtual Studio Review

LEARNING FROM NATURE
Bingyu Guo

Today the city is filled up by the non-stop extending grids. Learning from nature breaks the serious and stable urban fabric, starting a new dialogue between people and the city. Philadelphia green area breaks the grid system of Philadelphia and provides people a new way to read their native city. The artificial landscape nature in Philadelphia "Railway Park" designed by Bryan Hanes using the past railway and make a figural cut into to Philadelphia city map. This natural figural cut reactivates the city spatially and materially. Not only the city of Philadelphia, but also the city of New York and Tianjin in China, both artificial landscape and natural riverbank profile disordered the existing grid system and multiplied the way of reading the city. Based on the map study, the case study of the national football hall by Venturi developed another dimension of reading nature. Nature, as a member of urban texture, broke the existing and stable disciplines and produced multiplicity. The billboard, from national football hall as media, delivered the information that all humans can read. It is also related to the argument from *Learning from Vegas* that architecture is not served for specific form or function but a free reading that all people can be sharing, which implies the attitude of democracy.

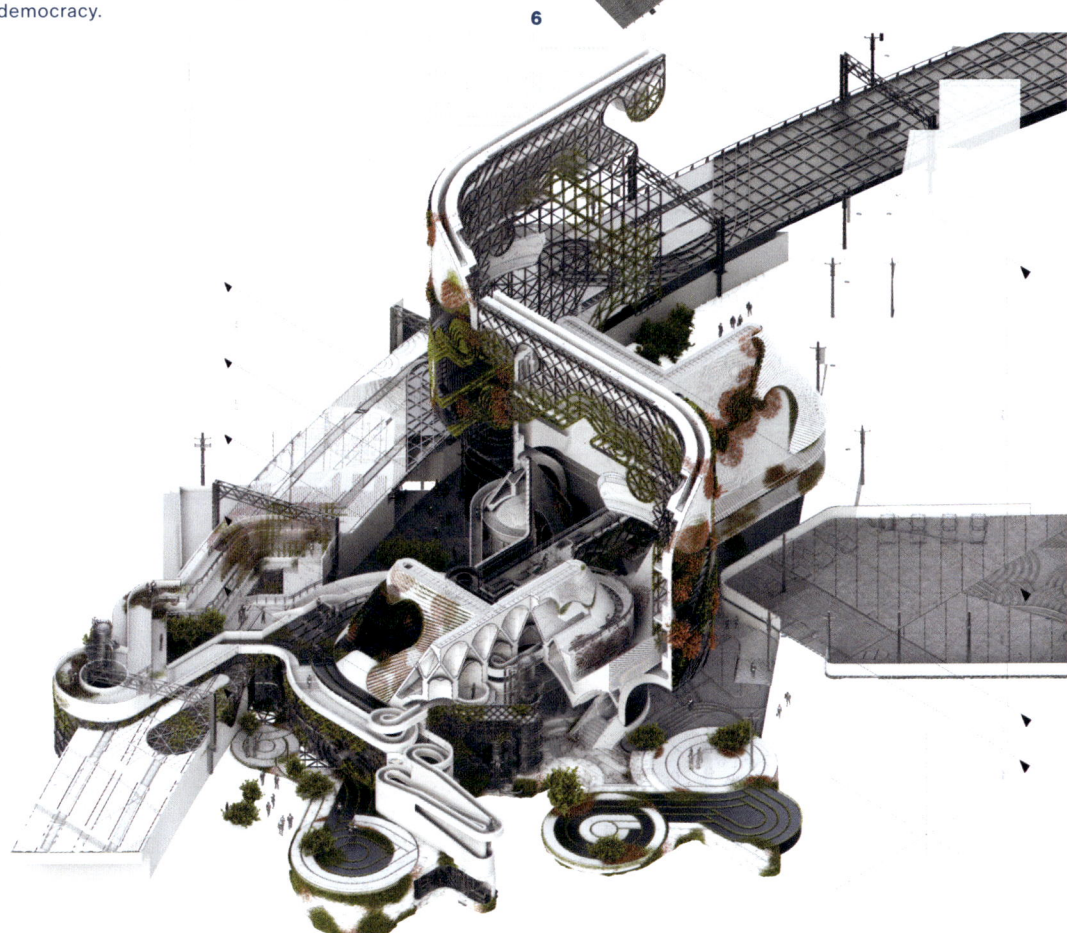

6 – *Learning from Nature* by Bingyu Guo, Final Plan

7 – *Learning from Nature* by Bingyu Guo, Final Iso

IN BETWEEN
Maria Sofia Garcia

During the 1900s, the neighborhood of Callowhill presented a strong connection between urban areas and residential regions. The current situation seems to be much more isolated. The blend of the qualities found in the city analysis and explorations of primitive precedents generated the design intent for a project that could propose the same close connection the city had but now at the neighborhood scale.

The proposed market aims to create a deep link between exterior and interior spaces, as well as public versus private moments. This relationship is achieved by the creation of overlapping programs: production and distribution of wine, aquaponics, and public spaces flexible enough to accommodate for different programmatic needs.

Vineyards are distributed throughout the intervention often extending to its facade, blurring the distinction between public and private spaces. Wine aging facilities are exposed to public activity as well as wine fermentation procedures. The emphasis of free and open public spaces becomes an important factor with the overlapping of the second program, aquaponics, where the introduction of a large reflective pool in the main plaza not only serves as a functional aquaponic element but also enhances the public experience.

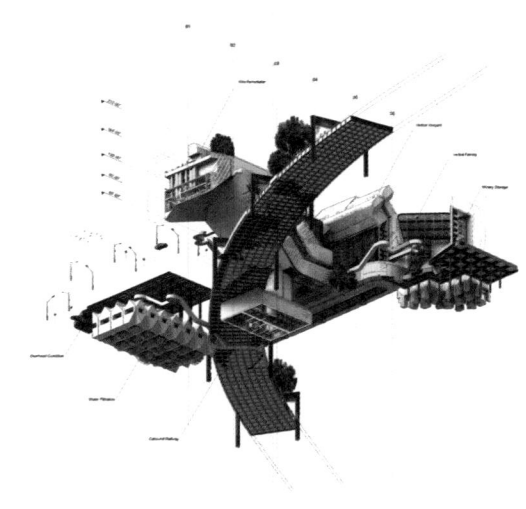

8 – *In Between* by Maria Sofia Garcia, Choissy

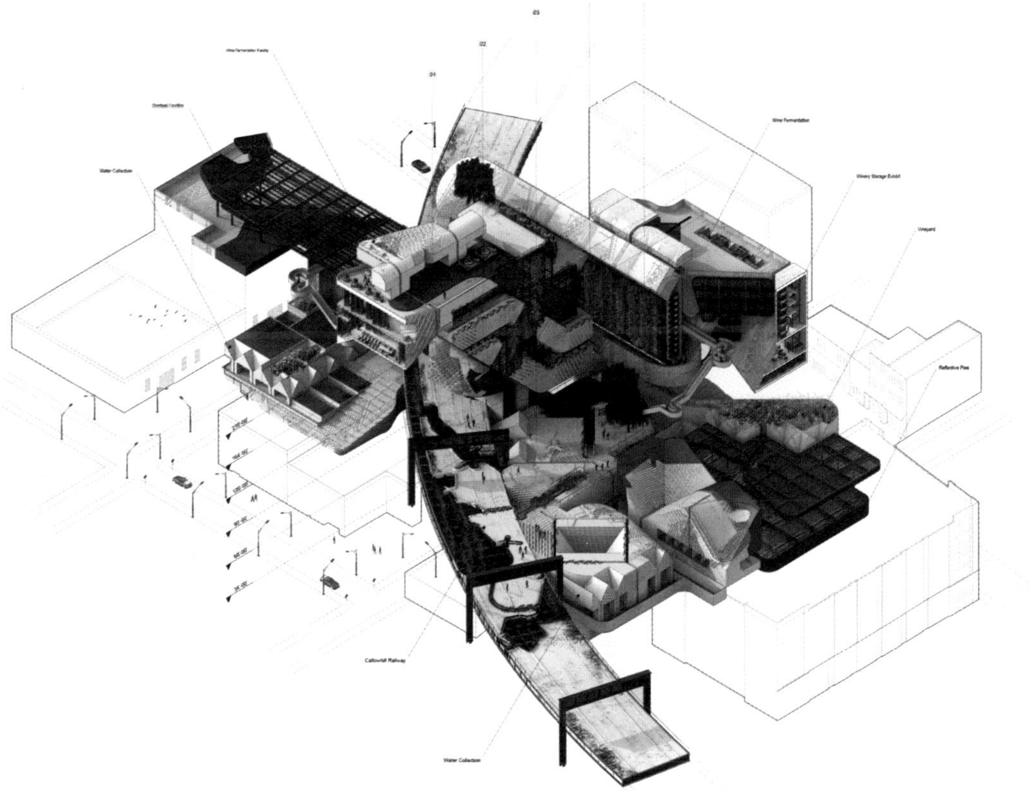

9 – *In Between* by Maria Sofia Garcia, Iso

BETWEEN CATEGORIES

Andrew Lucia (LECTURER)
Daniel Yang (TA)

Andrew Lucia: (Lecturer) LUCITO, Founding Principal – Andrew Lucia (Solo Art Practice) – 2015-17 Cass Gilbert Visiting Fellow, University of Minnesota – University of Pennsylvania, M. Arch, 2008 – University of Minnesota, B.A. in Architecture, 2001

This studio section approaches the city and typology of the urban market as assemblages comprising distributed elements through time—aggregate collections of material, data, qualities and experiences. Considered in this manner, the market as an urban condition can be seen as a collage, an amalgam of disparate qualities and spatial/material moments assembled, erased, exposed...(repeat). Collision, imposition, contamination residues of the past persist as artifacts, echoes whose permanence give rise to an overarching sense of composite identity and character.

1   COLLAGE MARKET
       Siwei Zhu

This project looks at the opposing character of the back and front facade conditions of urban residential blocks in Philadelphia. Drawing on Rowe and Koetter's discussion of these conditions in *Collage City*, "...with the representation of the public realm and its public facades, compromised not only the pleasurable possibilities but, worse than this, the essential sanitary bases of that more intimate world...the facades should not designate any effective frontier between public and private. They are evasive." Taking up this observation, the project blends the tidiness of the front with the playful and personal space of the back not only visually but spatially. Additionally taken in the context of *Collage City*'s critique of rational modernist urban planning, the project exists as neither a field of objects nor as a reified collection of objects in a field, rather operating between categories as a distributed market strewn throughout the residential towers and landscape. Here, the territories of the market and residential units of the towers blur the lines between front and back; what is interior and exterior is intentionally broken throughout the towers' facades and internal open courtyards. To this, the patterned facades and market program of the towers peel off and throughout the surrounding urban groundscape, further disintegrating the boundaries of object and field alike.

2

As a society primarily mediated via the image, we are arguably in a process of transition from one governed by a regime of orthographic geometric protocols to one comprised of vast distributions of information, image, and spatial data. With this digital remediation comes new material residue ripe to be mined for its aesthetic potential —the virtual stuff of surface, texture and territory. This digital terrain may be crude, to be sure, but only so as a factor of the scale and fidelity at which this particulate world of spatial data is rendered and experienced.

When approached as a question of scale and texture, the process of zooming in to an analog image, quantized image or a material architectural/urban condition reveals mid-scale boundaries that give way to hazy densities of microelements; their figures only revealed when observed outward at the macro level. Architecturally speaking, this could be read as a poche condition defining a

1 – *Collage Market* by Siwei Zhu, Interior Render

2 – *Collage Market* by Siwei Zhu, Render

filigree of interior spaces within the confines of an architectural object, while on an urban scale the poche serves to reveal objects within a field or field of objects within a city—in a state of potential that is neither and both, between categories.

3   CUBIST COLLAGE OF URBAN INTERSECTIONS
Yifan Shi

4

The project presents itself as a cubist collage of urban intersections, a guiding principle fusing ecological brewery production, market and garden whose foundations draw from market typologies, the spatial conditions of urban intersection, brewery production and its functional requirements. The idea comes from the extraction and combination of "intersections," a comprehensive notion for both actual urban spatial characteristics, and more conceptual programmatic and social considerations. There are two main systematic organizations that generate this market through their intersection. The first is a water purification system that collects both storm water and wastewater around the site, transferring them to a usable stage for further production. The second is the brewery system that includes multiple functions and activities beyond the basis of integrated brewery production such as public gathering, retailing, visiting, resting, entertaining, etc.

Through the intersection of these infrastructural and industrial systems, new social and spatial conditions are created demonstrating a range of loosely bounded zones across multiple scales of urban fabric. A variety of blurred urban spaces emerge, hierarchical in program yet flatted through pattern, oscillating between any fixed reading of space, sequence or function. This new collaged condition questions the understanding of urban boundaries while stitching industrial programs with the social features of a market. Through overlay and overlap, multiple possible intersections arise, and with them new experiences, offering a range of spatial and social interplay through this collage of urban infrastructure, brewery production, market, and public garden.

5

6

3 – *Cubist Collage of Urban Intersections* by Yifan Shi, Project Description
4 – Studio Review
5 – *Cubist Collage of Urban Intersections* by Yifan Shi, Bricollages and Prototypes
6 – *Cubist Collage of Urban Intersections* by Yifan Shi, Elevation Rendering

7 – Andrew Lucia in Studio Review
8 – Studio Review

MARKET MEANDERING
A HUB FOR A MOBILIZABLE VENDER
Shan Li

If we draw an analogy between a city and a market, the circulation within the market can be seen as road systems and the market stalls as urban blocks. The site is one of urban spaces that have been shaped by turning points of the road system. To explore this kind of irregular urban quality, the turning point of the road system and the surrounding urban fabric are studied and drawn upon. To further understand the cell of a market, different market stalls are collected and deployed. In a conventional market system, we usually see the vendor as the permanent host while the buyer is the customer and visitor who circulates. The objective of Market Meandering is to challenge the permanency of vender, introducing a continuous linear route, occupiable by both mobilizable vender and public while providing a more dynamic interaction between seller and buyer. The project resides between categories, as a synthetic form of urban infrastructure reminiscent of the banalities of parking ramps, yet with a densely layered market fabric strewn about its skeleton.

9

10

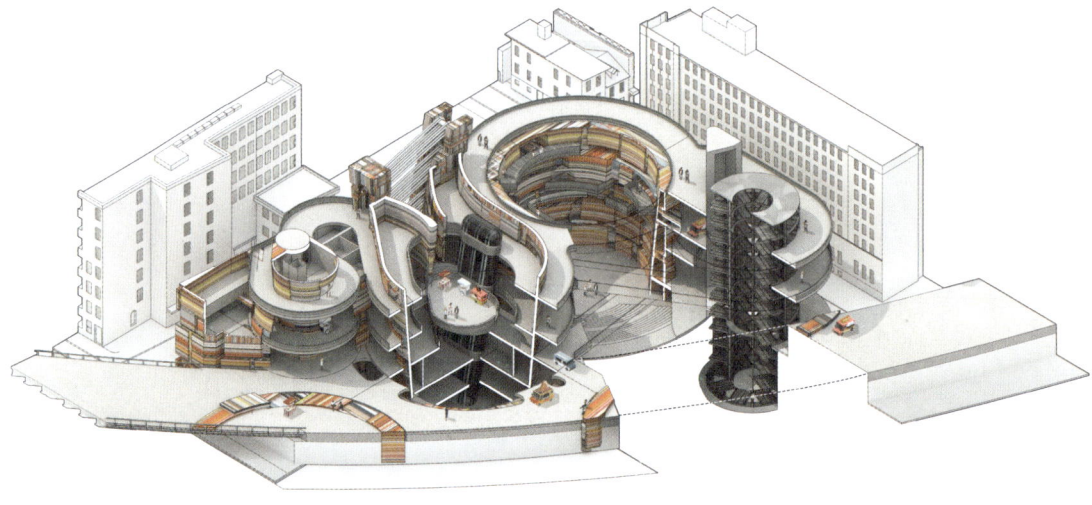

11

9 – *Market Meandering* by Shan Li, 3rd Floor Gathering Spot

10 – *Market Meandering* by Shan Li, Year 10
11 – *Market Meandering* by Shan Li, Isometric Visual Study

PHILADELPHIA MASQUE
Yuxiang Qi

Amid the chaos and noise of the city, the arcade has for centuries given back a secret place, light-filled and quiet. It is a transitional zone stitched into the urban fabric, between the private interior world of an urban block and the public life of the street, blurring the boundaries between these two arenas, between categories. The arcade is not only a distribution center for goods and people, but also an important urban space node operating as both figure and ground. Can this ancient urban element play its role in cities today?

Considered as a small urban condition, a miniature urbanism, the market is composed of different systems and collections of lived experiences. It is here that the project resides, not existing as an isolated object set within an urban lot, but as a collaged condition of urbanity comprising a multitude of follies whose characteristics have been derived from the leftover fabric of the city's layered history. It is here, within this collection, that we rediscover the arcade, asking whether this ancient market prototype can be revived in the present site, bringing new vitality and possibilities to its ad hoc urban surroundings. A cohesive whole has emerged, yet one that embodies the unpredictability, diversity, and complexity of the city.

12

13

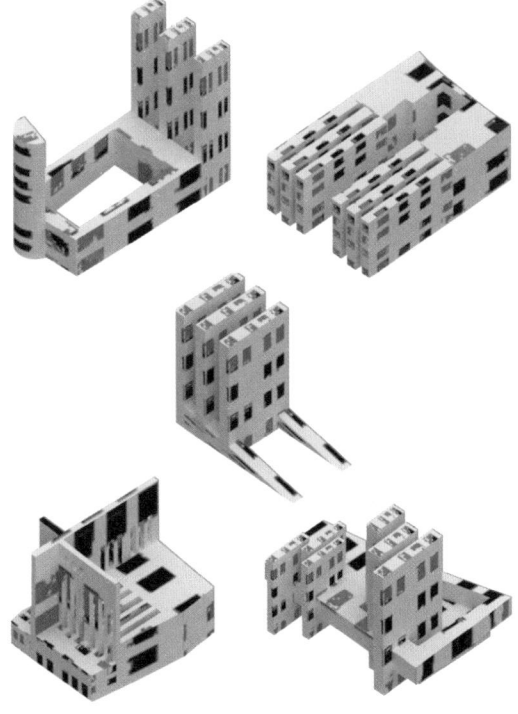

14

12 – *Philadelphia Masque* by Yuxiang Qi, Bridge View
13 – *Philadelphia Masque* by Yuxiang Qi, Exhibition View

14 – *Philadelphia Masque* by Yuxiang Qi, Texture Strategy

ARCHITECTURES OF COMMONING VOL.2: POLITICIZING TYPES WITH COMMONSPOLY

Eduardo Rega Calvo (LECTURER)
Eliana Weiner (TA)

Eduardo Rega Calvo: (Lecturer) Founder of Architectures of Refusal – Editor at urbanNext, Actar publishers – M.Sc. in Advanced Architectural Design from Columbia University, GSAPP – M.Arch from Polytechnic University of Madrid, ETSAM – B.Arch from University of Las Palmas de Gran Canaria

In an attempt to offer an alternative to Monopoly, the game that celebrates huge economic and real estate accumulation and collective bankruptcy, Commonspoly was recently released to illuminate, through play, alternative non-exploitative processes of city-making. For its capacity to broadly educate on the general dynamics of urban development by questioning current regimes of property, our 502 design studio this semester aims to redesign the Commonspoly board game to reflect the specificities of Chinatown North in Philadelphia. Chinatown North's Commonspoly serves as a launchpad for our critical discussions around architecture's entanglement in the systems of power that produce the city. Through the act of playing, and generating various scenarios, our studio explores systems of exchange and forms of ownership, where profit is replaced by benefit, market value by use value, and where accumulations of capital and private property are challenged by the collective reclamation of the commons.

1   COMMONS IN CRISIS PHASE 03: [RE]COVER
     Tuo Chen

Everyone has been touched by effects of the virus, even if they didn't contract it. With a death toll in the United States of 750,000, many lost loved ones. The collapse of the economy has left many without a job and without financial security. Many government funded initiatives have been cut by the conservative government, leaving many without access to basic services. Anger and insecurity leads to a growing movement of unrest within the community. The government increases police presence in the neighborhood, resulting in a disproportional arrest rate of those most in need.

Youth Art and Self-Empowerment Project (YASP) now steps into the spotlight to aid in the rehabilitation and recovery of the battered community. Due to FEED's extensive influence within Chinatown North, YASP becomes a partner in this co-operative. Although urban agriculture remains a key program of the site, the immense mobilization is no longer required. Portions of the site become covered and enclosed to create interior space to function as cultural and recreation space. The cultural programming by YASP aims to prevent criminal behavior as well as provide support for those previously incarcerated.

The emergency funding that had been supporting the initiatives of FEED during the pandemic was halted by the conservative government once the virus was deemed eradicated. This meant that the co-operative had to adopt a profit-based model to continue operation. To continue providing food to those in need, excess produce is sold at farmer's markets. To provide free cultural programming, larger ticketed events and activities are also held in the space. This dual function—programming for both a low-income population as well as middle to high-income—establishes the site as a community hub for all. The inclusivity strengthens bonds, not only rebuilding a community that once existed but improving it.

2

This year's 502 general syllabus takes the market as its main program. In its origins, the market is also the center of political life in the city, the Agora. In Commonspoly, like in occupy movements and popular revolutions across the world, the agora also names the space where collective uprisings against corrupt states and corporate domination are frequently staged. Our studio therefore treats the market as an Agora, a typology where principles of distribution, cooperation and access prioritize public benefit and oppose private profit maximization. Critically engaging

1 – *Commons in Crisis Phase 03: [RE]COVER* by Tuo Chen, Project Description

2 – *Commons in Crisis Phase 03: [RE]COVER* by Tuo Chen, Perspective

with the market's open and expanded functions and it's potentially strong relations with the city (beyond stalls, loading docks and arrangements of produce), we study its potential as the organizational center of Chinatown North's commons: an urban political activator, an open cooperative, a micro-factory, an urban community garden, etc. Our expanded Market-as-Agora is both a platform for, and a trigger of alternative modes of governance, ownership and local economic development that can support the neighborhood in resisting upcoming real-estate speculation and the threatening wave of gentrification.

Commonspoly, our studio's methodological backbone, operates as a tool that politicizes architectural types by inserting them in a game that can simulate the socio-political processes that produce them. The game provides an environment for collages of architectural types that play out post-capitalist narratives.

URBAN REGIMES OF SANCTUARY
PHASE 02: REGRESSIVE
Madison Tousaw

The right-wing government's unresponsiveness to the COVID-19 pandemic led to the use xenophobic rhetoric to shift the blame. These political and media driven campaigns against migrants leads to an increase in racially motivated harassment across the country. In an already difficult time, immigrants no longer feel safe in their communities. The widespread impacts of COVID-19 also trigger a regime focused on creating spaces for pandemic response. New building regulations are passed across the US as a result of the pandemic requiring all new construction to implement pandemic control and flexibility and adaptability requirements. Two organizaitions focused on equitable development and migration, Philadelphia Chinatown Development Corporation and Nationalities Service Center come together to take on a new role as real estate developers under the new ultra conservative government. With this new role as a front, they remain devoted to helping migrants and their struggles underground. While appearing to be open and transparent, the new building regulations can be used to produce spatial blindspots, escape routes for migrants under threat.

Under the new building regulations, a grid of water and energy access covers the city, rendering most space buildable, taking over buildings and pedestrian areas where necessary. Pandemic control regulations require that architecture remains flexible and adaptable to respond to any program of emergency whenever needed. This also produces an architecture capable of transforming its program with agility based on the dictates of the market. Under this system of fast program transformation, when there is no emergency, space can be constantly rented out at different times maximizing its financial performativity. Under this profitable spatial regime for capitalists, architecture and urbanism are defined by a basic service grid (water and energy), a collection of components that include columns, slabs, stairs, beams, furniture units and walls, and a series of combinatory protocols. Together these components are to be clustered at a variety of scales and plugged into the grid system allowing for a dynamic range of profitable activations of space and giving an appearance of transparency. As double agent architecture, however, the new architectural cluster regulations leave blind spots in various densities of components able to hide vertical circulation in order to provide escape routes for undocumented migrants when threatened by ICE. These hidden spaces provide access to spaces of sanctuary throughout the city.

3 – *Urban Regimes of Sanctuary—Phase 02: Regressive* by Madison Tousaw, Project Descritpion
4 – *Urban Regimes of Sanctuary—Phase 02: Regressive* by Madison Tousaw, Overlay Landscape Chunk

5

6

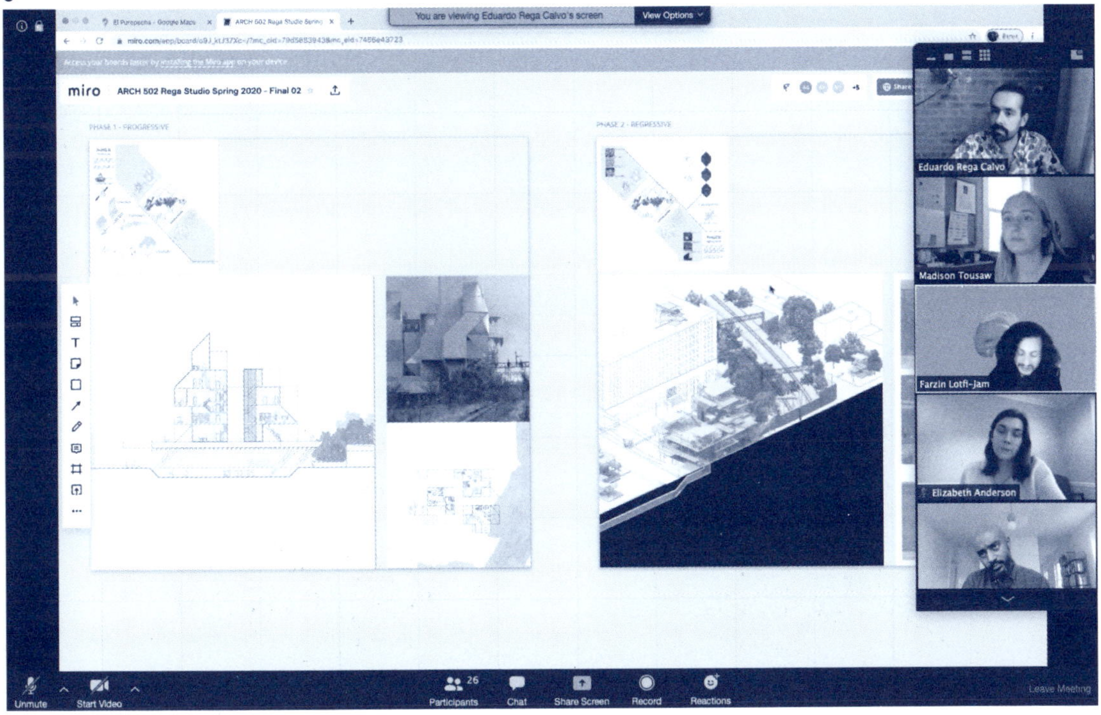

7

5 – *Urban Regimes of Sanctuary—Phase 02: Regressive* by Madison Tousaw, Render—Entry Emergency
6 – *Urban Regimes of Sanctuary—Phase 02: Regressive* by Madison Tousaw, Render—Entry Hidden
7 – Studio Review

ECO-FEMINIST NEW DEAL:
PHASE 01: INITIATE, ACTIVATE THROUGH ACUPUNCTURE
Nicholas Houser

Using the Acupuncture design strategy, the beginning phase is meant to setup the Eco-Feminist New Deal and test ideas for the Politics of Care deployment in Chinatown North. Phase 1 establishes the most pressing programs and infrastructure that must be developed through this overall plan. Neighborhood assemblies begin to take place to learn about the immediate needs of the community. Once this is done, the government funding is allocated to each program. Overall, this phase is designed on the basis of temporary and deployable infrastructure that not only makes use of the immediate site but also begins to redefine what could happen in other neighborhoods around the city, state, and country.

This phase begins to test sustainable systems under the theme of "Experiment – Deploy – Regenerate." One of the main areas of testing focuses on water extraction from the surrounding urban environment through water runoff. This water is then run through initial purification systems that can confirm the model that will be used in future phases. Phase 1 also attaches/punctures into buildings within the site context to test if the existing infrastructure could benefit the overall efficiency within the Politics of Care deployment. These portions of the design can increase total square footage of existing buildings or provide utility services and production. For example, wind and solar energy or deployable greenhouses that can be used to grow food and feed a family unit. The explorations will magnify and grow as the phases continue, eventually leading to production that can be distributed beyond the community.

7

8

9

10

7 – *Eco-Feminist New Deal: Phase 01: Initiate, Activate through Acupuncture* by Nicholas Houser, Axo
8 – *Eco-Feminist New Deal: Phase 01: Initiate, Activate through Acupuncture* by Nicholas Houser, Final Render
9 – *Eco-Feminist New Deal: Phase 01: Initiate, Activate through Acupuncture* by Nicholas Houser, Chunk 1
10 – *Eco-Feminist New Deal: Phase 01: Initiate, Activate through Acupuncture* by Nicholas Houser, Chunk 2

ECO-FEMINIST NEW DEAL:
PHASE 02: TRANSITION THROUGH ARCHIPELAGO
Anabella Gilbert

With the completion of testing in Phase 01, Transition through Archipelago begins a demonstration of the Politics of Care: Eco-Feminist New Deal as a Self-Sustaining Island. This Phase of implementation is expected to be built using leftover funds from Phase 01 in addition to what it was initially allocated by the Politics of Care campaign. Put simply, the Phase 02 goal is to demonstrate, sustain, and evolve. The design is deployed on the Chinatown North site, but it also proposes a strategy that can be expanded across other neighborhoods throughout the city. Each of these deployments would be government-funded and led by site-specific, grassroots organizations (similar to Project Home and Grounded in Philly) that can help lead the infrastructural and care-based decisions. Overall, Phase 02 focuses on the most vulnerable and fosters interconnected, cooperative programs of care: affordable housing, healing environments, community greenhouses/urban farms, and educational spaces.

The program selection is rigorous in its variety, but they work together by each prioritizing the most vulnerable. Each island on the Chinatown North site is made up of a greenhouse paired with an additional program of care. These islands are very open in plan to allow for an adaptable reuse of spaces. The greenhouses transition from their interior environments to the outdoors through a circulation of urban farms. Each island attempts to offer equal variety of program to promote collaboration and cooperation within the community.

11

12

13

11 – *Eco-Feminist New Deal: Phase 02: Transition Through Archipelago* by Anabella Gilbert, Final Iso
12 – *Eco-Feminist New Deal: Phase 02: Transition Through Archipelago* by Anabella Gilbert, Close Up

13 – *Eco-Feminist New Deal: Phase 02: Transition Through Archipelago* by Anabella Gilbert, Vignette 1

CALLOWHILL RELIEF

Andrew Saunders (ASSOCIATE PROFESSOR OF ARCHITECTURE)
Madison Green (TA)

Andrew Saunders (Associate Professor of Architecture, Director of Baroque Topologies): Principal of Andrew Saunders Architecture + Design (2004) — Received an M.Arch from Harvard GSD with Distinction for work of clearly exceptional merit. (2004) — B.Arch from Fay Jones School of Architecture, University of Arkansas (1998) — Winner of The Robert S. Brown '52 Fellows Program (2013)

"THIS IS HOW LIFE BECOMES NOTHING AND DISAPPEARS. AUTOMATIZATION EATS THINGS, CLOTHES, FURNITURE, YOUR WIFE, AND THE FEAR OF WAR."
— Viktor Shklovsky, Art, as Device (1919)

A charge of the studio is to take on the legacy of Colin Rowe and Fred Koetter through their major work of architectural and urban theory, *Collage City*. In particular we will build on the concept of collage: a deliberate variety of space and object, neither in exclusion from each other. To begin the studio constructs reliefs based on both existing and archeological urban artifacts from the Callowhill neighborhood of Philadelphia. Parallel analysis of Louise Nevelson's assemblages informs formal and compositional conditions of framing, grid, edge, figure, ground, light, shadow and Euclidean figuration. The studio explores the flexibility and discrete conditions of Nevelson's assemblages, her arrangements and how they are motivated by flexible interpretations of Mondrian grid compositions. Like *Collage City*, Nevelson's work deals with space and object, but on a much smaller scale. Additionally, the collage seeks to defamiliarize urban artifacts by severing their form from their original place and function.

Defamiliarization as Contextual Trope

In his essay "Art as Device" Viktor Shklovsky outlines a literary trope of defamiliarization as a technique for bring awareness to aspects of culture that have been taken for granted or automatically perceived. By slowing down perception and making "strange" the familiar, a refreshing perception renews the familiar and draws attention to the artistic procedures operating on the it. Building on the reliefs in the initial exercise, the studio becomes immersed in the material cultural context of Callowhill, both existing and archeological.

URBAN SWARMSCAPE
Lauren Hunter

Urban Swarmscape is a 21st-century market that takes the form of a new parceled landscape within the city of Philadelphia. The parcels were drawn from and align with edges of the existing city and site. Variability between the frames result in a rereading of Philadelphia's morphological structure. Parcels each host different programmatic elements that all relate to the raising and selling of honeybee products. Some parcels frame intense, floral bee stations that are both artificial and natural hubs for honeybee activity. Below this upper landscape frames continue to occupy the site at different sectional layers. Urban Swarmscape helps contribute numbers to the depleting honey bee population and offers a new, local source of naturally made products. Thus, offering a mutually beneficial relationship between honeybees and the city of Philadelphia.

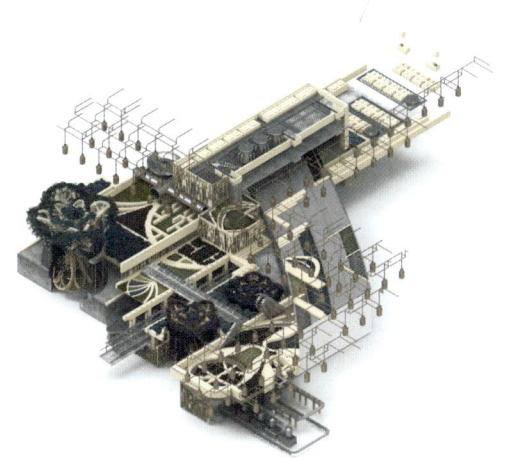

1 – *Urban Swarmscape* by Lauren Hunter, Program Chunk
2 – *Urban Swarmscape* by Lauren Hunter, Entry Render

3 – *Urban Swarmscape* by Lauren Hunter, Project Descritpion

Entrepreneurial Programming

With increasing interest in reviving the fortunes of struggling communities, older industrial cities represent promising regions for strategic investment and critical centers for promoting inclusive economic growth. The project of the studio is an urban market. The program of the market is defined individually by each student—a market for what? With a rich history of turn of the century booming industry, the studio will poses the question of what new industries could spark social and economic growth in Callowhill in the 21st century? Through an entrepreneurial approach, each student researches and proposes a contemporary program for the market. The entrepreneurial programs draw from both traditional guilds of Philadelphia as well as emerging models of industry. Each specific program informs the nature of the new urban market fostering a new typology of unexpected exchange with the community.

4

5

6

HEMP TECH GARDEN
Umar Mahmood

The Callowhill district in Philadelphia city has a new market that provides the much-needed facilities of hemp and marijuana products for the city. The market is designed by building, carving, and rebuilding reliefs from defamiliarized neighborhood artifacts. The market is serving the city with sustainable, environmentally friendly and ethical products. It carves its identity in the city as the density of ubiquitous elements while having unique courtyards of rare figures.

The market has five quadrants, each has a mat density of crisscross Cartesian elements which break their own limits and intersect with elements in adjacent quadrant. The main difference between each quadrant are the unique figural artifacts wrapped in dense Astroturf. Functionally, the market operates on four sections. The retail space, the industrial section, the harvesting area and public gardens. Each program operates on different level. The market has an industrial and synthetic programmatic interaction with the city. Moreover, it inhabits nature by providing urban farming platform.

4 – *Hemp Tech Garden* by Umar Mahmood, Material
5 – *Hemp Tech Garden* by Umar Mahmood, Elevation Daylight

6 – *Hemp Tech Garden* by Umar Mahmood, Project Description

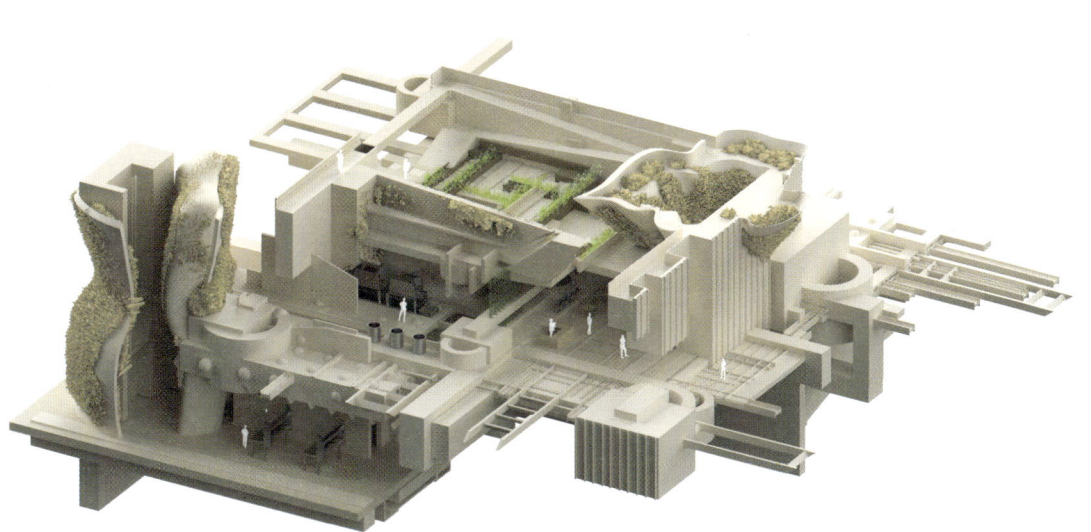

7 – *Hemp Tech Garden* by Umar Mahmood, Program Chunk

8 – *Hemp Tech Garden* by Umar Mahmood, Scene Exterior

BRICOLAGE
Anna Lim

This project introduces the industry of large-scale 3D printing to Philadelphia, and at the same time recalls the city's history as a leader of brick production in America during the 19th century. The design plays with methods of relief, collage, and defamiliarization on varying scales. From the street, dense moments of machine-like relief appear as works of sculpture, as a declaration of what 3D printing technology can achieve for the built industry. Above ground, similar figures operate as actual machines containing moving extruders, filament systems, and operating towers. Below ground are busy research labs and recycling facilities. An open marketplace sprawls across the ground floor, neighboring blocks, and viaduct, as individual vendor stalls are constantly recycled and reprinted for the community's needs. The complex is therefore self-sustaining as both an economic center and as a physical construct, able to serve a wide variety interest groups throughout the year.

9

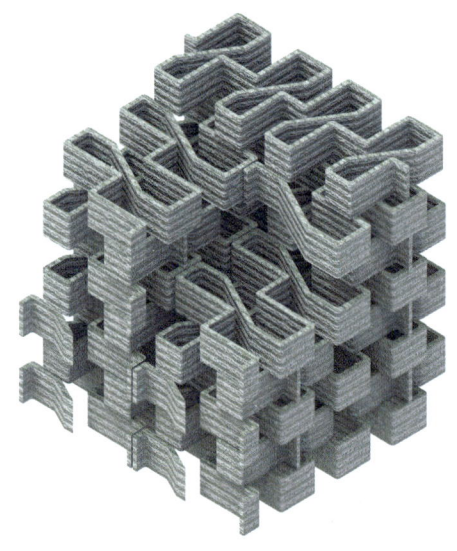

10

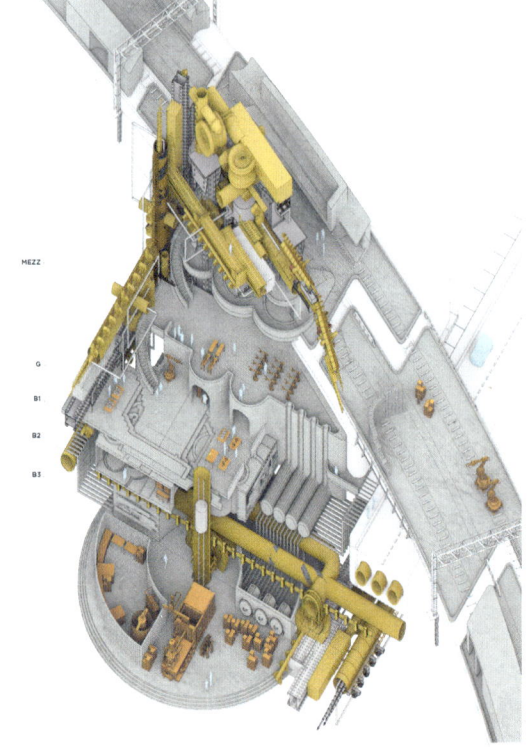

11

12

9 – *Bricolage* by Anna Lim, Elevation Year 10
10 – *Bricolage* by Anna Lim, Material

11 – *Bricolage* by Anna Lim, Viaduct View
12 – *Bricolage* by Anna Lim, Chunk

ARK OF RELIEF
A MARKET AS AN ANIMAL SHELTER
Dongqi Chen

People are ignoring moral doubts over the cruel usage of animals. Even with comprehensive laws designed to protect animals, or organizations devoted to enforcing those laws, the region is still struggling to extend adequate protection to its precious life.

With the salute for the efforts in the chronological transition of animal conservation in Philadelphia, the ark constructs defamiliarized manners for tectonic relief moments under Callowhill's artificial contexts and creates different zones housing the animal crematorium, pet market and gene lab. Ramps and bridges are performing as connectors between chunks and the sunken gardens while the relief elements blur the edges between them. The language that is dominating the project is a result of calibrating what is restricted and what is liberated, a process that assimilates and ultimately ends with a new understanding of an ark for animal.

13

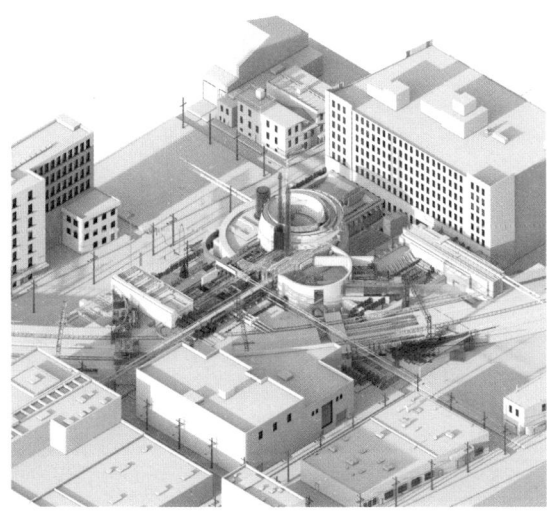

14

15

16

13 – *Ark of Relief* by Dongqi Chen, Elevation Render
14 – *Ark of Relief* by Dongqi Chen, Isometric
15 – *Ark of Relief* by Dongqi Chen, Views 1
16 – *Ark of Relief* by Dongqi Chen, Section

EVENTS

**September 4, 2019
BUILDING AND ALMOST BUILDING
Mimi Hoang, Eric Bunge**

Principals Eric Bunge and Mimi Hoang founded nARCHITECTS in 1999 with the aim of addressing contemporary issues in architecture through conceptually driven, socially engaging and technologically innovative work. The letter "n" represents a variable, indicating our interest in designing for a dynamic variety of experiences within a cohesive approach. In this spirit, we embrace challenges and scales of work ranging from buildings to public spaces to interiors, and across cultural, residential and commercial uses.

"We like cutting holes into buildings, creating erasures from the shallow to the deep, to compound the limits between buildings and their contexts."

nARCHITECTS has been listed in the top 10 firms in design in the US by Architect Magazine for the past three consecutive years. In 2012, World Architecture News named nARCHITECTS "part of a select group crowned to lead the next generation of designers in the 21st century." National and international recognition includes an American Academy of Arts and Letters in Architecture Award, an AIA National Institute Honor Award, AIA NY Design Honor and Merit Awards, a New York City Public Design Commission Award, The Architectural League of New York's Emerging Voices, the Canadian Professional Rome Prize, Architectural Record's Design Vanguard and two New York Foundation for the Arts grants.

Keller Easterling is an architect, writer and professor at Yale. Her most recent book, *Extrastatecraft: The Power of Infrastructure Space* (Verso, 2014), examines global infrastructure as a medium of polity. A recently published e-book essay titled *Medium Design* (Strelka Press, 2018) previews a forthcoming book of the same title. *Medium Design* inverts an emphasis on object and figure to prompt innovative thought about both spatial and non-spatial problems.

Other books include: *Enduring Innocence: Global Architecture and its Political Masquerades* (MIT, 2005) which researched familiar spatial products in difficult or hyperbolic political situations around the world. *Organization Space: Landscapes, Highways and Houses in America* (MIT, 1999) which applied network theory to a discussion of American infrastructure, and *Subtraction* (Sternberg, 2014), which considers building removal or how to put the development machine into reverse.

September 11, 2019
MEDIUM DESIGN
Keller Easterling

"Being right is too weak. It doesn't work against dangerous political superbugs."

[ARCH 512] HISTORY THEORY II
Sophie Hochhäusl

How did architecture and city building reflect the dominant social, economic, political, and environmental changes of the post-war period and how did architecture and urbanism aid in that materialization? How did postwar vast geopolitical shifts such as the Cold War, corporate capitalism, Neoliberalism, and New Nationalism shape architecture culture? How might architecture culture respond to its resistant variants, anti-imperialism, decolonization, and even anti-fascism? How did interwar critical frameworks become revised through the lenses of feminist, ecological, postcolonial, and critical race theory in postwar architectural production? And which strategies of making and thinking architecture and urbanism corresponded to critical theories that actively resisted dominant forms of power? This course provides an introduction to the major developments in architecture and urban culture from the 1930s to the present. In a series of lectures the course traces the proliferation of modern architecture in the world and how it became shaped by locally and regionally specific political, social, economic, and environmental circumstances. While we will trace instances of architecture and city planning that corresponded to dominant ways of thinking and making politics, we will also consider modern architectures of a "third way" and forms of urbanism that actively resisted dominant power regimes.

[ARCH 522] VISUAL STUDIES II
Nate Hume

The coursework of Visual Studies investigates architectural representation as the primary means for communication and development of an architect's position. Representation serves not just as a means for building documentation but is crucial to the generation of thought and of projecting arguments and concepts out into culture. The Visual Studies courses allow for continual evolution as mediums emerge, the courses contain an underlying discussion of the way we develop, consume, and interact with drawings, images, and photographs. Alongside the development of fundamental skills are weekly lectures on the history of representation from the Renaissance to today exploring the introduction of new technologies, drawings relation to culture, and impact on practice of representational turns. These lectures fold in contemporary discussions of visual culture extending the historical themes into fashion, industrial design, art, graphic design, and film. The historical development and use of representation by architects over the past five centuries provides a lens to understand current tools, techniques, and conventions and how they can be productively deployed. The courses compliment studio projects to further explore the ideas and design work through representation. 521 works through documenting objects and space through orthographic projection and isometric drawing while also moving between virtual and physical space with means including photogrammetry and 3D printing. 522 emphasizes drawings as generative devices which project possibilities not just document design decisions. Assignments explore image construction through photography and rendering and the construction of a large cutaway section drawing which speculate on the development of the studio project. 621 integrates more dynamic modeling, texturing, and rendering applications to synthesize and propel work from the earlier modules. To avoid tropes and the inherent biases of the tools, the theoretical and political implications of representation decisions need to be fully comprehended. The three semester arc provides an understanding of contemporary drawing, modeling, and visualization techniques while also creating the necessary grounding in the historical context needed to position one's work to engage and critique larger discussions in the field as well as to shape and impact culture and the built environment.

[ARCH 532] CONSTRUCTION II
Franca Trubiano

Construction Technology II is an advanced course in building technology that informs, instructs, and demonstrates the extent to which industrialized building systems and innovative building technologies impact and guide the architect's design process. The course focuses on multistory buildings whose complexities require the adoption of varying material, constructional, and informational technologies; all which, are never standard, typical, or obvious.

Construction Technology II is focused on exploring and understanding the reciprocal relationship that binds design to construction and construction to design. Designs can be conceived to produce spectacular constructions and construction can be organized to produce ever more wondrous designs.

Construction Technology II advances the idea that architecture is, in fact, an art of building. The success of any design is predicated on the success of its materials, construction practices, and the means used to communicate both. The architect's competent and innovative choice of building materials, (concrete, stone, wood, steel, and plastic) assembly techniques, and methods of fabrication assures a building's success. So too does the architect's choice of representational means.

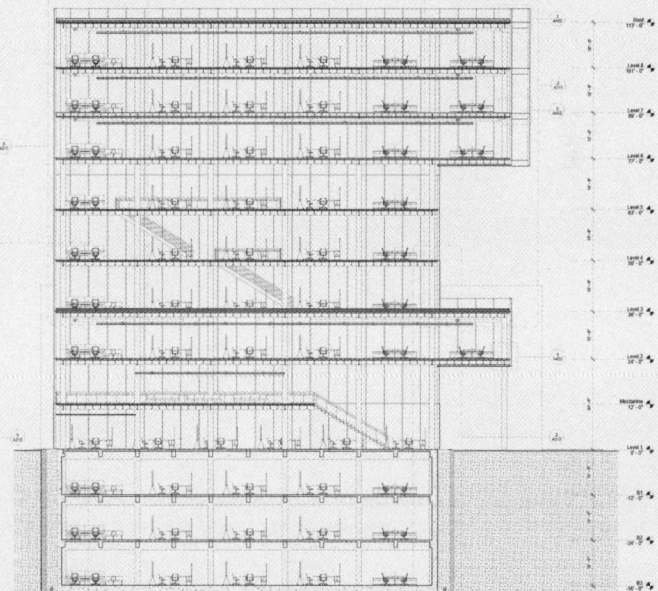

[ARCH 536] STRUCTURES II
Richard J. Farley

The Structures courses serve multiple purposes within the program. Fundamental structural principles of systems, elements and materials are related to the study of morphology of structure. Methods are taught to develop skills, knowledge and intuition for the application of structures to architectural design, including form-finding. The students are propelled to apply analytical digital skills directly to architectural design and to pursue structural optimization in subsequent seminars and design studios, carrying out into the profession.

Structures II—the course furthers structural analytical and form-finding techniques in anticipation of future structural explorations enhancing structural skills and knowledge to be applied to architectural design. The course culminates with the introduction and implementation of three-dimensional design using digital analytical techniques including a class project to analyze a structural system, given a prescribed set of conditions or implementing the student's design studio project.

EVENTS

LINDSAY FALCK (1934-2020),
architect and teacher

"In the spring of 1983, Lindsay was invited to teach at University of Pennsylvania's Graduate School of Fine Arts (hereafter Penn) as a visiting critic. For several years, he split his teaching between UCT and Penn before moving to Philadelphia in the fall of 1986 on a full-time basis as a Lecturer. Although Lindsay was never standing faculty at Penn, he did serve administrative roles as Associate Chair for the Department of Architecture under Adèle Naudé Santos and Alan Levy (1986-1995) and, under Dean Gary Hack, as the Assistant Dean for Facilities Planning (1995-2003). In addition, Lindsay taught part-time evening classes to working students at Drexel University's Westphal School of Media Arts and Design, where he served as an Adjunct Professor for 29 years (1988-2017). Lindsay's knowledge and experience in building construction and technology enabled him to teach across Penn's programs in Architecture, Landscape Architecture and Historic Preservation. He twice received Penn's G. Holmes Perkins Award for Distinguished Teaching (2005 & 2013). He retired from full-time teaching at Penn in June 2018 after 32 years and continued part-time thereafter right up to March 2020 when his deteriorating health brought an end to his long and impactful teaching career."

William Whitaker,
Curator of the Architectural Archives

"In the 2020 graduation ceremony held on May 16th, the faculty and graduating students of the Department of Architecture joined me in a tribute for Lindsay Falck. We were the lucky ones to have Lindsay for over 37 years in the Department of Architecture. His teaching and especially his case study course was legendary and the physical student models lining the hallways of Meyerson were phenomenal. Each year Lindsay would refresh them, and let us all know: "I could remove them anytime." Of course, this never happened as we all loved those models, and the amazing precision and dedication they presented.

In 2014, during my second year as chair, Lindsay turned 80. We produced a book for him as a present, and the reactions blew me away. We sent a note to all the faculty, current students, and alumni from many many years ago, and We were amazed that almost instantly we received a storm of messages, drawings, and beautiful notes. We bound all these in an 83 page book that we presented on his birthday. It was an amazing celebration with Lindsay, his friends, colleagues and family.

As we said goodbye to all of our graduating students and we welcome them as alumni, we did not know we were also saying our farewell to Lindsay as we were thanking him for the amazing time he spent with us... Lindsay was the most fantastic and warm person, an amazing teacher who we will miss dearly."

Winka Dubbeldam,
Miller Professor and Chair of Architecture

Lindsay Falck at the Gordion archaeological site in Yassıhüyük, Turkey, 2009 (Center for Architectural Conservation)

Entwined Tangents by Jamaica Reese-Julien
Critic: **Maya Alam** [p.87]

Through the Roof by Danny Ortega
Critic: **Annette Fierro** [p.81]

GALLERY

Bricolage by Anna Lim
Critic: **Andrew Saunders** [p.110]

Crepta by Ana Celdran
Critic: **Brian De Luna** [p.89]

Market Meandering by Shan Li
Critic: **Andrew Lucia** [p.98]

Within and Against: Self-Exoticism and the Erosion of Mad Max Development by Hayoung Nho
Critic: **Eduardo Rega** [p.100]

EVENTS

CORE 601

Hina Jamelle. Coordinator
Senior Lecturer, Director of Urban Housing

The Core 601 Urban Housing Studios define new contemporary modes of living in an urban environment.

In a world of increasing demand on existing resources there is newly focused attention on adaptive reuse and the expansion of existing facilities. Each Urban Housing studio section positions the housing project relative to an existing structure. The student proposals will be required to engage with this existing building condition—with 1/3 of the proposed project interacting directly with the existing structure while the remaining 2/3 to be new construction. A goal is to encourage the production of hybrid forms, programs, and architectural conditions that interrogate relationships between new and existing conditions. All Studio Sections develop housing projects of 50,000 sq. ft. on an urban lot with a minimum of two facades. The housing project is designed as a hybrid form of housing/dwelling with a commercial or cultural program that can co-exist with housing. Other key objectives include the study of a building's massing and the physical impact it makes on the city with a highly detailed facade.

Across all studios there are two separate event weeks: Plan Week immediately precedes the mid-review and addresses unit design, clear divisions of public and private spaces, building circulation, and preliminary documentation of life safety, egress, and ADA requirements. The Section and Facade Week immediately follows the mid-review and addresses an understanding of vertical and horizontal circulation, building program distribution, facade design, and documentation. The studio faculty are also practicing architects of note: Kutan Ayata of Young & Ayata, Jonas Coersmeier and Gisela Bauerman of Buro NY, Scott Erdy of Erdy McHenry, Hina Jamelle of Contemporary Architecture Practice NY SH, Ben Krone of Gradient Architecture, and Brian Phillips from Interface Studio Architects.

Taught concurrently are Professional Practice by Phillip Ryan and Environmental Systems by Dorit Aviv, which use the Urban Housing Studio Project as a basis of investigation. Professional Practice augments the studio project to bolster the student's understanding of their project through the lens of budgeting, team formation, scheduling, articulating a design vision, and formulating a hypothetical design practice ethos. The Environmental Systems course considers the impact of building designs on the environment and human comfort via three topics: Daylight and Solar Gain, Facade Thermal Performance, and Water and Energy Harvesting. Through drawings and numerical analysis of multiple proposed iterations, the students learn about their studio project's facade performance in relation to material conductivity, insulation, and condensation.

SHIFTING HYBRIDS:
ADAPTIVE REUSE OF THE SUNSHINE THEATER ON THE LOWER EAST SIDE OF NYC.

Hina Jamelle (SENIOR LECTURER, DIRECTOR OF URBAN HOUSING)
Caleb Ehly (TA)

Hina Jamelle (Senior Lecturer, Director of Urban Housing): – Architect and Director, Contemporary Architecture Practice, New York (2002) and Shanghai (2014) – Awarded Fifty Under Fifty: Innovators of the 21st Century. (2015) – Awarded Architectural Record Design Vanguard Award (2004) – Author: Elegance. Architectural Design, John Wiley and Sons Inc., London. (2007). – M.Arch from University of Michigan

This studio will examine part to whole organizations and its potential for architecture by offering the tools to create effects that exceed the sum of their parts. An exceptionally sophisticated part to whole relationship is one which resolves the integration of materials, structure, scale and spatiality to allow for the overall formation to appear suspended, or possessed of a particular lightness and elegance. In terms of formal appearance, this lightness includes qualities of fineness and daintiness, determined within the multiple individual elements and parts that constitute the building design. The scale of the part to the whole will be attenuated, adjusted with precision and refinement, in order to produce the desired affect. When the relation of part to whole is attuned, elegant sensations—rather than chaotic ones—may be achieved at the point of transformations.

The program for the studio is a new residential building on the site of the Sunshine Theater, located on the Lower East Side in downtown Manhattan. The student proposals will be required to engage with this existing building condition - with 1/3 of the proposed project interacting directly with the Sunshine Theater while the remaining 2/3 to be new construction.

1

THE FIGURAL DISCRETE
Megan York

The emergence of a new program and form manifested from a historic site and region of the Lower East Side of Manhattan generates a unique dialogue between an existing state and the evolutionary. By extracting existing datum and reference
lines associated with the Sunshine Theatre and adjacent buildings as well as analyzing the site's orchestration of deep texture through graffiti, lineaments were designed to create a relationship between the new form and the already-built geometries. The ground floor of the structure remains as an active viewing stage, but the intervention of a secondary program throughout the public regions of the structure reacts to the advancements of the moving image industry, involving the so-called new "magic" involved in the power of cinematic graphics. As the form progresses upward and inward, skeletal seams and depth of layering materials begin to interact and grow symbiotically throughout the volume; units are shifted in scale but yet read as a single profile, similar to the exterior geometries of the new, creating a unique profile against the Lower East Side sky line.

2

Our Studio is joined at key junctures by Martha Kelley from Goldman Sachs. Her division—the Real Estate Principal Investment Area [REPIA] makes direct, opportunistic equity and credit investments in real estate assets and portfolios around the country.

Each student refined their particular program and strategy for the new building business model during the course of the semester. The intended result is a project exhibiting innovative architectural organizations and strategies for market and affordable housing using topological surfaces, unit arrangements and patterns scaling from an individual room to the entire building with different spatial and material qualities contributing to the development of architecture.

1 – *The Figural Discrete* by Megan York, Project Statement

2 – *The Figural Discrete* by Megan York, Main View

3 – *Deep Texture Towards New Social Living* by Matt Kohman, Aerial

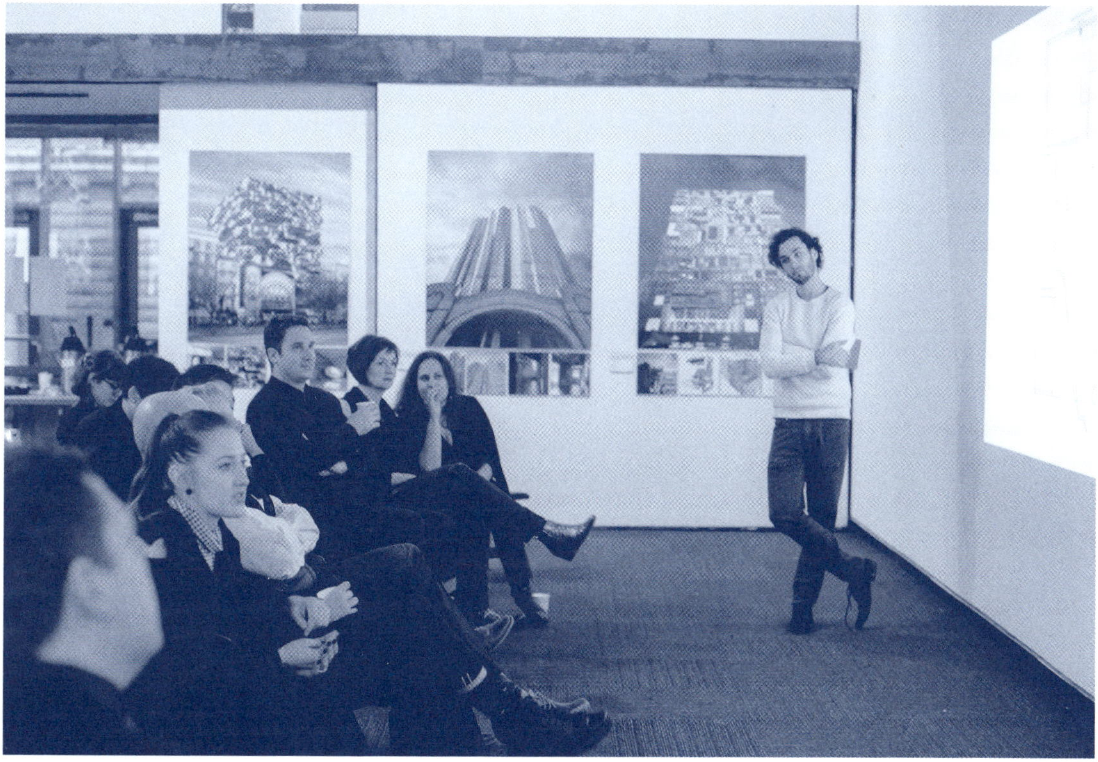

4

5

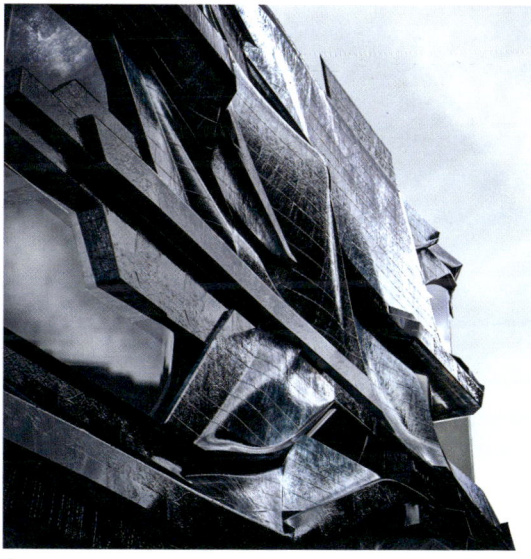

4 – Studio Review with Hina Jamelle (far right)
5 – *The Figural Discrete* by Megan York, Angle View

SHIFTING HYBRIDS
Kerry Hohenstein

This design aims to grow neighborly communities within urban typologies typically focused on isolative spatial conditions. A formal language of spatial pockets that shift from areas of public, private and shared distinctions are organized to give value to the interrelationships that form between different living styles throughout the structure. The existing grid of facade is extended upwards into a shifting language of rectilinear faces wrapping the structure with a secondary language of textured linear mass connecting these faces. As the interconnections between the unit groupings change as your wrap around the building, so do the balance of visual languages.

Pursuing a theater collection in homage to the building's prior use, a bold introduction of a multitude of theater sizes and typologies for diverse presentational and production conditions are organized to mimic the exploratory nature of the units above. Shared elements from the original structure such as the box office, marquee, {1} movie theater, and brick coursing are to remain in addition to the new programmatic spaces. Pockets of potential spaces for social communities to be formed is the ideal behind this project to reconstruct the typology of urban theaters and address the faults of the building's prior use.

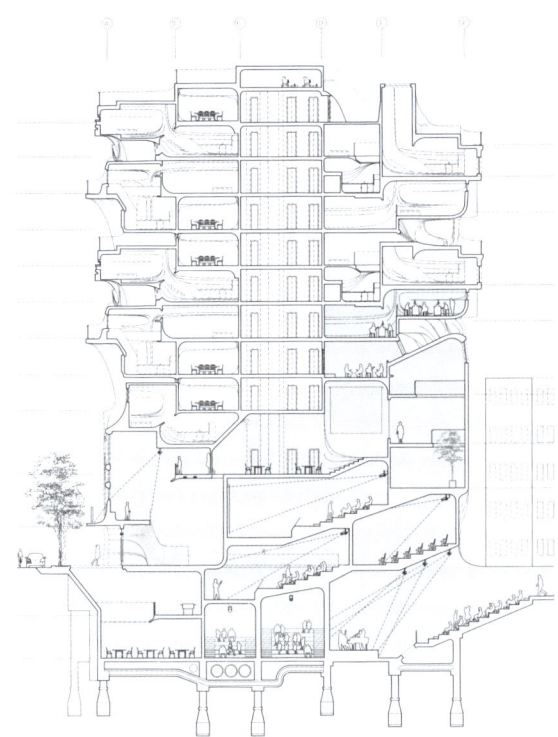

6 – Shifting Hybrids by Kerry Hohenstein, Section
7 – Shifting Hybrids by Kerry Hohenstein, Render
8 – Shifting Hybrids by Kerry Hohenstein, Render Corner Detail

DEEP TEXTURE TOWARDS NEW SOCIAL LIVING
Matt Kohman

This innovative housing reuse of the lower east side's Sunshine Theater considers novel spacial and programmatic organizations through an embedding and layering of urban textures. Counter to existing on site strategies of juxtaposing new and old, the Sunshine Theater's iconic facade is preserved by embedding it into the primary floor public volume, carving out a plaza/performative space to engage adjacent Houston st. The plaza builds a continuous circulation system that extends through the ground floor amenities to each home. Upper floor housing is organized as semi-detached Miesian units connected in enfilade through a sequence of circulatory seams which create deep, spacial pockets within the structure. These spacial continuities explore messy, emergent housing conditions from multi-generational arrangements to couch surfing culture and aim to capture and expand on the textural qualities of an area in transition from an artistic neighborhood to one of commerce.

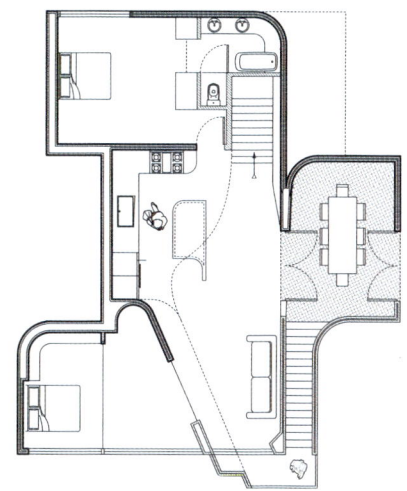

9

10

9 – *Deep Texture Towards New Social Living* by Matt Kohman, Unit Plan

10 – *Deep Texture Towards New Social Living* by Matt Kohman, Section

MEGA-BLOCK REDUX IV
"LIFE IN THE CIRCLE"

Kutan Ayata (SENIOR LECTURER)
Ryan Henriksen (TA)

Kutan Ayata (Senior Lecturer) **:** Co-founded New York-based architecture firm, Young & Ayata (2008) – Young & Ayata are winners of The Architectural League Prize (2014) – Received a MArch from Princeton University (2004) – Bachelor of Fine Arts in Architecture from Massachusetts College of Art in Boston (1999)

1

One of the most significant impacts of 20th-century modernist urbanism in dense urban environments was the implementation of mega-blocks. Mega-Blocks can be described as very large urban blocks comprised of combined (regular scale) urban blocks to enable large scale interventions, originally for social housing ambitions within densifying urban areas through the means of welfare state, later for concentrated expansion of private capital through the channels of neo-liberal economic policies. As modernist visions of new utopias for the city ambitiously attempted to redefine the city by replacing its small-scale fabric with large interventions in the name of "new living", their less finessed and realized versions, in most cases regardless of their location in the world, created mostly undesirable consequences; segregation, lack of density, urban discontinuity, increased crime, lack of urban character, homogeneity to name a few. Majority of these realized projects can be seen as black holes in the city, sucking out all potential urban life in and around them. They are too big to fail; they are deeply rooted and most likely here to stay. They are products of our own discipline, occupying a significant territory in the discourse of architecture and urbanism. They have been imagined with noble intentions and realized with endless optimism; things just did not go according to the plans. What do we do as a discipline to deal with our own garbage? To treat tabula-rasa with tabula-rasa at this scale seems like a pointless exercise and a massive material waste. Perhaps the response needs to be more surgical.

2

3

1 – *Mega-Block Redux IV*, Aerial Render Fall, Circle 2

2 – *Mega-Block Redux IV* by Peik Shelton, Close Up
3 – *Mega-Block Redux IV* by Peik Shelton, Looking Up

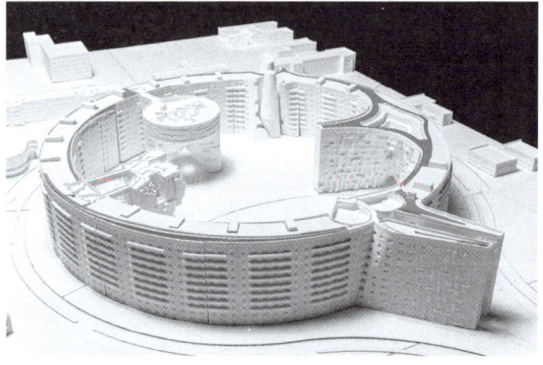

5

6

As city centers around the world continue to densify and grow their populations, new strategies of densification for urban housing are needed. While we can build taller and bigger, this does not necessarily guarantee a positive urban experience across population spectrums. While point interventions can be charming and progressive, their ambition lacks a larger vision of urbanism. How can we reengage the urban scale through specific design acts? At this juncture, mega-blocks with their low ground coverage ratio simply offer a fertile and available territory to consider new opportunities for densification.

4 – *Mega-Block Redux IV* by Paul Germaine McCoy, Approach
5 – *Mega-Block Redux IV*, Collective Model, Circle 1
6 – *Mega-Block Redux IV*, Aerial Render Spring, Circle 1

7 – *Mega-Block Redux IV* by Zhou Jinqyi, Exterior Image

Perhaps no other place has seen more of this typology implemented than Soviet Russia. The studio will work collectively to transform the current condition of two "round buildings" in Moscow; each nine story mega-structure, containing 956 apartments in a circular plan layout. Built originally for the 1980 Moscow Olympics, symbolizing one of the rings in the Olympics logo, Round Houses have been a fully occupied building since their completion. Our ambitions were to focus on to its future potential as we considered new lifestyle, demographic, political, economic, and social realities of the near-future. Unlike the modernist strategy of tabula-rasa to replace what has been previously implemented, we looked to fully embrace the permanence of the physical context and accept all that it has as a three-dimensional site to operate on. What is there remained there to initiate the next stage of urban development. We added, subtracted, intersected, fused, gut, grew, bridged the existing building to produce new masses, new characters. Each student worked on 60-degree slice of the circle in plan and generated a proposal with their self-generated housing agenda to create an alternative urban environment beyond just housing. This required strong communication and coordination among each member of the studio who were working on adjacent territories. The collective effort of the studio aimed to define a prototypical urban densification strategy for this mega-structure type.

8

9

Students:
Eric Sobek Anderson
Ximing Du
Alexander Lee Jackson
Paul Germaine McCoy
Yu Qiao
Peik Bennett Shelton
Heyi Song
Xiaojing Yuan
Xianlong Zeng
Jinqyi Zhou
Molly Elizabeth Zmich

8-9 – Studio Review

10

11

10 – *Mega-Block Redux IV* by Alexander Lee Jackson and Yu Qiao, Duet Image

11 – *Mega-Block Redux IV* by Zeng Xianlong, Elevation Render

MAXIMUM (EFFECT)
MICRO (IMPACT): PROTOTYPE

Gisela Baurmann (LECTURER)
Tim Tsui-Lun Wang (TA)

Gisela Baurmann (Lecturer): Founding partner of Büro NY – M.Arch with honors from Columbia University as a Fulbright Scholar – Has taught at Princeton University, Columbia University, Pratt Institute, and the Technical University Berlin – Finalist and first runner-up in the World Trade Center Memorial Competition (2004)—New York State Council of the Arts Fellowship (2004) – Nominated for the MoMA PS1 Young Architects Program (2003)

Besides the notion of creating "natures" through an architectural construct, this studio aims to speculate on human and other living organisms' needs to thrive under different conditions.

Beyond the anthropocentric idea of housing, the studio develops spaces for co-habitation of human and non-human dwellers. Each project defines one non-human species to live in a non-domesticized environment in spatial proximity to humans. The "other" living organism maybe be from the kingdom of animals, plants, fungi or protozoans.

orchid. The orchid family has thousands of species that have each evolved to attract different species for pollination, the nooks and crannies formed in the labellum are what informed the design of the residential units. The juxtaposition of small enclosed spaces with slivers of light against airy high ceilings with suspended furniture offers the human a variety of living conditions, similar to the spider, within their own home. The unit aggregation can be read from the undulating facade that gives way to pockets of outdoor space.

The design reference to the gothic is a means of offering comfort that can be felt and experienced in a psychological manner. A level of emotional comfort can be evoked through nostalgia and the way in which we feel when we associate places or things to our childhood, memories and places of the past.

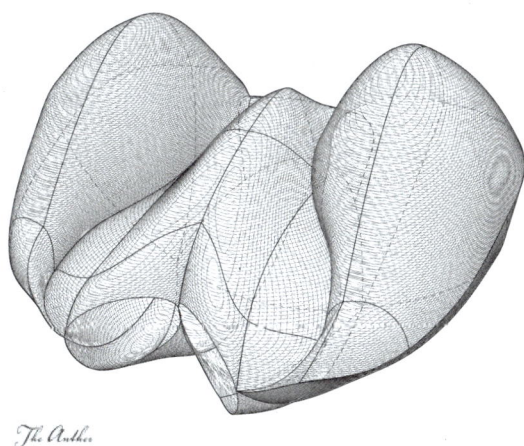

1

ARACHNIDA
Christine Eichhorn

Arachnida brings to light the coexistence of an ever-present organism that lives with humans every day. It is estimated that within the average human household there resides 61 spiders. In fact, there is most likely a spider within reach of this piece of paper right now. Arachnida is a symbiotic residential project that moves beyond the human home and elevates the typical dwelling of the spider.

The site-specific residential block consists of residential towers that are connected by a series of bridges that occur only where the crossroads meet the site. These bridges house the arthropod dwellings and observatories where silk can be harvested for scientific, medical and material research.

The mass and units are inspired by an in-depth plant study and generative remodeling of the

2

The living communities may operate in parallel and independently from one another, or they might assume unexpected forms of symbiosis beyond the hierarchical master-servant relations of man/pet, man/décor or man/nature. The search for novel ideas of comfort opens opportunities to rethink boundaries as defined by normative housing and leads to unexpected cross- species interiorized urbanities. Ideas of wellness in the context of dense urban living are redefined, while primary housing considerations as light, air and circulation are reconsidered through the lens of two species. The studio seeks to formulate different

1 – *Arachnida* by Christine Eichhorn

2 – *Arachnida* by Christine Eichhorn, Spider Render

ideas of comfort through the interrogation of these concepts:

Connectivity:
RELATE INSIDE AND OUTSIDE SURFACES TO THE INTRICACIES OF DOMESTIC SPACE

Surface to volume studies:
POCHÉ VOLUMES SCRUTINIZE ARCHITECTURAL BOUNDARIES AND BUILDING SKINS, AND

Programming:
DEVELOP IN-BETWEEN HABITATS FOR HUMAN AND NON-HUMAN LIFE FORMS.

Rethinking standard sizes and scales, as well as assumptions of comfort and luxury enables the formation of architectural natures that are beneficial to our minds as well as our bodies through social, proportional and material configurations.

3 THROUGH WATER: A SYMBIOSIS WITH CORAL
Robert Schaffer

In nature, organisms coexist together in every sense, working in tandem with one another in order to survive. As humans, we've grown to put ourselves above nature and our environment, creating a hierarchy that places our well-being above all others. This interspecies housing studio challenges the traditional idea of "humans first" and examines the results and benefits that can come from a cooperative, non-hierarchical relationship between two species living together.

A living precedent study was used as an introductory to the co-habitant housing. An analysis and examination of elements in nature was done to create a better understanding of embedded organizations and systems found within the natural world. The study of the organism involved with this project began as an inquiry into the mundane but essential species of grasses. In addition to the vertical nested system of the plant, a formal inspiration and typology evolved from the blooming organism. This study served as a basis for creating the residential housing units that would make up the urban site.

Choosing a species to coexist alongside humans, coral came to mind as posing both a multitude of opportunities as well as challenges. With a focused interest on the idea of public versus private space, water introduced a mediator, blurring the edges between the two realms. Concept ideas bloomed to imagine coral flowing between the aggregation of units, creating a connection as well as a barrier for those living inside.

As a system of vertical circulation, the housing units aggregate upwards, nestling together in a similar fashion to the vertical growth and efficiency of the grass family. Within the volume between the units, the structure provides a scaffolding for the coral to latch on to and grow.

The result of this housing complex challenges our traditional idea of comfort and poses the idea of an equalized co-existence. It pushes the boundary between fantasy and reality and challenges old ideals that may need questioning.

4

3 – *Through Water: A Symbiosis with Coral*
by Robert Schaffer, Description

4 – *Through Water: A Symbiosis with Coral*
by Robert Schaffer, Plant Render

5 – *Through Water: A Symbiosis with Coral* by Robert Schaffer, Render

6 – Gisela Baurmann in Studio Review

PUSH AND POD
Hanqing Yao

The project aims to find a new way to define living and comfort condition in such a high density and "over developed" city like NYC. The residential tower is on top of a historically valuable building, trying to make connection with the site and the urban premise.

Starting from a study on Maple Seeds, a design idea emphasizing the contrast between volume and surface is developed into three different design languages, which are later developed into three different units (living conditions). Based on the geometry of the units developed, a "interior core tower" is generated by stacking units on top of each other. When the units "go up" they automatically rotate and support each other structurally. Then, responding to the street condition and the city grid, an sculpturistic urban envelope is designed to shelter the units inside, meanwhile the envelope turns and folds with it interact with the three streets meet the building that it will create a new condition wherever it interact with street to allow visibility and connectivity. The envelope of the tower is further developed by three different scales: units, urban and community scale representing three to four floors of units in which amount units repeat themselves. The form of the tower is developed by such "community scale," by pushing and pulling on each side of the tower. The interior units tower then rotate 45 degrees against the envelope so the units can have chance to stick out of the tower to acquire more light and air, in other words, a more comfortable and humane living conditions.

The project also considers the relationship between human and other organisms. Mimosa, which is also known as shaming plants because their feature of closing leaves when being touched, are cohabiting with human beings where the walls are about to intersect and space gets narrower. These narrow space were supposed to be not welcomed, yet because of the presence of mimosa, they can be interacting walls that can bring fun and fresher air due to mimosa's air cleaning feature. Despite mimosa, there is also an orchid garden goes all the way through the tower that can be understood as a half of the void space in between the solid unit space and the envelope that can largely save the space and bring nature inside.

Finally the facade is designed as a collage of all the elements mentioned above, it is a projection of the inside solid space but also an extension of the void space.

7

8

9

7 – *Push And Pod* by Hanqing Yao, Axon Chunk
8 – *Push And Pod* by Hanqing Yao, Axon Chunk

9 – *Push And Pod* by Hanqing Yao, Model Units

40°43'39 N 74°0'33 W HOUSING EXTENSION
Merrick Castillo

This project explores housing units encased within an urban envelope, allowing people to navigate private swamp and garden spaces as well as urban infrastructure; all existing on top of a historic UPS warehouse. The units cluster and misfit together, allowing opportunities for new spaces to emerge within these joints, public gardens and swamps inhabit these spaces. Gardens spread through the housing units connecting public to private and allowing opportunities for private residences to merge with the scale of the city. Blending scales and program throughout the space. The urban envelope forms public landings for people to occupy, for events to be held and as a new gathering space for the city, connecting back to the existing city grid and providing views over the street. The units and the envelope are connected through reveals which merge in and out of private and public and materiality which blends the two. Creating a precise relationship between a single studio apartment and a large public infrastructure. Each Unit explore different scales and needs of users, from studio to two bedroom apartments. Users can have garden units which incorporate private gardens and swamp spaces creating truly private green space. Each unit allows for circulation between, allowing users to interact, hallways are embedded with garden spaces as well which serve as public gardens between apartments. The scale shift in gardens from apartment to public shifts outward to the urban envelope. Where the inside of the roofscape is huge public garden space for the city to occupy. These shifting scales allow users and visitors to explore different experiences all within one complex system. Allowing people to move around, but also exist within their own private sphere. These scales shift with the form, the exterior volume understood from the street is a radically different experience than what the user has inside the apartments.

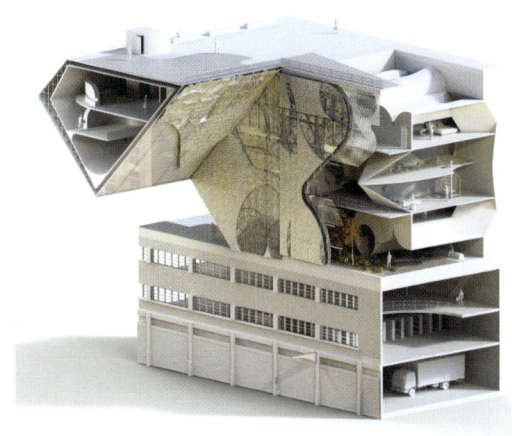

10

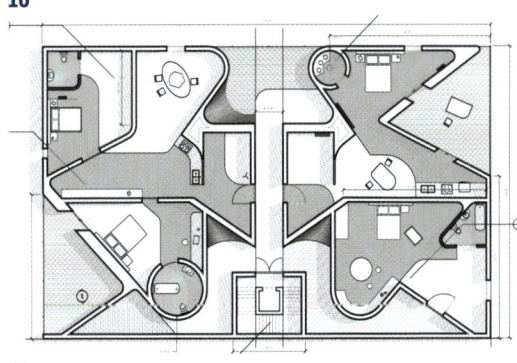

11

12

10 – *40°43'39 N 74°0'33 W Housing Extension* by Merrick Castillo, Facade Axon

11 – *40°43'39 N 74°0'33 W Housing Extension* by Merrick Castillo, Plans

12 – *40°43'39 N 74°0'33 W Housing Extension* by Merrick Castillo, Render

LOLUX HUB

Jonas Coersmeier (LECTURER)
David Forero (TA)

Jonas Coersmeier (Lecturer): Founded Büro NY, NY (2004) – M.Arch from Columbia University GSAPP (2000) – Received an engineering degree from TU-Darmstadt (1998) & MIT Architecture (1996) – Teaches studios & research seminars at Pratt & serves as guest critic at Princeton and Columbia GSAPP

HOUSING: LoLux Hub simultaneously focuses on the two primary growth markets of New York City real estate: luxury condominiums and affordable housing. It discusses these two extreme segments in context, probes into their interaction and systematically works out areas of synergy in order to add value for various stakeholders and for the community at large. The studio encourages the discussion of socio-economic and political issues of urban housing, and how they relate to architectural responsibilities and desires.

DENSITY: Massive population increases can no longer be supported by urban sprawl. Cities must grow inward and densify, not just for ecological, but also for socio-spatial and economic sustainability. The search for new forms of densification is driven as much by the urgent necessity to create space and resilient structures for habitation, as by the desire for density itself. Density is an architectural quality that registers as spatial sensation through aesthetic categories. We are looking for strategies of urban intervention that heighten this quality.

1

MESOCOSM
Sami Samawi

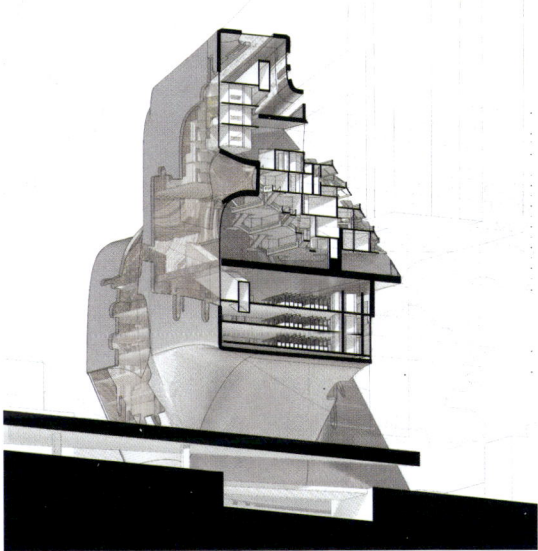

2

Mesocosm introduces a new scale to the urban fabric. It is not to be understood as a building, but rather a piece of infrastructure extending the urban landscape in the vertical and comprising of public urban spaces, various housing types with an integrated farming component and a transit hub underground. In being with the times, mesocosm responds to aspirations of a sustainable and self-sustained structure. The farmed food is produced and cooked in bulk by the tenants, giving the community access to cheaper organic home-cooked food for commuters in a city where time is of the essence as well as sustaining the tenants and life of the mesocosm. The structure deploys Rem's idea of Bigness at a different scale, giving the building a monolithic reading as well as a mechanical one responding to both the need for the building to be an Icon in the skyline as well as providing dense intimate spaces through the tectonics of the structure.

CONTEXT: The studio critically discusses the notion of context without relying on past conventions of contextualism. It studies models of densification that are invested in the autonomous reality of the city. Urban interventions are assessed by the architectural quality they produce, not merely by the degree to which they sustain the city's current condition or its historical continuity. Massive artifacts arrive as aberrations in the urban fabric and define a new kind of urbanity at the scale of a Brooklyn superblock.

1 –*Mesocosm* by Sami Samawi, Material Studies

2 –*Mesocosm* by Sami Samawi, Section

MATERIAL: The studio takes a material approach to the post-digital project in current architectural discourse. It ascribes design intelligence to matter and encourages deep material explorations in search of organizational and aesthetic principles. It suggests that we can fully move on from the digital project only by dissolving the deep-seated notion that human-machine-material interactions are always hierarchical. Material alchemy plays an active part in the process; it sparks moments of design innovation we learn to embrace. Physical models are the primary means of exploration in the studio.

4

and can allow for the area to become a social hub for the future (along with the renovation of the Brooklyn Navy Yards within walking distance). With a housing complex close to the location of the hub, it would be a convenient spot for commuters to live and enjoy their time. With city life being so greatly concerned around work and eciency, a subway station would be great for the area those coming or going to Brooklyn.

REUSE: We take a proactive approach to adaptive reuse, allowing for radical urban and architectural interventions. We consider this a form of real preservation, which is forward looking, as it creates a new life cycle for the existing building structure.

3

TERRACING TOWERS
Calli Katzelnick

As a secondary program for my site, I want to create a transit hub that can span over and under the BQE. With the highway constantly congested, I think an additional means of transportation would be benecial for commuters. There is already the road for the cars, but a spot for subways or trains would further help ease the trac. An area of food will also be located in the station to create a gathering spot for the local commuters. Those who live in the complex already can enjoy the many new restaurants as well as get to their own jobs with ease. More people will run through this portion of Brooklyn,

3 –*Terracing Towers* by Calli Katzelnick, Core Detail   4 –*Terracing Towers* by Calli Katzelnick, Render

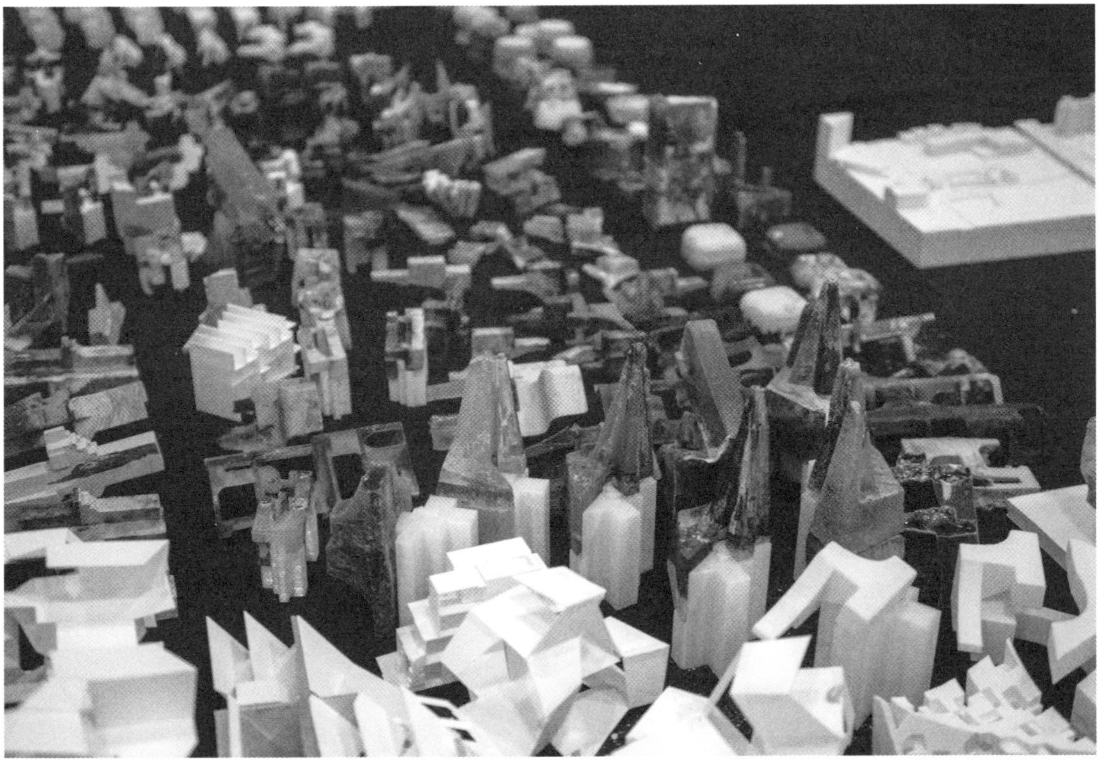

5

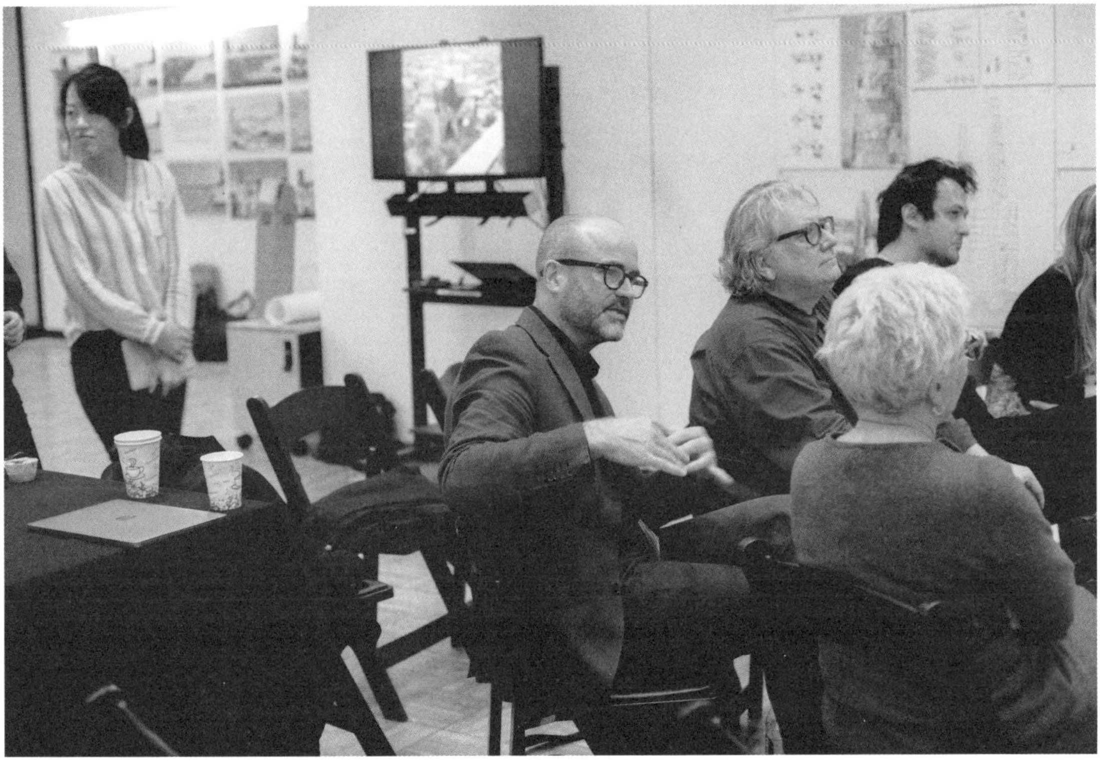

6

5 –Studio Review

6 – Jonas Coersmeier in Studio Review

HEARTH
Glenn Godfrey

The proposed housing tower integrates both permanent and temporary housing with cremation services, as well as a public columbarium to display ashes of the deceased. The added public program provides a place of rest for the dead, and a solution for the sacredness of space in an increasingly densifying city such as New York. The building's program is reflective of our need to embrace death and find opportunities in our daily lives to remember those we have lost. In the search for an architectural representation of this duality, the project integrates both large and small spaces for remembrance such as a cathedral, and small chapels adjacent to private rooms for individual mourners. Serving two user groups, private residents and visiting mourners, the housing tower and block contain units for both permanent and temporary residents. In achieving a continuity between housing and cremation, solid poche material casts ribbon throughout both areas to represent a kind of respect for ancestral passing as well as a tangible material representation of our celebration of both life and death.

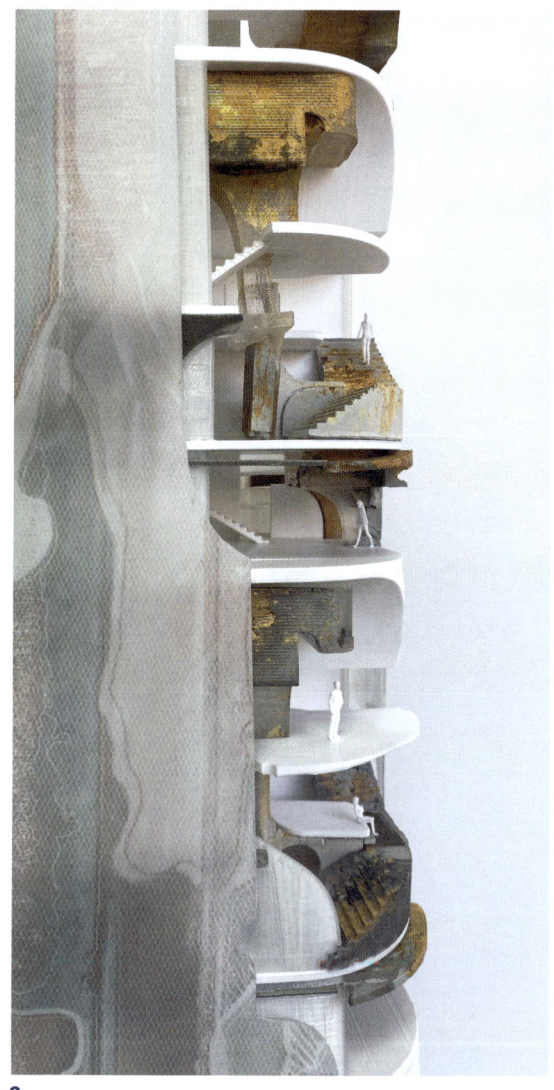

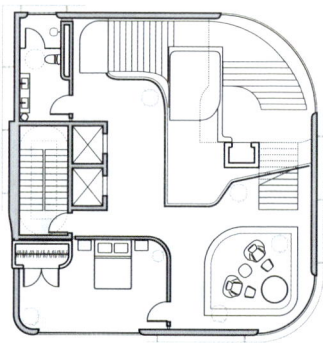

7 – *Hearth* by Glenn Godfrey, Material Study
8 – *Hearth* by Glenn Godfrey, Final Model

9 – *Hearth* by Glenn Godfrey. Render
10 – *Hearth* by Glenn Godfrey, Plan

PEAK HOUSE
Saina Xiang

The project aims to create multigenerational housing with market to provide a space to hang out, live, and exchange for the local community.

The space offers people who rarely hang out together in real society a chance to live and share their life. Focusing on the student, young family, and elder, the apartment incorporates four different housing types: single-loaded corridor, double-loaded corridor, matt building, and tower typology. Different housing types are interlocked to provide an intimate relationship between various user groups. The joints of the different housing types are dedicated to common space.

The project is also designed in an aggressive curvature modern envelop that adapts to the rectilinear existing building. Challenging the skyline of the Navy Yard Pier but by employing the brick texture, the building wishes to both integrate and include the old and the new. The old is being appreciated, reevaluated and inspired by the new modern massing, lifestyle, and energy.

11

12

11 – *Peak House* by Saina Xiang, Model

12 – *Peak House* by Saina Xiang, Elevation

HOSTEL COOP

Scott Erdy (LECTURER)
Xuefeng Li (TA)

Scott Erdy (Lecturer): Principal, Erdy McHenry Architecture — AIA Philadelphia Gold Medal (2001) — AIA Philadelphia Silver Medal (2004)

Food and Housing are two fundamental needs of any stable society. This studio investigates ways to provide more affordable, cost efficient and sustainable housing that supports today's transient population while addressing the acute need for food security.

Unfortunately, many in this country struggle to obtain these basic necessities. The average American spends more than two-thirds of their income on food and shelter alone, leaving few resources available for clothing, transportation, healthcare, or savings. For lower income individuals, this percentage is much higher—with up to 65% of income diverted toward shelter. Food Insecurity is another major issue in the United States. The limited and uncertain availability of nutritionally adequate and safe foods is exacerbated in stressed urban settings where access to quality food is limited due high cost, logistics or by social conditioning.

1 READING COLLECTIVE
Nathan Mollway

The Reading Collective centralizes the reinvestment in cooperative sustainability and urban heritage for downtown Philadelphia. The adaptive reuse of the 915 Spring Garden site decidedly preserves much of the existing Reading Railroad Office headquarters, as well as the adjacent— and dilapidated—elevated train station. As a master plan, the new direction of 915 Spring Garden must holistically engage the immediate neighborhood by creating a center for the productive growing of crops, assembly, and dissemination of skills. Beyond this, the project must activate the disused viaduct to as a locus of sustainable urban identity for all Philadelphians.

Equalizing the importance of food and shelter, The Reading Collective negotiates the value of historic urban spaces with the needs of the 21st century. The re-purposing of extant site structures is necessary for the project's holistic success, acknowledging sustainable practice as greater than the isolating vision of "green" technology. What more, The Reading Collective master plan boasts a community of 65 low-income housing units, artisan studios, medium-to-large open plan office spaces, and an expanded brewery and restaurant. With communal spaces as points of connection throughout, the density of this versatile program ensures a successful ecosystem of inhabitants. Functioning throughout the year, the growing apprentices will not only provide an abundant source of local produce to residents, but also rehabilitate the industrial viaduct in the decades to come. This system will mark the physical passage of time, highlighting the ecological and economic value of such a cooperative, and acting as a call-to-action for more to come.

Based on principles put forward by Chef José Andrés and the Think Food Group, we use food to empower communities and strengthen economies. The new self-contained HOSTEL COOP addresses food security and shelter by creating a place where residents can live for short or long periods of time while cultivating and preparing the food that they and the community will eat.

2

1 – *Reading Collective* by Nathan Mollway
2 –*Reading Collective* by Nathan Mollway, Elevation

While the project will focus on exchanging "work for food and shelter," the real exchange will happen through the educational transference of practical urban farming techniques passed between short and long-term residents. The design of the housing units will reflect this ambition in their size, appointments and organizational strategies, taping on ways that architecture can enhance social interaction and teach its function through its form.

4

Within the confines of a 50,000 sq. ft. building project, students develop a self-sustaining strategy for housing that incorporates energy efficiency/generation and food production. The goal of this research is to demonstrate communal strategies for housing that are not only self-sufficient, but can also be deployed in urban areas across multiple cultural and environmental regions around the globe.

3

ENFRAMING
Yuhao Zhang

The strategy of this project is eliminating the boundary between old buildings and nature. In addition, another aim of this project is attracting people's eyes back to this place, which would not only solve the crowed urban population pressure, but also rekindles the new energetic life for old buildings. The concept of this project is about enframing. It gives a possibility to connect old buildings and nature environment together. In other words, it reframes a new relationship. When we have the frame, the new urban residential life with farming, gardens would be the painting in this frame.

The studio begins with the design of the Summer Camp: a deployable single occupancy dwelling that will provide a compact, self-sustaining shelter that accommodates the basic human needs of providing food and shelter. This analytical study provides the conceptual basis for the development of the living module that will be adapted for the parasitic occupation of an existing urban structure. The interaction with an existing artifact promotes a logical approach that leverages the embodied energy of an existing building and the cultural memory that it represents.

The project incorporates urban adaptive building reuse and site reclamation strategies. Set within an existing structure (Reading Railroad Offices and Station) together with the abandoned high-line rail, the project challenges normative assertions of value, seeking to be a bridge between old and new.

3 – *Enframing* by Yuhao Zhang, Model

4 – *Enframing* by Yuhao Zhang, Render

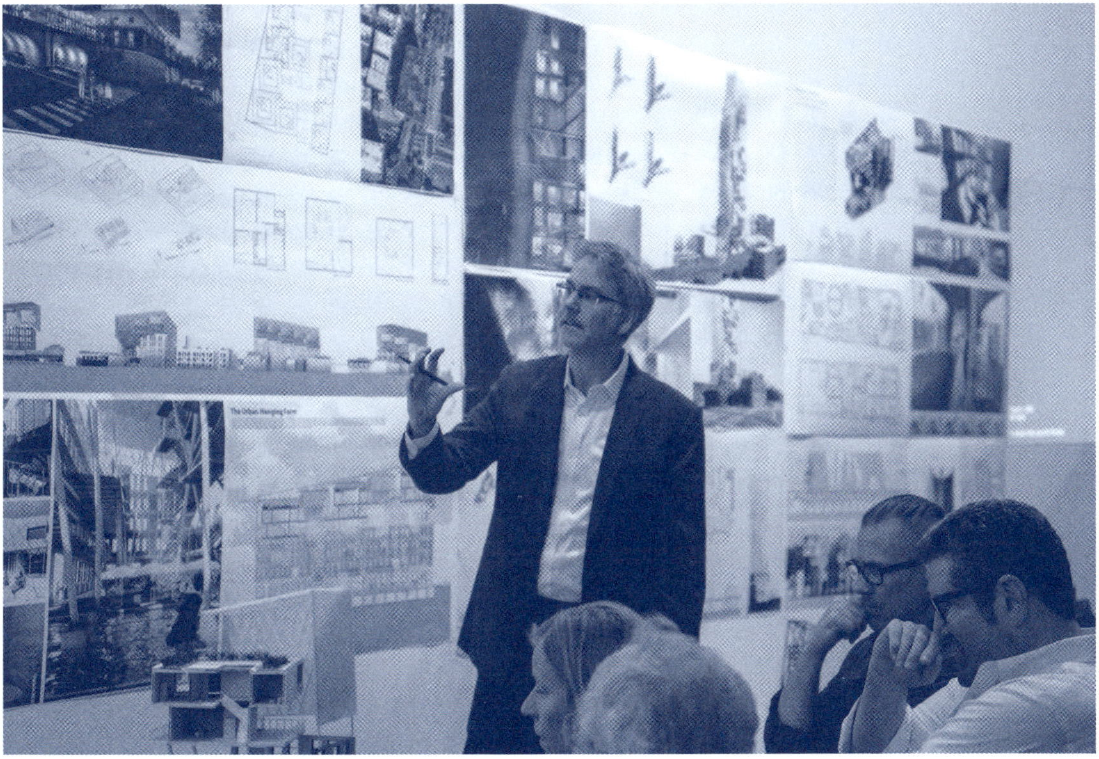

5

6

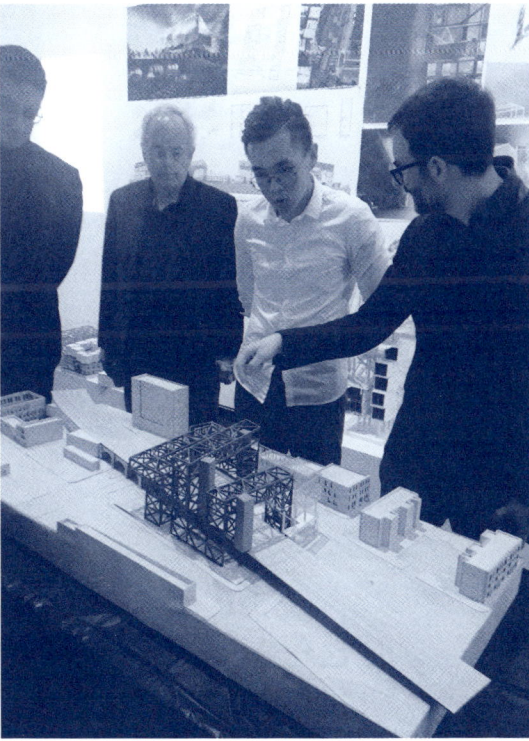

5-6 – Scott Erdy Studio Review

BIOTOPIC SYNERGY
Maria José Fuentes

This project aims to create spaces of community through spaces that bridge the intersection between living and giving life. This building creates an ecologically equitable building that houses the needs of all inhabitants; fish, human and plant. Peter Zumthor once described the atmosphere as buildings as containing more sensitivity than deliberation. "Atmospheres have an integral character that does not result from linkage, which would preserve distinctness, but a consolidation that gives rise to a single effect, several voices harmonized as one." The atmosphere of a place creates a space that is memorable, vibrant, powerful and visible. The floor plans create a landscape of living that allows for fluidity through the circulation of each building's floor plan. The building footprint was determined by using the original circulation paths and creating a scheme that fit within the five foot grid that was used to create the dimensions of the cones. The building becomes a crossroad between community, light, hope, and service. The cones of the building become visual representatives of the light that penetrates the building from above. As these lights allow for connectivity with the natural, there are additional vertical lights installed within each cone that allow for a fruitful and year-round growth for the vegetation. The vegetation's water is filtered by the fish and in turn, the plants help purify the water for the fish. Through this Closed Recirculating System, the system uses 20-40 percent less water and fertilizer than open systems. The process becomes a sacred event for the residents to experience. Those that enter the building are able to experience a space filled with tremendous voids of light, flickers of water, and the embodiment of a community rooted in ecological co-existence.

6

7

8

6 – *Biotopic Synergy* by Maria José Fuentes, Process Elevation

7 – *Biotopic Synergy* by Maria José Fuentes, Biotopic Hall Interior

8 – *Biotopic Synergy* by Maria José Fuentes, Long Section

ELEVATED GARDEN
Yangkenan Li

The loss of farmland and increasing populations are placing immense strain on the world's food supply. As food security in cities becomes an ever increasing problem, urban farming is emerging as a plausible solution. This project speculates on the future of urban living by growing food alongside living spaces. The traditional system combine with new agriculture but she was lies is poly carbonate the sides aquaponics in vertical farming technologies within residential units would allow for efficiency, density, and availability, Using such technology to respond to the anticipated food crisis is project speculate on the future of urban living were residence entire diet would be grown alongside their living space. The traditional system combine with new agriculture but she was lyses poly carbonate massage Aquaponics in vertical farming technologies within residential units with allow for efficiency, density, availability, conservation, and consistency in the residence customizable pescatarian food supply. The new housing units are located on top of the existing building and supporting structures fixed on the foundation of the existing structure to provide a large area of public space. Households cooperate to grow crops in order to meet the caloric needs of the entire cooperative. The original building acts as a market within the food court to guide the surrounding neighborhoods to participate in these public activities, which turns the site into a dynamic regional Center, and also spread the urban farm cooperative model to the public and influence is the way we live in the future.

9

10

9 – *Elevated Garden* by Yangkenan Li, Site Plan   10 – *Elevated Garden* by Yangkenan Li, Elevation

IN RESIDENCY

Ben Krone (LECTURER)
Catherine Shih (TA)

Ben Krone: (Lecturer) Founded Gradient Design Studio, NYC (2006) – B.Arch from the University of Florida (1999) – M.Arch degree from Columbia University's Graduate School of Architecture, GSAPP (2004) – Winner of McKim Prize for Excellence in Design & the Sol Kaplan Traveling Fellowship.

Traditionally, new housing development acts as an accelerator in making neighborhoods in New York unaffordable for longer-term residents. The studio sets out to prove that through community-based programming and the expansion of a specific neighborhood-focused artists in residency program, multi-unit housing has the capacity to expand a neighborhood's core constituents through the creation of new housing that integrates and educates outsiders into the rich history and sense of place that makes the neighborhood, specifically Red Hook, what it is.

with the more deserted areas of the East making an art and manufacturing corridor providing affordable housing and creative working spaces. Here I am using the Grain Terminal as a reflection chamber. A mirror and multiplier of its surroundings both physically and metaphorically as a connection to pioneer works and the community of the western edge of red hook. The idea is to create a new anchor point on the edge of Red Hook to become a catalyst for everything that exists on the two edges with the intent to create a new creative corridor rather than the island that currently exists there. Thinking these inserted volumes as creative spaces, they start to reflect around as to create a feedback loop of creativity and inform the dynamic process existed within.

The studio integrated into an existing, abandoned grain elevator on the Red Hook/Gowanus, Brooklyn Border. It is 12-stories tall, 70-feet long, and 429-feet wide. It was constructed in 1922 and decommissioned in 1965. It has sat abandoned since. Today, it is primarily used for film shoots and occasional artists performances.

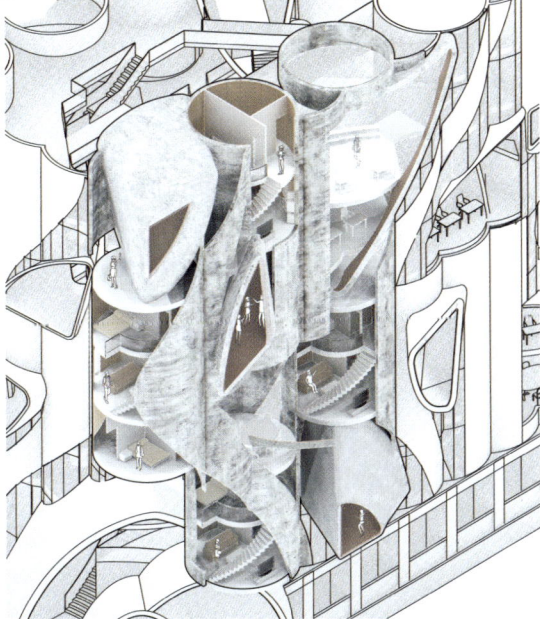

1 LOOPING REFLECTION
Baoqi Ji

Red hook has tons of industrial working space in the west. However, this side of Red Hook does not. East of Dwight street the character of red hook changes from mixed manufacturing and residential to empty lots demolished or undeveloped plots and areas of contaminated soil that has stifled development in this area of red hook Gowanus border. As one of the most significant building in Red Hook, with its unique geometry and massive volume, the Grain Terminal building can be a place that stitch the two distinct areas of red hook together essentially bridging the art and manufacturing communities of west red hook

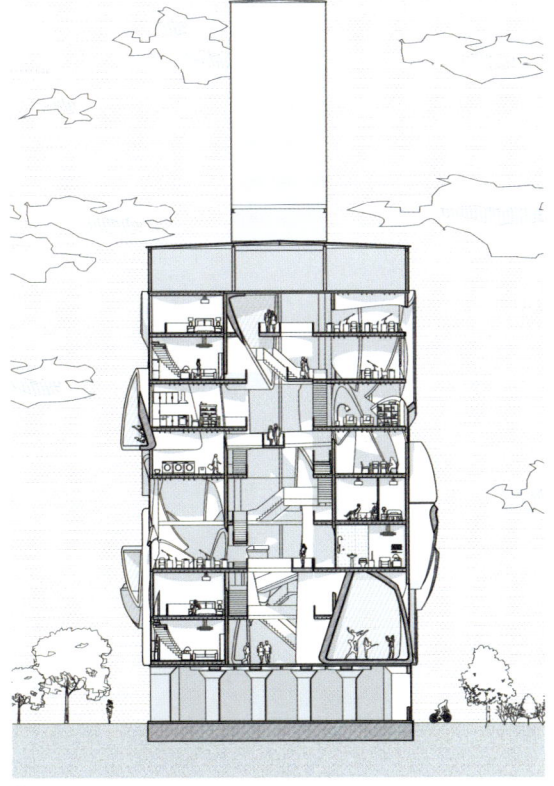

2

1 – Looping Reflection by Baoqi Ji, Chunk

2 – Looping Reflection by Baoqi Ji, Short Section

RED HOOK LIVING WATERS
Hillary Morales Robles

Bathhouses has been a community program typology since ancient Rome. Those spaces became a social condenser, where everyone interacted with each other about their age and identity. In other words, water have the potential to behave as a social mediator.
Red Hook Living Waters strives towards the same idea. In what ways water can be placed and intersect in between housing, workspaces and activate the community through different public programs? While remaining public, how can pools can generate different degrees of intimacy in order to keep the existing relationship of public/private within domesticity?

With the design of a pool system, the GBX is surgically treated and use the silos as niches (similar to bathhouse's layout). The niches are conceived to locate housing units, workstation areas for *Pioneer Works* artists in residence, administration and pool sharing areas. The circulation concentrated in the center helps to create connectivity between them and bleeds through the different pool typologies. The pools are the main community public program. They are placed strategically across the building to prevent program segregation. They are connected at some extent and responds for different purposes. The pools are for recreational, sensory deprivation, reef restoration, aquaponics, aquaculture, robotic/technology testing, among other uses. All of them can be assessed from a public or private source point, which leaves room for everyone to interact and be part of a larger community.

Studio Partnership
PIONEER WORKS

A non-profit cultural center in Red Hook, Brooklyn that builds community through arts and sciences by providing practitioners a space to work, tools to create, and a platform to exchange ideas. The housing studio is an extension of Pioneer Work's community and residency program.

3 – *Red Hook Living Waters* by Hillary Morales Robles
4 – *Red Hook Living Waters* by Hillary Morales Robles, Render – Domesticity Facade.

5 – Drone photo of the Building Site: Red Hook Grain Terminal

6 – Group working together to assemble the final site model of Red Hook **Students:** Zhenxiong (Daniel) Yang, Baoqi (Miki) Ji, Veronica Rosado, Jasmine Chia-Chia Liu, Alexander Brown, Amber Farrow, Chuanqi Gao

7 – **Final Review** Amber Farrow, **Professor:** Ben Krone, **Critics:** Daniel Markiewicz, Chico MacMurtrie, Angeliki Mavroleon, Jack Brough, Kate Larsen

PROXIMAL TERMINAL
Chia-Chia (Jasmine) Liu

The word NIMBY "not in my backyard" is the idea that people tend to feel threatened when something or someone may encroach within certain proximity of the individual. NIMBY is commonly associated with the negative connotations of gentrification of neighborhoods, such as RedHook, the site of our housing proposal.

My housing proposal is a mixed housing for both resident artists of Pioneer Work and the low-income groups. I attempt to tackle the notion of NIMBY by getting to the core of the issue of adjacency and attempts to celebrate proximity rather than to attempt to create boundaries or divide between socioeconomic groups. Translating from the analogue models, which focused on the study of spatial adjacency conditions, the "boot shaped" aggregation of my housing units create interesting adjacencies and gaps between residents, which lead to larger interior courtyards. There is no NIMBY in my project, every resident shares their backyard and are guided to interact and celebrate the adjacencies.

The program of the housing is a science lab, where the community of RedHook learn that art is inclusive that involves technology and science, which corresponds to the inclusive housing. Viewers are able to enter through a different entrance from the residence entrance, follow the catwalk to view the science labs as well as enjoy the industrial atmosphere of Grain Terminal. and enjoy the roof garden as the final destination.

8

9

8 – *Proximal Terminal* by Chia-Chia (Jasmine) Liu, Model

9 – *Proximal Terminal* by Chia-Chia (Jasmine) Liu, Exterior Night View Render.

IN RESIDENCY
Veronica Rosado

New housing development traditionally acts as an accelerant to making neighborhoods in New York unaffordable for its longer-term residents. In response, this adaptive reuse and housing project, located in the GBX terminal in Red Hook, comes as an extension of the work of Pioneer Works and their Ecologies of Transition Roundtable Series, advocating for projects that intersect design, science and ecology. These three things become assets meant to strengthen the housing and the residency program of the building. In order to achieve this, I dealt with a continuous element (the ribbon) that moves throughout and in-between the silos organizing the space based on openness and enclosure, public and private, shared and intimate environments. The openings throughout the building create a visually shared space that promotes an ambiguous condition between the housing and the workshops, the interior and the exterior; meant to force the intersection of different social groups that already coexist in Red Hook: artists, designers, activists, young entrepreneurs, nuclear families. This then provides flexible spaces for making and exhibiting projects related to water resilience and its relevancy when living on the waterfront.

The "ribbon" defines the ambiguity or determinacy of the spaces as it also makes a monument for water once it reaches the roof and the ground of the building. The goal is to intersect the housing program with the work of organizations like Marisa Prefer's *Invisible Labor and Resilient Red Hook*. Potentially turning the *Ecologies of Transition Roundtable* discussions in physical outcomes that thrive the adoption of policies in favor of long-term urban ecological thinking and conservancy of the Gowanus Canal.

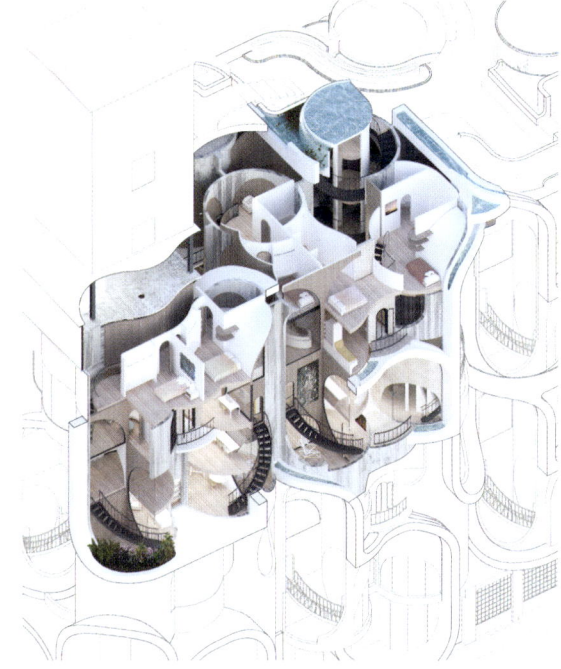

10

11 12

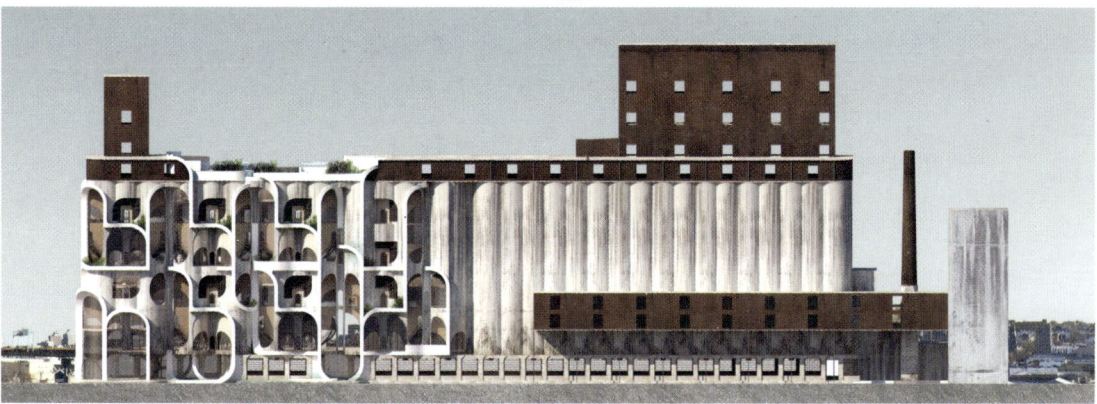

13

10 – *In Residency* by Veronica Rosado, Section
11 – *In Residency* by Veronica Rosado, Render 1
12 – *In Residency* by Veronica Rosado, Render 2
13 – *In Residency* by Veronica Rosado, Section

DOCKED

Brian Phillips (LECTURER)
Perry Ashenfelter (TA)

Brian Phillips (Lecturer): Founded Interface Studio Architects (ISA), Philadelphia (2004) – Master of Architecture University of Pennsylvania (1996) – BSED University of Oklahoma (1994) – Pew Fellowship in the Arts (2011) – Architectural League of NY – Emerging Voices (2015) – AIA National Housing Award (2017) – AIA Philadelphia Gold Medal (2018) – AIA Pennsylvania Firm of the Year (2019)

While many cities have embraced their waterfronts as luxury, lifestyle-driven housing zones, Philadelphia remains tentative about it. The vast majority of Philadelphia's high-end housing is located in the central core and close-in neighborhoods which provide decidedly urban, walkable, mixed-use experiences. The city's development indifference to the Delaware River stems from its industrial wharf legacy, which positioned the waterfront as a primarily non-residential infrastructure in the 20th century, and later, from the replacement of that industry with an interstate highway (I-95) cutting between the urban fabric and the riverfront.

affordable housing and creative working spaces. Here I am using the Grain Terminal as a reflection chamber. A mirror and multiplier of its surroundings both physically and metaphorically as a connection to pioneer works and the community of the western edge of red hook. The idea is to create a new anchor point on the edge of Red Hook to become a catalyst for everything that exists on the two edges with the intent to create a new creative corridor rather than the island that currently exists there. Thinking these inserted volumes as creative spaces, they start to reflect around as to create a feedback loop of creativity and inform the dynamic process existed within.

The studio thought broadly about the possibilities of the Delaware River waterfront leveraging its marginalized character to create innovative attainable housing on the site of a pier currently used as an arts and culture destination. The story of the pier is one of operating in the margins of markets, neighborhoods and physical fabric to realize unique urban qualities. The studio took this opportunity seriously as a method for converting an under-defined urban leftover into an affordable, creative, entrepreneurial mixed-use residential zone. Projects looked to connect with deep aspects of existing conditions and elevate them as defining characteristics.

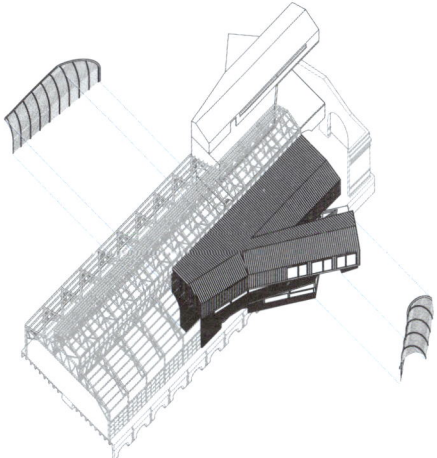

1

THE SOWER
JooYoung Ham

Red hook has tons of industrial working space in the west. However, this side of Red Hook does not. East of Dwight street the character of red hook changes from mixed manufacturing and residential to empty lots demolished or undeveloped plots and areas of contaminated soil that has stifled development in this area of red hook Gowanus border. As one of the most significant building in Red Hook, with its unique geometry and massive volume, the Grain Terminal building can be a place that stitch the two distinct areas of red hook together essentially bridging the art and manufacturing communities of west red hook with the more deserted areas of the East making an art and manufacturing corridor providing

2

1 – *The Sower* by JooYoung Ham

2 – *The Sower* by JooYoung Ham, Model

MILLENIALS INC.
Lingxin Feng

As housing prices rise in desirable urban neighborhoods and millennials struggle to afford personal apartments, co-living becomes a solution. Already comfortable with Uber and Airbnb, sitting on a sofa with a stranger is not a big leap for millennials. Characterized by a median age of 36, often without children, the Old City neighborhood is largely defined by young people who values experiences, creativity and being socially connected. Co-living on Cherry Street Pier is a way of meeting new people, engaging with local artists, accessing local food culture, all while enjoying the view of the waterfront.

The proposed wedge-shaped over-build structure organizes co-housing in a thin mat building hovering over the pier. A recreation ramp loops up and around the wedge connecting residents and the broader city along a spectacular entry experience. A key public destination is a dramatic river overlook at the top that loop. The wedge stays clear of most of the existing pier creating provocative interstitial spaces between the old and new construction elements.

3 – *Millenials Inc.* by Lingxin Feng
4 – *Millenials Inc.* by Lingxin Feng, Render
5 – *Millenials Inc.* by Lingxin Feng, Exploded Chunk

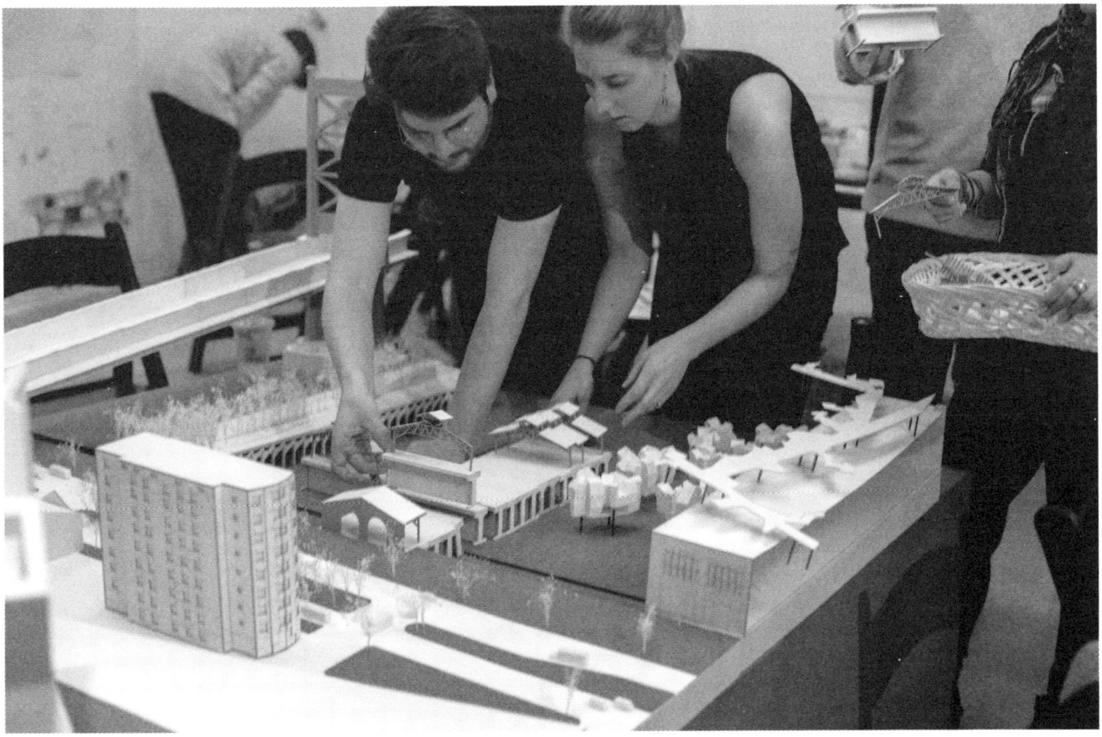

6

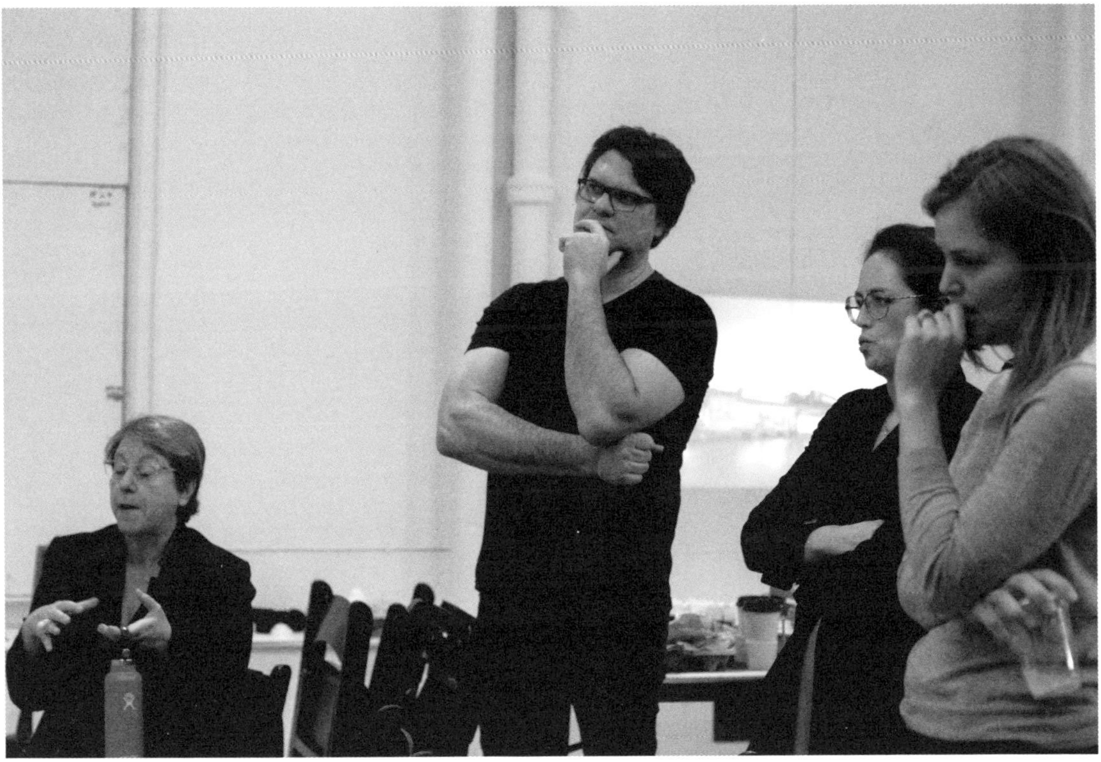

7

6 – Studio Review

7 – Brian Phillips in Studio Review

DOCKED: TIDE POD
Cindy Zheng

The new residences proposed at Cherry Street Pier will act as an interactive water filter for the Delaware River, providing unique spaces and habitats for residents and visitors to explore. The Tide Pod is designed to showcase eco-friendly best practices for clean water management, utilizing natural and biological systems for filtering river water into a clean swimmable recreational pool as well as integrating a non-potable water reuse system for in-house residential uses. The swimming pool extends into the Delaware River, placing users in a unique position to experience the river that is otherwise unswimmable, while bringing awareness to the polluted condition of the existing river water. The semi-submerged residence units line the sides of the filtration ponds for the pool, acting as both a mechanical and visual step for the filtration process. They provide residents direct views of the tidal river waters as it feeds into the ponds. The project will serve as a step forward in promoting co-existence with the natural waterscape along the Delaware River.

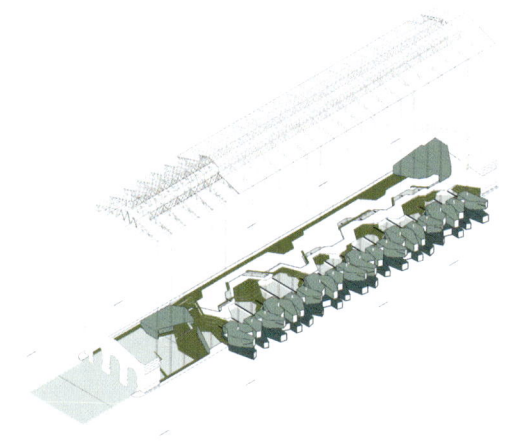

8

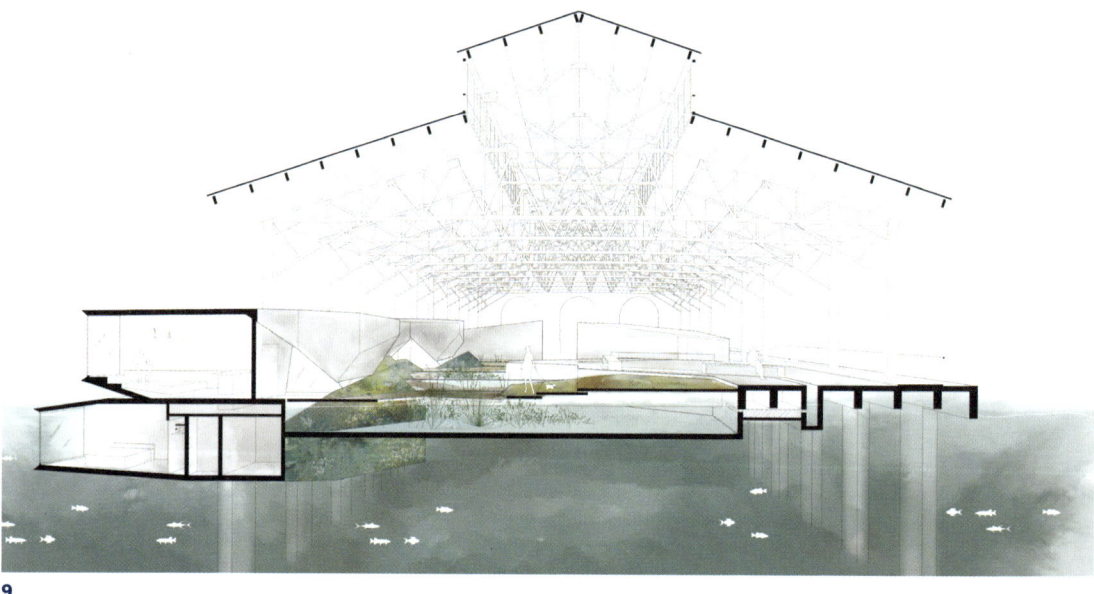

9

10   11

8 – *Docked: Tide Pod* by Cindy Zheng, Axon
9 – *Docked: Tide Pod* by Cindy Zheng, Section Perspective
10 – *Docked: Tide Pod* by Cindy Zheng, Render
11 – *Docked: Tide Pod* by Cindy Zheng, Render

CURATED DECAY
Tianhui Zhang

Cherry Street Pier, an aging industrial building directly situated on the Delaware river waterfront, has more design opportunities in its deterioration than in a full restoration. Curated Decay proposes a light-touch approach to housing which provides residents with a uniquely local and specific view into the past of the city's industrial and natural contexts. The process of decay is synthesized through formal moves into the spatial experiences of the project.

Housing units and shared living experiences are articulated through their relationship to the truss structure of the pier, as well as the poetic qualities found in the tensions between the eroding industrial pier structure and its contact with water systems.

In the public realm, the eroding pier creates a changing piece of public landscape connecting residents and the city-at-large to the water in a unique way.

12

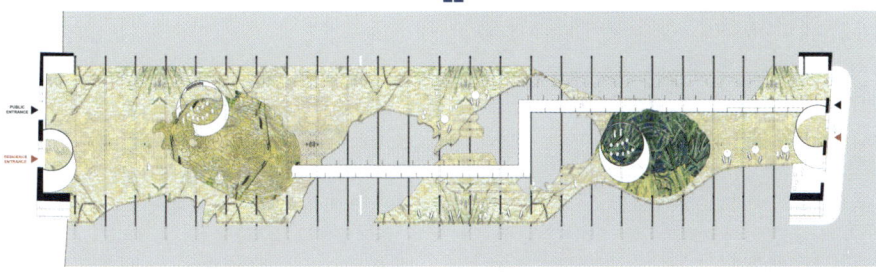

13

14 15

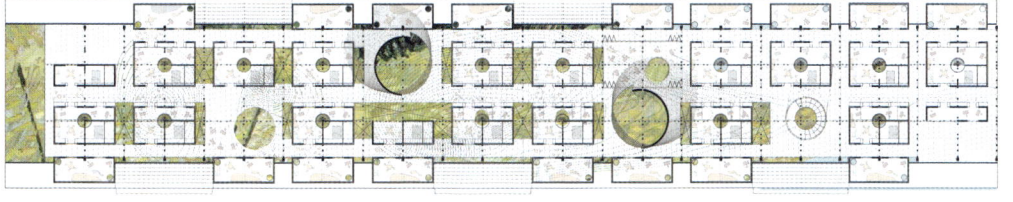

16

12 – *Curated Decay* by Tianhui Zhang, Plan Level
13 – *Curated Decay* by Tianhui Zhang, Floor Plan
14 – *Curated Decay* by Tianhui Zhang, Render
15 – *Curated Decay* by Tianhui Zhang, Render
16 – *Curated Decay* by Tianhui Zhang, Typical Plan

[ARCH 611] HISTORY AND THEORY III
David Leatherbarrow, Sophie Hochhäusl, Carson Chan

This is the third and final required course in the history and theory of architecture. It is a lecture course that examines selected topics, figures, projects, and theories from the history of architecture and related design fields during the 20th century. The course also draws on related and parallel historical material from other disciplines and arts, placing architecture into a broader socio-cultural-political-technological context. Seminars with teaching assistants complement the lectures.

[ARCH 621] VISUAL STUDIES III
Nate Hume, Brian De Luna

The coursework of Visual Studies investigates architectural representation as the primary means for communication and development of an architect's position. Representation serves not just as a means for building documentation but is crucial to the generation of thought and of projecting arguments and concepts out into culture. The Visual Studies courses allow for continual evolution as mediums emerge, the courses contain an underlying discussion of the way we develop, consume, and interact with drawings, images, and photographs. Alongside the development of fundamental skills are weekly lectures on the history of representation from the Renaissance to today exploring the introduction of new technologies, drawings relation to culture, and impact on practice of representational turns. These lectures fold in contemporary discussions of visual culture extending the historical themes into fashion, industrial design, art, graphic design, and film. The historical development and use of representation by architects over the past five centuries provides a lens to understand current tools, techniques, and conventions and how they can be productively deployed. The courses compliment studio projects to further explore the ideas and design work through representation. 521 works through documenting 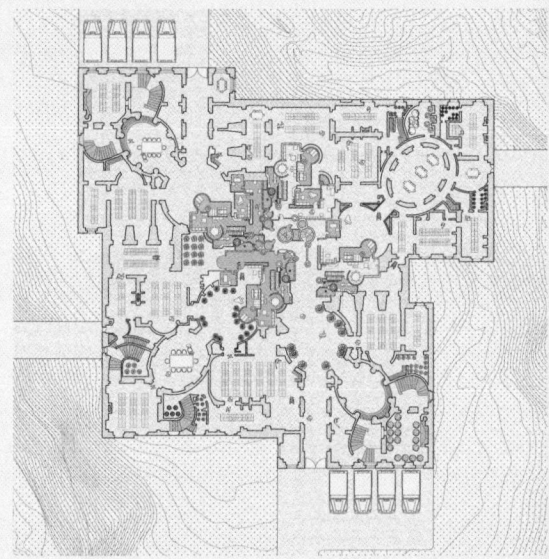 objects and space through orthographic projection and isometric drawing while also moving between virtual and physical space with means including photogrammetry and 3D printing. 522 emphasizes drawings as generative devices which project possibilities not just document design decisions. Assignments explore image construction through photography and rendering and the construction of a large cutaway section drawing which speculate on the development of the studio project. 621 integrates more dynamic modeling, texturing, and rendering applications to synthesize and propel work from the earlier modules. To avoid tropes and the inherent biases of the tools, the theoretical and political implications of representation decisions need to be fully comprehended. The three semester arc provides an understanding of contemporary drawing, modeling, and visualization techniques while also creating the necessary grounding in the historical context needed to position one's work to engage and critique larger discussions in the field as well as to shape and impact culture and the built environment.

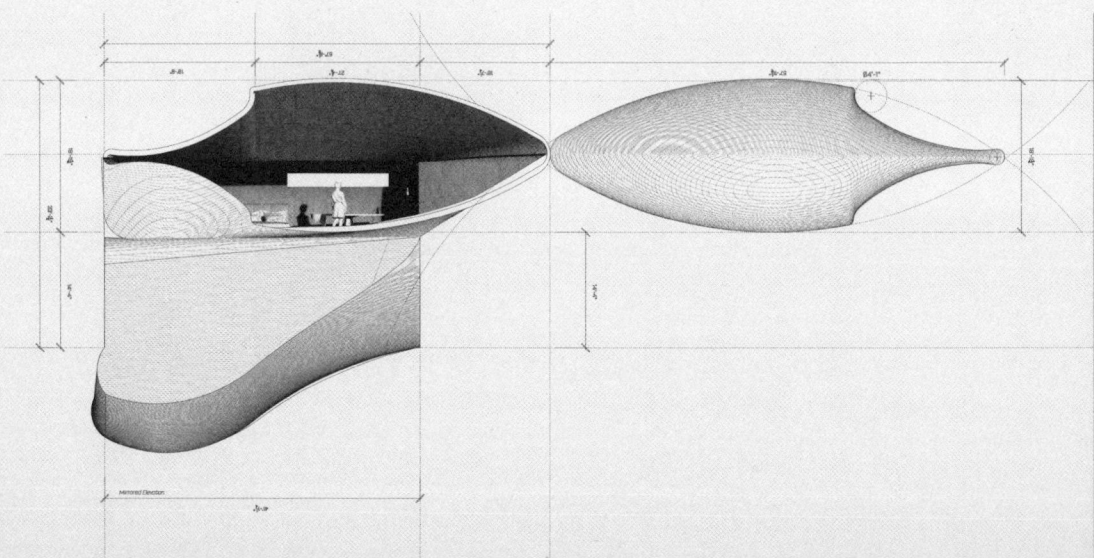

[ARCH 631] TECHNOLOGY CASE STUDIES I
Lindsay Falck

The course is intended to focus on the rapidly developing trends in the new technologies being applied to the design and construction of contemporary buildings. As a basis for understanding these new developments we will use the Geddes/Mumford framework of analysis of materials, tools, skills, and energy systems, studying their changes over time. To these four criteria we will add a fifth, relating to information transfer between the various contributors to the construction process. When looking at materials we will study the new materials that become available for building construction at an ever increasing rate, such as ETFE and other tensile membrane materials, polymers, intelligent or phase change materials, etc, but also look at how new tools and other conversion processes have revolutionized how we can use existing materials such as wood, concrete, metals, etc, thus extending the vocabulary available to designers.

Tools used for the extraction of raw materials from the earth and for their conversion in manufacturing processes are also going through major changes and developments. Digitally programmed saws, drills, lathes, etc, are in everyday use for heavy structural components as in steel-framed buildings. CAD/CAM cutters, routers, milling machines, robotic fabrication and on-site assembly are in ever growing use today. Water-jet cutters, spark erosion systems for large and small elements are now installed in most fabrication plants.

Skills are progressively evolving from the hand-eye-brain skills to the more advanced computer-integrated on-site and off-site operations. However, the skilled manual operator of tower cranes and other heavy industry equipment will always be an integral part of the construction industry, as will the highly skilled plasterer of complex ceiling or wall moldings and the "finish-wood" carpenter or cabinet maker working in wood, synthetics or metalwork, remain as ongoing contribution to the building industry.

Broader issues of sustainability, embodied energy, carbon footprints, LEED certification etc will be a prime focus for the class as will be the implications of climate change, rising sea levels and storm surge conditions of coastal areas as effecting street and basement levels of buildings. We will also address the challenges of providing shelter and general infrastructure for rapidly growing informal sector settlements in edge urban or rural conditions. The class will encourage very open debate so that the experiences of students working and living in various and different environments can share experiences with the whole class.

It is hoped that studio critics in both the 601 studio classes and others in the School of Design can contribute to the class, particularly in selecting projects for study in the class. It is also the aim of this Case Studies class to contribute into the 601 and more particularly, into the 602 studios of the spring semester where more detailed investigations of structure, building envelope and service systems are made in student work.

[ARCH 633] ENVIRONMENTAL SYSTEMS I
Dorit Aviv

The Environmental Systems I course's main learning objectives are first, to understand building systems within the context of macro and micro ecological cycles, and second, to consider the interaction between architectural elements and environmental forces and the consequences of this interaction to the human experience of space.

During the course, students are exposed to novel sensing technologies that make it possible to characterize dynamic thermal environments. The students build and deploy sensors that report real-time data on environmental factors in the space they inhabit.

As the course coincides with the Urban Housing Studio, it is designed to allow for the students to explore environmental systems in buildings through their studio projects, in a series of assignments that correlate with the studio's progress. Through these, the students investigate the intrinsic relationships between formal and material strategies and environmental impacts.

1. DAYLIGHT AND SOLAR GAIN:
While the students are conducting studies of the residential unit plan and aggregation strategies for multiple units, they are asked to conduct digital and physical simulations measuring the impact of each design iteration on daylighting and solar heat gain within the urban site context.

2. FACADE THERMAL PERFORMANCE:
During the week in which the studio is focused on facade and sectional design, the students are asked to consider the overall facade design and the wall-section details, specifically as they pertain to the conduction of heat. Through drawings and numerical analysis of multiple proposed

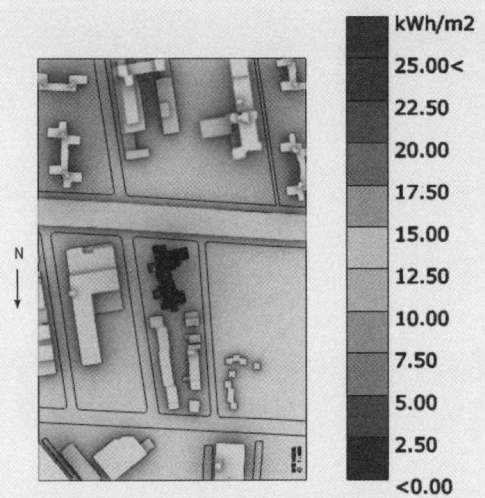

Radiation Analysis
New_York_Central_Prk_Obs_Belv_NY_USA_1977
12 DEC 10:00 - 31 DEC 16:00

iterations, the students learn about the facade performance in relation to the use of conductive and insular materials within the wall section, and how the wall assembly and temperature gradients impact the risk of condensation. They also explore how the ratio of different materials in the facade, opaque and glazed, can significantly impact the cooling and heating load of the building during different seasons.

3. WATER AND ENERGY HARVESTING:
The students learn of storm water mitigation strategies in urban areas through investigation of the potential of their building envelopes for channeling and collecting rainwater. They are also asked to think about the potential to use the building surfaces for solar energy harvesting. These exercises allows students to explore how surface geometry can channel climatic forces.

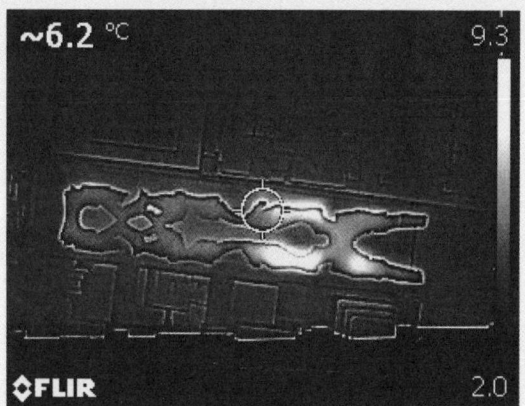

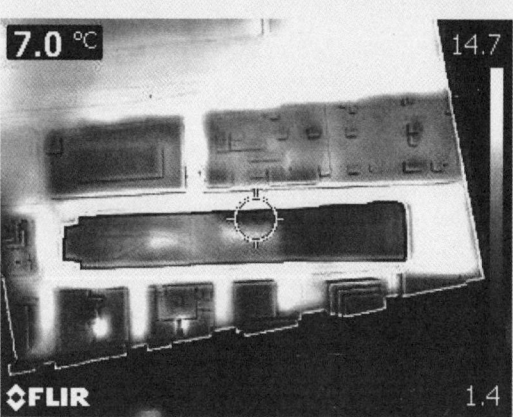
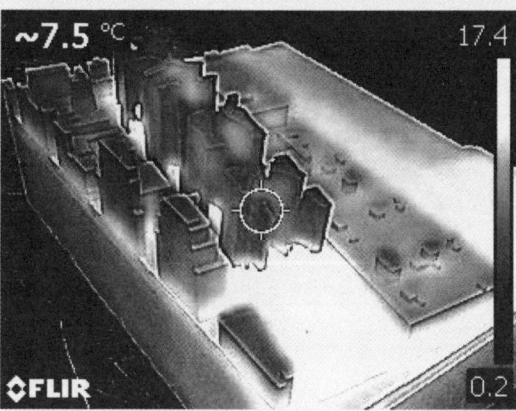
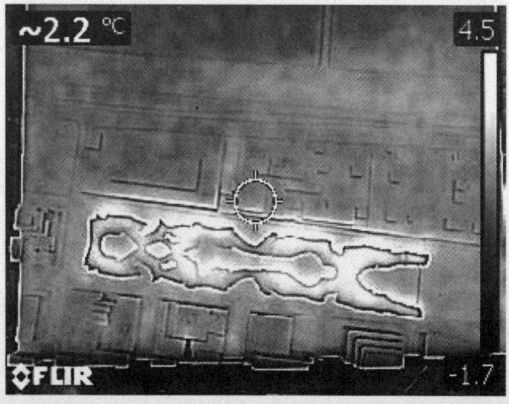
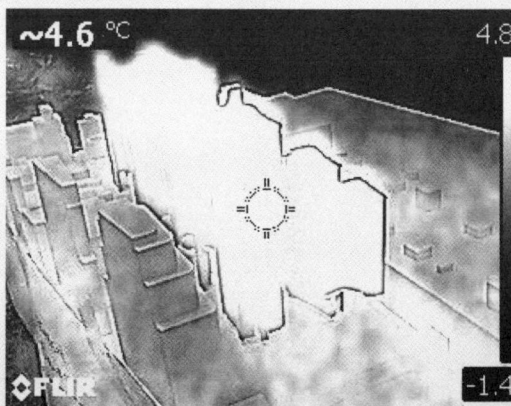

Arachnida by Christine Eichhorn
Critic: **Gisela Baurmann** [p.141]

The Sower by JooYoung Ham
Critic: **Brian Phillips** [p.165]

Elevated Garden by Yangkenan Li
Critic: **Scott Erdy** [p.157]

Red Hook Living Waters by Hillary Morales
Critic: **Ben Krone** [p.160]

shifting hybrids by Kerry Hohenstein
Critic: **Hina Jamelle** [p.130]

Mega-Block Redux IV by Paul Germaine McCoy
Critic: **Kutan Ayata** [p.134]

August 28th, 2019
IN CONVERSATION
Thom Mayne and Wolf Prix
Moderator: Winka Dubbeldam

Moderated by Miller Professor and Chair Winka Dubbeldam, the Department of Architecture was pleased to host Thom Mayne and Wolf Prix in conversation.

Thom Mayne is the Founder and Design Director of Morphosis and Cret Chair Professor of Practice at the Weitzman School of Design.

Mayne has been the recipient of the Pritzker Prize (2005) and the AIA Gold Medal (2013). He served on the President's Committee on the Arts and Humanities under President Obama.

Wolf D. Prix is the Co-Founder, Design Principal, and CEO of COOP HIMMELB(L)AU. Prix was a guest instructor for a 701 studio in Fall 2019.

Prix is a member of the Österreichische Bundeskammer der Architekten und Ingenieurkonsulenten, the Bund Deutscher Architekten, Germany (BDA), the Royal Institute of British Architects (RIBA), the Architectural Association Santa Clara, Cuba, as well as Fellow of the American Institute of Architecture (FAIA).

CORE 602

Simon Kim, Coordinator
Associate Professor of Architecture

The cumulative fourth semester core studio is a design course integrated with Structure, Environmental Design, as well as Visual Studies, and Histories and Theories courses. My role in shaping this studio is in the implementation of disciplinary networks: Structures Week and Cladding Week require collaboration with engineers and consultants. The Master Lecture series introduces the students to experts or leaders in the allied industries. Included in the Master Lectures are: Hanif Kara at AKT II, Marc Simmons from Front Inc., Martha Tsigkari from Foster and Partners, Wolf Mangelsdorf at Buro Happold, and Alex Klein at the ICA.

Under the direction of emerging and well-established design instructors, the ARCH602 students enfold the Structure and Cladding assignments, as well as the Master Lectures, into a public / private facility at a site that we see as a place for experimentation and projection. The successful design of an urban building is its assembled systems that ratify, challenge, or explore architecture as a cultural product, its role in discourse, and its milieu in history. For this intent, our past polemics have ranged from synthetic natures, entanglement, mobility, and non-human agencies. Our cohort is made of talented faculty who are also practicing architects of note: Kutan Ayata of Young & Ayata, Miroslava Brooks and Daniel Markiewicz from Forma NY, Nate Hume of Hume Coover Studio, Simon Kim from Ibañez Kim, Ben Krone of Gradient Architecture, and Danielle Willems of Maeta Design. Each of us bring consultants of our own, such as Arup, Heintges, WPM, to engage with the pedagogies of our studio sections, typically made of twelve students divided into teams. Each team works with their consultants, aided by the course assignments and Master Lectures, to develop a project that is resplendent in form, planimetric drawing, in detailing, atmosphere, and in physical model.

Here are a few powerful excerpts from our Master Lecturers and Consultants:

"PERHAPS THE BETTER QUESTION IS NOT 'HOW TO BEND TECHNOLOGY TO SERVE YOUR DESIGN NEEDS' BUT INSTEAD TO ALLOW DEEP IMPLEMENTATION OF REQUIRED INSTRUMENTATION, SO THAT TRUE EMERGENCE IS POSSIBLE."
— Martha Tsigkari

"ARCHITECTURE, OR WHAT WAS ONCE THE PURVIEW OF A SINGULAR MASTER-BUILDER, HAS BECOME POPULATED WITH SECONDARY FIGURES AND TRADES. WHAT THE FIELD OF ARCHITECTURE CAN CREATE IS DIRECTLY PROPORTIONAL TO THE SERVICES IT HAS LEFT BEHIND DUE TO SPECIALIZATION."
— Hanif Kara

"THE FACADE OF A BUILDING IS THE PRIMARY MEANS OF COMMUNICATING DESIGN INTENT TO THE PUBLIC REALM. THE DETAILS AND MATERIALS, AND THIS REQUIRES VIGILANCE FROM INITIAL DESIGN TO MOCK-UPS, IS WHERE IT TRANSCENDS SIMPLE ENCLOSURE TO PERFORMATIVE INNOVATION."
— Hanif Kara

The completion of this course provides a high platform from which the M.Arch student launches into the final year Option Studio or Thesis.

CUBLOIDS AND CYLINDS:
A SYNTHETIC NATURE

Simon Kim (ASSOCIATE PROFESSOR OF ARCHITECTURE)
Katarina Marjanovic (TA)
Erik Verboon and Gustav Fagerström, Hanif Kara (MASTER LECTURE)

Simon Kim (Associate Professor of Architecture): Co-founded Ibañez Kim Studio, PA & MA, (1994) — Graduated from the Design Research Laboratory at the Architectural Association (AA) — Taught studios and seminars at Harvard, MIT, Yale, and the AA. — Director of the Immersive Kinematics Research Group.

Founded in 1986, Socrates Sculpture Park is the only site in the New York Metropolitan area specifically dedicated to providing artists with opportunities to create and exhibit large-scale sculpture and multimedia installations in a unique outdoor environment that encourages strong interaction between artists, artworks and the public.

Socrates Sculpture Park was an abandoned riverside landfill and illegal dumpsite until 1986 when a coalition of artists and community members, under the leadership of artist Mark di Suvero, transformed it into an open studio and exhibition space for artists and a neighborhood park for local residents. Today it is an internationally renowned outdoor museum and artist residency program that also serves as a vital New York City park offering a wide variety of free public services.

1

SENSORIUM
Glenn Godfrey & Calli Katzelnick

The Sensorium releases one's self from the expectations of perception; to widen the senses beyond what we experience in the everyday. Visitors wander in between and throughout worlds within worlds to experience a multitude of sensorial abstractions. The building aims to explore, question, and alter the nature of perception as one's senses are enhanced, blended, or manipulated through a variety of architectural strategies. Each character contained within the larger "big box" structure of the Sensorium both performs and contains qualities of its interior function via its posture and interaction with human occupants. Orientations and relationships between characters is important to an evocation of their highly specific interior world. The homunculus explores temporal qualities of growth, decay, absorption, discoloration and movement as ink and fungi transform the object throughout its life. As figural and biological representations of the Sensorium, the homunculi demonstrate qualities displayed by and contained within the characters throughout the building and provide a glimpse into the sensory qualities of the project.

2

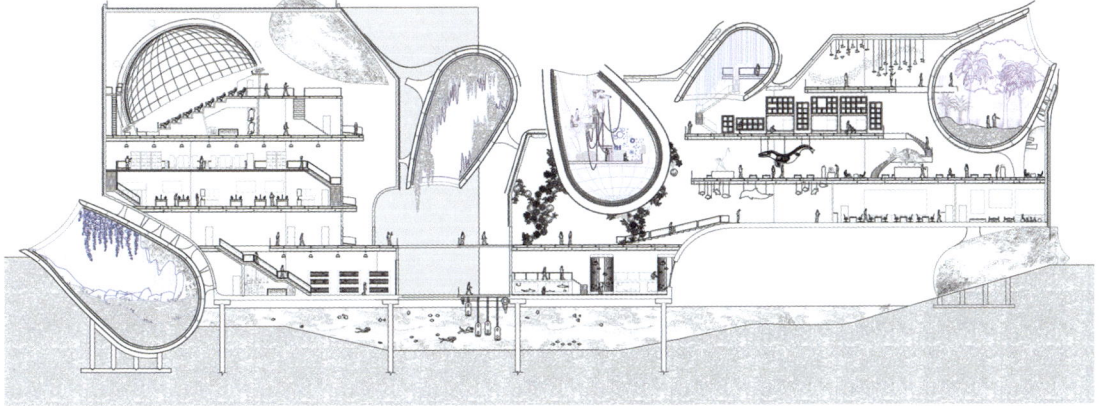

3

1 – *Sensorium* by Glenn Godfrey and Calli Katzelnick, Project Description
2 – *Sensorium* by Glenn Godfrey and Calli Katzelnick, Render Optic
3 – *Sensorium* by Glenn Godfrey and Calli Katzelnick, Section 01

Agenda

We will offer a support center in its adjacent site through the concept of Nature, Character, and Homunculi.

Characters require a certain separation from "looking like" a tree or a parent. An aesthetic shift is required to break the idea of representation, and replace it with active performance and interaction. A building does not look sad, nor does is cry. These are human-based projections onto agents and constructs of wholly separate behaviors and realities. A building may be considered soft because its materiality has selective degrees of pliability. Rather than "cry," a building may draw vapor from the atmosphere and channel its condensate across its facade. Connecting known architectural types and devices from the nature of unknown matter will create a methodology to engage a synthetic world of nonhuman characters and their behaviors.

Methodology and Program

We will focus on how to generate a meaningful understanding of space and tectonics that is based on the ideas of longspan and thick facade as transformation in order to generate total environments, fully immersive atmospheres. These will be in the training of novel structures, and response behaviors to participate in architecture of worldbuilding.

MY GROTTO OF ARCHITECTURAL DEATH
Hosung Jung and Pedro Medrano

Our project focuses on the aspect of death and decay through programmatic and formalistic explorations stemming from a critical use of renaissance architectural vocabulary. Located atop a former illegal landfill in Queens, NY our project centers around the idea of creating spaces for reflection and conversations about death along New York's beloved waterfront. Utilizing a courtyard typology, the building explores the notion of worlds within would as colonnades lead to fantastical courtyards inhabited by wildlife. In between the fantastical and the underground, one meanders through the halls of a music conservatory with a live-in residency program. Stairs not only ascend upwards towards skyline views but also downwards into the depths of New York's underground. As visitors descend downwards the layers of exposed earth reveal the false comfort of solid ground as a fabricated and unstable layer of the anthropocene is revealed to the viewer. This is a project not only of spectacle but also of impermanence, it is a project which forces us to grapple with the cultural consequences of our consumption and inevitable death.

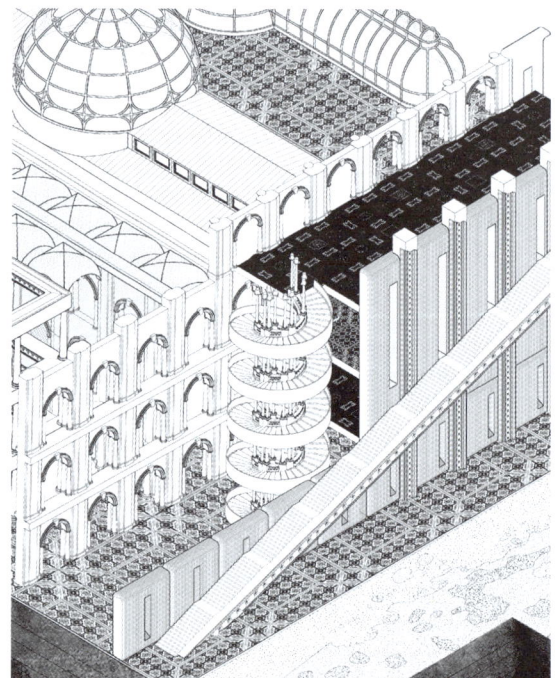

5

4 – *My Grotto of Architectural Death* by Hosung Jung and Pedro Medrano, Project Description

5 – *My Grotto of Architectural Death* by Hosung Jung and Pedro Medrano, Axonometric

6 – *My Grotto of Architectural Death* by Hosung Jung and Pedro Medrano, Axonometric Zoomed Out

HINTERLAND
Robert Schaffer and Christine Eichhorn

Buried beneath the earth, Hinterland appears as little more than a mound of earth to those passing by. Carved into the landscape, a single entrance and sequence restricts guests, prescribing their journey as they descend deeper into the ground.

Temporality and architecture tend to be two phenomenons not always cheerfully discussed in context with one another. We live in a world full of finite, beautiful, natural monuments and yet we shield our eyes to the idea that one day our buildings will follow suit. Hinterland embraces this and speculates on the nature of the building as it enters the post-human era. This transitory study begins with the creation of the building and moves forward in time hundreds of years to a world that post dates the human race. The descent follows the stream of water and moves through a cavernous cistern before opening up into the amphitheater beyond. This project doesn't look to create a building, but rather a foreign realm buried beneath us —a world within worlds.

7

8

9

7 – *Hinterland* by Robert Schaffer and Christine Eichhorn, Render
8 – *Hinterland* by Robert Schaffer and Christine Eichhorn, Render
9 – *Hinterland* by Robert Schaffer and Christine Eichhorn, Final Section—Shadow

POSTURED NATURES
Paul Germaine McCoy and Matthew Kohman

Postured Natures is a set up of three ideas that construct a palpable speculation of a new conservatory and performing arts center for Socrates Park:

Posture as a means to engage the site's ground condition and natural poche. Wood as a technique to exhaust structural specificity and aesthetic affect. Enfilade as a strategy to se!uence experience between the wild and the curated.

We drew a series of rooms that could touch, teter, or slip away. A partition schedule gives the postures uni!ue characters that react to one another and their surroundings. The ensemble of postures imply the ephemeral dualities of a changing shoreline and program development of Socrates Park. The nine s!uare grid is used to challenge the linear sequence of the theater program typology. The postures become animated with materiality as they navigate a scaled environment. Chonk as in objectness, and part-ness over whole. An unfolded sequence of section, detail, plan, and elevation.

10

11 12

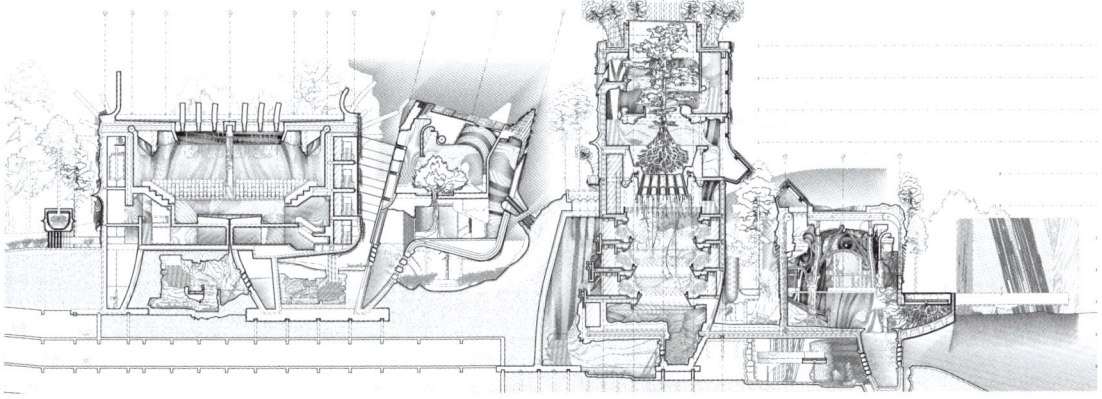

13

10 – *Postured Natures,* by Paul Germaine McCoy and Matthew Kohman, Chunker
11 – *Postured Natures,* by Paul Germaine McCoy and Matthew Kohman, Aerial
12 – *Postured Natures,* by Paul Germaine McCoy and Matthew Kohman, Enfilade
13 – *Postured Natures,* by Paul Germaine McCoy and Matthew Kohman, Section

THE DIVE-HOUSE

Kutan Ayata
Caleb Ehly (TA)

Kutan Ayata (Senior Lecturer): Co-founded New York-based architecture firm, Young & Ayata (2008) – Young & Ayata are winners of The Architectural League Prize (2014) – Received a MArch from Princeton University (2004) – Bachelor of Fine Arts in Architecture from Massachusetts College of Art in Boston (1999)

As our cities grow, the demands of contemporary urban life diminish the chance to explore outdoors on a regular basis. Certain outdoor recreational activities such as cycling, rowing, climbing, diving (and others) find new appropriations within the bounds of the city in the confines of constructed environments. These are building types which provide specific physical conditions as determined by the activity, enabling variety of challenges to be "tackled" by users. While the degrees of difficulty and thirst for fitness can be satisfied in a utilitarian manner in these artificial terrains, what typically cannot be experienced in them are the totality, sublimity, and majestic qualities of grand outdoors. Architecture's response to this interesting problem and challenge has been mostly a retrieval, where the architect is relegated to designing the shed around these artificial constructs created by "specialist experts."

Architecture's battle with nature is old and historically rich. The discipline of architecture (as well as the arts) has always been preoccupied with questions of representing/recreating/redefining/embodying "nature" through various strains of its histories, i.e. from Baroque, Rococo to Art Nouveau, from Modernism, to Biomimicry, and even recent tendencies of green, sustainable approaches continue these ambitions by foregrounding responsible relations with our environment. Without a doubt, all these approaches generated significant aesthetic arguments for architecture. The two most common pitfalls of all such aesthetics can be summed up as follows: either the design aims for a simulacrum of an idealized notion of "nature," resulting in literal visual interpretations of "what is commonly assumed to be natural" or aims for juxtaposition through absolute abstractions to posture against "the nature". Both these positions reflect the presumption of the commonly embraced nature/culture divide. What if we explore this problem yet again, but aim to operate away from these opposite poles? What if we claim that we can produce specific objects that can begin to undermine our assumptions about the culture/nature divide? What if we rather take the position that authentic "objects of nature" can be constructed and these constructions can cultivate their unique qualities, experiences, and cultures?

1   DIVING INTO THE BOXES
Saina Xiang and Kyunghyun Kim

The project tends to explore a unique diving experience by designing five extremely long, deep, and narrow boxes that are integrated on the top and radially branched out to the city. By introducing a cylinder shape structure on the bottom to elevate these rectangular diving pools, the project is also able to respond 360 degrees to the site including existing infrastructure and railway park. The project also studies the hybridization between circular and orthogonal shapes and creates an articulated transition terrace for other supportive functions such as spa and recreational pools. In terms of materiality, the Dive-House first reacts to the existing material, and then it generates its own character throughout the development. The bottom tries to emphasize the project's horizontality by layered earth tone stone in contrast with the top's verticality which is emphasized by vertical scratch apertures on the metal facade.

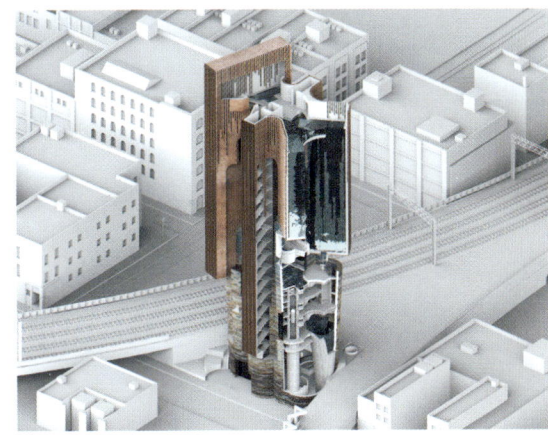

2

1 – *Diving Into The Boxes* by Saina Xiang and Kyunghyun Kim, Project Description
2 – *Diving Into The Boxes* by Saina Xiang and Kyunghyun Kim, Axon

The studio explored a freediving and bathhouse facility next to the Viaduct Rail Park. Formerly known as the Reading Viaduct, this piece of infrastructure was a railway which ran through various Philadelphia neighborhoods, sometimes as a tunnel, sometimes as an elevated platform. Its domestication is partly complete, its fate is sealed in predictable mediocracy. We speculated on an alternative building types which attempted to define their characteristics somewhere between architectural and infrastructural aesthetics.

4   THE DIVE-HOUSE
Yi-Hsuan Wu and Jooyoung Ham

Our design aims to capture the spirit of freediving sensation: control and concentration. To keep this idea, we started off with simple geometries, and used a series of controlled merges to connect the geometries and created the overall form of the building. Four separated legs contain the three pools and egress merge to the top as one public space. The bottom public spaces are populated with stepping flower beds that cascade down from the rail park level to the street level, connecting the circulation of the park and street. The pools inside are designed with ledges every 10 feet to guide the divers, and the shape of the pools are designed to serve the best diving experience without hindering the free dive experience.

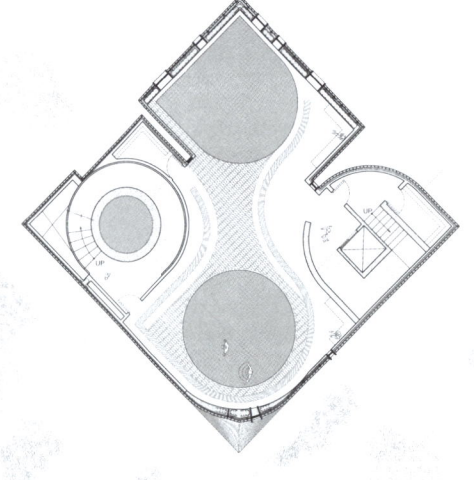

5

6

3 – *Diving Into The Boxes* by Saina Xiang and Kyunghyun Kim, Pool Interior
4 – *The Dive-House* by Zhiqi Sheng and Megan York, Project Description

5 – *The Dive-House* by Zhiqi Sheng and Megan York, Plan Upper Level
6 – *The Dive-House* by Zhiqi Sheng and Megan York, Render Elevation

7 – Collective Images

THE WATER TOWER
Luo Tao and Dekang Liang

The Water Tower is an urban water recreation facility that supports water diving, swimming, sauna, spa, and all other sorts of water related activities. The building takes the topology of typical water tower form to house three deep diving pools in different heights and a main body containing water related programs in the air. Its structure also takes precedent of how a water tower houses and supports water. Inside this landmark structure, people experience the feeling of touring around and inside of a water tower: a fantastic, heterotopia world of water.

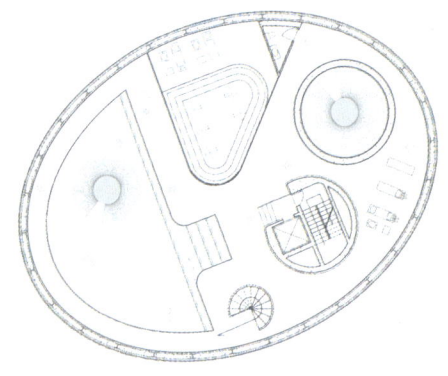

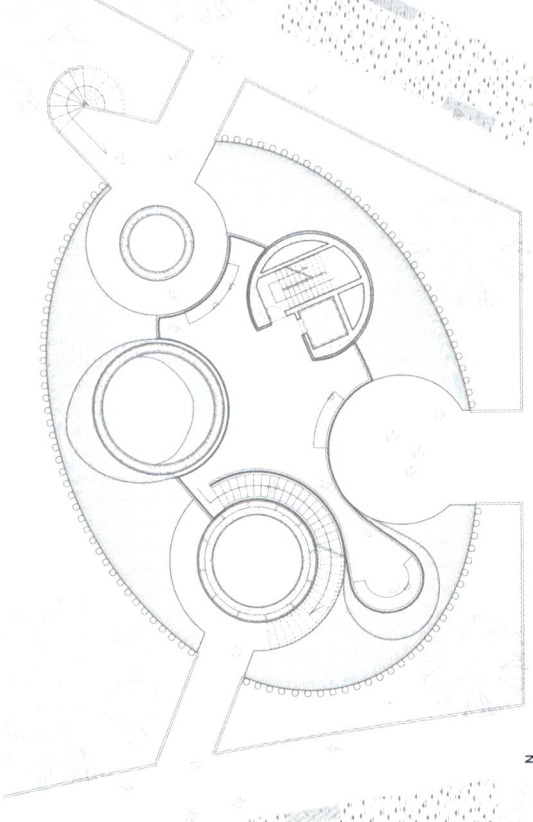

8 – *The Water Tower* by Luo Tao and Dekang Liang, South East View
9 – *The Water Tower* by Luo Tao and Dekang Liang, Plan Upper
10 – *The Water Tower* by Luo Tao and Dekang Liang, Cut Away Axon
11 – *The Water Tower* by Luo Tao and Dekang Liang, Plan Railpark Level

THE DIVE-HOUSE
Zhiqi Sheng and Megan York

As our cities grow, the demands of contemporary urban life diminish the chance to explore outdoors on a regular basis. Certain outdoor recreational activities such as cycling, rowing, climbing, diving (and others) find new appropriations within the bounds of the city in the confines of constructed environments. While the degrees of difficulty and thirst for fitness can be satisfied in a utilitarian manner in these artificial terrains, what typically cannot be experienced in them are the totality, sublimity, and majestic qualities of grand outdoors.

By hybridizing a contemporary program of recreational free-diving pools with the aesthetic typology of the Bernd and Hilla Becher Water Tower series, a new urban artifact emerges from its urban context. The object of the interior free-diving pools is encased within the overall reptilian exterior object of the building itself.

Everyday materials that we are already familiar with (i.e. exterior shingles and interior pool tiling) is further manipulated to create a more bizarre aesthetic, such as polymer printing the shingles to look dramatically aged and weathered and lining an iridescent film over the interior pool tiles for a more "sublime" aesthetic. Looking into Baroque topologies in plan, the recreational program of the pools are primarily condensed into a singular core near the center of the design with program acting on the perimeter. The central core of the program becomes inversed towards the top of the structure with a singular oculus, creating a level of sublimity rarely found in the design's urban context.

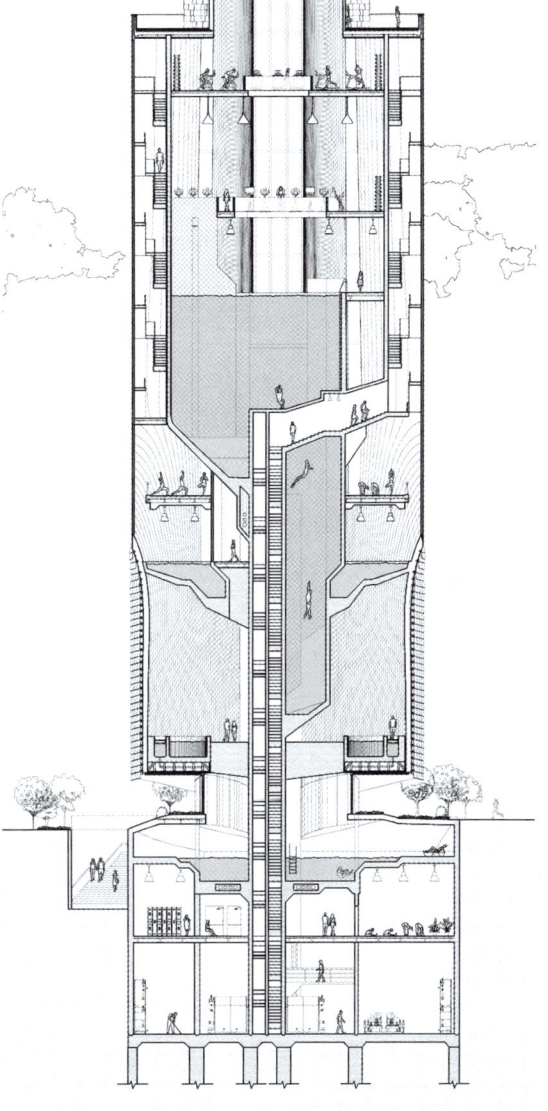

12 – *The Dive-House* by Zhiqi Sheng and Megan York, Section
13 – *The Dive-House* by Zhiqi Sheng and Megan York, South East Render
14 – *The Dive-House* by Zhiqi Sheng and Megan York, Interior Pool Perspective

MUSEUM HYBRID

Miroslava Brooks (LECTURER)
Marta Llor (TA)
Erleen Hatfield and John Hodder (ENGINEERING CONSULTANTS)

Miroslava Brooks (Lecturer): Founding partner of FORMA - an architecture practice based in New York City – holds a Master of Architecture from Yale University, where she was awarded the William Wirt Winchester Travelling Fellowship – school's most prestigious prize – Graduated Summa Cum Laude from The Ohio State University with a Bachelor of Science in Architecture – Has taught design studios and seminars at Yale School of Architecture – worked as Project Designer and Research Assistant at Eisenman Architects

Last year alone, many cultural institutions saw a surge of exhibitions and events focusing on our fractured relationship with the natural world. From *Eco-Visionaries: Confronting a Planet in a State of Emergency* at London's Royal Academy of Arts, *Nature* at Cooper Hewitt in New York, and *Broken Nature: Design Takes on Human Survival* at the Milan Triennale, it is clear that contemporary artists, designers, architects, curators, scientists, and philosophers are trying to grapple with the profound awareness of climate change, engaging in questions that are grounded "in the understanding that the ecological crisis is a symptom of something bigger, deeper, older: our alienation from labor, our colonization of nature, our enslavement of each other, our crisis of humanity." [a]

Historically, museums were places of authority where knowledge was collected by a few disciplinary experts, clearly categorized, and presented to the public. Such authority was often conveyed through a building's facade via symmetry, monumentality, and historical (Western) references. Today, cultural institutions are rethinking their institutional identities in order to expand their audience through cross-disciplinary thinking and risk-taking programming.

The task of the studio was to design a new addition to the canonical museum designed by Marcel Breuer in New York City. Starting with image collections, collages, and relief models, the students were asked to: 1. harness the representational capacity of architecture —the means by which a building communicates with the public—focusing the design on what is arguably the building's most public interface: the facade, and 2. to utilize the section as the primary medium through which multiplicity of spatial conditions are organized in productive spatial adjacencies. Ultimately, the hope was for the students to formulate their own critical position and research agenda through the design of a building, and in doing so outline the bases for one's own architectural project.

1   NATURE RELINKAGE-WOODEN MUSEUM
         Baoqi Ji and Yuhao Zhang

The project intends to bring wood structures back into the city through this new addition to the existing Met Breuer Museum. 'Growing' from the gab between the museum building and the adjacent historical brownstones, the new addition expands vertically, as a tree might. We started by looking at specific spatial and structural conditions of a real tree and how those could be translated to new ideas for a building. As an extension to the Met Breuer, the proposed exhibition spaces have much higher ceiling heights, are varied in size, and connected with branches of circulation that lead visitors to explore the interlocked interiors of the new museum. The facade consists of wooden louvres and wooden panels that have a change of scale from top to bottom and a color gradient, like the clusters of leaves on the tree. The vertical louvres not only provide proper shading to the exhibition spaces, but just like the texture of the bark is multidirectional, the louvers also change direction and rotate gradually outwards towards the surrounding site.

2

a – https://www.aam-us.org/2019/02/01/curator-as-catalyst-how-an-interdisciplinary-fellowship-inspired-a-new-way-of-doing-museum/

1 – *Nature Relinkage-Wooden Museum* by Baoqi Ji and Yuhao Zhang, Project Description
2 – *Nature Relinkage-Wooden Museum* by Baoqi Ji and Yuhao Zhang, Interior Render

THE URBAN CANYON
Maria Jose Fuentes and Veronica Rosado

Our project proposes to re-create and infiltrate traditional gallery spaces with environmental biomes and art residencies to create a new hybrid typology for the 21st century museum. We define biomes as place-making rooms of environmental change which oscillate between natural and artificial. This is seen through the lens of non-anthropocentric agencies. These biomes could be Virtual Biomes, plant incubators, or homes to synthetic art. Paola Antonelli's Broken Nature exhibition influenced the project's ethos, which stresses the positive outcome of museums being curated through a fluid institutional approach; encompassing both the natural and the imaginative in order to accumulate an applicable data set to mindfully continue conversations surrounding the anthropocene.

3

Our collection of images reflects on Borasi's *Museum Is not Enough* concept of "grey areas." This allowed us to think of a museum institution more fluidly; as a series of biomes that allow for different natural moments to exist in muddled binaries with the artificial.

The urban canyon sets out to carve out a public space for the pedestrians on the street level, as well as informing inhabitants of what could be artificial, what is nature, and how we find ourselves in the mix as humans.

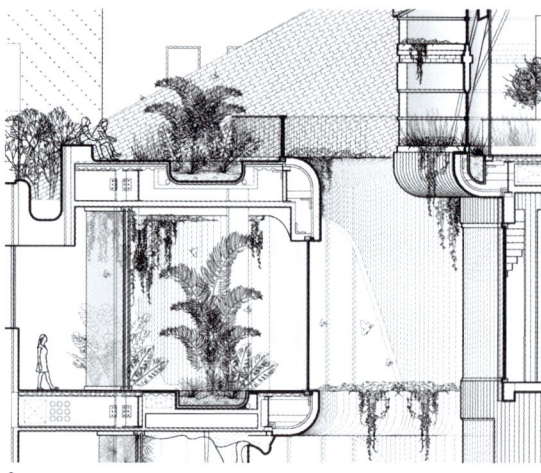

4

5

3 – *The Urban Canyon* by Maria Jose Fuentes and Veronica Rosado, Elevation
4 – *The Urban Canyon* by Maria Jose Fuentes and Veronica Rosado, Section Close-Up

5 – *The Urban Canyon* by Maria Jose Fuentes and Veronica Rosado, Render

STRANGELY, FAMILIAR: MUSEUM OF FAKE REALITIES
Alexander Jackson and Kevin He

This project is an exploration of the replica through the *near miss*. We wanted to explore how the idea of fake realities could be explored through architecture by replicating the existing building designed by Marcel Breuer on the adjacent site. We were interested in how elements of the original building can start to spin an entirely new system, similarly to how one small piece of truth can spin many new tales of fiction. With the front aperture of the existing Met Breuer building being the most iconic image of the project, we sought to represent these through a spatial near miss. The apertures become large spatial voids and organize exhibition spaces inside the new interior. The iconic figure is now radically transformed from within. Situated in parallel to the original Met Breuer building, the elevational experience presents the addition on equal footing with the museum to the point where one may question which is the original.

6

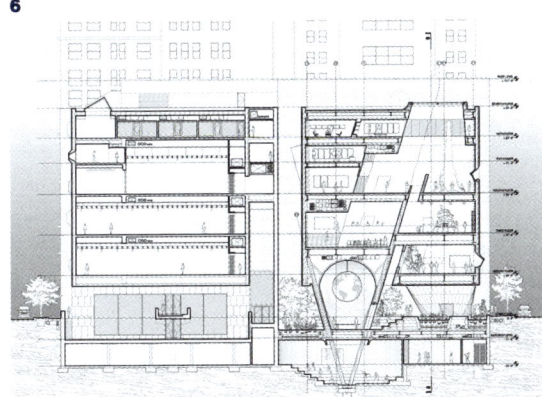

7

8

6 – *Strangely, familiar: Museum of Fake Realities*, by Alexander Jackson and Kevin He, Elevation

7 – *Strangely, familiar: Museum of Fake Realities*, by Alexander Jackson and Kevin He, Sections

8 – *Strangely, familiar: Museum of Fake Realities*, by Alexander Jackson and Kevin He, Render

OUTSIDE IN

Nate Hume (SENIOR LECTURER)
Ryan Henriksen (TA)
Eddy Roberts, Jamison Guest, and Michael Tortella (ENGINEER AND FACADE CONSULTANTS)

Nate Hume (Senior Lecturer) MArch Yale University - Principal Hume Architecture - Founder SuckerPunch

Eddy Roberts, Jamison Guest and Michael Tortella

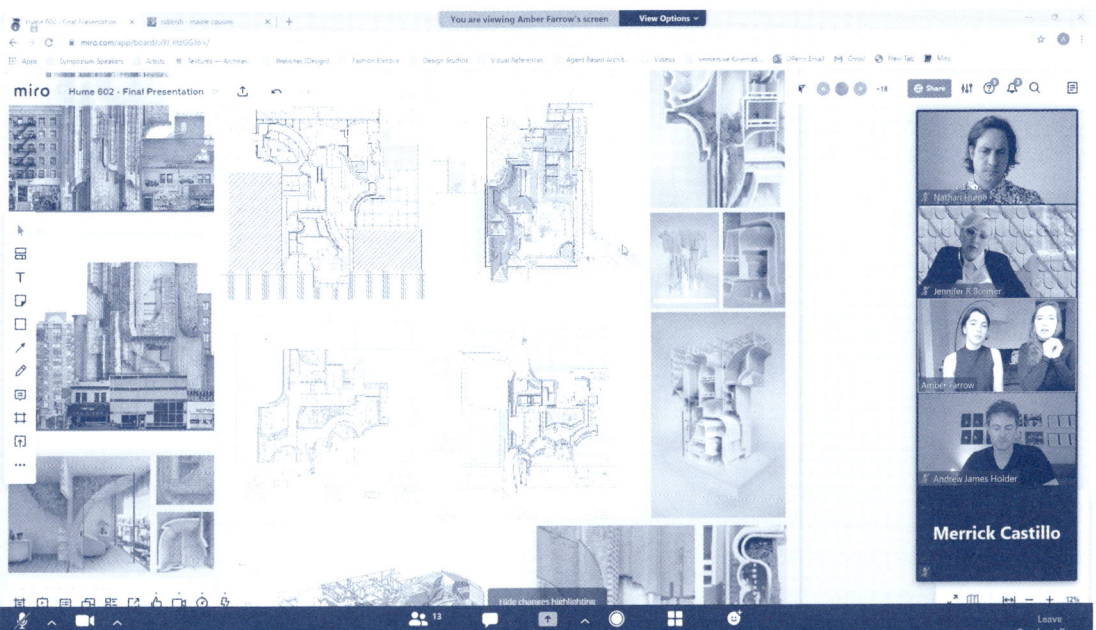

1

The studio was interested in looking at the expanding palette of building materials which break down the traditional distinction between the natural and the artificial. Historically, building materials have either been sourced from nature or produced artificially, with natural materials being conceived of as ones that come from raw, organic matter, and artificial materials being produced from chemical or factory processing. Today's material culture exists largely in a liminal territory between the two states. Composite materials hold multiple properties of the raw and the processed, not only questioning what is natural but also producing new natures and aesthetic effects. The hybridization of these materials are formed through several means including laminating, embedding, and compressing organic and inorganic matter. The strategies are extracted from the composition of the materials to be mined for spatial and tectonic strategies. Banding, stacking, and clean delineation give way to patches, peeling, embedding, growing, and accumulating in all directions. The material effects move form the zoning of the cladding to re-conceiving the spaces of the building as the projects look for inhabitable rustication. The wall becomes not just a traditional division between what is conceived of as the interior and exterior but as a mediator between slippery notions of the public domain of the city and the private as well as nature and the constructed inner world of buildings. The strategies developed through looking at material composition serve to find provoke relationships in the mediation that exist between these binaries to arrive at new architectural conditions.

To explore these notions the studio designed a headquarters for a food startup, specifically one dealing with shortages or surpluses. Ones looking to replace depleted food sources with ones alternatively grown or bred in abundance or produced from waste

1 – Studio Review

surplus. Similar to material palette expanding and blurring the natural and processed there is intense need for new means of producing food whether it is through artificial lab grown items or natural foods produced in new ways. Tastes and textures get mixed and recalibrated to produce seemingly contradictory items such as plant based shrimp, bacon made from mushroom roots, animal free eggs, or insect burgers. Or elements removed from the waste system such as fruit skins, coffee waste, leaves, and husks become key ingredients for alternative flours, meats, and dairy. Architecture can produce environments to complement the synthetic worlds of these new production spaces. The wild spaces of the unknown may no longer be the mountains and seas but instead warehouses of robots growing beef, dense urban hydroponic arrays of vegetables, and towers of sensors monitoring urban apiaries. The buildings are a dynamic facility with spaces for test kitchens, production, storage, and public events. The center will look to attract and engage with a public curious about the future of food production, cooking, and culinary adventure. Growing, cooking and eating food are social acts capable of producing community. We will look at the success of events such as MAD, Smorgasburg, and spaces such as Refettorio to think about the cultural contribution a building like this could foster. This building should look for ways to act as a generator of activity not just in its immediate site but throughout the neighborhood and city as well.

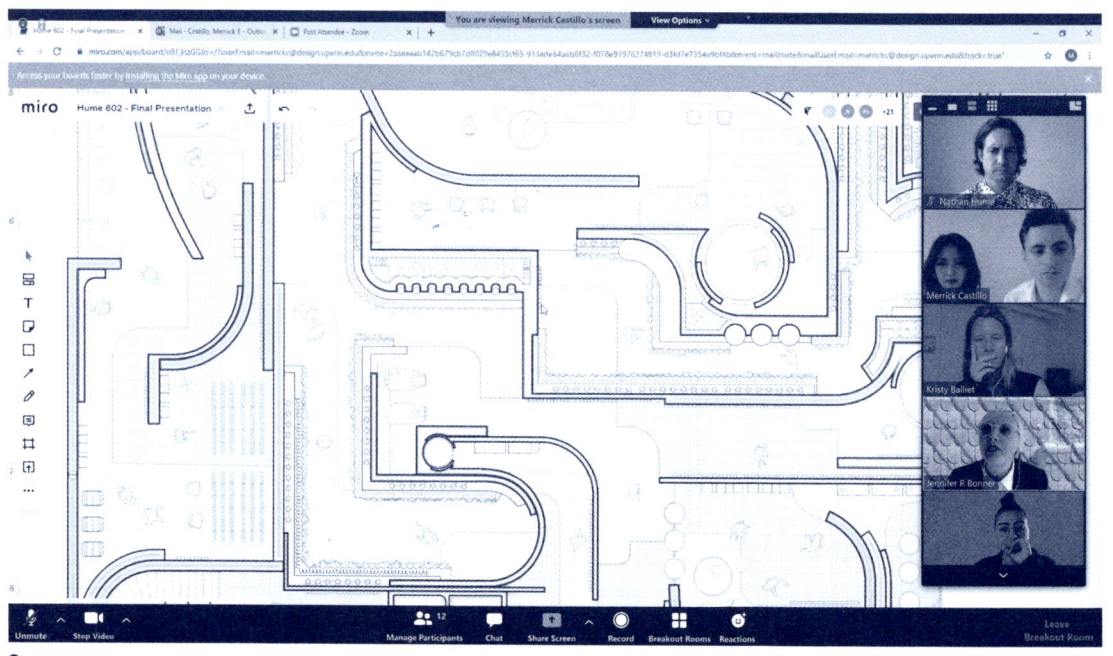

2 – Studio Review

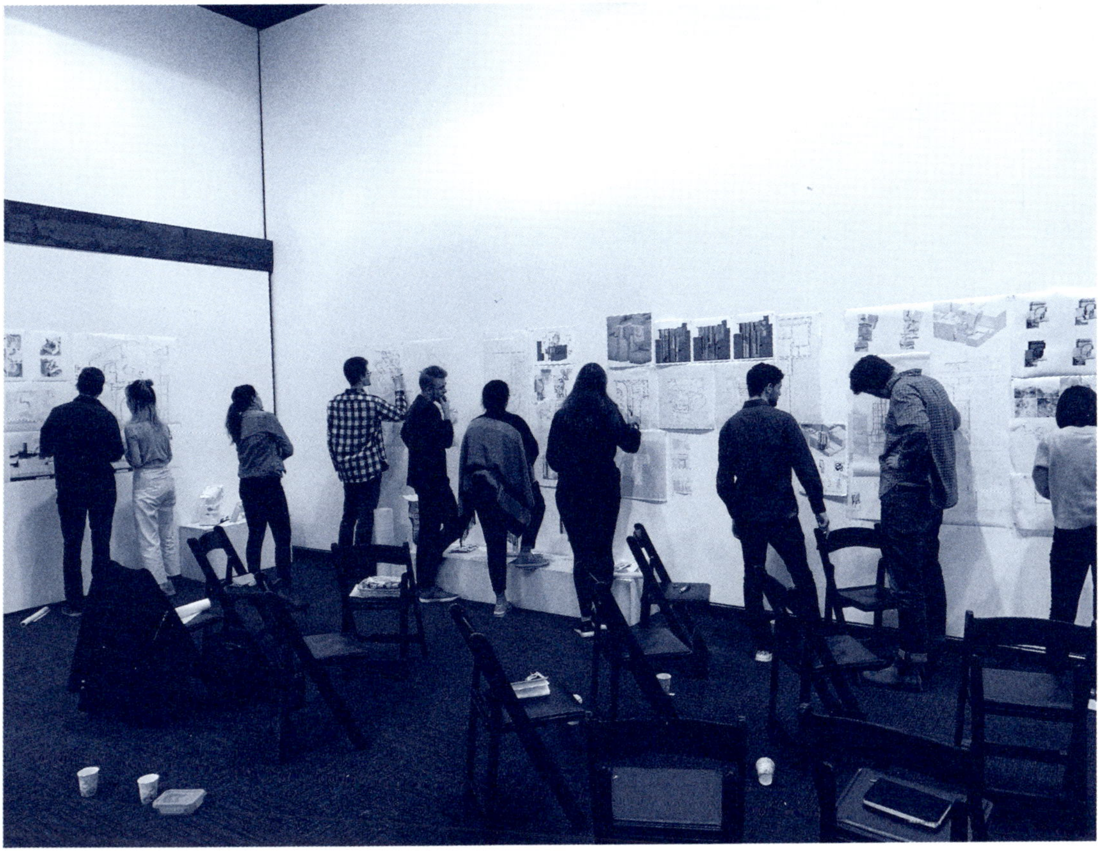

3

4

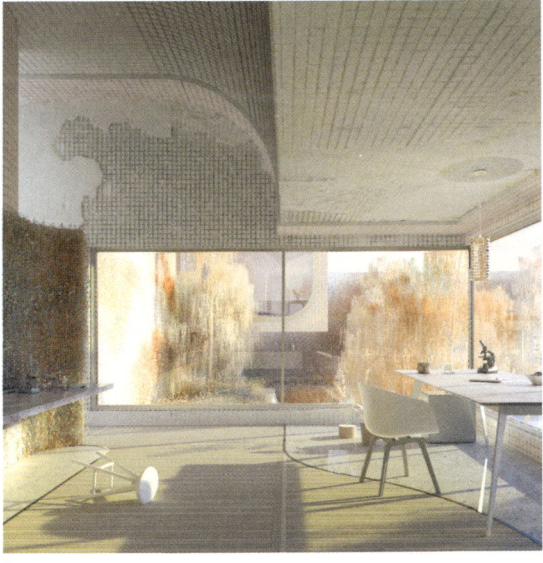

3 – Studio Review
4 – *Suspended Environments* by Merrick Castillo and Hanqing Yao, Scene

TRASH-TO-TABLE
Amber Farrow and Molly Zmich

Our innovative compost reuse facility challenges the role of the wall and its perception of boundary and thickness as barrier. This reinterpretation exists not only in the construction methodology but also through manipulating the relationship between threshold and habitation within the project. By interpreting a common language of slippage and delamination in massing and spatial organization, the ideas and notions of inside and outside are called into question.

Through textural experimentation, spatial layering, and the blurring of interior and exterior condition, this project calls into question the notions of the synthetic and the role of nature in the urban setting. Often the interaction between nature and the city-dweller is one of control and manicured artifice. Much like the role of the grotto in renaissance times, our intention is to challenge this relationship, showing the rough edges and the space of the "in-between." By bringing the waste of the city into the project, and repurposing it in a contemporary way; the public is now able to develop a new relationship with nature in a setting that examines the definitions of both grotesque beauty, exterior inhabitation, and the limits of the synthetic.

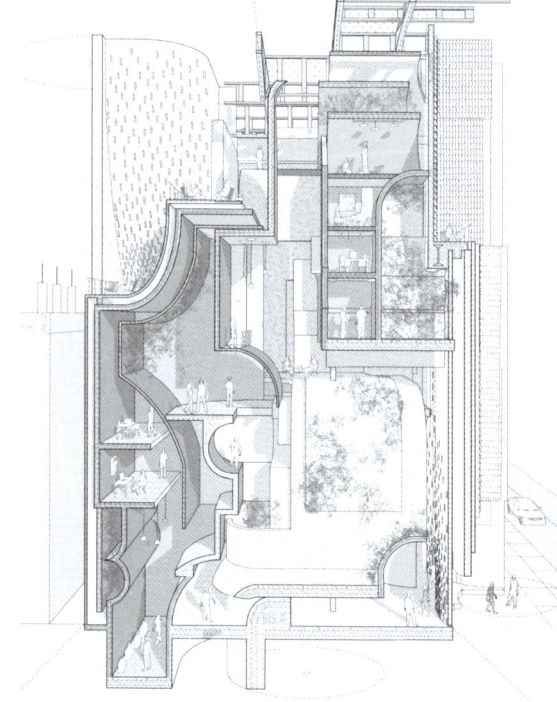

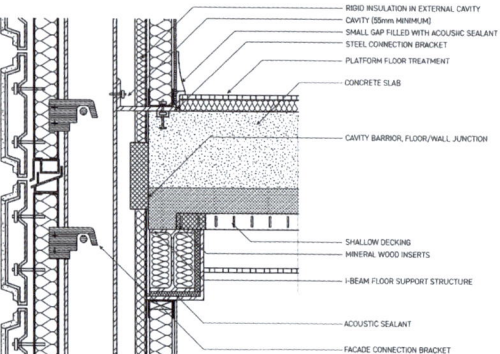

5 – *Trash-to-Table* by Amber Farrow and Molly Zmich, Section
6 – *Trash-to-Table* by Amber Farrow and Molly Zmich, Final Elevation
7 – *Trash-to-Table* by Amber Farrow and Molly Zmich, Section Detail
8 – *Trash-to-Table* by Amber Farrow and Molly Zmich, Section

SUSPENDED ENVIRONMENTS
Merrick Castillo and Hanqing Yao

Suspended Environments explores the role of nature in the city; questioning precedents such as The High-Line and Ford Foundation on their treatment towards landscape as a single layer. Our project creates suspended volumetric nature visitors can inhabit. Landscapes and liners create parks that push their way through the building forming gardens for the public and poche for growing and freezing food. As the landscape pushes its way through the facade, a billboard emerges towards Delancy. The park embeds itself into the building using walls as liners encased by soil which allows people to see moments of natural and mechanical environments as they are pulled into new hyper-conditions.

As the landscape moves through the building it allows for programmatic space to emerge, the program is freeze dried food, where the food is grown within the landscape and frozen throughout. Freeze dryers are large in nature and the mass of these machines manipulates the poche pushing their way into the landscape, creating their own mechanical environments. The frozen reality of the machine contrasts the light airy environment of the park and as they mix they produce new natures. The plant life within the park overgrows, yet in moments creates profiles along the materials. Mimicking geometry from the machines, creating a new form of landscape.

As people move down delancey street the elevation reveals a large billboard where there is a slippage of synthetic material layers and different depths of the landscape can be seen. This elevation takes on the graphic nature of the billboard, using vegetation and material layers to create figures displayed to the city. The materials slippage create inhabitable space for both human and plant life. People are in constant contact with the landscape. As they approach the building they see blurred figures of nature, as the landscape cantilevers over the airspace of the neighboring building. Once they enter the lobby, glimpses of landscape are suspended above them. As they move towards the park they are pushed into a tray where trees are growing around them and they are placed in a completely new world.

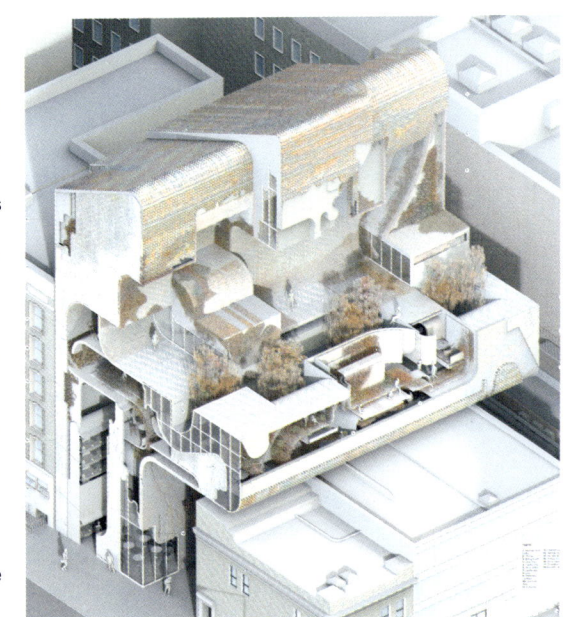

9

10

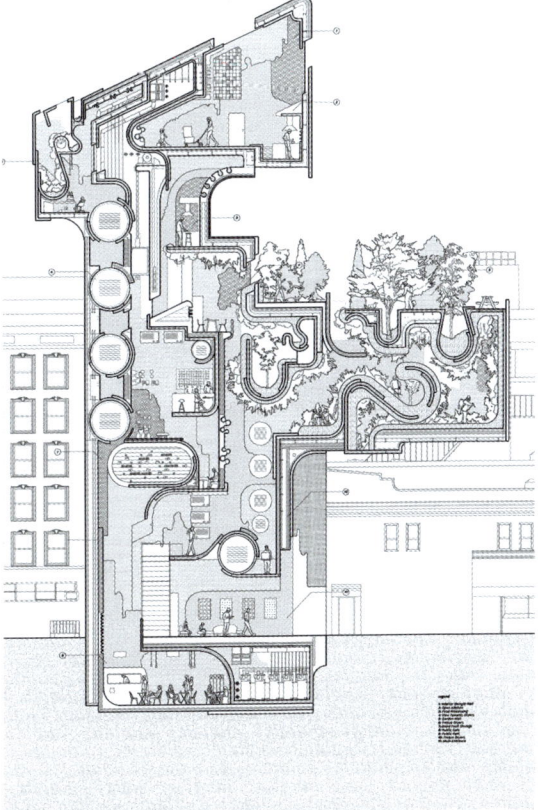

11

9 – *Suspended Environments* by Merrick Castillo and Hanqing Yao, Cutaway Axon

10 – *Suspended Environments* by Merrick Castillo and Hanqing Yao, Scene

11 – *Suspended Environments* by Merrick Castillo and Hanqing Yao, Section

THE LIVING LABORATORY: GOVERNOR'S ISLAND CENTER FOR CLIMATE ADAPTATION AND POLICYMAKING

Ben Krone (LECTURER)
Jon Kontuly (STUDIO CONSULTANT)
Catherine Shih (TA)

Ben Krone (Lecturer): Founded Gradient Design Studio, NYC (2006) – B.Arch from the University of Florida (1999) – M.Arch degree from Columbia University's Graduate School of Architecture, GSAPP (2004) – Winner of McKim Prize for Excellence in Design & the Sol Kaplan Traveling Fellowship

Jon Kontuly (Studio Consultant), Senior Architect at MAD

Research on the effects and potential solutions to climate change has become a worldwide endeavor. The global effects have nearly every major university and numerous independent research entities analyzing both the effects and potential solutions. Not since WW2's Manhattan Project laboratory established in Los Alamos has there been a coalescence of research, science and policy making centered in a single location. The Governors Island Climate Center establishment will be the first of its kind and should set a precedent for the future of dealing with these global crises. Both in its unique physical location and proximity to Lower Manhattan—the most populous of coastal cities likely to experience the effects of climate change, Governor's Island has already established itself as an early adopter of some of the landscape principles associated with climate sensitive modifications. As reported in the New York Times, The Governors Island Trust which manages all aspects of the island's resources and its development is proposing that the island become a home for every aspect of research and testing of Climate Change and its effects on urban centers. The proposal for the center will include research-based schools and universities, a conference center for hosting climate summits, laboratories for monitoring its effects as well as testing new potential solutions. The island also plans to use the center for public advocacy and policy making. The idea of a Living Laboratory is to have a place to deploy potential solutions in a real-world environment. To take one of the most vulnerable places to the effects of climate change and make it a physical manifestation of its effects and solutions.

SITE

Governor's Island Western Development Zone

Governors Island is situated at the base of Manhattan's Southern tip across the mouth of the East River. It has become a major destination for both local New Yorkers as well as Tourists in the summer months due to its fantastic views of the city, its rolling park landscape and number of eco tourist and art tourism sites. The Governors Island trust has selected their Western Development site (Aprox 7 acres) for our studio to work on. This is one of the major future development sites for the future Climate center and has been selected by the Trust due to its relevance to the studio goals as well as its sweeping views of the city and Statue of Liberty.

1

MICROPLASTIC RESEARCH AND COMMUNICATION CENTER
Yu Qiao and Ruichen Xu

Microplastics that pollute the environment and threaten both marine and terrestrial organisms are created through photodegradation of plastic debris. The amount of methane, which makes up 20% of all greenhouse gases, released during the breaking down process is one of the factors that deteriorate climate change. A microplastics research and communication center on the Governor's island researching on possible ways of microplastic collection and reproduction can help raise the public's awareness of the pollution as well as the importance of plastic reuse and recycle.

Based on the photodegradation and reproduction of the microplastic reuse cycle, we select two tectonic terms to create spatial organizational strategies of this project, subdivision, and reformation.

1 – *Microplastic Research and Communication Center* by Yu Qiao and Ruichen Xu, Second Floor Render

The rigid rectangular massing sits on the edge of the island breaks down into two pieces to adapt to the ocean currents. A dynamic central piece that stimulates active public engagement bonds them together and reforms to a new structure. The three pieces function together as a gigantic machine that filters microplastics inside both seawater and rainwater. Public can enjoy the space and pockets created by the umbrella collectors in different scales and on different levels.

The vertical louvers on the lab facade express the falling rainwater. They also echo the vertical frame of the umbrella collectors, which help to mitigate the tension created by the different spatial quality of the three parts. The facade design also conveys the idea of exposing the hidden scientific research process in the labs. Besides function as sun-shading devices, the louvers also control the views and interactions between public and researchers in labs, which helps the public to involve in this filtration process. The labs in this research center are not unreachable. Visitors can see what's happening inside the lab and experience in person in the educational spaces for lectures and labs.

THE ANALOG MODEL
Spatial, Conceptual, Geometric Studies

The studio began by groups considering one or several immediate endangered ecological systems relevant to the climate crisis. This research formed the foundation of each team's conceptual approach towards programming, and ultimately became the basis for defining "the living laboratory" as a new building typology.

Through analog investigations of space, geometry, and various manual techniques of weaving, stitching, stacking, molding etc., complex geometric systems were generated, embedded with the DNA for both spatial and geometric innovation that may be applied at various scales and utilized to test a host of programmatic functions.

2

3

2 – Class analog model

3 – *Microplastic Research and Communication Center* by Yu Qiao and Ruichen Xu, Elevation Render

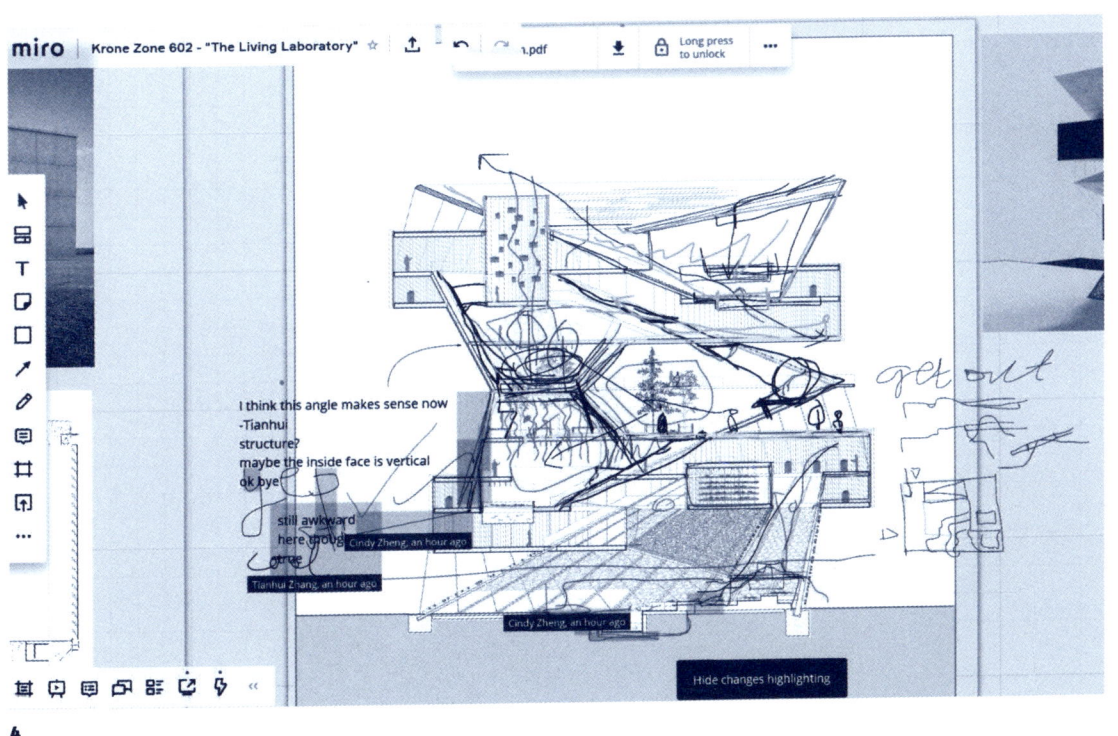

4 – Collaboration through *Miro*

THE CLOUD MACHINE
Aaron Stone and Tone Chu

This project is a climate change research and demonstration center which focuses on geoengineering and decarbonization. It aims to raise the public's awareness of the urgency and enormous scale of the climate crisis and hence is itself also a performative machine. Applying Marine Cloud Brightening and Direct Air Capture of Carbon Dioxide technologies, the project manifests the concepts of "capture, binding, and dispersal" through both form and function. Combining architecture and landscape architecture, it responds to the prevailing winds, wave actions, and the river flow, creating an immersive environment of dynamic ecologies on site. Taking advantage of Governors Island's visibility and prime location, the Cloud Machine serves as a beacon in the age of climate change.

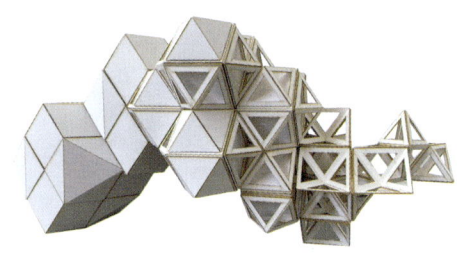

5

6

7

8

5 – *The Cloud Machine* by Aaron Stone and Tone Chu, Concept Model
6 – *The Cloud Machine* by Aaron Stone and Tone Chu, Interior Render
7 – *The Cloud Machine* by Aaron Stone and Tone Chu, Interior Render
8 – *The Cloud Machine* by Aaron Stone and Tone Chu, Render

THE LIVING LABORATORY
Huadong Lin & Wenli Sui

Conceptual development
The project started from the study of global ocean current circulation, also known as the "ocean conveyor belt", which has major impact on mitigating climate change in a global scale. The conveyor belt contains large amount of heat mass and transport the energy due to injection of freshwater, mainly from melting iceberg and river. Governor Island – the site for The Living Laboratory, locate in the estuary of Hudson River and the East River, which is an ideal location for monitoring the composition and the dynamic state of ocean conveyor belt. This project was dedicated for studying the global ocean current in a local scale.

Form development
The project was defined as a composition of static and kinetic elements as the conveyor belt was translated into architecture language. The continuous horizontal bars, divided into upper and lower parts, implicate the static components, and inhabit immobile elements such as laboratories, offices, archives, and public plaza. The ziggurat columns in between implicate the kinetic components, collect and transport the seawater and rainwater to the lab.

Response to climate change
The equilibrium of the conveyor belt impacts the sea level. Facing imminent threat of losing land area to the ocean, the awareness and actions of the public are in need. The project intends to make an immediate response to the rising of sea level by magnifying the impact of tidal change, part of the public area was lowered to a height that is sensitive to different tidal conditions and divided into several platforms according to the height of different tidal states. During high tide, the silhouette of the public plaza would be reshaped and lose area to the ocean, forcing the public to confront with the instantaneous change of sea level and adapt their activities in different time of the day. The inclined ground level also marked the projected sea level in the span of 15 years to raise awareness of how much the building would be invaded by ocean in the imminent future.

9

10

11

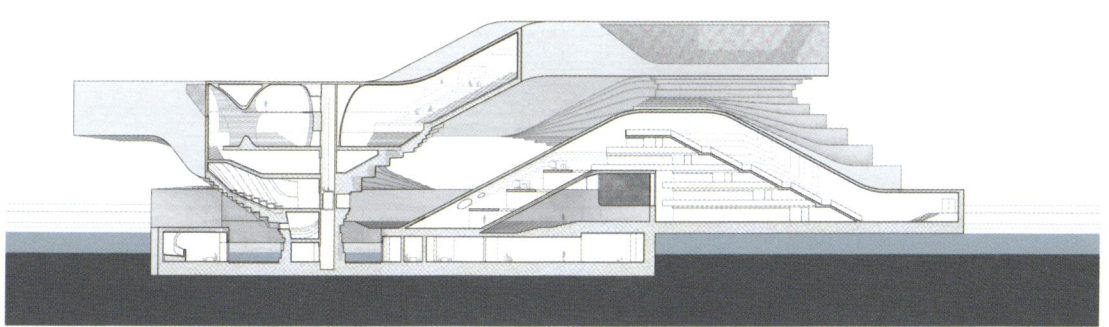

12

9 – *The Living Laboratory* by Huadong Lin & Wenli Sui, Water Garden
10 – *The Living Laboratory* by Huadong Lin & Wenli Sui, Flood
11 – *The Living Laboratory* by Huadong Lin & Wenli Sui, High Tide
12 – *The Living Laboratory* by Huadong Lin & Wenli Sui, Section

MIS-FIT-MAKING

Daniel Markiewicz (LECTURER)
Ellison Turpin (TA)
Vishwadeep Deo (FACADE CONSULTANT)
Andrew Blasetti (STRUCTURAL ENGINEER CONSULTANT)
Chris Sheridan (MECHANICAL ENGINEER CONSULTANT)

Daniel Markiewicz: (Lecturer) – Partner of FORMA Architects PLLC – M.Arch from the Yale School of Architecture – B.S.E. in Civil Engineering/Architecture from Princeton University

SOMEONE WHO IS NOT ACCEPTED SOCIALLY BY OTHER PEOPLE BECAUSE HIS OR HER BEHAVIOR IS UNUSUAL OR STRANGE:
I WAS A SOCIAL MISFIT, THE KIND OF KID NO ONE PLAYED WITH.
– Cambridge Dictionary

The art world is full of misfits; it is in fact a world where misfits are often celebrated. Contemporary artists today must, seemingly without exception, question norms, push boundaries and operate outside of conventions. Who better to accept these responsibilities of an artist than someone whose behavior, thinking and point of view is naturally unique? Who better than a misfit? Students will be asked to develop their own unique points of view using the tools of anamorphic project and material contrast. Ultimately, this studio will examine "mis-fit-making" by exploring what it takes to "make a misfit" or rather what is takes to educate an artist through the design of a new graduate Art School on Roosevelt Island.

The work of artists George Rousse and Felice Varini will provide a conceptual and formal starting point for the studio. Through the use of anamorphic projection and graphic contrast between bold color and rich material these artists have created spaces that force viewers to question their position in the world. Rousse's work in particular has been mainly disseminated through photographs and questions the way in which we interpret 2D visual material in an image-rich world.

The site for the project on Roosevelt Island, in New York City has itself been described as an island of misfits. It is a sliver of land between Manhattan and Queens with a rich and varied history of use including providing a home for Disease hospitals, Mental Institutions, Housing developments, athletic facilities and a number of Public Parks. It is home to one of the worlds few pneumatic garbage collection systems, can be accessed by an elevated gondola and was once the site of New York City's primary prisons. That extremely varied history continues today with the ongoing development of the Cornell Tech Campus just to the south of the 59th Street Bridge. In the context of this studio, the development will continue even further with the design of a new Art School that balances the scientific innovation of "tech" with the creativity of art performance and cultural production.

1

INVADED ISLANDS
Jingchu Sun and Bin Liu

Roosevelt Island is isolated from the Manhattan and the Queens area by the Hudson River. However, at the same time, the construction style of this island is highly affected by these two areas. Therefore, this location provides a hybrid spatiality combining with isolation and connection. In order to provide the same atmosphere for the occupants in the art school on Roosevelt Island, we are designing buildings being wrapped by the circulation tubes which allow visitors to roam around different buildings and watching the working process of student artists. However, on the other hand, the public space and studios in the art school are highly isolated from each other by physical gaps and solid walls to create a misfit atmosphere for the art students to focus on the artwork. Through the combing of isolated buildings and connected circulation tubes, this architecture system meets the requirements of different occupants in the same building for two states of separation and connection.

1 – *Invaded Islands* by Jingchu Sun and Bin Liu, Chunk

Many educational buildings tend toward an insular or privatized attitude—socially, culturally, and architecturally—but the addition of this new program on Roosevelt Island will attempt to disrupt this trend. The Arts Complex will be designed chiefly as a highly public and open institution with a significant portion of the building devoted to gallery space that is publicly accessible. Both the program and the site selection of this project will require critical thinking on how this project addresses the institutional Cornell Tech Campus to the North and the open Public Park to the south (including the ruins of the historic Smallpox Hospital and the new Franklin D. Roosevelt Four Freedoms Park). While a significant portion of the program will be spaces of learning reserved for students, an almost equal portion of the building will be dedicated to spaces of presentation and performance open to the public. Students will be required to answer questions about the role of art education: what types of spaces and amenities are needed to produce contemporary art today? How should private institutions interface with the public realm?

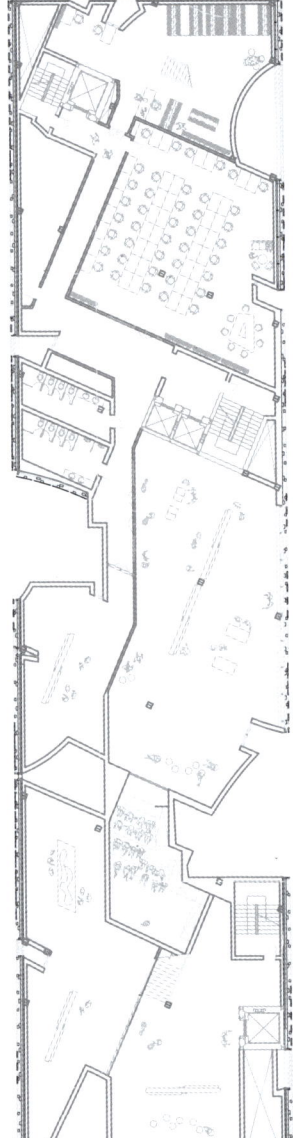

2

MISFIT TO MISFIT
Shiqi Ming, Jinghan He
and Katharine Vavilov

Anchored in the history of Roosevelt Island, we noticed that the concept of Misfit was defined by proportion and perspective. Misfits are classified by their relationship to "the standard" or "the normal". And they are always outnumbered by the "conventionally accepted."

Iteration by iteration, we explored architectural design languages to demonstrate this concept through the alteration of the two principle systems and through the contrast of material color and texture. This conceptual relationship plays out through the carefully crafted experience, where users may observe the same volumetric feature from different perspectives and may notice the role of the misfit alternating between the two principle systems as their proportions change in the space.

3

4

2 – *Misfit to Misfit* by Shiqi Ming, Jinghan He and Katharine Vavilov, Project Description
3 – *Misfit to Misfit* by Shiqi Ming, Jinghan He and Katharine Vavilov, Plan

4 – *Misfit to Misfit* by Shiqi Ming, Jinghan He and Katharine Vavilov, North Rendering

5

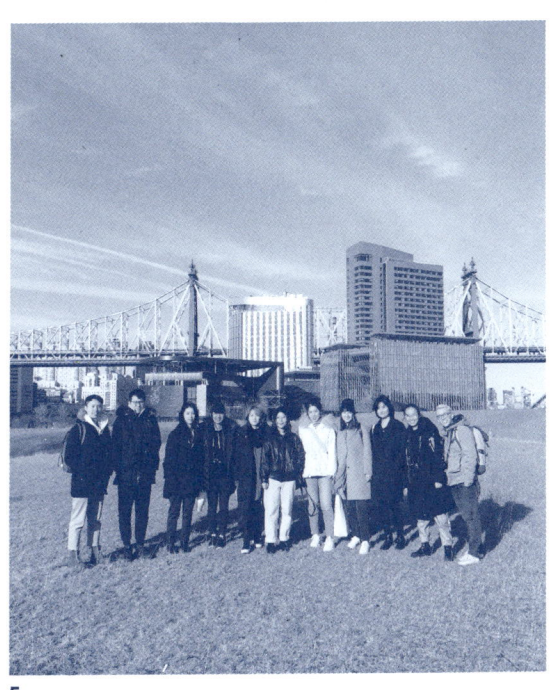

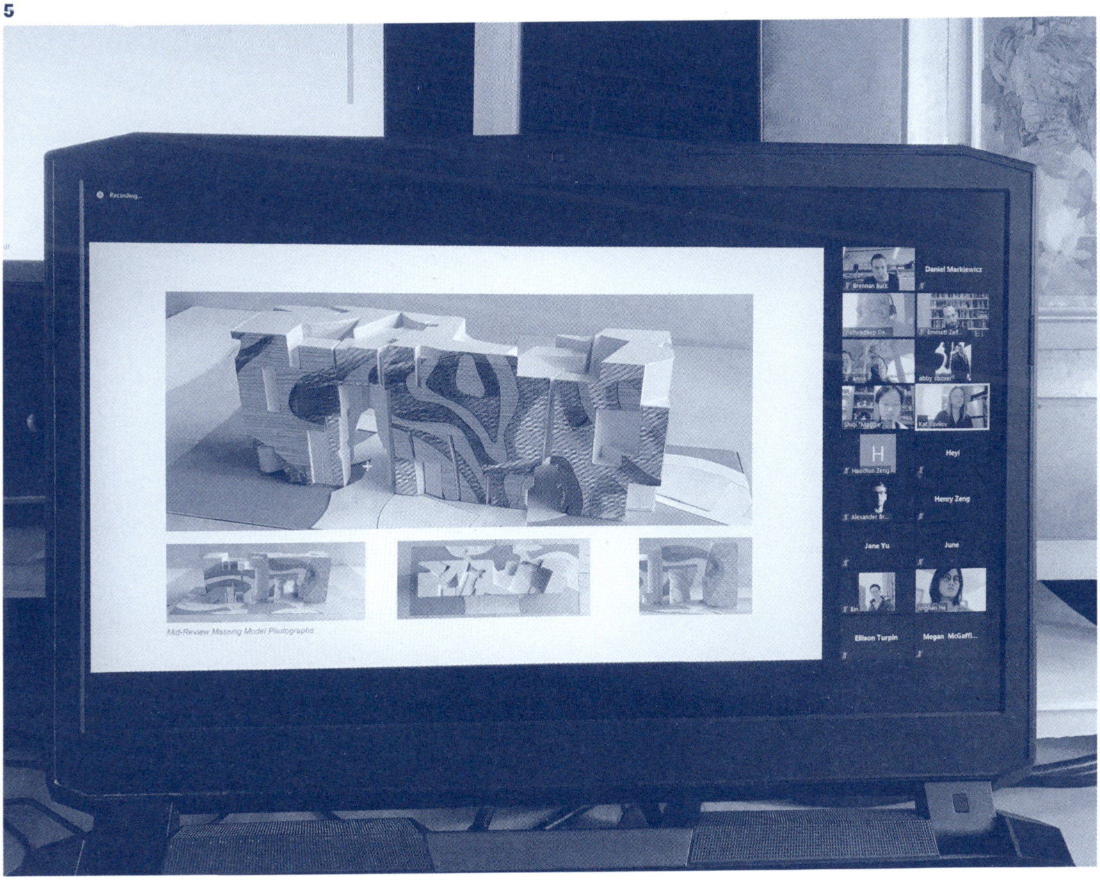

6

5 – Studio Visit
6 – Studio Review

TRANSFORMED ARCH
Heiyi Song and Haochun Zeng

The project starts from discovering the relationship between Manhattan and Roosevelt island. The initial collage developed our insight on the shadow of Manhattan on Roosevelt island and how the shadow encourages the appearance of the new figurations.

Roosevelt island used to live under the shadow of Manhattan, receiving patients/prisoners from Manhattan and trying to fit into Manhattan by copying the similar planning and architecture strategies. The influence of Manhattan on Roosevelt island, either promising or advise combined with the unique history of Roosevelt island formed a new configuration and bring a new identity to Roosevelt island.

Translating to the concept massing model from collages, the initial massing model negotiates the condition of figural objects and figural voids through the insertion of the new figures coming from collages. We think more about the site condition with the aim of breaking down views towards Manhattan and extract certain focus taking the advantage of figural voids.

The figural voids are used as the major structural elements to hold the building weights, as well as elements to shape the plans by making divisions of the interior spaces. The figures translated to arch structural system and marks a separation between students' educational part and public exhibition part. The landscape shows an extension of the figural voids and perform in different functions.

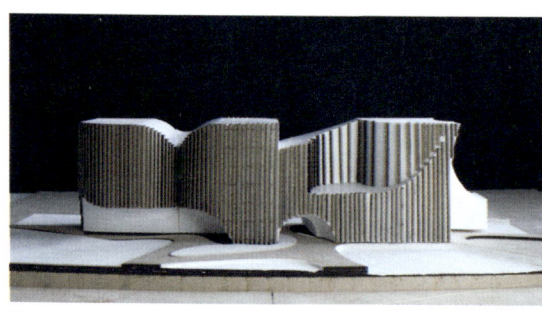

7

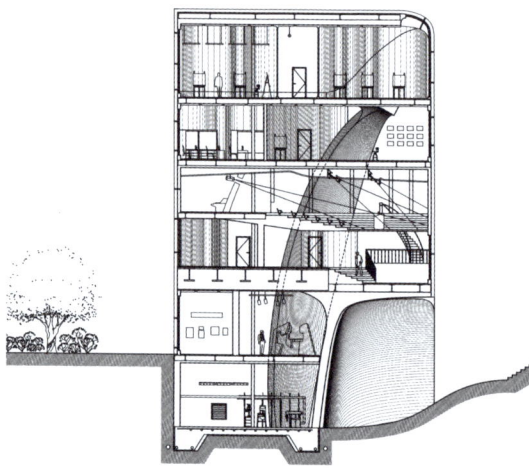

8

9

7 – *Transformed Arch* by Heiyi Song and Haochun Zeng, Middle Review Model
8 – *Transformed Arch* by Heiyi Song and Haochun Zeng, Short Section
9 – *Transformed Arch* by Heiyi Song and Haochun Zeng, Exterior rendering, Ferry Entrance

CORNELL ART SCHOOL
Chenyang Yu and Mingyang Yuan

This project is based on our investigation on the separated but intertwined relationship between Roosevelt Island and Manhattan. Historical and onsite research on the transportation revealed a separated but intertwined relationship between these two islands from long time ago, and continue to exist today. Specifically, the traditional ways of transportation such as Queensborough bridge serves to isolate Roosevelt Island instead of connecting, while the tram, a unique way of transportation which actually connects these two islands, serves also as a touristy attraction, offering new reading of the two islands from a different altitude.

Using such a distinct contrast of materials wood and glass, the form of the building represents the reinterpretation of such an interesting relationship that from the exterior the wood faceted piece seems to be separating the two glazed masses while from the interior the wood piece is actually connecting the two masses. Furthermore, the connecting wood tissue served more than a connection, but a multi-function active space for people to travel through, stop at, gather, communicate, learn, and peak into the spaces at different levels.

The facade was designed as a series of faceted wood panels with operable wood louvres that may open or close, allowing control of different light effects in order to serve different functions of the center space, and create theatrical experiences when necessary.

10

11

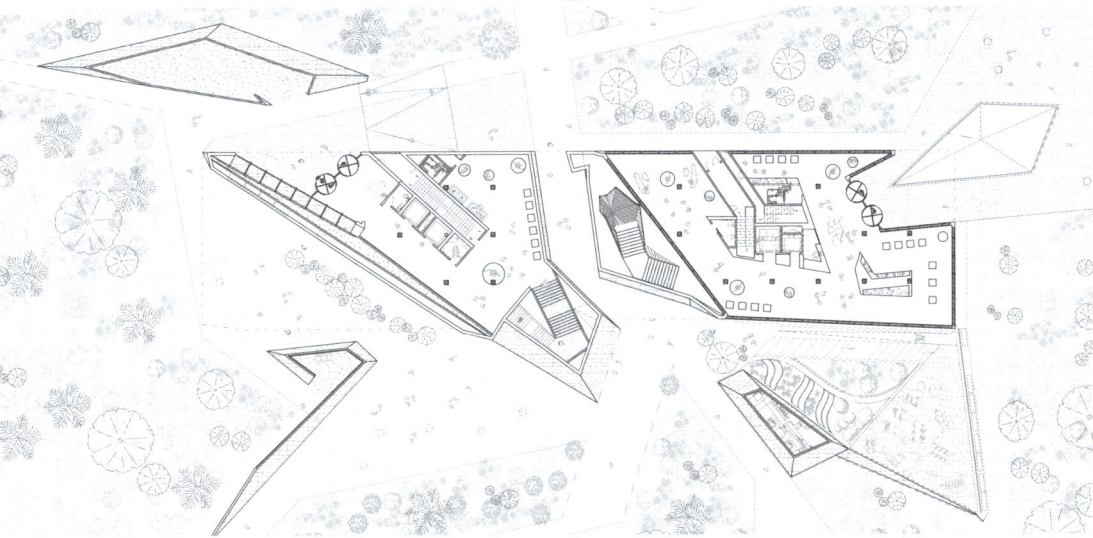
12

10 – *Cornell Art School* by Chenyang Yu and Mingyang Yuan, Model
11 – *Cornell Art School* by Chenyang Yu and Mingyang Yuan, Exterior Entrance
12 – *Cornell Art School* by Chenyang Yu and Mingyang Yuan, Site plan/Ground Floor

MONOLITHIC, MACHINIC HYBRIDS

Danielle Willems (LECTURER)
Daniel Knee (TA)
Zachary Jones (TA)
Florian Meier (STRUCTURAL ENGINEER CONSULTANT)

Danielle Willems (Lecturer) Co-Founder of Mæta Design (2008) – Visiting Professor at Pratt University, Brooklyn NY – Earned a MArch from Columbia University, GSAPP (2007)

Florian Meier (Consultant) Associate with Knippers Helbig – Advanced Engineering

This studio Monolithic, Machinic Hybrids focused on the development of a Data Center and Data Museum as an exciting opportunity to rethinking the architectural typology of Infrastructure/Exhibition and Material/Computation.

The contemporary paradigms of robotic manufacturing, augmented reality, blockchains and artificial intelligence, are going to have profound repercussions for our discipline. Our world is increasingly being understood as an emergent outcome of complex systems. Similarly, both analytical and generative tools for the definition of spatial and architectural complex systems have been established within our discipline. The research of the students started by reconsidered the Cenotaph, being both "monolithic" and ancient, these impressive vessels of void, and utilized this as a generative point of departure to re-conceptualize a new type of artifice in relationship to the typology of the data center.

The thesis of this studio ventured into an investigation that was extremely sensitive to existing models of self-organization in material, cognition and physical data systems, the intention could not be further than the mere replication of "matter" nor "nature". On the contrary, with the deployment of non-linear computational design methodologies this studio explored new singularities in the extended territory of contemporary architectural production. At the same time, this research allows for the transcendence of traditional disciplinary architectural boundaries since our focus in complexity itself is an emergent language shared between multiple scientific and artistic fields.

Monolithic, Machinic Hybrids - Ontological Data Formation is an investigation into multi-scalar definition of computational constructs and ultimately attempts to merge architecture and composites materials into direct relationships with what will appear more and more as artificial materials.

1

SLANTING THRESHOLD
Xinyi Chen and Jingyi Zhou

Monolithic does not only present to us as a single object. It generates a discussion of the relationship between micro and macro. Like substances are made of particles, the monolith is also made of something small. On the macro scale, the monolithic is one. On the micro scale, the monolithic is all. The transition between micro and macro remains responsive to the thinking mind, which has similar fluidity as the information data. This realization connects us from machinic to monolithic, where small pieces, sometimes even seem trivial, make a continuous whole in a constantly changing state.

On the other hand, We define machinic not by physical entities but by the physical phenomenon of electromagnetism, as well as the potential to create a brand new virtual reality for humankind. Thus we are interested in another kind of materiality—the virtual one. However, reality and virtuality have never collapsed into one, and the gap between these two worlds has always remained ambiguous. For us, just like the flow of information data, such ambiguity is not static and will never be; its fluidity is extremely unique. It intrigues us to capture such threshold and inspires us to create a medium for the public to understand its existence, therefore, define this in-between space in their own terms.

Since the last half century, digital technology has greatly changed peoples' lives. Not only it

1 – *Slanting Threshold* by Xinyi Chen and Jingyi Zhou, Interior Render informs people a new way to look at the world, but also challenges our established concepts of reality. Media, electronics, information data have become the second nature of human beyond the existing reality. People are connected by the invisible flow of information. This realization has greatly changed human's perception of the world. Nowadays, people switch back and forth between superficial and reality constantly, and it leads us to ask: what is in between?

As digital technology continues to blend into reality and becomes an inevitable and inseparable part of life, a question has been raised to the users: does information data require any threshold or additional layers before it enters into the reality from a digital space? As a result, the architectural combination of a data center and a digital art museum could shine some light on the problem. This data center/museum hybridity will serve as a medium connecting the virtual reality and the existing reality. The data center would expose its complicated system of servers and mechanics to the public. The art museum would enlighten the public with machinic potential through artists' creations. The in-between space thus becomes a bridge and a neutral ground for the visitors to establish their own definition of the threshold.

2

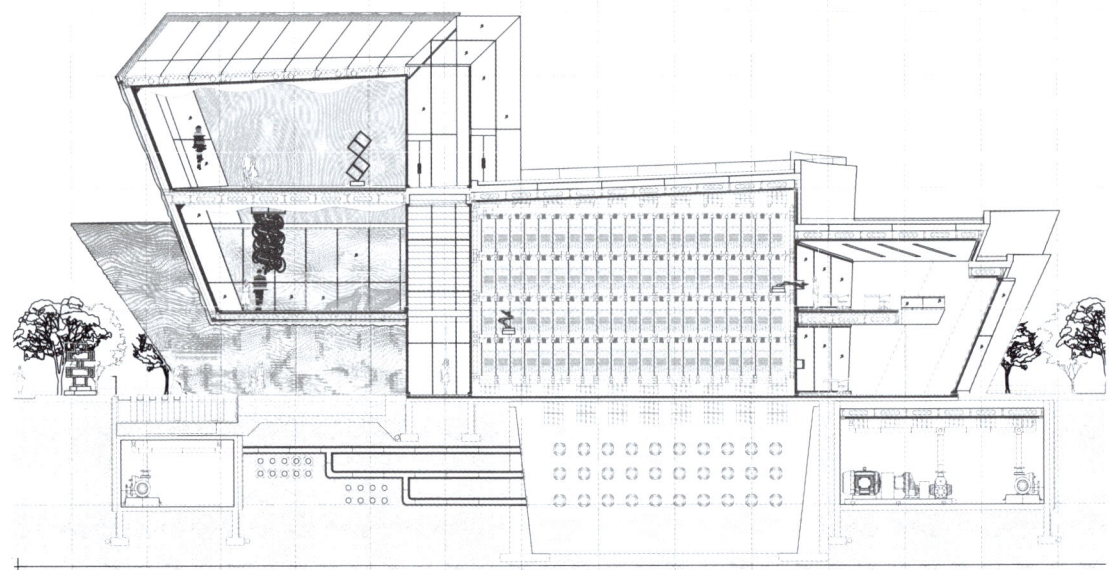

3

2 – *Slanting Threshold* by Xinyi Chen and Jingyi Zhou, Elevation

3 – *Slanting Threshold* by Xinyi Chen and Jingyi Zhou, Section

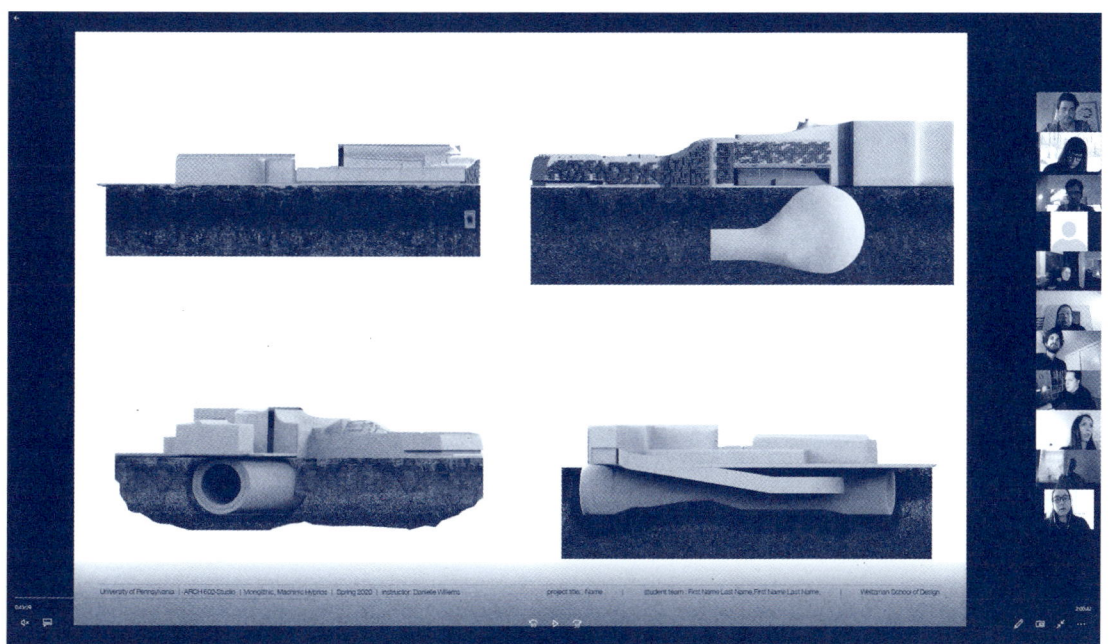

4

5

4 – Studio Review
5 – Danielle Willems in Studio Review

THE CUBE
Xinyi Huang and Chia-Chia Liu

Data is ubiquitous yet hidden from society. In contrast to the era of information, people have little understanding of the potential of technology developed from data. The project seeks to showcase the power of data to the world—challenging the nature of data center being secretive and hidden, displaying and emphasizing the machinic space, and visualizing the informational age with a powerful and monolithic statement.

The Cube stands monolithically both within its own and in the urban envelope. Containing two different kinds of programs—data center and museum, the project seeks to link and open up the data center (secured and machine-centered) to the museum (public, educational, and human-centered) while still maintaining a sense of division.

5

6

7

5 – *The Cube* by Xinyi Huang and Chia-Chia Liu, Elevation
6 – *The Cube* by Xinyi Huang and Chia-Chia Liu, Landscape Pipe
7 – *The Cube* by Xinyi Huang and Chia-Chia Liu, Render, Across the River

THE BUNKER
Abdullah Alsahafi, Michael Niklas Caine and Kerry Hohenstein

The united nations has been dissolved. All that remains of the organization are millions of electronic memos, pieces of paper, and video documents. These documents are rapidly deteriorating and will not be around for the next generation due to the toxicity of the air.

To ensure that these documents will be around, archivists have been avidly scanning the remains and transferring the data onto silica discs and keeping them secured in a museum in long island city. What can be salvaged from the computers of the united nations has been transferred onto silica discs as well. The knowledge held within these walls can hopefully chart out the way to peace between sovereign nations in the future, and learn from the mistakes we have made attempting to achieve that very goal. The only way to learn from the past is to actively prevent falling into the same footsteps and those who had come before you. This archive of the human condition and policy is to educate the next generations of diplomats and world leaders…

8

For security reasons, the data center is disconnected from the outside world and the only accesspoint to view the documents stored within the vault is in the museum's library. That is not the only threat the museum faces. Machine vision and aerial surveillance poses a risk of becoming a target of attack. To combat the threat of machine vision, the data centre employs hexagonal paneling to disrupt form-finding, and heat tracing from any aerial surveillance by breaking up the massings and giving false edges to make the building view as a collection of multiple smaller buildings. The roof pattern is derived from the previously existing buildings and street outlines. The anti-monolith…

9

10

8 – *The Bunker* by Abdullah Alsahafi, Michael Niklas Caine and Kerry Hohenstein, Close Up Render
9 – *The Bunker* by Abdullah Alsahafi, Michael Niklas Caine and Kerry Hohenstein, Render
10 – *The Bunker* by Abdullah Alsahafi, Michael Niklas Caine and Kerry Hohenstein, Render

[ARCH 634] ENVIRONMENTAL SYSTEMS II
Efrie Escott

In the spring portion of Environmental Systems, we consider the environmental systems of larger, more complex buildings. Contemporary buildings are characterized by the use of systems for ventilation, heating, cooling, dehumidification, lighting, communications, and controls that not only have their own demands, but interact dynamically with one another. Their relationship to the classic architectural questions about building size and shape are even more complex. With the introduction of sophisticated feedback and control systems, architects are faced with conditions that are virtually animate and coextensive at many scales with the natural and manmade environments in which they are placed.

The task of the semester is to establish an understanding of how the concept of "high performance" shapes the design of modern buildings, building on the basic concepts of energy transfer and thermodynamics covered in Environmental Systems I. Through case studies, we will interrogate approaches to building enclosure, dynamic interaction between active and passive systems, air quality, acoustics, and material performance.

[ARCH 636] MATERIAL FORMATIONS
Robert Stuart-Smith

Material Formations introduces principles of generative design into the discipline of architecture, providing opportunities for architects to synthesize multiple performance criteria within design and robotic production in the context of additive manufacturing. Participants develop an approach to design-computation that questions relations between form, structure and material across a number of scales, with robotic production and material dynamics also explored as active agents in design rationalization and expression. Lectures covering technical and research/project case-studies are supported by practical tutorials that focus on the incorporation of material-physics simulation, generative computation, and robot fabrication concerns within design and in partnership with structural analysis. While production is traditionally viewed as an explicit and final act of execution, the course explores the potential for aspects of building production to participate within the creative design process, potentially producing performance and affect. Students will develop skills and experience in computer programming, robot motion planning with geometrical and structural adaptation and material-physics simulation. Throughout the semester a number of discrete assignments are undertaken that facilitate the development of a design synthesis between form, structure and material considerations alongside robotic production constraints.

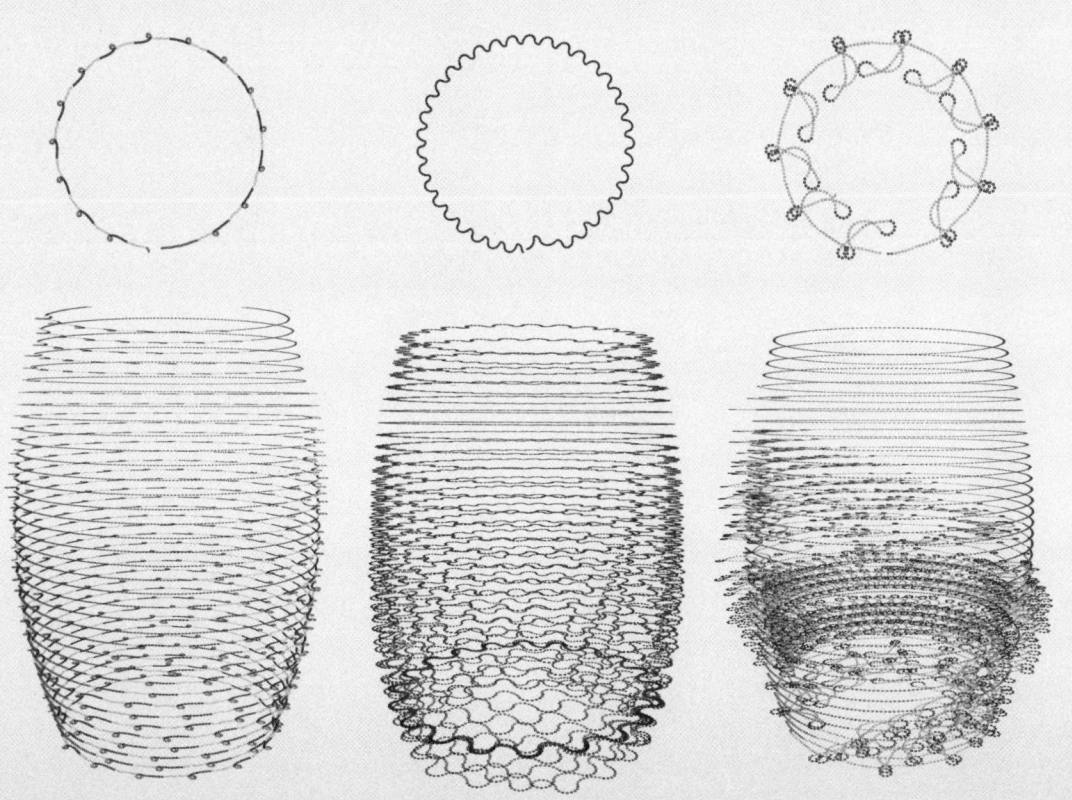

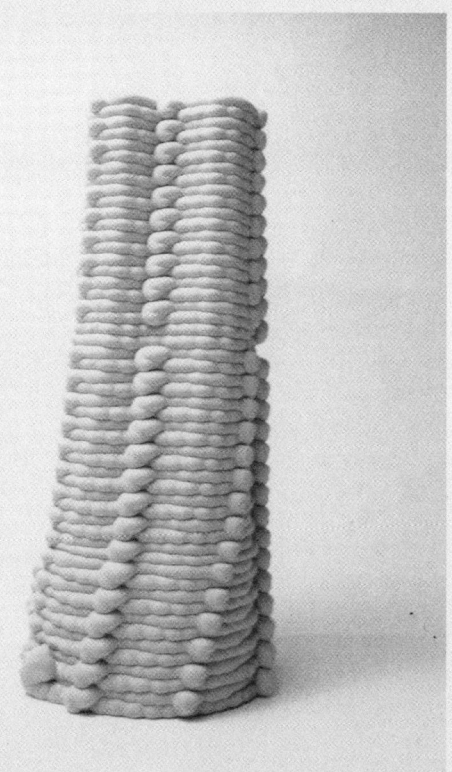

[ARCH 671] PROFESSIONAL PRACTICE I
Philip Ryan

Professional Practice discusses the issues and processes involved in running a professional architectural practice and designing buildings in the contemporary construction environment. The course will describe the methods involved in getting, designing, and constructing a building project. Lectures will delve deep into the mechanisms for articulating a design vision visually and verbally and the systems employed to insure successful implementation of that vision. The lectures will draw connections between the student's studio design knowledge to date and the instructor's experience in practice including local building examples and guest lectures by relevant professionals.

MATTER, MAKING & TESTING:
DESIGNING WITH NEXT GENERATION PRECAST CONCRETE

Lecturer Richard Garber's ARCH 732 fall seminar partnered with Northeast Precast (NEP) in New Jersey to produce a series of panel prototypes for wall assemblies that respond to structural, thermal, and water-proofing performance. Students developed a delivery workflow utilizing digital tools to communicate with and transmit panel, assembly, and formwork concepts to NEP staff, fostering a collaboration opportunity for students that is not regularly experienced in architecture school.

Students included Amanda Gruen, Catherine Shih, Karen Toomasian, Yiling Zhong, Yuan Zhang, Yu Mao, Eric Jiacheng Gu, Shangzi Tu, Zhaoyi Liu, Lauren Hunter, Yongkyu Hong, Alexander Jackson, Ian Lai, Quan Huynh, David Forero, Abdullah Alsahafi, Huadong Lin, Xiaoyi Peng

All materials and manhours sponsored by Northeast Precast.

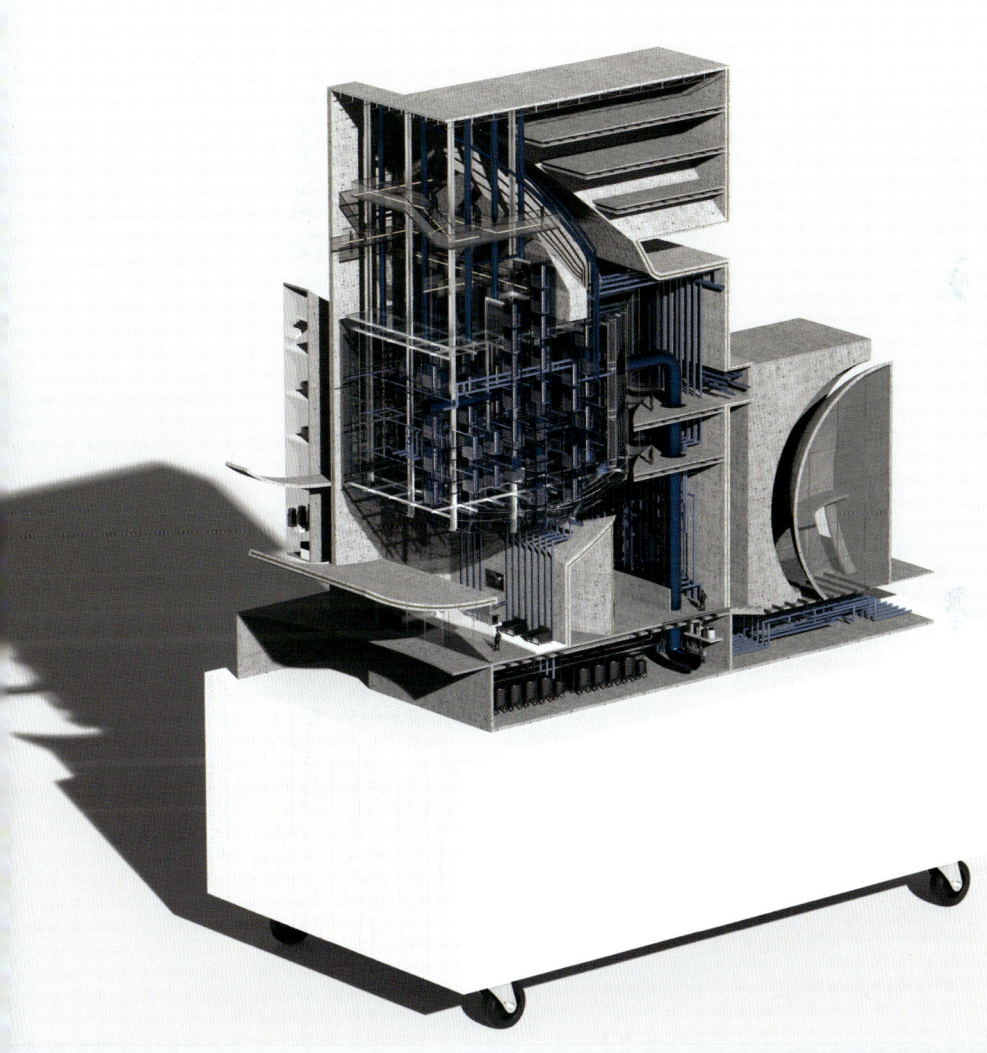

The Cube by Xinyi Huang and Chia-Chia Liu
Professor: **Danielle Willems** [p.222]

The Living Laboratory By Huadong Lin & Wenli Sui
Professor: **Ben Krone** [p.211]

Transformed Arch by Haochun Zeng and Heyi Song
Professor: **Daniel Markiewicz** [p.216]

The Dive-House by Zhiqi Sheng and Megan York
Professor: **Kutan Ayata** [p.195]

Hinterland by Robert Schaffer and Christine Eichhorn
Professor: **Simon Kim** [p.188]

The Urban Canyon by Maria Jose Fuentes and Veronica Rosado, Professor: **Miroslava Brooks** [p.198]

OCT. NEWS

WEITZMAN STUDENTS PARTICIPATE IN HACKATHON TO ADDRESS GLOBAL REFUGEE CRISIS

Students participated in a day long design charette called "hackathon for good," hosted by USA for UNHCR and the innovation hub New Lab, in Brooklyn on October 26. The event brought together architecture students, architects, urban planners, and civil engineers to develop new solutions to improve the lives of refugees around the world. Eighteen students from Associate Professor Franca Trubiano's seminar, Matter + Energy, Building in Crisis: Climate Change and Refugee Housing, participated in devising solutions for some of the most pressing design problems faced by architects today. The seminar and charette are focused on the design and construction of shelter in a time of climate crisis.

SIMON KIM AND WEITZMAN STUDENTS FEATURED IN 2019 SEOUL BIENNALE

Associate Professor Simon Kim and Weitzman students from his 2018 701 studio are featured in the 2019 Seoul Biennale of Architecture and Urbanism: Collective City. Kim's project, "TYOLDNPAR: The Heterotopial City," was submitted by his firm, Ibañez Kim. It aims to address the following concerns:

1. MASTERPLANNING:
Single visions of urbanism and architecture could not be more out of touch.

2. CITIZENSHIP:
In a postmodern society, there are as many forms of communication as there ㄹㅏㅓ are social groups, and truth can no longer be the alibi of one ruling class of citizen.

3. NATURES:
In a posthuman environment, there are no longer separate identities of human-nonhuman, wild and civilized, public-private, inside-outside. To address this, a crypto-city made of familiar places is the location of new collective commons, synthetic natures, and hybrid environments. As a heterotopia, this city compresses elements of real metropolises into incongruities and opportunities that reveal our current human nature, and suggests alternate actions.

"Montreal, Sensate and Augmented" was created by Kim's 2018 701 studio:
Architecture of a city as a proposition or a form of intellectual investigation is tethered to a built, shared environment. Its implicit and explicit meanings and affects are to be developed in material and also in behavior over time. To do this, we will imbue architecture and urbanism with duration, with its own agency and self governance in the location of Montreal. Montreal's history in Expos and Olympics places it as an ideal postindustrial model with an apex towards advanced thinking of new environment and eco-intelligence. Rather than determining architecture from a top-down application of function and use, we are more interested in a durational and temporal occupation of space that is for both the human and nonhuman.

Participating Weitzman students include Mostafa Akbari, Yunyoung Lina Choi, Wenna Dai, Zihao Fang, Yuting He, Wenqi Huang, Mikyung Lee, Chuqi Liu, Bowen Qin, Yingke Sun, Si Yang Xiao, Weimeng Zhang, and Chengyao Zong. Kim and previous 701 students also participated in the 2017 Seoul Biennale.

ARCHITECTURE MAKES TOP 10 IN DESIGNINTELLIGENCE RANKING

DesignIntelligence has released its annual rankings of America's Top Architecture Schools and the Department of Architecture at the University of Pennsylvania Stuart Weitzman School of Design earned two Top 10 rankings:
    #9 Most Admired Graduate Programs
    #5 Architecture Programs Most Hired From

Survey participants were asked, "What schools do you most admire for a combination of faculty, programs, culture, and student preparation for the profession?" and "From which schools have you hired the greatest number of students (graduate and undergraduate combined) in the last five years?" These rankings are determined by surveys sent to recent graduates, hiring practitioners, and department deans and chairs. This year DesignIntelligence received nearly 12,000 responses.

ARCHI-TECTONICS INCLUDED IN MOMA REINSTALLED COLLECTION GALLERIES

Work by Miller Professor and Chair of Architecture Winka Dubbeldam is now on view in the newly reinstalled collection galleries at the Museum of Modern Art in New York following a major expansion. "Suspended Armature" and "Twist Me" were produced by Dubbeldam's firm, Archi-Tectonics. The designs were originally exhibited in collaboration with the MIT Media Lab at New York's Frederieke Taylor Gallery as a holographic installation studying the transformative qualities between object and environment. They were based on the firm's prior work with a private home in Upstate New York.

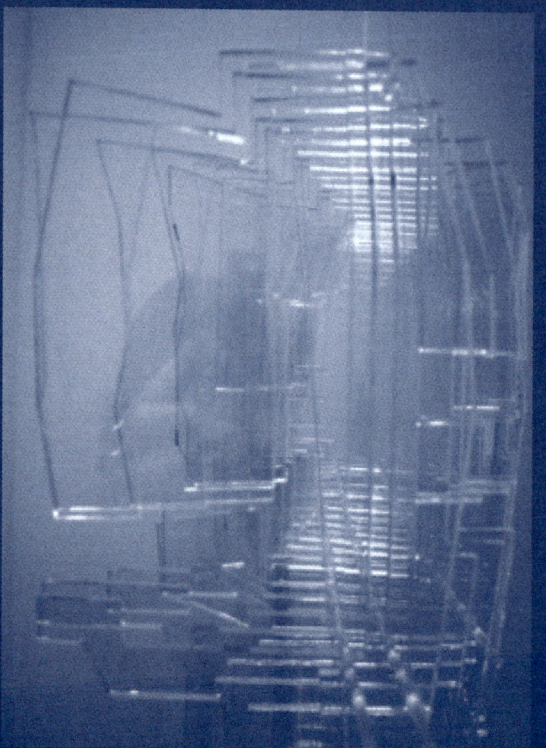
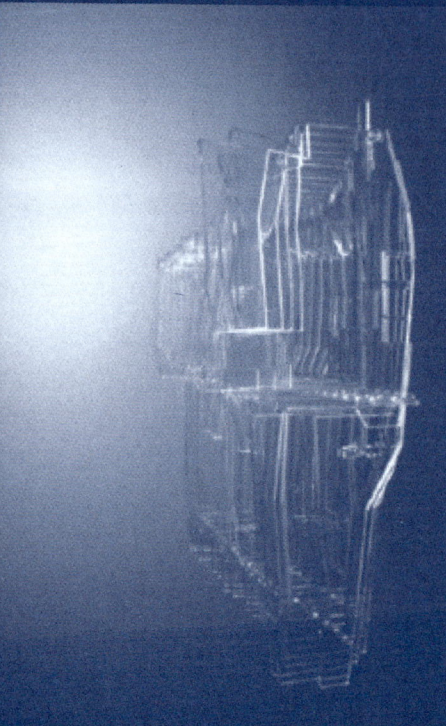

NOV. NEWS

WEITZMAN ALUMS PLACE THIRD IN JAPAN'S CENTRAL GLASS INTERNATIONAL DESIGN COMPETITION

Recent Weitzman alumnae Justine Huang (MArch'19) and Anya Sinha (MArch'19) earned third place in the 54th Central Glass International Design Competition in Tokyo, Japan. Their submission, titled Residue: Charms of the Sakariba, originated as a project for Lecturer Florencia Pita's 704 studio in spring 2019. The competition theme was "Architecture That Generates New Sakariba." Sakariba are described as "lively places where crowds gather." Huang and Sinha's proposal "seeks to reform the 'leftovers' of postindustrial sites and radically energize these social habitats." Competition judges included Hiroshi Naito, Kengo Kuma, Jun Aoki, Yoshiharu Tsukamoto, and Weitzman alumni Tadao Kamei (MArch'78) and Goichi Kamochi (MArch'89).

PORTIA MALIK WINS LONDON FESTIVAL OF ARCHITECTURE CONTEST

Former MArch student Portia Malik is one of five winners in the London Festival of Architecture's contest to design a series of £1,500 benches across the Royal Docks in London's East End. The Pews & Perches competition called for a "fun and creative place to sit, rest, and play." Portia's project, Peekaboo, is located at the dock edge in front of The Crystal:

"With the increasing popularity of open water swimming in the Royal Docks, Peekaboo is a playful seated changing space for swimmers, providing privacy when changing in and out of wetsuits. The sweeping freestyle stroke-inspired arm enclosures envelope and structurally support the users, while also incorporating hooks for a towel." Peekaboo will be on site for a year. Judges included LFA director Tamsie Thompson, Dan Bridge of the Royal Docks Team and David Ogunmuyiwa, principal at ArchitectureDoingPlace.

DEC. NEWS

LAURA COLAGRANDE (MARCH'18) MAKES FORBES 30 UNDER 30

Recent Weitzman graduate Laura Colagrande (MArch'18) and Wharton graduate Haley Russell (W'18) landed on the Forbes 30 Under 30 list in honor of their startup Chippin, which sells pet food made from sustainable proteins like cricket powder.

Colagrande and Russell met through Penn's Integrated Product Design (IPD) program, which connects students from the School of Engineering and Applied Science, the Wharton School, and the School of Design to collaborate on innovative new products and experiences.

In 2018, Chippin won $55,000 from Penn's third annual iDesign Prize competition, which helped launch the product in stores and online.

MARION WEISS SELECTED TO LEAD MASTER PLAN OF LA BREA TAR PITS

WEISS/MANFREDI, the New York-based design practice co-founded by Graham Chair Professor of Architecture Marion Weiss and Michael Manfredi, won an international design competition for the La Brea Tar Pits by the Natural History Museums of Los Angeles County. The world's only active paleontological research facility located in a major urban area, the La Brea Tar Pits is situated within the eastern portion of Hancock Park in Los Angeles's Miracle Mile district.

The proposal for the La Brea Tar Pits and Museum Master Plan is titled "La Brea Loops and Lenses." The project redefines Hancock Park and the Page Museum as one continuous experience. As flexible armatures, loops and lenses connect and reveal, forming an open-ended journey that tells the story of the La Brea Tar Pits and Museum: the continuum from prehistoric time to our contemporary moment. The museum treasures will be revealed to visitors, bringing the museum to the park, and the park into the public imagination.

PROFESSOR OF ARCHITECTURE DAVID LEATHERBARROW AWARDED 2020 AIA/ACSA TOPAZ MEDALLION FOR EXCELLENCE IN ARCHITECTURAL EDUCATION

The AIA/ACSA Topaz Medallion honors an individual who has been intensely involved in architecture education for more than a decade and whose teaching has influenced a broad range of students.

For nearly four decades, Leatherbarrow has trained reflective practitioners through his graduate and undergraduate courses exploring the interdependence of design and theory. One of the world's leading experts in the history and theory of architecture, he has supervised 30 dissertations and advised an additional 30 that included prominent leaders from around the world. As many of his students will attest, his energy and optimism for the built environment are infectious, and his positive vision is ceaselessly inspiring.

At Penn, where he has taught since 1984, Leatherbarrow created a foundational culture that persists to this day. For 20 years, he led the Weitzman School's first-year studio, which he coupled with a course focused on his signature integration of design and theory. In addition, he has taught the required first-semester course in the school's PhD program, and his instruction has established fluency in architecture's theories and history for countless scholars and teachers. His academic leadership at the Weitzman School includes service as chair of the Department of Architecture and two decades as chair of the PhD in Architecture program.

ADVANCED 701

Winka Dubbeldam, Coordinator
Miller Professor and Chair

An integral part of the 701 studio is collaboration with real world experts, like governments, developers, and other universities,. They have become an integral part of how the studios operate by inviting students to visit and perform in-depth research locally. Important examples are Ferda Kolatan's research-design studio, "Oddkin Architecture Istanbul III: Remaking the Büyük Valide Han in Istanbul, Turkey," sponsored by the GAD Foundation. Another great example is Simon Kim's "Seoul: Compound Beings, Devious Typographies," sponsored by alumnus Young Kyoon Jeong (MArch'89). Both studios propose radical and innovative architectural and urban schemes that provoke new social, cultural, and aesthetic understanding of the Future City.

The historical transformations of large cities around the world, from modern metropolises to postindustrial megacities, have radically impacted our urban environments and how we live within them. Globally networked markets have produced new economic and political realities leading to unprecedented forms of regulatory frameworks, urban growth patterns, and hyper-densification. Infrastructural and technological innovations have changed the ways we build, move around, and communicate in and with the city. Ecological awareness is revising our understanding of design by privileging organic and symbiotic strategies over static and categorical ones and by acknowledging the importance of nonhuman factors and agencies in the processes of design.

These changes, among others, have a profound impact on the complex material and cultural system we casually refer to as the city. In fact, the term "city" operates today mostly by approximation without clearly defined physical or conceptual boundaries, a specter of sorts. The ever-intensifying confluence of technology and capital in the 21st century has created the utterly strange phenomena of an urban realm where age-old territories blur, contradictions thrive, and novelty arises. This urban realm, however, does not only provide an arena for architecture's latest design ambitions, be they pragmatic, experimental, or utopian, but it also demands a more fundamental rethinking of the contemporary city, its meaning and definitions, its politics and aesthetics, its potentialities and challenges. Thom Mayne's "Madrid Nuevo Norte" studio deals with the urban realm in its vast scale as a city of multiplicities. Matthias Hollwich also looks at the supersized systems with his "Unforgettable Urbanism" studio. Matthijs Bouw's resilience examines "Undoing/Redoing 20th Century Working Waterfronts" as a new way to resist water level changes. Also focused on resilience is Joe MacDonald's studio "Stockholm Resilience Centre" with rigorous research and provocative solutions. We find in Wolf Prix's studio an understanding that "Iconic Buildings for a Future Society" are essential attractors for future city life that gives buildings agency to act upon the city.

The 701 Design Research Studios, in the widest sense, explore the complexity of current cities and seek to formulate architectural positions that deal with the multi-facetted ramifications of contemporary culture. "Future of Cities" is not an urban design or a planning studio. Rather, the goal is to develop design ideas that operate on a distinctly architectural scale, as building, city-block, infrastructure, park, etc., but also to reflect on the pressing themes of today's urban life with new thought models. After all, the term "city"—just like the term "nature"—is still largely understood and instrumentalized within a modern paradigm while our current circumstances point to a vastly different reality. To remedy this gap, or to deal with it productively, is an important aspect of this studio. Two examples come to mind: Robert Stuart-Smith's "Multifarious Matters: Les Halles 2030" and Karel Klein's "Cyborg Pareidolia." Klein's studio looks to AI to re-imagine a new city future and critically re-examines new realities that collapse or collide with existing city structures, catapulting the city as we know it in another realm.

These are just a few examples of our 700 faculty, visiting faculty, research projects, and collaborations, all adding nuanced discourse to the Design Studios as a whole.

UNDOING/REDOING
20TH CENTURY WORKING WATERFRONTS
In Collaboration with the Department of
Landscape Architecture and Regional Planning

Matthijs Bouw (ASSOCIATE PROFESSOR OF PRACTICE)
Ce Mo (TA)

Matthijs Bouw: Associate Professor of Practice,
Weitzman School of Design – Director of Urban Resilience
Certificate Program – McHarg Center Fellow for Risk
and Resilience – Founder, One Architecture & Urbanism
(Amsterdam/New York)

The premise of this studio was that we need to drastically redesign our coastlines in the face of climate change, and that this redesign requires us to rethink industry, logistics and infrastructure, and its impact on communities. By looking at two industrial waterfront sites on two continents (New York, USA and Semarang, Indonesia). we can learn to understand vulnerabilities and development cycles, compare approaches, and look at global relationships.

Drastically rethinking the coastlines and the working waterfronts requires partial retreat from rising seas, and creating space for nature-based solutions for coastal defense and stormwater flooding (which also improve bio-diversity, act as a carbon sink, and allow for new approaches to waste water management).

abandoned military zone. In the first site, we introduce constructed wetland as natural system and mechanical system at the same time as wastewater treatment system. And use it as an educational park for communities. In the latter site, we propose a retention basin with a floating market. The new retention basin can increase the polder's retention capacity, and the floating market that can improve the social standing of waste pickers.

In other areas within the polder system, we introduce minor intervention because of land limitation. We created three types of constructed wetland along the street to treat household wastewater, three types of boardwalks to cross the seawall, and four types of public realm along the canal.

By doing these simple and low-cost components and typologies, we are trying to encourage communities to participate in building a better living environment for themselves and be able and willing to build consistently in the future.

1   RETHINKING INFRASTRUCTURE: FROM ISOLATION TO INTEGRATION, Jinyu Zhang and Abinayaa Perezhilan

We are redesigning existing infrastructure to increase community resilience in Semarang. Banger Polder is an existing polder system locates right behind Tombark Lorak, the most vulnerable fishing community in Semarang. After analyzing the risk of Banger Polder, we identified four essential elements of a polder system, which include seawalls, pumping stations, canals and retention basins, as points of leverage. To build a robust Banger Polder, we set the following six goals: increase pumping and retention capacity, improve sanitation and water supply system, activate public realm and encourage community engagement.

We identify two sites for more intense intervention within Banger Polder, one is the site of the existing pumping station, and the other is the subsided

3

2

1 – *Rethinking Infrastructure: From Isolation to Integration* by Jinyu Zhang and Abinayaa Perezhilan, Project Description
2 – *Rethinking Infrastructure: From Isolation to Integration* by Jinyu Zhang and Abinayaa Perezhilan, Section
3 – Travel Photo, Water project management project visiting Jakarta.

A reduced footprint for industrial functions forces us to increase density by stacking and combining functions, leading to new architectural typologies. These changes in the building stock allow for a re-thinking of energy systems, materials and processes.

With these impending changes, the question of how the transition takes place becomes critical. It is clear that top-down planning approaches and big corporations, real estate firms and utilities have failed to deliver, and that we need to look into community planning practices, decentralized infrastructures and local agency to deliver equitable and resilient outcomes.

4   INDUSTRIAL SPONGE ZONE:
         FROM ISOLATION TO INTEGRATION
         Quan Hao Huynh and Robert Irwin Romo

This project reflects the historic and current needs of the Newtown Creek, heavy industry and clean water. These needs have been at odds and in designing for the future, we believe these needs can coexist. Sea level rise and economic transitions provide a catalyst for change in this part of New York City. Industry can and should be reorganized in a more efficient, more intense, and more environmentally conscious way.

The project imagines the Newtown Creek being reconstituted into several islands of concentrated heavy industry. The buffer zone created by this land reclamation will clean the creek, give residents recreation space, and protect the neighborhood from flood events of increasing regularity and intensity. Also part of the project is a reimagining of urban logistics. Facilities like the one proposed will combine high-intensity warehousing and transportation with wholesale retail and a new public access points to a previously hidden creek.

In the studio, students learned about urban resilience. We looked at its concepts, at how resilience is a critical component of climate change adaptation, at the tools that are used to build resilience, and how a holistic approach to resilience links to other aspects of urban development. In the studio, students linked the natural, built and social environments, and thought through both global and local scales.

The studio worked on two sites in two continents in very different cycles of development: New York City and Semarang, Indonesia. In an initial research phase, three groups worked on different research topics and projected them on the sites. In the design phase, teams articulated an opportunity for design that links climate adaptation, industrial transformations and strong communities in either New York's or Semarang's working waterfronts and develop this into an integrated project.

The studio trip took us to Jakarta and Semarang in Indonesia, as well as to Singapore. During the trip the students explored sites, but also engaged with city agencies, universities and local communities.

4 – Industrial Sponge Zone: From Isolation to Integration
by Quan Hao Huynh and Robert Irwin Romo

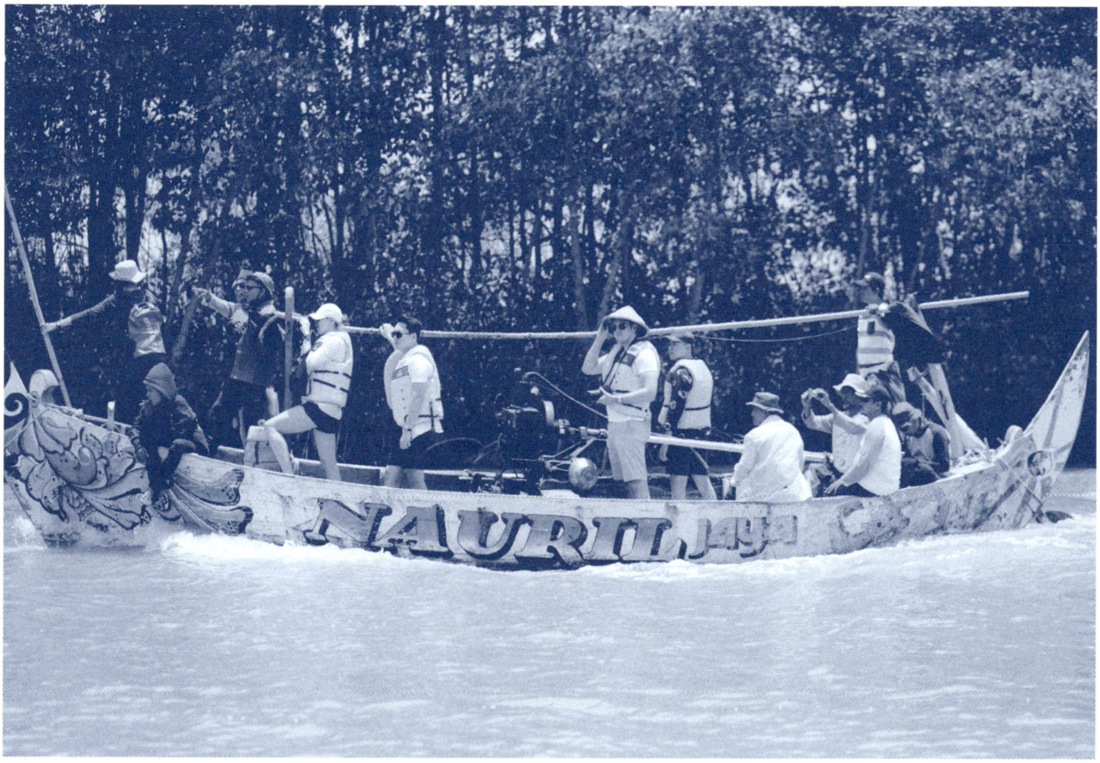

5

6

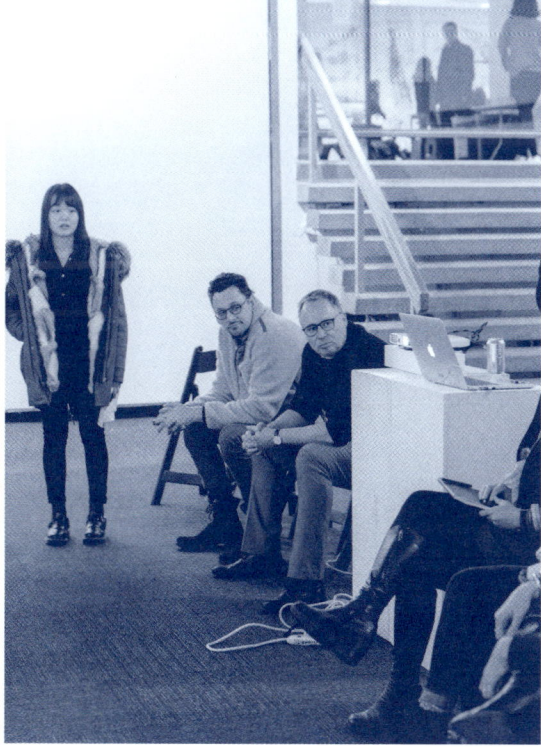

5 – Travel Photo, Mangrove Restoration
Nature based solutions
6 – Matthijs Bouw in Studio Review

THE ADAPTIVE WATERFRONT VILLAGE
Perry Ashenfelter and Lingyu Peng

How can we leverage existing relationships between people, place, and water in order to develop a sustainable community approach to living on the water, while acknowledging the dynamic nature of water as both risk and resource?

As we cannot predict the exact impact of sea level rise and subsidence, it is necessary to plan for significant waterfront inundation at the coast of Semarang. The combination of these risks requires a resiliency plan that accommodates retreat while also maintaining enough coastal land for the fishermen who rely on the water for their livelihoods. Our strategy of retreat and reorganization through a dynamic and adaptive project allows for these vital connections to be maintained for an extended period.

Specifically, we are looking to utilize restoration processes to stabilize and increase mangroves as a coastal buffer and economic driver through nature-based solutions, while also reimagining the interdependencies of people and place through a waterfront village integrated with market and small local businesses in the form of constructed terraces, buildings designed for disassembly, and green infrastructure that empowers the community to be able to incremental adapt to their changing environment, as well show social infrastructures can be adopted in the new village typology.

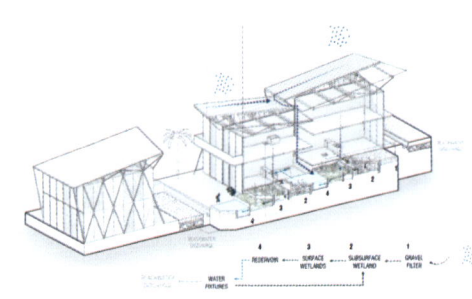

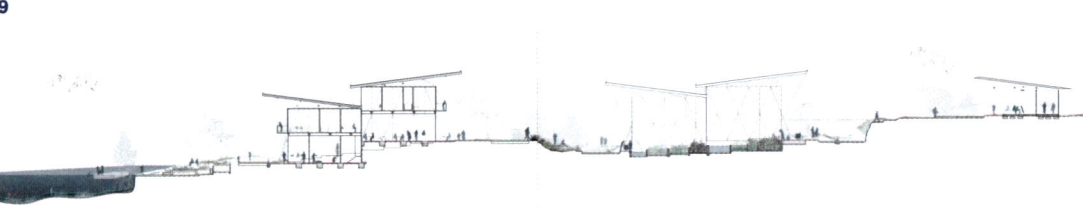

7 – *The Adaptive Waterfront Village* by Perry Ashenfelter and Lingyu Peng, Overall Plan
8 – *The Adaptive Waterfront Village* by Perry Ashenfelter and Lingyu Peng, Axon
9 – *The Adaptive Waterfront Village* by Perry Ashenfelter and Lingyu Peng, Render
10 – *The Adaptive Waterfront Village* by Perry Ashenfelter and Lingyu Peng, Cluster Section

REACTIVATE THE TANJUN EMAS PORT
Tsui-Lun Wang and Jiachang Ye

With the sea level keeps rising, there are significant needs to understand the risks related to subsidence and climate change that diminish access to land and clean water resources, especially for the most defenseless communities and industries at the coast.

The Tanjun Emas Textile Port is aiming at rethinking the port as the forefront of the response to climate change and environmental risks in the City of Semarang. It is also vital for us to understand the severity and interdependencies of the sea level rise, land subsidence, water extraction, and coastal erosion in order to identify potential industries or zones that need to migrate or reorganize and maintain a sustainable environment for the Semarang coastal community and industry.

11

12

13

11 – *Reactivate the Tanjun Emas Port* by Tsui-Lun Wang and Jiachang Ye, Landscape
12 – *Reactivate the Tanjun Emas Port* by Tsui-Lun Wang and Jiachang Ye, Section
13 – *Reactivate the Tanjun Emas Port* by Tsui-Lun Wang and Jiachang Ye, Rendering

SITE / NON SIGHT
at the Architectural Association School of Architecture in London

Homa Farjadi (PROFESSOR OF PRACTICE)
Pierandrea Angius (TA)

Homa Farjadi (Professor of Practive): Principal of Farjadi Architects (1987) — Received a Graduate Diploma from the AA School of Architecture in London and an MArch with distinction from Tehran University — The work of her office has been exhibited and published internationally.

METHODOLOGY:

History of architecture has had many instances of reformulation, of renewals of its parameters and of its models. Many have happened through actual design in building, others come through theoretical formulations of new beginnings. The two texts offered in this studio both in works and in words, can be seen as two instances of such reformulations. One in Art and one in Architecture the two are brought together side by side to engage in a dialogic encounter to frame the design parameters for a new contemporary project. the statement can be read as follows:

'TO CREATE A NEW PRECEDENT IS TO SPEAK ARCHITECTURALLY CREATING NEW POSSIBILITIES, NEW PROBLEMS EVEN.'

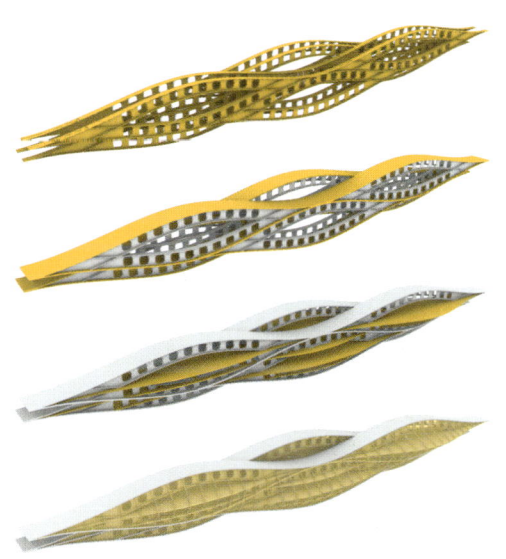

1   ENTROPIC EXPANSE: A NEW DATUM FOR THE CITY OF LONDON
Megan McGaffigan and Ellison Turpin

We are testing the limits of the wall as the driver for understanding space and time. By exploring walls at the extremes of design (both the absence and overwhelming presence), we can understand how "human" behavior impacts perception of space. How does the design of walls create fluctuations in space from the orderly to the disorderly?

1 – *Entropic Expanse: A New Datum for the City of London* by Megan McGaffigan and Ellison Turpin, Chunk Structure

TOPIC:

Land Art works- When discourses of Land Art movement were being developed during the 1960s and 1970s the issue of "site" along with what was termed by Robert Smithson as "non-site" created a central focus. On the one hand the site for a work of art was challenged by taking it outside of the institutional setting of museums and galleries as objects under the control of artists. On the other a radically different set of parameters and scales entered the work of art positioned in faraway, open horizons physically and conceptually. Unbound by human development these we may call *'found sites' that on the one hand foregrounded natural processes and their exchange and effect on man-made works bracketing the limits and role of authorial control, and on the other brought forth a super scale of nature which would challenge the boundaries of objecthood of the work of art designed in its relation to human body, where land is not the setting but part of the work.*

Rem Koolhaas's *Elements of Architecture* divides architecture in its elements, door, window, floor, wall, ceiling etc. a work of analysis of parts, discussion of conventions, regulations, technology are offered as prompters of their historical development. This work's focus on elements can be read as an attempt to dislodge the contemporary emphasis on the work of the image foregrounded by digital processes of design. Hence *no-sight* can challenge the primary drivers of design to engage with elements of architecture and their processes of production and performance in a building/design with a bias on elemental accumulation rather than authorial composition of the image. Project of Elements can be seen as an effort to an emptying of form from its imagistic content so easily at hand by the contemporary tendencies in digital processes of design in favor of hidden motivations and rules to be found everywhere in our environment.

THE SITE:

The London Studio project site takes the site of Alison and Peter Smithson's Robin Hood Gardens project which is currently being demolished. Its iconic approach to design of social housing as an urbanism is but an inspiration point for the treatment of this east London site.

HEAP
Su Wan Park and Mana Nampanwiwat

Inspired from A Heap of Language by Robert Smithson, his project reinterprets the pictorial, semantic, and performative aspects of a 'heap' (an untidy pile or mass of things), creating a pile of words and communicating through its formal arrangement over the meaning of each word presented. Taking on this act of defiance of conventional systems as well as the unexpectedness behaviour of a "heap," our project attempts to create a non-separated arrangement of programmes and a non hierarchical organisation of spaces through loose packing of rooms and series of non-symbolic, structural facade that is ever-present in the project, creating an indistinguishable faces on the interior and exterior.

A catalogue rooms (basic rooms, long rooms, tall rooms, and big rooms) composes a packing organisation which are then redistributed to create a loose packing organisation within the Vierendeel structural system that allows for light, circulation and ventilation.

Our proposed programme is a hybrid building of housing, public performance spaces, and supporting smaller spaces such as rehearsal rooms and performance schools, whereby the interior of the larger spaces are informed by the smaller, supporting ones

2 – *HEAP* by Su Wan Park and Mana Nampanwiwat, Project Descritpion

3 – *HEAP* by Su Wan Park and Mana Nampanwiwat, Final Model

4 – Review Photo at AA London

ALOGON
Jingshuang Wang and Ninghsin Chuang

The project considers the logic of arches into creating dynamic sense of spatial experiences and in emphasis, the project brings a monumental sense of architecture and explains that dramatic geometry arrangements challenge human perception through perspective illusion. At the initial researching stage, the project dive into Robert Smithson's Monument Proposal of Antarctica and Element of Architecture focusing on the element of roof. The project focuses on concepts of "Alogons" and roof geometry focusing arches in understanding structure and spaces in term of scalar, perception and view of perspectives. Through exploring the logic of structure and the logic of space, the project seeks to structurally embed the logic of arches such viaduct into structure but at the same time create a sense of sandwiched spaces incorporating the geometry. As means of integrating these two logics, the project seeks to achieve a result that override the logic of both in which the structure that holds the ceiling and slab together and integrates slab and roof to create a spatial logic. The occupiable space becomes a result of both logics integrated. Depending on different sizes of units, there are multiple programs on each floor to create similar views for people with the changes of spatial perception in the meantime. Considering the pollution on the site, the project also aims at migrating the vegetation from the park to the other side of the tunnel, programs such as roof gardens and greenhouses make the best use of the open space and different daylighting conditions among the Alogons.

5

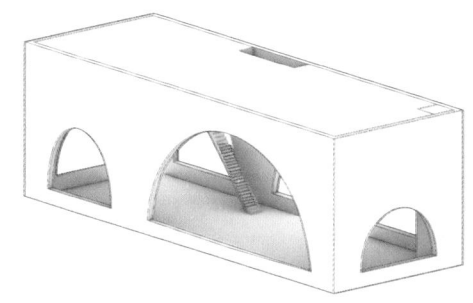

7

5 – *Alogon* by Jingshuang Wang and Ninghsin Chuang, Ground Plan
6 – *Alogon* by Jingshuang Wang and Ninghsin Chuang, Matrix
7 – *Alogon* by Jingshuang Wang and Ninghsin Chuang, Render

FOUND ITINERARIES
Kalob Morris and Tynx Xebeca Taneja

Rem Koolhaas' Door and Robert Smithson's idea of non-site led to the making of Found Itineraries, a faux labyrinth, meant for users to find their way through eight blocks of residential buildings organized together. Replacing Alison and Peter Smithson's Robin Hood Gardens, this project is a shared housing project providing private spaces amidst a sea of shared ones in the mathematical Truchet tile. Each user occupies a wall, which lofts into the space above. Users have their own private bathroom and bedroom space but share a kitchen and a series of public shared spaces. The ground floor houses more public and retail spaces and the other floors are more residential. The roof space is occupiable. The ground and second floor act as connectors between the eight blocks. The projects engulfs the entirety of the site and is meant to be a playful yet logical maze.

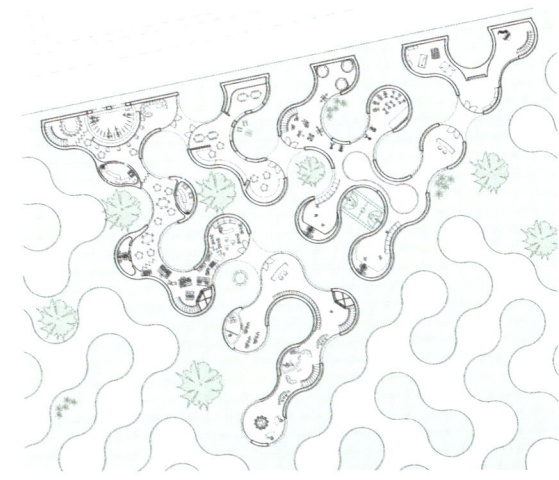

8

9

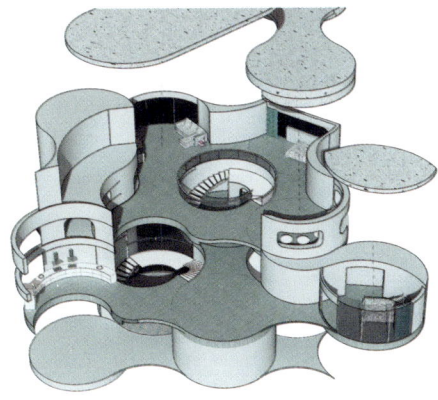

10

11

8 – *Found Itineraries* by Kalob Morris and Tynx Xebeca Taneja, Ground Floor Plan
9 – *Found Itineraries* by Kalob Morris and Tynx Xebeca Taneja, Exterior Render
10 – *Found Itineraries* by Kalob Morris and Tynx Xebeca Taneja, Chunk
11 – *Found Itineraries* by Kalob Morris and Tynx Xebeca Taneja, Interior

FUZZY AGGREGATES
SPECULATIONS ON NEW FORMS OF MIX-USE

Georgina Huljich (LECTURER)
Marcelo Spina (LECTURER)
Miguel Abaunza (TA)

Georgina Huljich and Marcelo Spina (Lecturer): Georgina Huljich and Marcelo Spina are partners of P-A-T-T-E-R-N-S based in Los Angeles. Georgina is Associate Adjunct Professor at UCLA Marcelo is an instructor at SCI-Arc. Their work has been exhibited globally, including the Venice Biennale, The Chicago Biennial, the Art Institute of Chicago, SFMOMA, and the MAK Museum in Venice.

The studio will center on the tension between multiple, discrete, even disparate parts or elements and indeterminately vague and even mysterious fuzzy aggregates. The impossibility to unify parts with whole, or the necessity of many wholes will be the unresolved questions posed by the studio. Rather than only understanding parts as essential, we will also imagine them as physical agents within both architectural volumes and surfaces. These two large and maybe opposing tendencies will arise in the studio, and will work either in parallel, against or in complete disregard of each other.

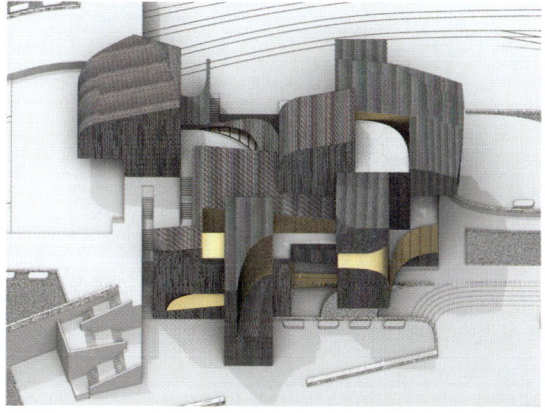

1   FUZZINESS, INTERLOCKING AND OBJECTHOOD
Yingxin Zhang and Yuhe Zhao

Located in a historically central location, adjacent to the Gothic Quarters and the Olympic Villa, the project aims to take the opportunity to make and expand the city's urban fabric. Sited in an area which was bustling before but kind of isolated nowadays, we intend to change the isolation and connect the two distinguished districts through our mix-used cultural center project. Confronted with the difficul-ties of train tracks, highways and altitude differences, a series of amphitheaters and outdoor spaces are incorporated in our manipulations on the ground.

Inspired by local architecture, the extreme abstract geometry, the variation of composition and strong intension of materiality are extracted and considered in our project. Conceptually, the project is a "fuzzy aggregate", a series of autonomous parts not quite cohering into a whole but not fragmentary either. There is a set of strong recognized profiles in our aggregate which consist of the DNA of our project. Even though they seem like a series of simple geometric outlines, they are able to create various of different but similar "parts." This is not without ambiguity, since it implies a synthesis of disparate elements, sharing a degree of consistency in the combination that allows them to still be distinguished within the aggregate. Through those manipulations of synthesis, the project expectedly expresses the qualities of fuzziness, interlocking and objecthood.

As an urban cultural center, this project also aims at achieving the mix-used pro-gram including performing art theaters as well as residential apartment for young artists. Besides these programs we also incorporate some institutional spaces like classroom and conference room open for public. In order to satisfy the spatial characteristics of public and private spaces, we try to mediate the relationship be-tween each program and the "parts" we have. The profile and material of different parts are used to indicate different program. By carefully manipulating the profiles and composition of aggregate, we tend to establish a clear and related connection between parts and programs which is implied from the outside articulation as well.

The relationship between parts and whole can also be revealed from materiality of this project. The combination of concrete and perforated metal panel helps to create a kind of ambiguity between different "parts," also imply the exploitation of curved profiles in the aggregate. In addition, we have two kinds of technique on concrete material, which add another layer of detail on the facade and increase fuzziness of the aggregate.

The studio will concentrate on an ensemble of architectural objects geared towards the generation of an urban node. Each project will develop a dissonant whole, an urban consortium of inharmonious, independent and interdependent objects [and also programs and maybe systems] within a larger and expanded site as well as a more refined architectural intervention on the given site. Simulating and subverting a traditional process of master planning followed by that of often distinct architectural interventions which by including different architects, add both a distinct character and aesthetics to each

1 – *Fuziness, Interlocking, and Objecthood* by Yingxin Zhang and Yuhe Zhao, Oblique Plan

project, the studio will aim to generate a new kind of urbanism, aggregate and fuzzy, intensive and extensive. Beyond the formal and aesthetic aspect raised by the studio, projects will also include the design of the programmatic and problematic components constituting the aggregate. The program will include various emerging arts institutions with an emphasis on performing arts, dance, theater, artist studios, schools and other educational programs and as well as ancillary activities such as cafes and restaurants. Understanding that in the shift from the scale and scope of designing architectural objects to articulating an urban ensemble, there are both quantities and qualities that substantially change, the studio aims to generate a discourse that is critically progressive, engaging of both long-standing architectural typologies as well as current development tendencies.

The studio will be looking at a large site in the City of Barcelona, Spain. The studio project will be situated in a historically central location, adjacent to the Gothic Quarters [and The Born] and the Olympic Villa from the Olympics Games of 1992. With all the merits and failures one could consider in retrospective, and from a point of view which is now very old in terms of what the Olympic Games mean, Barcelona's case was an exceptional one wherein the global opportunity was used to make and expand the city's urban fabric with remarkable architectural objects. The actual site is located at the edge of the Parc Zoologic de Barcelona, bordering The Villa Olympica del Poblenou, and adjacent to La Barceloneta, the project completes an important urban part of the city, already much consolidated. The site, with a tapering shape which follows the edges of the railways, comprises more space than it's actually needed for the building. This excess, aims to account for much needed open public space in and around public buildings.

2

2 – *Fuziness, Interlocking, and Objecthood* by Yingxin Zhang and Yuhe Zhao, Perspective View

3

4

5

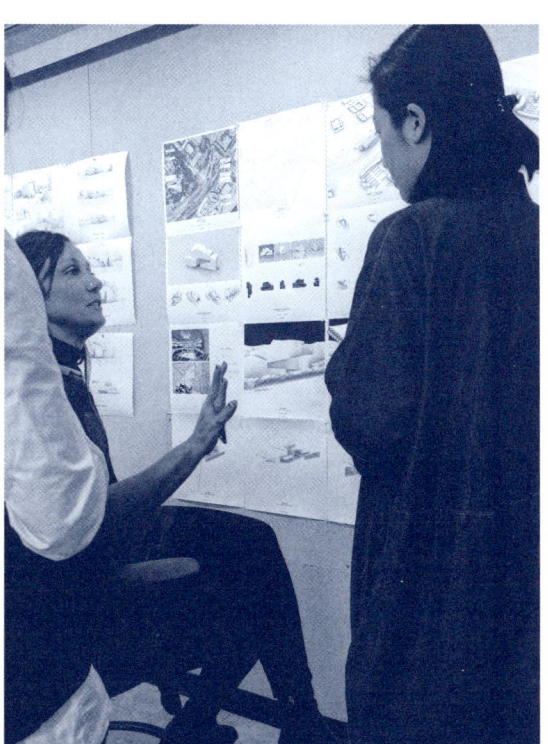

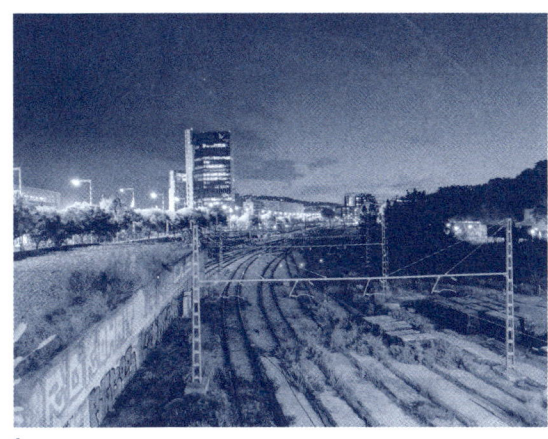

3 – Georgina Huljich in Studio Review
4 – Site Photo

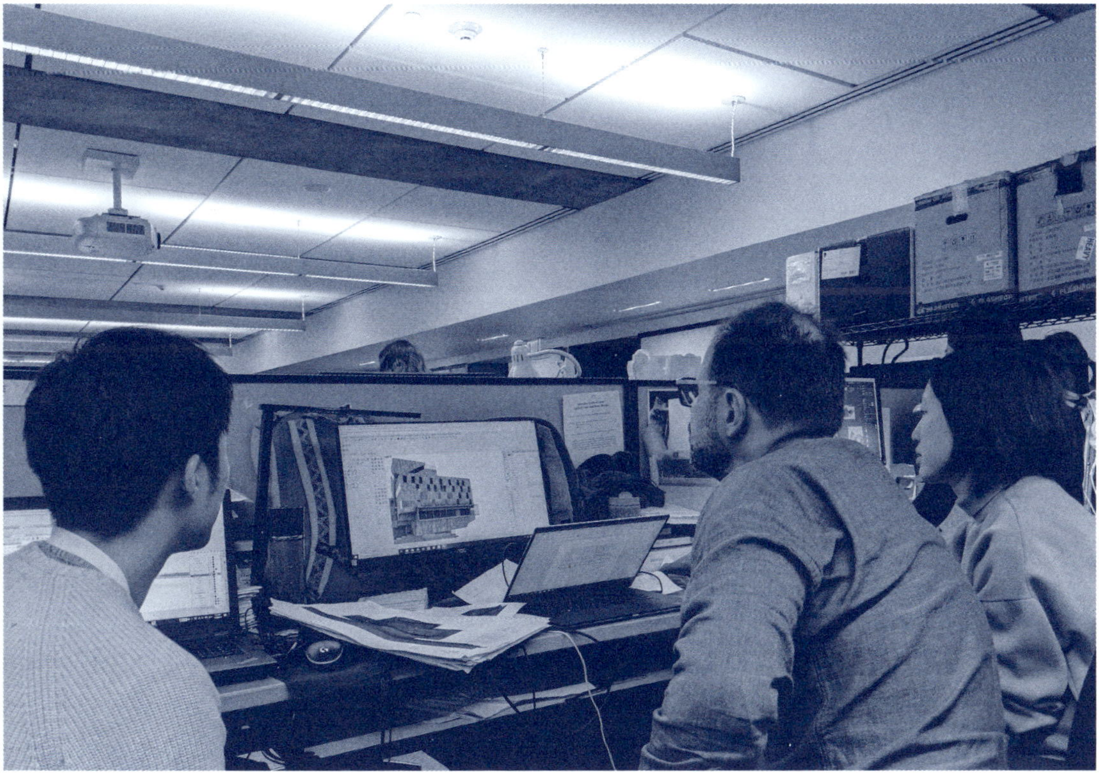

5 – Studio Photo with Marcelo Spina

MIRA'M
Marta Llor and Catherine Shih

Mira'm disrupts the symbiotic notion of the observer and observed through the programmatic juxtaposition of performance arts and social infrastructures. Catalan social systems rely on social interactions whether physical, visual or perceived which architecture facilitates. Balconies, terraces and slivers allow for observers to engage with their context through varying degrees of freedom: from full visual exposure to subtle surveillance.

Mira'm uses terraces and slivers to activate the building as it becomes part of the social fabric. People on the streets catch a glimpse of life, a snapshot of the stories that inhabit the space, which becomes reflected on the exterior, making up the building, infusing life into it from outside. The building becomes an active participant in the fabric of the city, engaging its context through an invitation to be seen. Performances originate within nodes of interaction, moments in which the quotidian life of the building's inhabitants mixes with the school of the arts' curriculum, blurring the boundaries between entertainment and activity.

Positioned between the city and the sea, [the project] falls within a break in the urban grid, being in a unique position to connect the disrupted flows of the Port Olímpic neighborhood. Through the articulation of the landscape, the project blurs the harsh lines between the existing park and the street, mediating circulatory flows and opening up impromptu performance spaces. The urban fabric is vertically recontextualized through terraces, slivers, materiality breaks and programmatic adjacencies. Observers, the observed, arts, education, community, tradition, and urbanity become synthesized within [the project] to shape a new paradigm for mixed use urban developments.

6

7

8

6 – *Mira'm* by Marta Llor and Catherine Shih, Section
7 – *Mira'm* by Marta Llor and Catherine Shih, Top Perspective
8 – *Mira'm* by Marta Llor and Catherine Shih, Elevation

FLOATING VALLEY
Qianni Shi and Han Zhang

The relationship between parts and whole is the starting point of this project. The parts are basic elements of the building which give the building its volume and mass. The variations among parts also give the building a certain character that we are interested in. The truncated and monolithic parts create a fuzzy aggregate that is pyramidal. The monolithic volume is balanced out by the huge cantilevers. The different components of our project share some common traits; however, they could not be put into simple categories since each one is different from another. Together, they contribute to a building that is both uniform and flexible. The flexibility comes from the diversity and variability of different components. The uniformity comes from the efforts to carefully arrange and aggregate these parts based on their characteristics.

In this project, we wish to create an exterior space that resembles the feeling of a valley. The outdoor stairs, platforms and amphitheaters are arranged to be semi-enclosed, giving visitors a feeling of both in the city and outside the city. Cascading terraces along the roof enable visitors to have a view of the adjacent zoo and the city. The volume of the building is also aligned according to the constraints of the site plan so that people could enter and approach this building following the flow of the natural urban fabric and the existing urban grid. Cantilevers allow trains to pass along the existing tracks beneath, and form the auditorium spaces in the building.

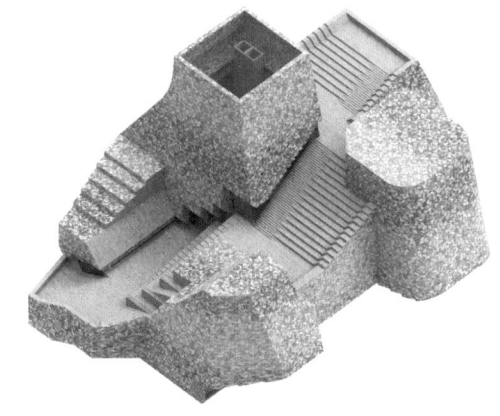

The interior spaces are arranged due to the logic of how the parts are aggregated. Different programs are clustered around certain volumes, where vagueness and ambiguity are created. Since the parts could never be truly separated from the building, the programs are allowed to mingle and mix among one another.

9 – *Floating Valley* by Qianni Shi and Han Zhang, Section
10 – *Floating Valley* by Qianni Shi and Han Zhang, Chunk
11 – *Floating Valley* by Qianni Shi and Han Zhang, Render

UNFORGETTABLE URBANISM

Matthias Hollwich (VISITING LECTURER)
Drew Busmire (TA)

Matthias Hollwich (Visiting Lecturer) Founder and Principal, HWKN Architecture DPC – Matthias Hollwich, AIA, is an architect who has established himself at the forefront of a new generation of groundbreaking international architects. – Matthias believes the key to successful architecture lies in finding new and exciting ways to create relationships between people and buildings. – He was recently honored in Fast Company's ranking of the world's top 10 most innovative architects and was on Business Insider's list of the top business visionaries.

In today's society we have shifted from owning to experiencing—but what happens when we forget? A product we own is physically with us for as long as we choose, whether that be a home, a car, or a keepsake, while an experience, if not remembered, is as if it never happened. But what is memory, and what makes us remember a single experience over thousands of daily impressions? New science emerging from brain research gives us clues about what makes us remember and what makes us forget. This studio explores the science of memory and how we can create unforgettable memories. The design strategy will not be about a style, a theory, or a form—it will be about the memories that we shape. We will create places that are not just Instagrammed, but remembered for a lifetime.

engage with the landscape, thus the landscape will have a strong sense of belonging to the main building. The public amenities, the building and the landscape are unified by the form, people would immersed in this intensive form and engage with it by having various kinds of activities which in turn would create emotional connection and long term memory.

With the world's population still rapidly increasing and livable space decreasing, we will explore ideas of maximum density. We will reach towards the sky to take advantage of new high-rise technology, while challenging typical living and working conditions by introducing micro, common, and collective ideas that allow to densify while socially activating. We will research, analyze, and design new types of apartment layouts including micro, shared, and coliving typologies, responding to shifts in society with boomers, millennials, and Gen Z at the forefront of change. Here, density is part of the program, but even more so, unforgettable experiences that shape friendships and lifetime memories through smart programming, design, and social programming.

Houston, a booming city in Texas, has an incredible competitive advantage to any other city in the US: It has no zoning laws. A developer can technically build whatever they want. A site can become a mixed use neighborhood, it can switch from residential to industrial to

FORM & EMOTION & MEMORY
Yuan Zhang and Yiling Zhong

Form is never just function as a visual pleasure. Form can arouse people's emotions when it was implemented to externalize the human activities, social connection and natural environment. It is medium that help express the power of building and transfer that power to human emotions. The fully engagement in that form turns emotions to our unforgettable memory.

In our design, we use different forms to highlight the public amenities inside the building and make them exposed to the outside which can be seen from the ground floor passer-by's. Thus, it will have a certain social connection between people inside and outside. We also use certain form to

External Partnerships: The studio would like to thank Eckpfeiler, Hines, Midway, Edens, Masterworks and National for their generosity spending time with the students

1 – *Form and Emotion & Memory* by Yuan Zhang and Yiling Zhong, Render
2 – *Form and Emotion & Memory* by Yuan Zhang and Yiling Zhong, Render

commercial and residential, and a building can be as high as the sky or as low as a single story. The only limit is the planner's imagination and the city's infrastructure capacity (traffic, water supply, drainage, and the power grid). New progressive ideas of off-the-grid infrastructure, zero car usage, hyper sustainability, and mix use strategies can also render this limitation mute. We will plan a 40-acre site in Houston using architecture to reduce traffic, eliminate grid dependency and shape memories.

3   URBAN STAGE
Yutian Tang and Bella Ding

The project is inspired by the fact that people on the stage will have longer lasting memories than the audience. Based on psychological study, we can understand this fact with the knowledge of semantic memory and episodic memory. The former is for the audience, the latter is for the people on the stage whose memory will be enhanced by the stage effects. And the mechanism is further developed into our key concept, to create hierarchical stages in everyday life for theatrical effects on people's behavior to simulate longer lasting memory. There are two paths to achieve this goal, first is to directly create programs on stages, and the second is to force people as the audience to respond to the stage, even transform the seats into stage.

And we looked into several specific theatrical spaces including theater and stadium and developed a center stage complex with new organizations of programs to trigger the interactive effects.

On an urban scale, the hierarchical idea is also applied in the relationship between the context and center object. One of the scenes is standing on the towers and looking through the "seats" to the center stage, transforming the seats to a stage for the towers in a certain way. The audience is pushed onto the stage for longer lasting memories.

The scheme is also an economic experiment since all the amenities of the context towers are concentrated in the center object. And the towers respond to the center object in a subtle way, with outdoor spaces and angled position. This new organization will also stimulate theatrical effects among these context towers, further enhancing the concept of urban stage.

4

3 – *Urban Stage* by Yutian Tang and Bella Ding, Project Description

4 – *Urban Stage* by Yutian Tang and Bella Ding, Perspective Section

5

6

5 – *Urban Stage* by Yutian Tang and Bella Ding, Rendering
6 – Matthias Hollwich in Studio Review

LUMISCAPE
Pengkun Wang and Yu Mao

Psychological experiments prove that the greater the contrast between the characteristics of things, the deeper the degree of perception, which creates more memory. People focused on contrast because its modulation has been shown to modulate the excitability of the visual cortex in a positive fashion. Specifically, incoming visual signal is more likely to reach perceptual threshold during maintenance of high contrast mental image. We try to create contrast in the flat Houston area by creating a mountain, which create the contrast in scale and profile, hoping to attract people from the surrounding areas to our site. We try to create nature to contrast with the city, whether it is the green slope or the central canyon is a tribute to nature. We create natural feelings with advanced architectural language, creating another kind of design language contrast. Exploring the possibilities of different developers in different plots enriches the masterplan and makes it different. It is both this uncertainty and the defined urban planning guideline that make every building unique and fun, while also keep the overall masterplan unified and harmonious.

6

7

8

9

6 – *LumiSCAPE* by Pengkun Wang and Yu Mao, Rendering
7 – *LumiSCAPE* by Pengkun Wang and Yu Mao, Section
8 – *LumiSCAPE* by Pengkun Wang and Yu Mao, Building Strategy
9 – *LumiSCAPE* by Pengkun Wang and Yu Mao, Rendering

ELEVATED PITCH
Ian Lai and Qiaomu Xue

Within the spectrum of typical residential and commercial architecture lies the elements of Living, Working, and Playing. We are familiar with the three, but is there a fourth that results in the intersection of all of these elements? What kind of architecture does this kind of fused space yield, or rather, what kind of form produces this programmatic intersection?

This project aims to investigate how two completely different building typologies meet to create one iconic form, and from the same footprint below, carve out a negative void that mirrors its above grade condition and produces public below-grade retail equally as unforgettable as it's positive opposite above. Situated between the city metropolis and the residential, this speculative model acts as a medium for the imagination of what could be an iconic fusion of three distinctly different programs, architecture, and lifestyles and the public space it can create.

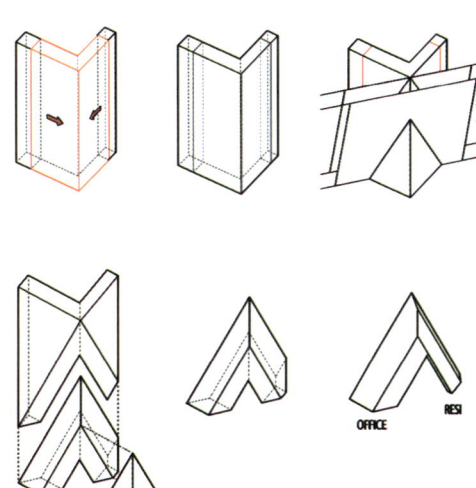

10

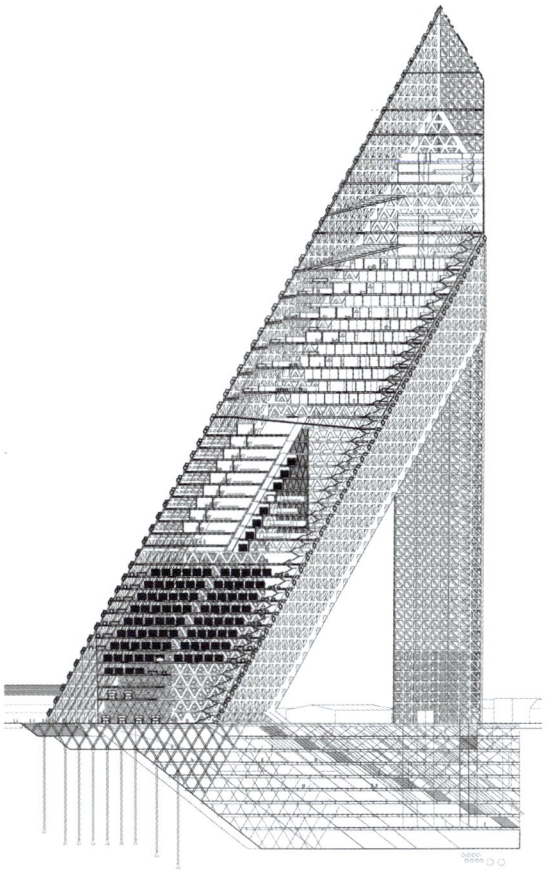

11

12

10 – *Elevated Pitch* by Ian Lai and Qiaomu Xue, Form Generation
11 – *Elevated Pitch* by Ian Lai and Qiaomu Xue, Office Section

12 – *Elevated Pitch* by Ian Lai and Qiaomu Xue, Rendering

SEOUL: COMPOUND BEINGS, DEVIOUS TOPOGRAPHIES

Simon Kim (ASSOCIATE PROFESSOR OF ARCHITECTURE)
Andrew Homick (TA)

Simon Kim (Associate Professor of Architecture): Co-founded Ibañez Kim Studio, PA & MA, (1994) — Graduated from the Design Research Laboratory at the Architectural Association (AA) — Taught studios and seminars at Harvard, MIT, Yale, and the AA. — Director of the Immersive Kinematics Research Group

Agenda

Architecture of a city as a proposition or a form of intellectual investigation is tethered to a built, shared environment. This may be expanded into terrain and even terra-forming where outside-inside is not easily divided. Its implicit and explicit meanings and affects are to be developed in material and also in behavior over time.

To do this, we will imbue architecture and urbanism with duration, with its own agency and selfgovernance in Seoul at the intersection of historical Haebangchon and the recently decommissioned U.S. military base of Yongsan. With new media and new materials, it is not impossible to conceptualize the built environment of ground and building as a sensate and sentient field. Our role as designers and as inhabitants is to coordinate and live in this new city and new nature as a shared endeavor. Korea's rapid advancement in light and heavy industries places it as an ideal postindustrial model with advanced thinking of new environment and eco-intelligence.

This studio will break from the classical hierarchy of humancentric design and allow for nonhuman (all manner of flora, fauna, and matter) authorship and stewardship. Rather than design from a compositional position, and to dwell in a seamless zone of human comfort, this studio will engage in a design process with transformations over time, to produce environments that change and behave for otherthan-human requirements (such as seasons, water, air, animal).

We will consider the postwar projects of Gordon Pask, Nicholas Negroponte, and the writings of Timothy Morton and Donna Haraway, while rejecting the mechaideologies of Archigram and Evangelion. Architecture that is sensate and nervous do not need to look like giant robots, and projects based in nonhuman agency should not be simplified to an easy reading or cliche.

If the term Anthropocene defines the global impact of human activity, the city is at the concept's core. Although on one hand a 'humancentered' approach to urbanism can generate positive discussions on the quality of life, all too often it is used to place humans at the hierarchical apex of the ecological

1   HRAKAHN
Sanxing Zhao and Hanning Liu

As a starting point for the agency between human and non-human spaces, this design mainly discusses whether the boundary between human and non-human could be blurred by the self-development posture in this context. If so, coexistence could be achieved. Also It creates and channels steam for Seoul as an infrastructure, but also as a cultural servant.

In this regard, instead of embracing the formation of buildings led by people, but let the building expand spontaneously through the external environment and its own attributes. The organic growth process is similar to the expansion of roots, but due to the nature of its architecture, the specific process of expansion is not identical to roots, but rather similar to the growth of crystal caves.

At the same time, in terms of function, we have shaped it into an engine, or seed, for changing a range of micro-ecosystems. When he was planted, based on the support of the geothermal energy system, water vapor was used to release heat, moisture and nutrients into the surrounding soil, atmosphere and water, while planting through the plants in the incubator. In turn, those plant also perform photosynthesis to produce oxygen and balance humidity.

As an intention, spices indicate the complex components rich in water vapor, and also indicate that the building is in a state of continuous outward propagation to change the environmental components.

Studio Sponsor: Heerim Architects and Planners and CEO Young Kyoon Jeong (MArch'89)

1 –*Hrakahn* by Sanxing Zhao and Hanning Liu, Project Description

system. Therefore, rather than a holistic vision of the city, massive imbalances continue to degrade the global ecology; paradoxically massive social inequalities also escalate as wealth accumulation becomes a geopolitical game of subdividing the city as 'realestate.' In fact modernist planning classifies the city along functionalist lines of housing, business, retail, production, and the like fragments that on the surface seem to define humancentered activities, but in practice can easily be captured by power structures. A. Zaera-Polo

Goals:
On Immersive Architecture

The premise of the studio will be to accelerate the urban growth of a new model of synthetic nature, augmented architecture, and compound beings so that there is no sense of a critical distance. This polemic denies a separation of environment and occupant to be encompassing and immersive. We will develop behaviors and duration in architecture and ground, and apply it to a new model of Synthetic Nature and Augmented Architecture. The scope of the work in fall option studio is the large urban scale. To that end, we will (1.) disrupt the separation of topographic ground and building. We will then (2.) focus this world into a protocommunity of synthetic beings made of people, flora, fauna, and new technologies who operate and dwell as a conservatory of new bodies of knowledge and forms of life.

If the tasks for Immersive Architecture is to remove the anthropo-centric model of architecture, and replace it with a networked synthetic nature and ecology, then the challenge is to define the narrative of common space or the public. These may be presented relationships that are seamless, or difficult as topographic ground yields not only inside and outside but also topside and underside. The site of Yongsan and HaeBangChon is at the center of Seoul, and is historically poignant. The military base sits on open terrain in the city center, and is juxtaposed by high-density urban fabric of mid-size buildings. The site can undergo another transformation where the biodiversity, biomes, and ecosystems are not only fully engaged, but have a role in: human industry, non-human cultures, and history. For this reason, the dimensions of politics cannot be ignored.

2

2 –*Hrakahn* by Sanxing Zhao and Hanning Liu, Axon

3-5 –Seoul Studio Travel

THIS IS [NOT] A HIVE
Nick Kalantzopoulos and Wenhao Xu

The hive is a framework of coexisting worlds. Bees and humans operate side by side in an internal spring scenario, creating a heterotopic space of illusion, exposing every real space and thus establishing a microcosm of different environments.

The object seats in a basin in a forest, suggestive of a space that that needs to be discovered. Its spherical core generates both heat and steam, resembling a ritual or purification. Spaces are isolated and penetrable yet not freely accessible like a public place. Steam is an integral part of the architecture, acquiring space with more layers of meaning or relationships to other places, enabling the cohabitation of its occupants at the top, while, at the same time creating an aromatic chamber deep in the bowels of the building.

6 – *This is [Not] a Hive* by Nick Kalantzopoulos and Wenhao Xu, Section Final
7 – *This is [Not] a Hive* by Nick Kalantzopoulos and Wenhao Xu, Model

8 – *This is [Not] a Hive* by Nick Kalantzopoulos and Wenhao Xu, Model

MOTHER MYTHOLOGY
Agata Jakubowska and Katarina Marjanovic

According to Donna Harawy, "by the late 20th century in scientific culture, the boundary between human and animal is thoroughly breached." Looking at these systems of hybridity, we catalogued ideas of animals and human, animal and object, animal and parasitic artifacts. The idea of hybrid is the borrowing of multiple parts within a whole, existing in sequence with one another, and without hierarchy. Rather, a cholarchy of relationships feed off of one other, whether it be symbiotic, parasitic, or coexisting.

Ignoring the importance of nonhuman entities may lead to the downfall of human civilization. Since the first shelter was made as an architecture to protect from the wild, we have fought against nature as an Other that either must be kept away, modified or taken. We were struck by the ecology of Korea's wetlands, and how the DMZ has become a flourishing area of ecological prosperity. Even in the face of political tension, this area has benefited from little to no human interaction.

9

10

11

9 – *Mother Mythology* Agata Jakubowska and Katarina Marjanovic, Model
10 – *Mother Mythology* Agata Jakubowska and Katarina Marjanovic, Model

11 – *Mother Mythology* Agata Jakubowska and Katarina Marjanovic, Section

CYBORG PAREIDOLIA

Karel Klein (LECTURER)
Ryan Barnette (TA)

Karel Klein (Lecturer) Partner, RuyKlein – Faculty, Southern California Institute of Architecture – Visiting faculty, University of Pennsylvania, Weitzman School of Design – Visiting faculty, Pratt Institute, GAUD

Though some are panicking that AI is eventually going to replace human judgment, the more likely scenario is that human judgment will simply be altered and modified by the presence of AI "partners." Partners, perhaps, because the technology currently classified as AI does not comfortably fit our ideas of what a tool is. Because AI technologies seek to simulate our own capabilities, to say that AI is nothing but a tool would imply that we are also nothing but a tool. So, counter to this idea of AI being merely a new kind of tool would have to be the premise that AI is like us. Therefore, potential collaborators. This studio will be continuing an ongoing investigation into this potentiality. Using one or more networks from a new class of AI software, style transfer algorithms, cycleGANs (generative adversarial networks), etc., our studio will experiment with how this new automated process of "seeing" might begin to suggest both new architectural forms and expressions as well as new grounds upon which these new architectures would occupy.

Because these AI networks must be trained with images in order to learn how to "see," they can be introduced to architecture much in the same way that we study architecture, that is through images, drawings, photographs, etc. In other words, precedents. But, because machine vision appears to misalign or misinterpret precedents in an entirely novel way—one might say absurd, or uncanny—strange and exciting questions about the role of historical influence on the production of new objects begin to emerge. We will exploit these new potentials of precedent in our studio.

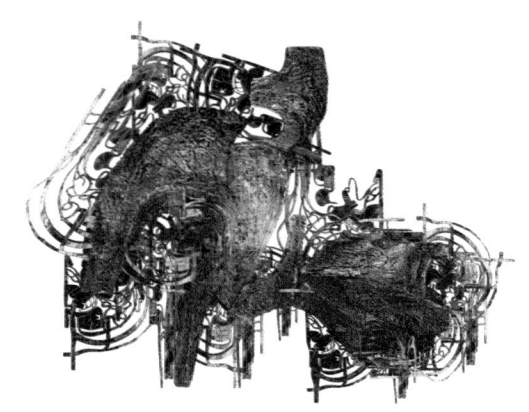

1 CYBIOC MORPHOLOGIES
Abdurrahman Baru

The Gothic features of redundancy and naturalism inspired this project through the catalyst of artificial intelligence, transforming the Gothic savageness into a collage of AI production flow. These technologies are viewed as partners, willing and able to shift the privilege of tracery and the machine. The gesture of the swirling tracery exists as the DNA of the New Tectonic, metamorphosizing from the precious scale of ornament to structural elements that craft a reading of surface and volume. An interplay of elements attributed to the features of the Gothic form conditions savage in quality. These new organizational and assembly logics generated by the machine, when paired with the Gothic create a relationship of strange associations with shifting edge conditions. The balance between figural and field relationships is shifted into a hybridized integral aesthetic of a New Tectonic interconnection. Different conditions of the New Tectonic are accentuated through this compositional shift. Relinquishing ownership from architecture to the machine, the AI generates a series of sectional variations depicting a novel representation style that straddles realism and drawing. A speculative interior populated with tectonic tracery produces a strange association with abstract wildness, leaving an impression of figural lines through the vision of the machine.

With regard to this mechanized misinterpretation, this studio continues the ambition to extend theories of artistic estrangement via these new technological regimes. The recent renewal of interest in Viktor Shklovsky and Harold Bloom suggests the ongoing relevance of the premise that creative expression is the result of a process of

1 – *Cybioc Morphologies* by Abdurrahman Baru

defamiliarization. In Art as Technique, Viktor Shklovsky argues that great works of art do their work by defamiliarizing normal reality and slowing down habits of perception in the beholder. Similarly, but with regard to difficulty of authoring great works, Harold Bloom asserts in The Anxiety of Influence that masterpieces are nothing more than creative misinterpretations of previous masterpieces—or precedents. The new question, however, is how these theories of estrangement are to be understood when it is not the human author doing the reading or the writing, or the seeing or the imaging, but the machine? Or even more convoluted is the same question relative to a hybrid human-machine author. The weird question of the studio is, how might a cyborg design architecture? This question should not be taken as a preposterous scenario of becoming a bionic designer as kitsch science fiction might like to imagine. As Donna Haraway points out, we are all already cyborgs. The studio will only ask you to recognize this and actively collaborate with our machines.

3

SYMPATHIES OF THE UNKNOWN
Patrick Danahy and David Forero

The architectural history of formal analysis within style, is echoed here by a non-stylistic neural network based formal analysis. Elements of existing styles that evoke space or signify larger architectural assemblages are preserved in combination with more abstracted formal assemblages. This combination acts in pursuit of new architectural surface. Rather than utilizing formal analysis to further understand historic architectures, neural networks are used to read these works formally through their own abstracted view of the architectural elements.

There are principles of space and representation being tested that at times flatten the subject into a space of universals, which is seemingly absent of style, while in other moments the elements assemble into objects and distinguish themselves from the background. This play of flattening of hierarchy is both representational and spatial and engages the architect to question how the subject operates in their spaces.

The gothic serves as a platform for testing familiarity in combination with unfamiliar or abstracted elements. This allows for noticeable columns to assemble into larger arcades and then disassemble into unknown architectural surfaces.

2

2 – *Sympathies of the Unknown* by Patrick Danahy and David Forero

3 – *Sympathies of the Unknown* by Patrick Danahy and David Forero, figure for plot, Project Description

4 – Karel Klein and Ryan Barnette in Studio Review

CORROSION
Tianjian Li and Jintong Mao

The form of the factory is not fully pregiven in a completed plan, nor the elements of the construction in standardized molds to be filled in with inert matter. The factory is empowered by artificial intelligence with opportunity and capacity to be self-evolving and self-representing. This sort of corrosion rejuvenises the factory by introducing uncertainty, changefulness, and spontaneity.

Changing the attribute of stone and steel, the burgeoning of corrosion spread out through the site. Although continuous in form, the corroded matters grow across "broken lines." At each step, their curvature might inflect, or they might bifurcate or merge. it varies and distributes them following the growth of form. Eventually, the factory becomes the repercussion of the corrosion.

entwining around each other, or changing direction in unison to avoid entwinement, every inch of the wall is moving and mutating to establish an inextricable, indivisible relationship between the interior and exterior.

All the possible iterations of interior integrate into one result that is moving and expanding toward the plane-filling limit. Harmoniously, a new blueprint of the factory? is born.

Exactly how corrosion eventuates is determined by the result of oxidation reaction, influenced by the factory's material and spatial characteristics. The work of artificial intelligence, in its encounter with the material, becomes an internal growth factor of the design.

5

6

7

5 – *Corrosion* by Tianjian Li and Jintong Mao, Object
6 – *Corrosion* by Tianjian Li and Jintong Mao, Section
7 – *Corrosion* by Tianjian Li and Jintong Mao, Site

THROUGH THE MACHINE'S THIRD EYE
Yangxunxun Zhou

Our brain is a filter. Tons of information goes into it and gets filtered when it comes out. Our worldview is generated based on our experiences, which is somehow filtered by our emotions.

Machines, at one point, are like humans. They think differently, see things differently based on their own consciousness. The only difference between human and machines, maybe, is that machines would not be controlled by emotions.

The machine can mimic, but what generated from it is not exact the same as the original one anymore. It is the misreading that causes the "unlike mimicry." But they do have similar qualities which allows the mimicry one simulating into the environment and merging in the surrounding.

The project is growing and it's hard to tell where it starts and where it ends. The mimicry of machine allows the site "enfolds, penetrates, and even passes through" what it contains. Eventually assimilated into the background. Continuously, infinitely.

I'm also misreading what the machine has misread before. Is this misreading really useless? Is this really meaningless to the machines consciousness?

It seems useless, but it's not. The back and forth misreading, respond, and feedback generate what I want and narrow the difference between me and the machine.

Eventually, we receive the feedback from each other, both of us could read the same thing. Collaborating through elaborating the misreading of the same content, this process includes a long back and forth conversation.

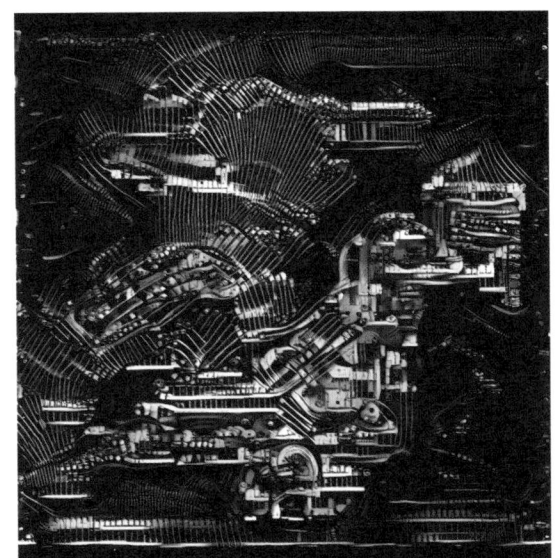

8

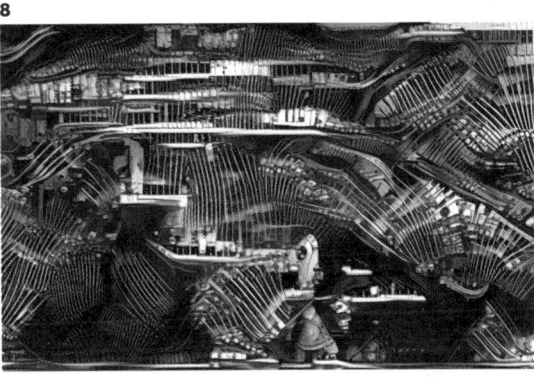

9

10

8-9 – *Through the Machine's Third Eye* by Yangxunxun Zhou, Research

10 – *Through the Machine's Third Eye* by Yangxunxun Zhou, Site Mix

ODDKIN ARCHITECTURE ISTANBUL III
REMAKING THE "BÜYÜK VALIDE HAN" IN ISTANBUL, TURKEY

Ferda Kolatan (ASSOCIATE PROFESSOR OF PRACTICE)
Michael Zimmerman (TA)

Ferda Kolatan, (Associate Professor of Practice) Founding Director of SU11 Architecture+Design—MsAAD, Columbia University—Dipl.Ing., RWTH Aachen, Germany

Studio Sponsor: GAD Foundation, Istanbul—Turkey

ODDKIN: BEINGS (AND THINGS) REQUIRING EACH OTHER IN UNEXPECTED COLLABORATIONS AND COMBINATIONS. BEING SITUATED SOMEPLACE AND NOT NOPLACE, ENTANGLED AND WORLDLY.
— Donna Haraway, Staying with the Trouble (2016)

"Oddkin" architecture seeks to develop design strategies by closely examining a site's idiosyncrasies and by mixing them into new types of hybrid urban objects. In philosopher Donna Haraway's words, the goal for this studio could be described as the design of "unexpected collaborations and combinations" in architecture, which —by being "situated someplace"— take on new meanings in regard to their place and origin.

In a time of frantic image proliferation through digital media, the nature of how we perceive a thing's originality has shifted profoundly. Confronted with the simultaneous presence of myriads of images with no detectable reference to type, scale, or history, our vision of the world is increasingly governed by acts of lateral mixing and meshing. Cities, curiously, provide the physical equivalent to this current phenomenon of our image culture. After all, cities are where we produce images through objects, where we mix histories, invert scales, and (re)originate types.

Oddkin architecture is foremost a coming to terms with the question of how we produce value in a world that is no longer contingent on linking images to their local and temporal context. If all things already-out-there can be used to remake new images, then what is the "new" in the first place? If there is no link to an origin, how can we be original? If all places and times comingle, then how do we know authenticity? The projects in this studio examine these questions through the re-origination of a historic Han in Istanbul, a city already strongly characterized by hybridizations of new and old, planned and random, mundane and precious.

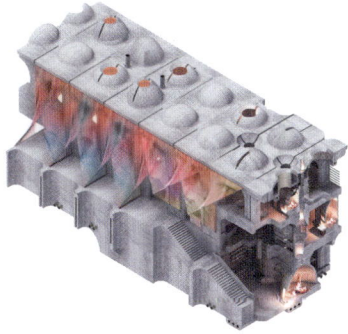

1

ARCHINESPHERE
Xiaoqing Guo and Jiacheng Gu

We studied the existing artisan spaces in the Buyuk Valide Han, noting their particular characteristics to create collaborations between the machines, the tools, designed objects, craftsmen, and workspaces within and around the existing Han structure. These new hybrid conditions reconfigure the spaces around the artisan workshops in order to produce a unique experience of color, texture, and material. In the case of the textile maker, colorful threads weave through space as the sound of the spinning machines hum along throughout the Han's colonnade. The machines, no longer bound to a utilitarian mode of production, make new configurations with the architecture and produce waterfalls of color along the facades within the courtyard. In another corner of the Han, a collection of chimney's combine, clustering the workshops and several blacksmiths. Vibrant light and heat spill out from their fireplaces, producing a shimmering gallery quality attracting to passersby. As these new artisan spaces grow, the entire Han transforms into a new kind of machine object meant for painting with color and light.

2

1&2 – Archinesphere by Xiaoqing Guo and Jiacheng Gu

UNFOLDED STORIES
Zoe Cennami and Margarida Mota

On a Saturday afternoon inside the courtyard of the Buyuk Valide Han, kids are running around kicking the football, elderly men sitting on benches under the Oak trees are discussing which type of bird is singing above their heads, and tourists scurry around every corner, taking photos and looking for a way to climb up to the roof for the best views of the city. Everything seems normal, like in any other Han in Istanbul.

However, things are not quite as normal as they seem. Activities and things unfold in unique combinations and the courtyard comes to life like some Ottaman miniature painting. The kids grow bored of playing football, and instead are mesmerized by a video playing from LED panels, filling the facade from top to bottom with bright, vibrant colors and images. The elderly men, unsure of what they just saw, notice more birds appearing from nests and geological crevasses within the Han's facade. A group of tourists forget about their journey to the roof once they enter the courtyard and discover a world bustling with activity and filled with unique combinations of colors, images, textures, birds, patterns, and many things they don't know how to describe. They leave the Han with more photos of the courtyard than of the views from the roof.

As the day comes to an end, the people all leave, and the bright lights and birds remain. This is not like any other Han in Istanbul. This one plays a different role within the city. From afar, it fits into its urban context within the surrounding Hans in the historic neighborhood. However, its courtyard presents a new urban interior that enables different stories to unfold.

3 – *Unfolded Stories* by Zoe Cennami and Margarida Mota, Project Statement
4 – *Travel Picture*
5 – *Unfolded Stories* by Zoe Cennami and Margarida Mota, Elevation
6 – *Unfolded Stories* by Zoe Cennami and Margarida Mota, Render Aerial

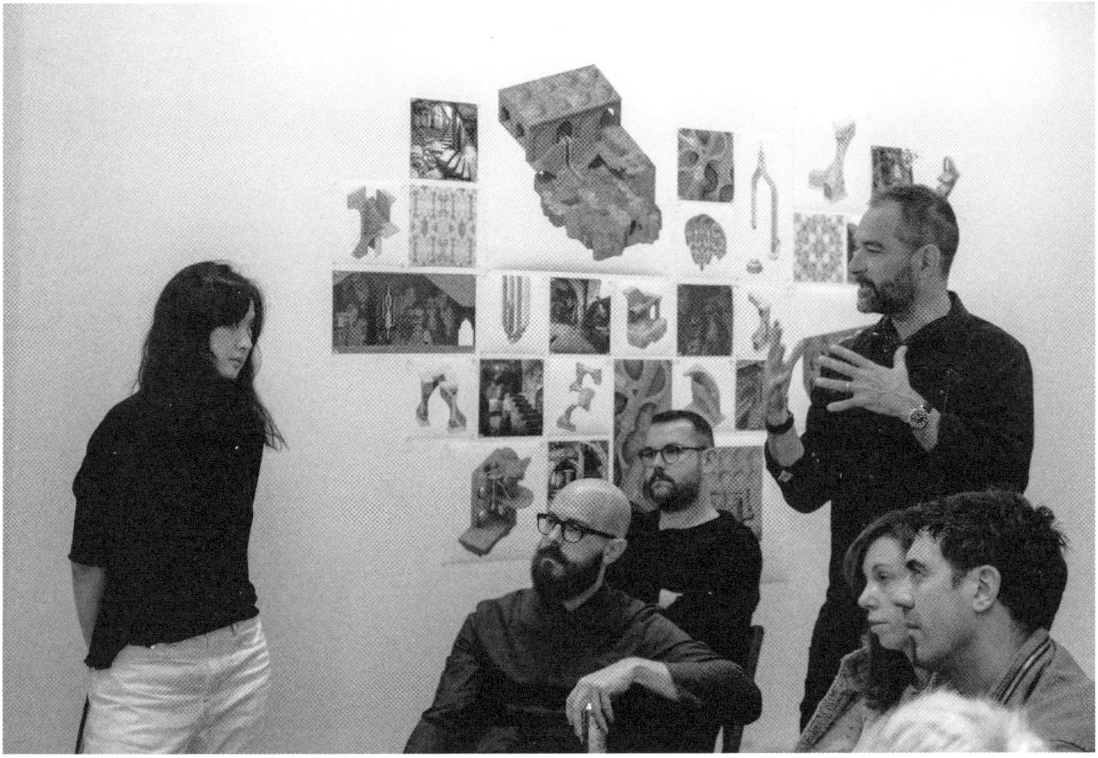

7

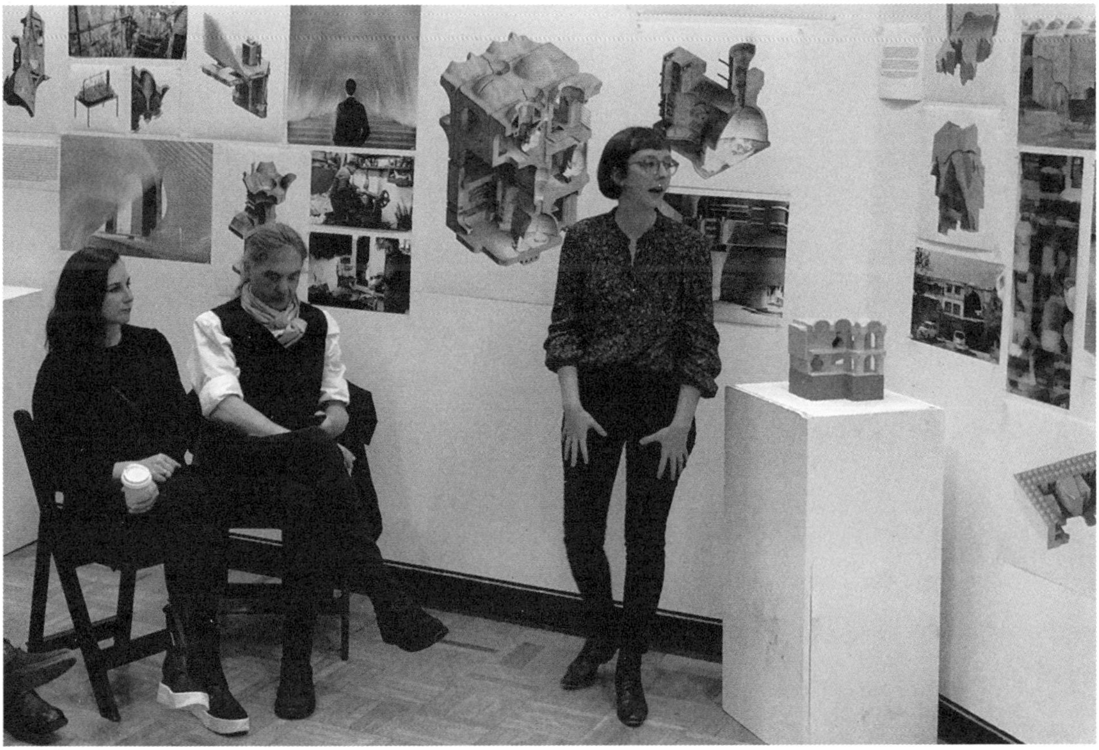

8

7 – Ferda Kolatan and Michael Zimmerman in Studio Review
8 – Studio Review

EMBEDDED SEQUENCES
Caleb Ehly and Joonsung Lee

As the Han developed through the centuries, its fluctuation of usage, space, and growth has rendered it almost unknown. This project seeks to reestablish the processional qualities that were once present as one would enter through a passageway, to an open courtyard, through another passageway, and again into an open courtyard, where in turn, the Han presents itself to its user. As our project develops in, around and under the existing, it takes on conditions through a buildup of details, both in the small and large scale. Articulation, color, and geometry fuse together through undulating sculpted metal inlays, taking over and reconstructing the threshold conditions between courtyards. Volume and space become synonymous with detail and articulation, developing a formal approach that accepts the resolution found within the historic culture, and hybridizes it with contemporary techniques using geometry, material, and texture. In doing so the project begins rendering new hybrid relationships and aesthetic qualities that dive deep into the cultural aspects of Istanbul, both in the day to day use, along with the introduction of a contemporary gallery. These functions, both in their tensions and similarities play a part in establishing a new role and identity to the Han's image culture, recalibrating the points of attention and attraction.

9

10

9 – *Embedded Sequences* by Caleb Ehly and Joonsung Lee, Model Photography

10 – *Embedded Sequences* by Caleb Ehly and Joonsung Lee, Garden Axo

PALIMPSEST
Ryan Henriksen and Tae Hyung Lee

Over the course of its life, the Ottoman Han has become a palimpsest of the programmatic needs of its successive occupants. Though the structure was initially purposed to hybridize urban lodging, commerce and stables, in its contemporary life the Han has undergone constant reconfiguration to suit an ever-changing role within the evolving city. New circulatory elements, introduced into the structure to service functional connections and programmatic re-appropriations, have created hybridized conditions present with the Han that entangle remnants of its multi-generational use. These circulatory moments, though estranged from the original architecture, develop unique Oddkin moments that exist inseparably from the contemporary character of the Han. It is around and amongst these existing hybridized stair conditions that our intervention takes form; spinning these functional circulatory appendages into new architectural configurations.

Palimpsest reinterprets and transforms existing circulatory moments into manifestations that embed new spatial conditions within the Han. This series of interventions and its programming is intended to extend and enhance the current usage of the Han. Ordinary elements such as stairs, arches, and domes collaborate with newly configured architectural elements giving life to unique episodic moments.

12

13

11

14

11 – *Palimpsest* by Ryan Henriksen and Tae Hyung Lee, Object
12 – *Palimpsest* by Ryan Henriksen and Tae Hyung Lee, Chunk, Corridor Stair

13-14 – *Palimpsest* by Ryan Henriksen and Tae Hyung Lee, Project Render

STOCKHOLM RESILIENCE CENTRE

Joe MacDonald (LECTURER)
Shayer Rahman (TA)

Joe MacDonald: (Lecturer) Joe MacDonald received his March from Harvard and BArch from the University of Washington. He is a founding principal at Urban A&O. Awards include IDEA International Design Excellence Silver Award for Environments for the WaterPlanet, China's Most Successful Design Award for the Johnson & Johnson Olympic Pavilion in Beijing, Architecture Magazine's Vanguard Award.

This studio is a design and research studio and Part II of one taught last Fall titled the Dubai Studio. We'll continue to study concepts around resilience through the lens of computational design. Sustainability in the Americas offers a narrow focus on building materials and assemblies as the primary solution to environmental stewardship while neglecting a more wholistic approach to living with and practicing resilience.

If we look to China and their effort to phase out carbon by 2050 and initiatives in Europe and Scandinavia, we see more radical, responsible and inventive research and planning to address global warming. Sir Tim Smit of the Eden Project in Cornwall and his team work across boarders with agencies such as Mistra and the Stockholm Resilience Centre developing progressive frameworks to address the crisis we are currently facing.

Centre site. By farming kelp in the lake, we can purify the polluted water and generate biofuel for the building. Diverse programs are included, which aims to create a chemical synergy for researchers, kids and machines.

Buildings are wrapped in an adaptive and consecutive ceramic mesh which can change density and form according to the sunlight and wind. The openness of a single unit depends on the program hiding behind. The use of grasshopper helps to create a set of variations on the facade.

2

Our studio will design a state-of-the-art net-zero operation for both power and water use as a replacement facility adjacent to the Stockholm Resilience Centre site.

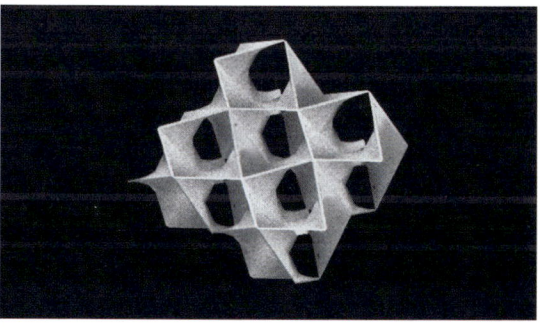

1

STOC-KELP HARBOR
Chengyang Wang

Sustainability should not only focus on building materials and assemblies as the primary solution to environmental stewardship while neglecting a more wholistic approach to living with and practicing resilience. We can explore more radical, responsible and inventive research and planning to address global warming.

My design is a state-of-the-art net-zero operation for both power and water use as a replacement facility adjacent to the Stockholm Resilience

Mistra

"The world faces major challenges associated with our environment, human use of natural resources and our impact on our surroundings. The Swedish Foundation for Strategic Environmental Research (Mistra) plays an active part in meeting these challenges by investing in the kind of research that helps to bring about sustainable development of society. This is done by investing in various initiatives in which researchers and users make joint contributions to solving key environmental problems."

1 – *Stoc-Kelp Harbor* by Chengyang Wang, Text Description

2 – *Stoc-Kelp Harbor* by Chengyang Wang, Snow

Through Mistra's vision, Stockholm Resilience Centre (SRC) was tasked to "make a difference for sustainable development by building a world-leading research centre that would take the interdisciplinary research on linked ecological and social systems significant steps forward" and provide "insights and means for the development of management and governance practices in order to secure ecosystem services." They took on this task with great excitement, asking new questions, collaborating across disciplinary borders, and generating new findings and insights of relevance for sustainability.

They regularly and flexibly adjust and restructure our research to stay at the frontier. Since the beginning this was essential because the science is moving rapidly. In their first ten years, research has accumulated on what it means to live in the Anthropocene —the age of humanity. Industrialized societies are shaping the Earth system at the planetary scale. Humanity has moved from being part of the biosphere —that thin sphere around the planet which supports all life on Earth—to the prime driver of change in the biosphere. Humanity is truly intertwined in biosphere processes from local to global scales. It is becoming clear that a resilient biosphere serves as the basis for just and sustainable development, for human health and well-being, and transformations towards global sustainability are necessary, definitely possible, and highly desirable."

3   SUSTAINABLE INCUBATOR
Jingwei Sun and Yihao Zhang

This is an incubator located next to the Stockholm resilience center. It mainly consists of five functional areas arranged in two connected blocks, one of which is the exhibition area of purified water process, the other integrates the catering and entertainment area, residential area, hotel area and start-up green tech companies.The building itself can be regarded as a water purification machine for sustainable development. Starting from the lake water on the other side of the road, the lake water is pumped and purified in first phase through the water pump. Then it is transported to the building for the second phase purification through solar energy and electrolytic cell. The purified water is used for all functions of the building, and the surplus water resources are transported back to the lake water. The whole process not only ensures the use of water resources in the building, but also purifies the lake water and protects the environment.

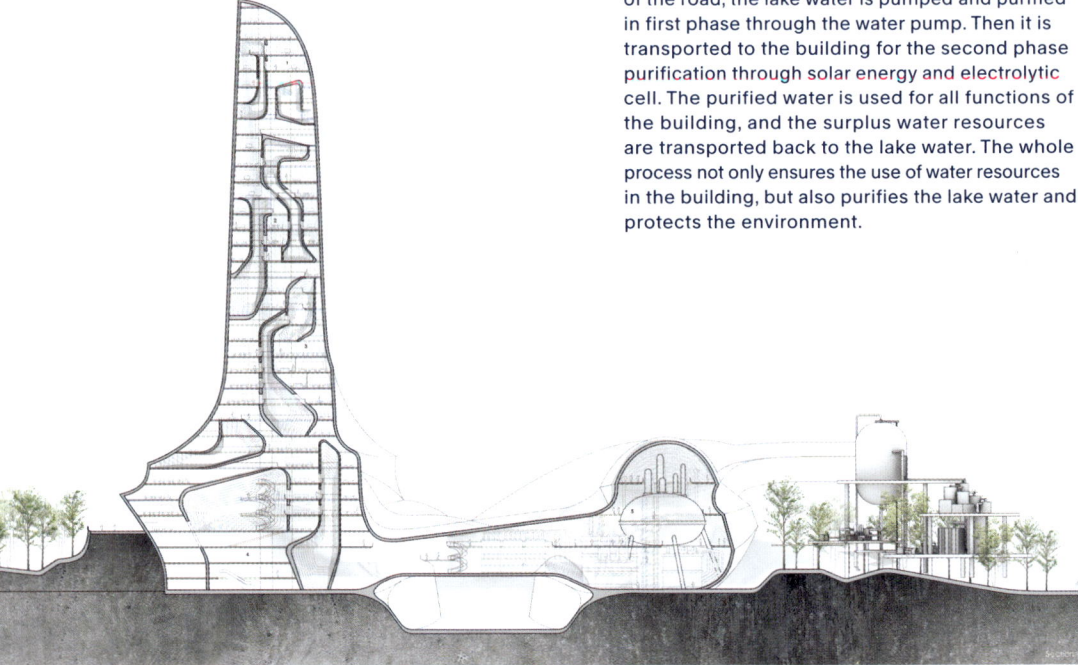

4

3 – *Sustainable Incubator* by Jingwei Sun and Yihao Zhang, Text Description

4 – *Sustainable Incubator* by Jingwei Sun and Yihao Zhang, Elevation

5 – Joe MacDonald in Studio Review

STOCKHOLM FOOD LABORATORY
Zhenqin Dong and Xin Yi Chen

In collaboration with Stockholm University's research in agriculture and food production, the project aims to promote resilient food system, by providing the city with an urban vertical farming, landscape farming and fundamental Biochar production infrastructures and research labs. The organic waste of agriculture produced by the project would be transformed into biochar, a chemical which enhances food quality and quantity, as well as reduces soil degradation. The biochar would be further used in the building's food production process, forming a closed system loop within the project scope. The two twin towers sweep up from the landscape with partially exposed vertical greenhouses orientated to maximize natural daylight. The interior spaces and vegetations are protected by a layer of metal mesh wrapping around the facade. The towers are interconnected with a bridge, one contributes to the production and research of biochar and innovative food systems, the other one contains public dining and researcher housings.

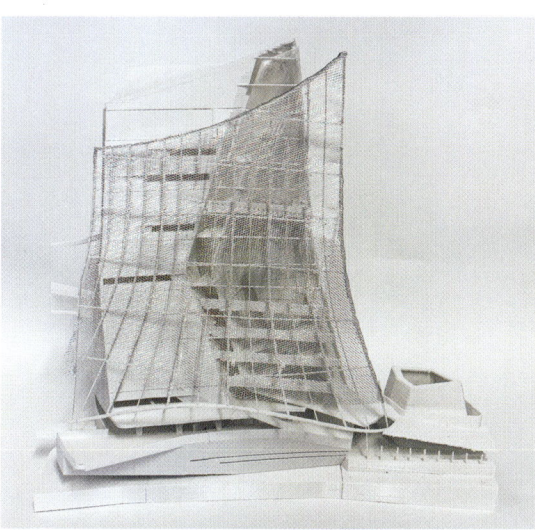

6

7

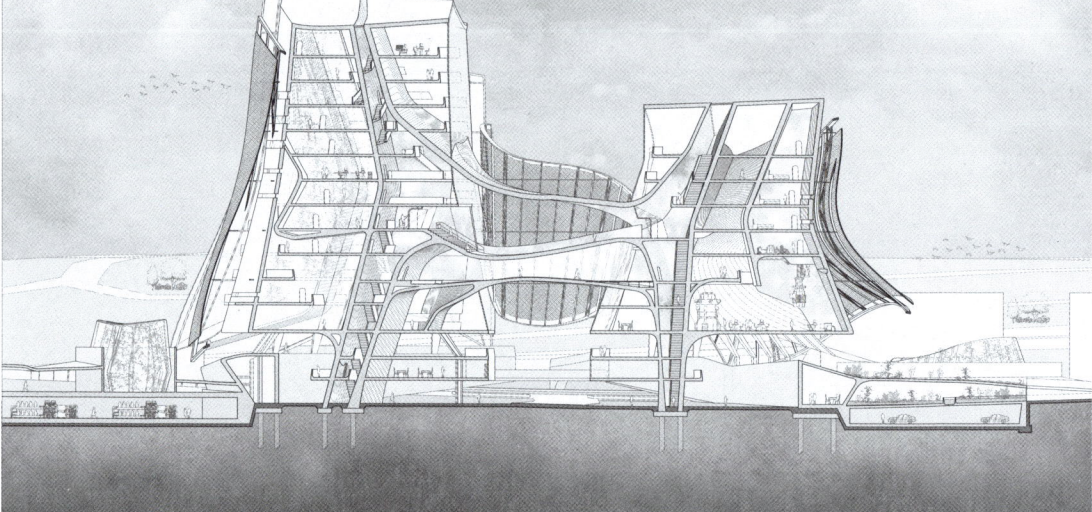

8

6 – *Stockholm Food Laboratory* by Zhenqin Dong & Xin Yi Chen, Model Chunk
7 – *Stockholm Food Laboratory* by Zhenqin Dong & Xin Yi Chen, Rendering
8 – *Stockholm Food Laboratory* by Zhenqin Dong & Xin Yi Chen, Long Section

STOCKHOLM PROJECT
Meng Zhen and Yiran Fu

The project is located next to a campus in Stockholm, where, as a result of the study, water pollution has been a persistent problem. What we want to focus on is climate crisis and the relationship between building and environmental impact. Our design is a machine driven by wind power to absorb the pollution in the seawater, while purifying the seawater and providing fresh water for the residential building on top.

This tower is a self-sustainable public infrastructure. At the same time, it also has the function of enjoyment. Tourists and residents can visit the process of energy conversion process. This project shows that sustainability is not a burden but should improve the quality of people's lives and could also be aesthetic and articulate to make a dynamic experience. It's built right in the middle of the sea and is now part of everyday activities. The tower is ecologically, economically, and socially sustainable.

9

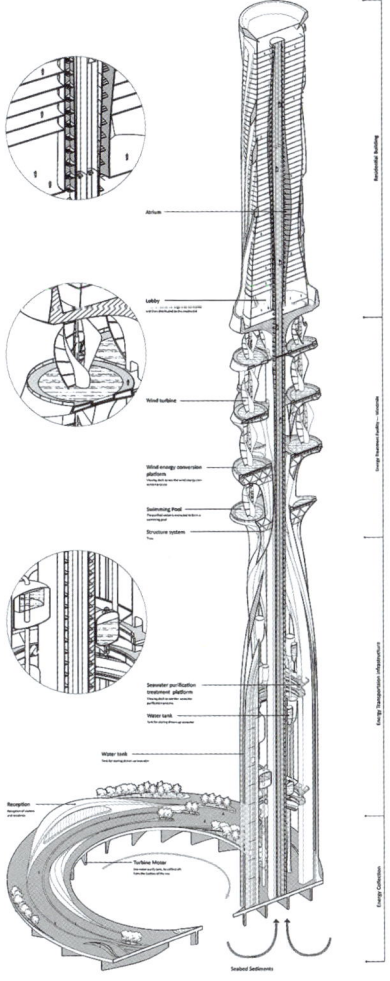

10

11

12

9 – *Stockholm Project* by Meng Zhen & Yiran Fu, Render Aerial
10 – *Stockholm Project* by Meng Zhen & Yiran Fu, Render Lookup

11 –*Stockholm Project* by Meng Zhen & Yiran Fu, Section
12– *Stockholm Project* by Meng Zhen & Yiran Fu, Infrastructur

MADRID NUEVO NORTE

Thom Mayne (CRET PROFESSOR OF PRACTICE)
Nicole Bronola (TA)
Eui-Sung Yi (TA)

Thom Mayne: (Cret Professor of Practice) Founded Morphosis in 1972. – Mayne's distinguished honors include the Pritzker Prize (2005) and the AIA Gold Medal (2013). – He was appointed to the President's Committee on the Arts and Humanities in 2009.

Heterogenous Ecologies of Combinatory Urbanism

Never static, the contemporary city is dynamic, unstable, and increasingly difficult to trace as a linear process. The true territory for innovation in urban architecture begins as a critique of the totalizing singularity that motivated modernist thought. Such a critique is possible through the design of the operational strategies that deal with the multiple and overlapping forces of a highly complex and entirely uncertain "collective form." This entails work that in both its physical and mental state identifies the particular, the individuality unique to each situation, maximizing difference, developing a coherency, a consistency made of the partial, of fragments or juxtapositions.

As architects, it is vital to understand the city as an evolving organism, an open-ended design that contrasts markedly with the closed-end assemblage that is associated with architecture. So how does one design for an open-ended ecology where the evolution is not authored or predicted at every detail? By designing the systems.

Combinatory Urbanism offers an alternative method of urban production that designs flexible frameworks of *relational and operational systems* within which activities, events, and programs can organically realign and redefine themselves. As such, Combinatory Urbanism, engages the premise of continuous process over static form, identifying the socio-political imperatives of architecture while pushing formal organizational possibilities.

Introduction to Madrid Nuevo Norte:

As the third largest city in the EU (after London and Berlin), Madrid's urban plan has supported and performed aggressively to address the complex infrastructural, social, and economic issues

1
Urban Jungle
Sirui Chen

100+ is a dense urban jungle envisioning a new relationship between the city and nature. The project is a car free prototype development covering the site with over 100% greenspace and simultaneously adds more residential, commercial, and facility space than the current proposal for Madrid Nuevo Norte. 100+ is the missing link connecting the new north to the existing parks of Madrid and the green loop providing a much needed urban lung to filter the air of Madrid.

2

1 – *Urban Jungle* by Sirui Chen, Josh Ketchum, Yi Lu and Xuezhu Sun, Description

2 – *Urban Jungle* by Sirui Chen, Josh Ketchum, Yi Lu and Xuezhu Sun, Plan

demanded by its residents and visitors. Anchored and defined by natural and man-made infrastructure, from the Rio Manzanares to the Paseo de la Castellana, the city's physical and spatial organization has demonstrated itself as being very capable, resilient and expandable. However, for the past 25 years, the city has not had the full machinations of all its available infrastructural sites. Despite the celebrated southern anchor of Atocha Station, its bookend northern counterpart, Chamartin station, suffered through an underperforming plan by defaulting to a large transportation wasteland that limited city life and prevented a healthy cohesion of the surrounding new suburban housing plans known as PAUs.

Now, after a quarter of a century, diverse community and political stakeholders have come together to agree on a new future to resolve the Charmartin issue. Located on an incredibly large site on the northern end of Madrid, the district recently rebranded MADRID NUEVO NORTE, will emerge as a dutiful anchor and receive the northern terminus of Paseo de la Castellana and offer itself as a cultural and business hub for the adjacent towns.

Madrid Nueovo Norte (MNN) is a rare opportunity to examine the premises of Combinatory Urbanism. Combinatory Urbanism's ability to establish its own planning raison d'etre through the interrogation of Madrid's diverse development strategies will be translated into operational, programmatic, and cultural systems.

3 – Studio Travel

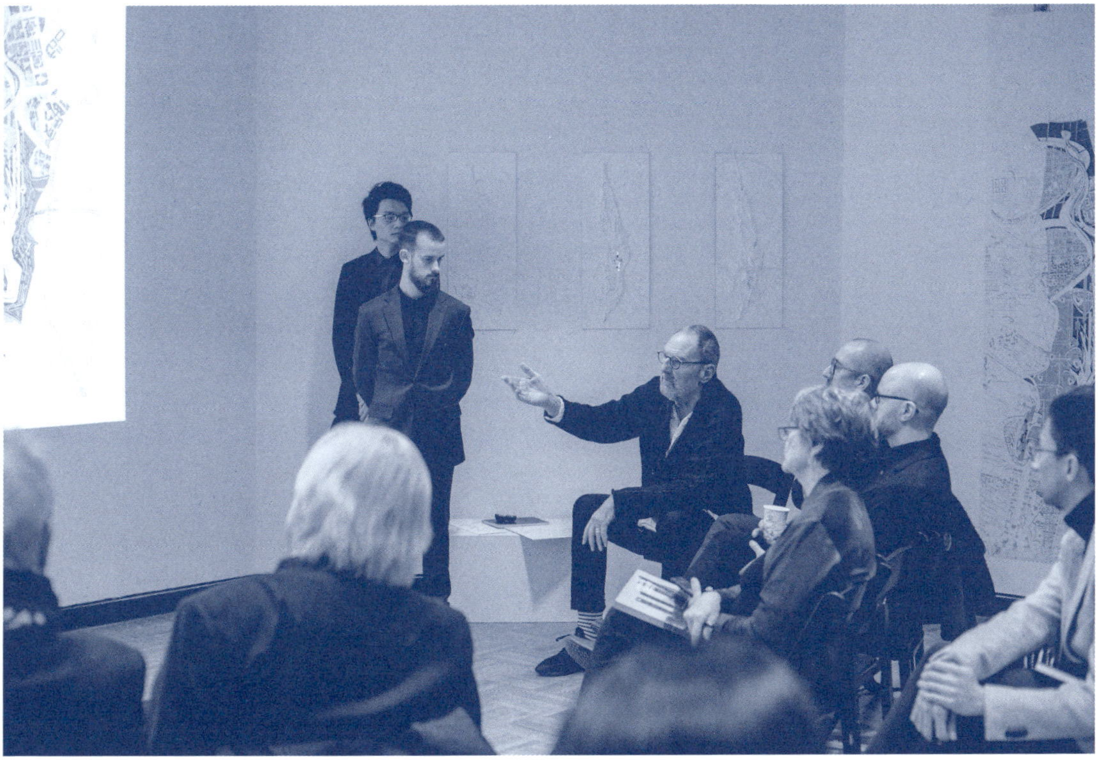

4

5

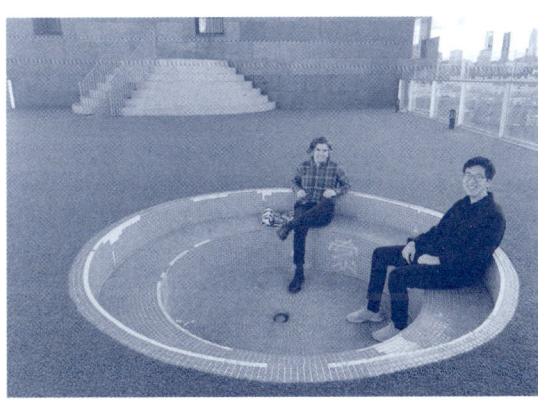

4 – Thom Mayne in Studio Review
5 – Studio Travel

CUADRIENAL DE MADRID
John Dun, Eliana Weiner and Kaiyi Cao

Increasing strain on the existing business and Gothic quarters of the city of Madrid cause: a relocation of commercial districts, an increase in residential density, and requires transportation capable of serving two distinct nodes of the city that are otherwise isolated from one another. The development of a second node calls for the creation of Retiro Norte, a large public park, which acts as the staging site for the Madrid Cuadrienal. The introduction of an exposition of architectural pavilions and transportation exhibits invites tourism, builds up existing communities, and puts Madrid in an exclusive class of international cities such as Milan and Venice.

6

7

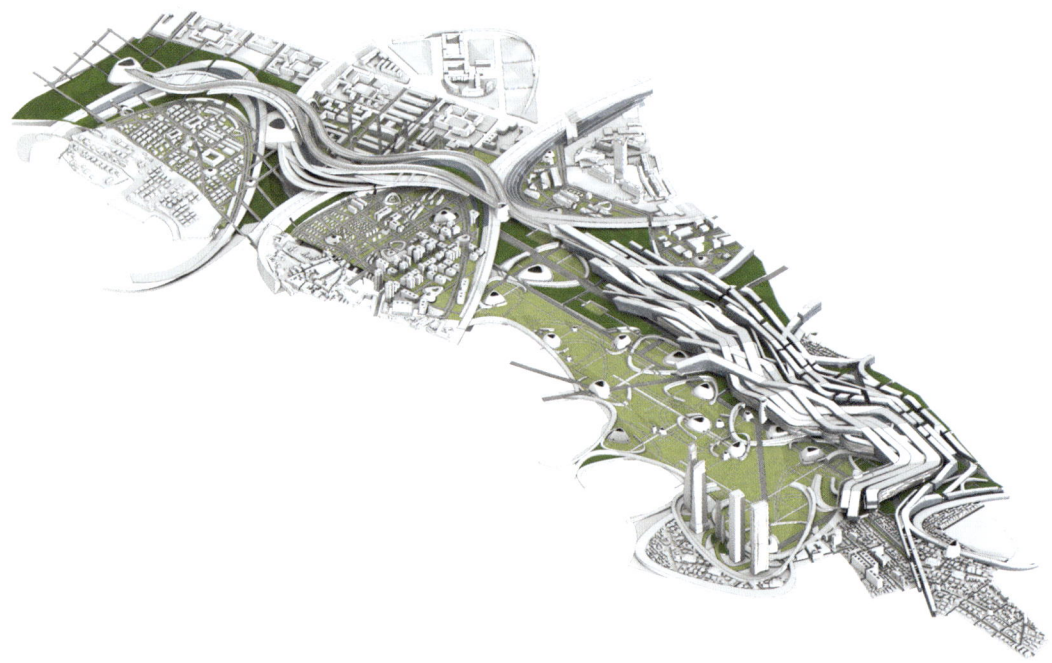
8

6 – *Cuadrienal de Madrid* by John Dun, Eliana Weiner and Kaiyi Cao, Render

7 – *Cuadrienal de Madrid* by John Dun, Eliana Weiner and Kaiyi Cao, Render

8 – *Cuadrienal de Madrid* by John Dun, Eliana Weiner and Kaiyi Cao, Overall Axon

PARALLEL CENTRO
Chanho Noh, Sien Hang Cheng and Yujie Li

The urban project situated in northern Madrid expands on the opportunity for the university extension while solving issues though transportation and interconnecting several programs throughout the site. The center circular areas are a part of the University District where a campus and hospital are connected to adjacent existing hospitals. To the south lies the central business district with office space, and the north with low rise residentials. The green space between the south and the north is to provide nature to the neighbor-ing population while serving both the residential and university districts. Together, the urban proposal transforms the northern end of Madrid to a new business and hospital community.

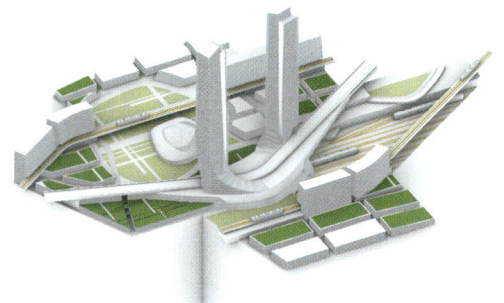

9

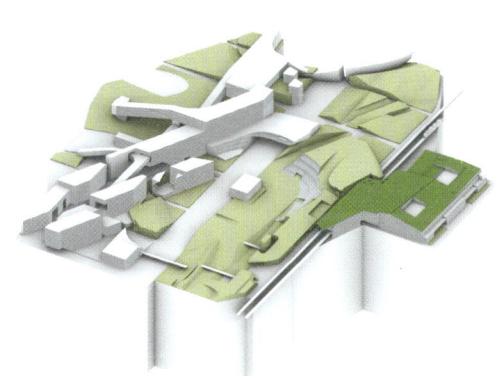

10

11

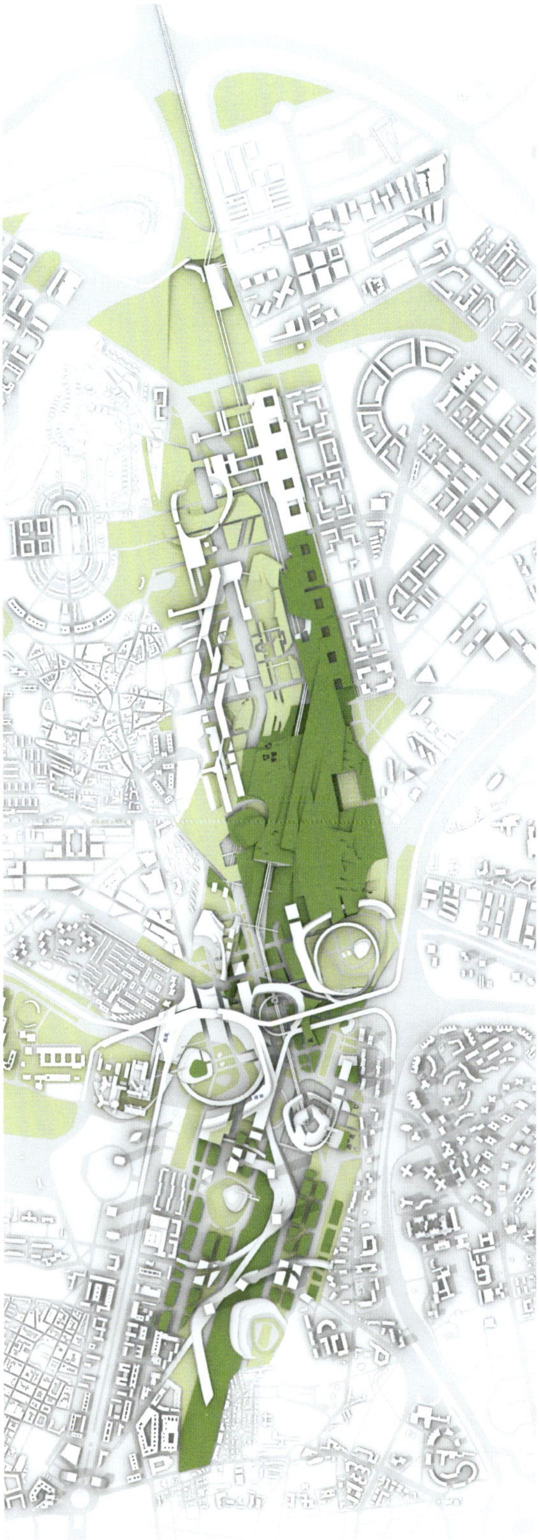

12

9 – *Parallel Centro* by Chanho Noh, Sien Hang Cheng and Yujie Li, Chunk CBD
10 – *Parallel Centro* by Chanho Noh, Sien Hang Cheng and Yujie Li, Chunk Residential
11 – *Parallel Centro* by Chanho Noh, Sien Hang Cheng and Yujie Li, Chunk District
12 – *Parallel Centro* by Chanho Noh, Sien Hang Cheng and Yujie Li, Plan

ICONIC BUILDINGS FOR A FUTURE SOCIETY
WHEN FORM BECOMES GESTALT

Wolf D. Prix (VISITING LECTURER)
Abigail Coover (TA)

Wolf D. Prix (Visiting Lecturer): born in 1942 in Vienna, is co-founder, Design Principal and CEO of COOP HIMMELB(L)AU. He studied architecture at the Vienna University of Technology, the Architectural Association of London as well as at the Southern California Institute of Architecture (SCI-Arc) in Los Angeles.

Fiberoptic facades, generative machines, green washes, artificially intelligent friends and optimistic dystopias characterize the exploration of Iconic Buildings for a Future Society throughout this semester. Is the near future a modifi-cation or our current reality or an idea that we cannot currently imagine? What is an iconic building? Does a building start as an icon of a society or does it become one through its relationship to its society over time? How can an existing city be redefined for the future? These are some of the questions that this studio has begun to contemplate.

Through a multifaceted design approach that included digital video clips, physical models, diagrams and collage, the studio has evolved through a linear series of steps:

1.
DESIGN PARTY PLATFORM FOR A FUTURE SOCIETY

2.
DESIGN ICONIC BUILDING FOR YOUR FUTURE SOCIETY ON A SITE OF YOUR CHOICE

3.
MERGE YOUR ICONIC BUILDING WITH AN EXISTING BUILDING

4.
ELOCATE YOUR ICONIC BUILDING TO LOWER MANHATTAN OF A NEW NEW YORK OF THE NEAR FUTURE

A project that began the semester as a cultural investigation has resulted in one that challenges and interrogates the future of urban city planning. New design methods have led to new ideas of building methods through destructive construction of transportation, education, housing, infrastructure, culture, and climate design reform in the production of a new unique and cohesive city plan.

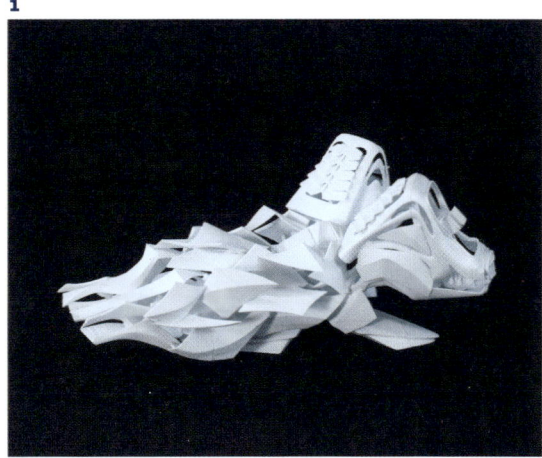

THE NEW DEAL
Rentian Liu and Frank Xuefeng Li

32.5344° N; 117.1227° W, there is a place called Friendship Park between Tijuana, Mexico, and San Diego, California. It is the only place along the Southern California border where families can legally reunite on both sides of the fence.

For us, building the Wall to separate people is an undemocratic approach. This political action reflects the bureaucratic and hierarchical structure we all face in today's modern society. So, can we have a society that has maximum democracy and freedom, minimum socioeconomic inequality? Can we create a public space where people from both sides could meet with each other, exchange their culture and ideas, creating a binational third place? With those inquiries, we investigated the ecological as well as sociopolitical potentials along the border, which shows that except for disconnecting people, the border wall will also disrupt wildlife refuges, threaten diverse landscapes and exacerbate flooding. Rather than building the Wall, we proposed a Green New Deal—a future building as a point of departure that can take down the fences and create a 2,000 miles green corridor for both sides. The linear corridor with a mix of green facilities such as solar

1 – The New Deal by Rentian Liu and Frank Xuefeng Li, Render
2 – The New Deal by Rentian Liu and Frank Xuefeng Li, Model

power, wind turbines, and desalination would have a historic positive effect for both nations, which will trigger unprecedented economic development at a different level. The proposed building will lead this transformation to come to life.

The proposed building is not only a new way to look at architecture but a new approach to solving our urgent environmental issues. The research has shown construction and demolition materials constitute a significant waste stream in the United States. These various C&D materials can be diverted from disposal and managed into new productive uses. A fascinating, moving part will depart from the main structure moving along through the border, eating the Wall and other materials, recycling them into newly engineered products. The architecture itself has become a big robot that plays a part in the construction process of future city planning, synthesizing nature, and architecture with advanced technologies. This new approach will allow us to design and plan our habitats to produce ecosystem services rather than depleting them. It is time to give back nature instead of taking from nature!

3

4

3-4 – Studio Travel

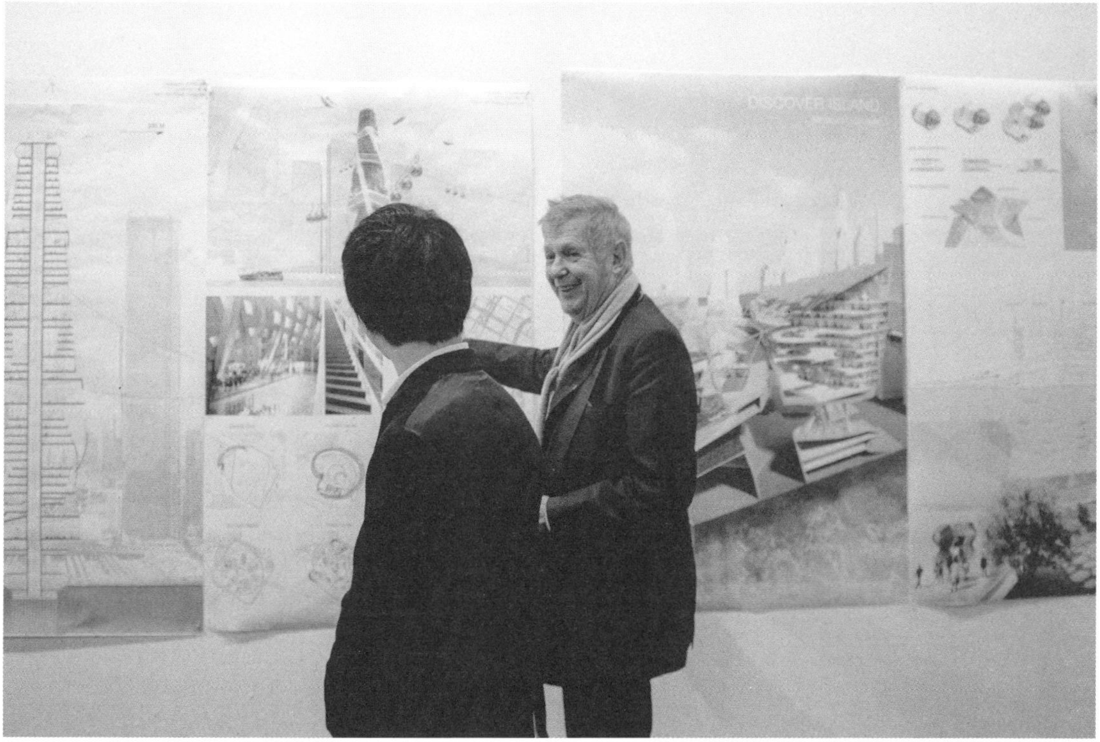

5

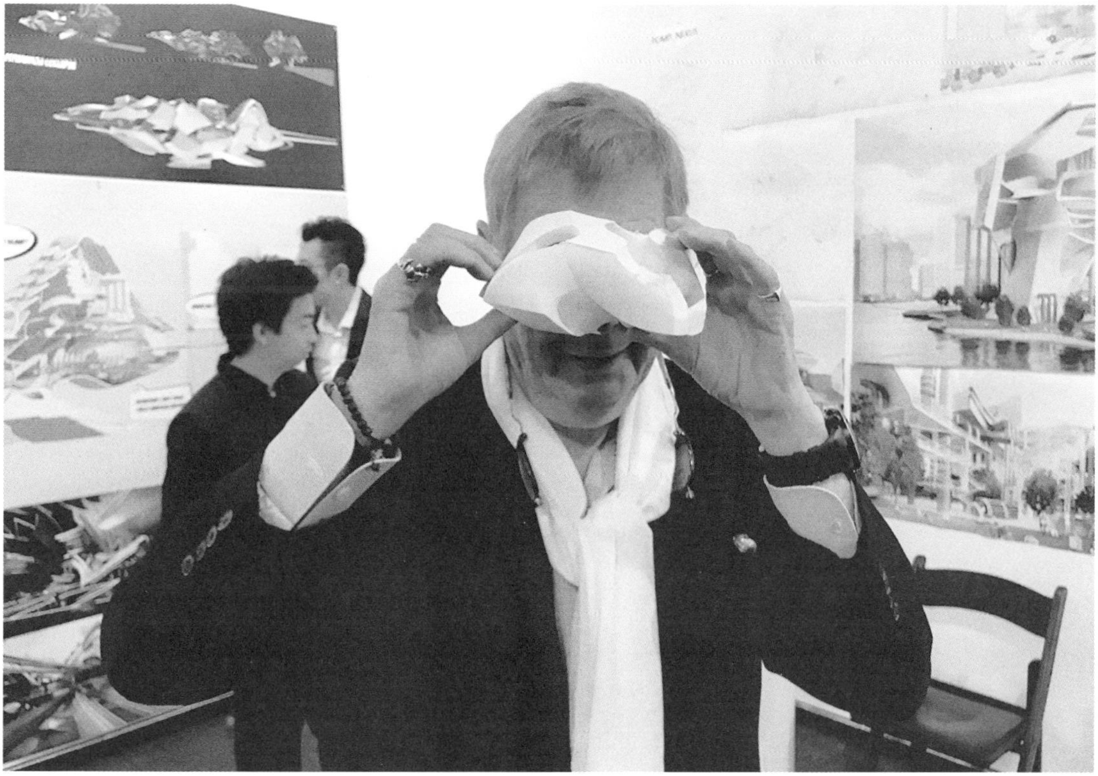

6

5-6 – Wolf D. Prix in Studio Review

POMP-NEXUS
Rui Lu and Neng Zhu

Pomp-Nexus: the ceremony and splendid display of a connection. In the future city, methods are taking to reduce the time for people to do their work. The pomp-Nexus is acting as the connection between existing buildings and the exterior, which becomes the place to embrace a life full of varieties. New adaptions connect the existing interior spaces of different functions, invade the city and break the limit of buildings. Spaces of different volume and appearances inside the future connections respond to a complexity of a slow life where human enjoys planting, relaxing, playing with the aid of technology. With infrastructures installed for robots in between new structures, technology replaced human forces to do supplementary works that help future human live more efficiently and alleviate the psychological pressure in the increasingly busy life. The ground is giving back to the greenery where people, with their robotic friends, can wonder and play. Thus, people in the futuristic community is connected in various ways within a lively, complex and iconic network.

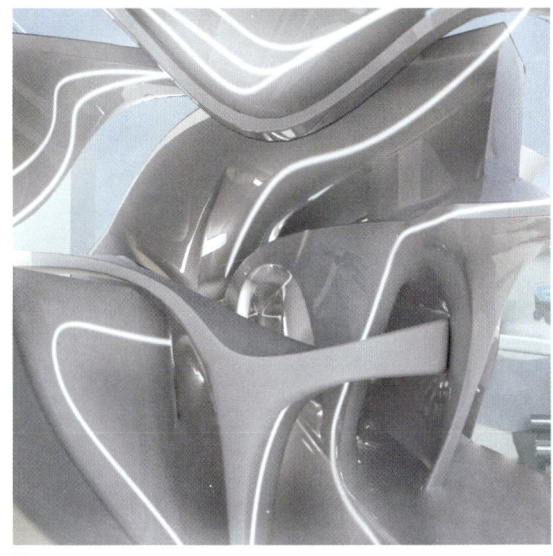

7

8

9

7 – *Pomp-Nexus* by Rui Lu and Neng Zhu, Interior
8 – *Pomp-Nexus* by Rui Lu and Neng Zhu, Section
9 – *Pomp-Nexus* by Rui Lu and Neng Zhu, Exterior

DATAPLEX
Ruxin Zheng, Matthew Price

Global warming has been an ongoing dilemma and is a looming crisis that will affect humanity's destiny. Ironically, it is caused by human activity, which is done primarily by the burning of fossil fuels that pump greenhouse gases into the atmosphere. While we need energy to survive, polluting fossil fuels are still the most accessible and economical energy resource. This presents an opportunity to find new ways of living by embracing current and futuristic technologies, which will allow humans to adopt to a rapidly changing world by utilizing renewable energy sources in a new way.

The DATAPLEX is proposing a new way to solve these crises by reforming Government into a self-governed and futuristic residential community with new, big-data technology, like Blockchain, to ensure information authenticity and transparency of their choices and effected living systems, all supported by a geothermal energy plant in the form of a new, iconic tower typology.

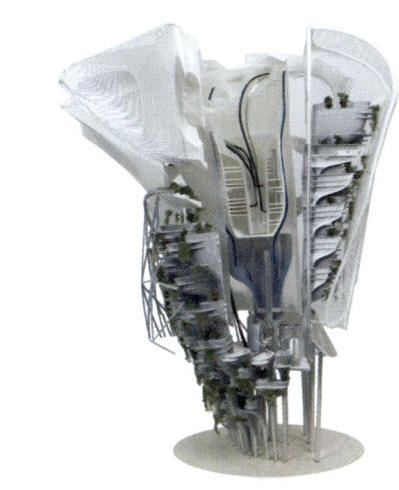

10

11

12

13

10 – *Dataplex* by Ruxin Zheng and Matthew Price, Model
11 – *Dataplex* by Ruxin Zheng and Matthew Price, Section Render
12 – *Dataplex* by Ruxin Zheng and Matthew Price, Interior
13 – *Dataplex* by Ruxin Zheng and Matthew Price, Elevation Render

MULTIFARIOUS MATTER: LES HALLES 2030

Robert Stuart-Smith (ASSISTANT PROFESSOR OF ARCHITECTURE)
Musab Badahdah (TA)

Robert Stuart-Smith (Assistant Professor of Architecture, Director of MSD-RAS): Robert is a founding director of rs-sdesign, a co-founding director of the collaborative research practice - Kokkugia and a Studio Course Master in the AA School's Design Research Laboratory (AA. DRL) in London. Robert studied architecture in the UK, France and Australia and holds a Masters in Architecture + Urbanism from the Architectural Association School of Architecture's Design Research Laboratory (AA.DRL). He has practiced architecture in the UK, USA and Australia

Urban retail is undergoing a significant transformation due to the rise of online shopping. Amazon Go is the first supermarket to allow customers to walk out without paying at a register, while a suite of new fashion boutiques utilize virtual assistants to deliver clothing to change rooms at the touch of a button. Beyond novelty, these applications of technology transform not only the experience of shopping, but also the square footage, fit-out, staffing, security, supply and delivery logistics. Apple's park-bench and tree-scape interiors, or Nike's half-court basketball facilities have become a destination in themselves. Extending beyond merchandise, these retail ventures priveleddge experience over sales, recognizing a sale could take place at a future date online. These experiential retail stores create a fuzzy edge to public space, capable of enhancing our urban experiences.

Inspired by Levi Bryant's *Democracy of Objects* and Stan Allen's *Field Conditions*, the studio operated through both object and field, embracing all site objects and actors as active participants in design expression and considering them as integral to architecture. Material considerations were also investigated through the designing of affects strategized through fabrication methods developed within a collaborative workshop at Cemex's Global Research Centre in Switzerland during Travel Week, and through proxy concrete pouring methods using Penn's ARI Robotics Lab. Multi-material concrete casting was explored within design propositions that addressed water flow, utilizing scomputer-simulations to strategically distribute soft-landscaping and Cemex's Pervia (porous) concrete within design proposals. Although the projects were significantly large in scale, a material scale is explored that relates to the larger scale urban and landscape proposals.

1   MULTIFARIOUS MATTER: LES HALLES 2030
     Akarsh Sabhaney and Dongyun Kim

The project draws inspiration from two seminal proposals for Paris's Parc De La Villette; Bernard Tschumi's field of follies and OMA's striated field of diverse landscapes. We re-imagine Les Halles as a three-dimensional heterogeneous field of public space compressed into a three sub-terranean layers that connect to Les Halles RER and Metro train platforms, and provide an outdoor park above.

for the offices of Lab Architecture Studio, Grimshaw Architects, Arup's AGU (Advanced Geometry Unit) and Balmond Studio as an algorithmic design consultant.
Collaborating Partner: Cemex Global Research HQ, Switzerland

Studio Travel: Biel, Switzerland and Paris, France
1 – *Multifarious Matter: Les Halles 2030:* by Akarsh Sabhaney and Dongyun Kim, Site Plan

The studio explored a speculative near-present future, a post-human retail and public space in the context of emerging autonomous transportation infrastructure including e-scooters, air-taxis and autonomous cars, in one of central Paris's most important transportation and retail hubs; Les Halles. Les Halles functioned as a market until a central and suburban railway station and shopping centre was constructed in 1971. The development was ambitious yet is considered a socio-political failure, and a venue for fastfood and drug addicts. Its inadequacies were addressed by the recent construction of a new retail centre. Berger Anziutti Architects's "La Canopée" enlarged the park, physically connecting it to a pedestrian concourse that crosses central Paris through to the Pompidou Centre in Beaubourg. While La Canopée is an improvement, it did not challenge our existing concept of retail. An opportunity remains in re-considering the nature of urban parks and retail as a post-human entrepreneurial proposition, which may involve a downsizing, up-sizing or a redistribution of space for shoppers versus goods and entertainment or wellness vs retail. While Paris has been the site of seminal urban park concepts, Bernard Tschumi and OMA's competition proposals for Park de la Villette are now 35 years old. The rise of Industry 4.0 may be potentially destabilizing to urban space as is currently known, yet it offers new opportunities for establishing complex and dynamic relationships between a park's myriad of occupants and events. The studio explored alternative concepts for re-casting public space adjacent to new models of retail in this socio-political and economically charged Parisian transportation hub.

2   MULTIFARIOUS MATTER: LES HALLES 2030
Xiaoyi Peng and Mo Shen

Paris is a one of the world's most active fashion centers. We propose to bring a unique form of fashion factory into the heart of Paris, and to make it available for use by all. With Industry 4.0, it is now feasible to rapidly produce individually mass-customized clothing centrally in a minimal amount of space. The proposal imagines that the ability to make factories small, and to incorporate mass-customization enables them to operate in more public environments. Our proposal situates the factory within a field of hard and soft landscaped public space. The factory is semi-submerged to reduce its overall height, while enabling accessibility and visibility into the factory spaces from both the landscape above ground, and the transport spaces below. The building comprises of three main activities: Customization, Fabrication, and Fashion Related Activities. Visitors can customize their own designs or other provided designs through an online interface after providing a 3D-scan of their body data (scanning is available on site). The customized design is then sent to a robotic production line, fabricated, packaged, and distributed through well-connected delivery systems. Adjacent public spaces are used for fashion-related activities such as workshops, fashion shows, etc.

2 – *Multifarious Matter: Les Halles 2030* by Xiaoyi Peng and Mo Shen, Render
3 – Concrete is not inert or monolithic. Penn Architecture students have been exploring ways to engage in material agencies, and enable design to operate through material dynamics and novel solutions to fabrication. Experiments with the phase-changing, viscous nature of concrete help us to speculate on larger acts of construction, and to operate with no abstraction between design and manufacture — just concrete action!

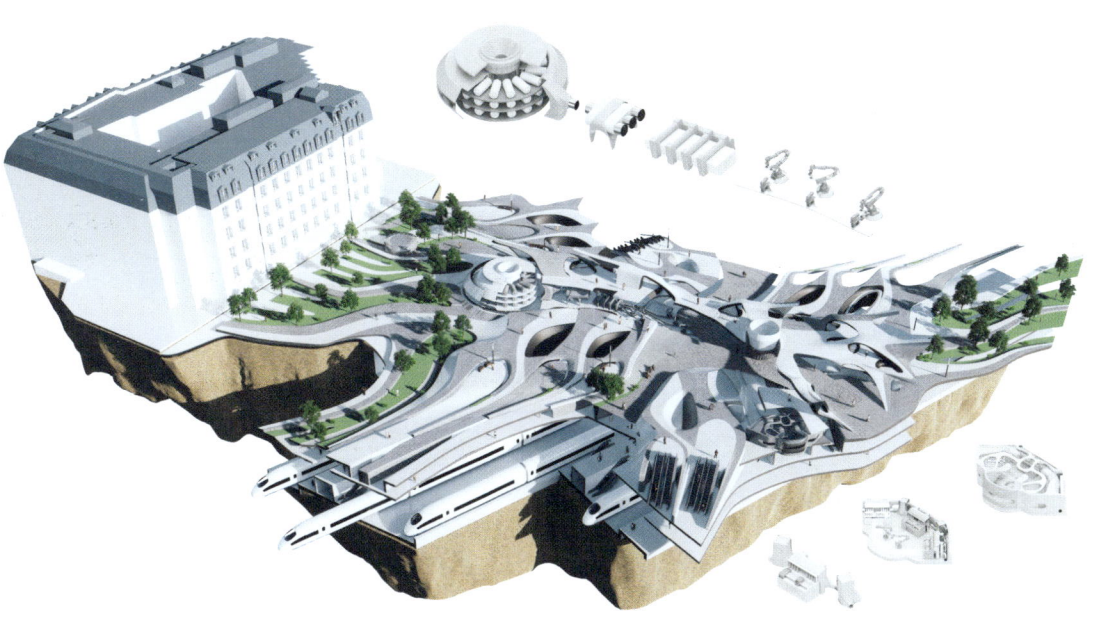

4 – *Multifarious Matter: Les Halles 2030* by Xiaoyi Peng and Mo Shen, Chunk
5 – Studio workshop at Cemex Global R&D, Switzerland

MULTIFARIOUS MATTER: LES HALLES 2030
Sihan Zhu, Lingyun Yang and Rui Huang

The project speculates on how new and emerging forms of transport might facilitate a high-speed physical shopping experience. Through the use of e-scooters and driverless cars, a drive-through retail and public space experience is proposed, where high-speed circulation and spatial organization drive alternative forms of architectural typology. Explored as a post-humanist architecture, the proposal incorporates many actors such as transportation vehicles and infrastructure are integral to the architecture itself.

6

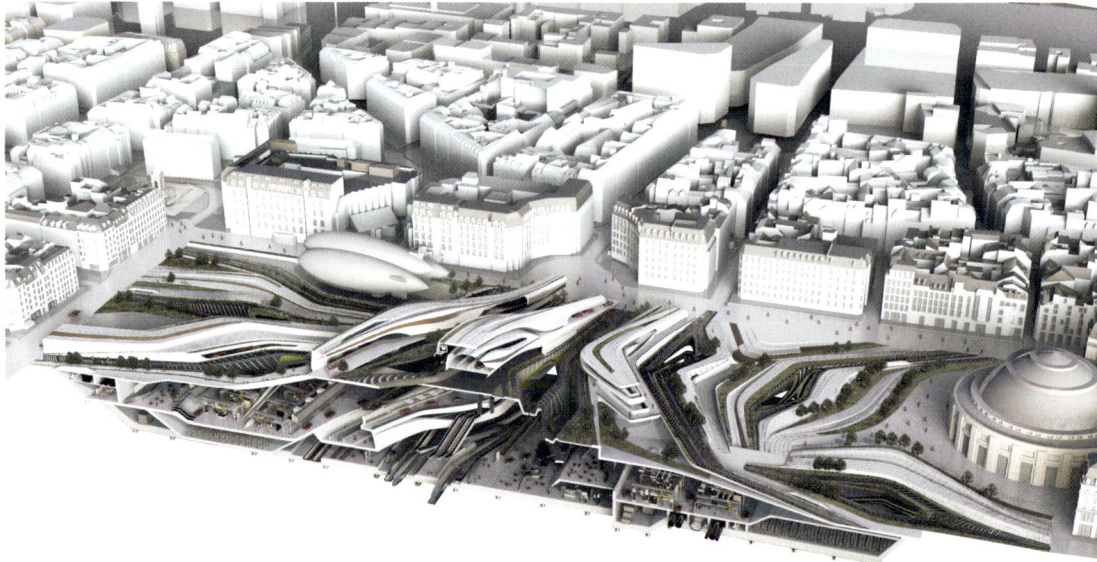

7

8

6 – *Multifarious Matter: Les Halles 2030* by Sihan Zhu, Lingyun Yang and Rui Huang, Perspective
7 – *Multifarious Matter: Les Halles 2030* by Sihan Zhu, Lingyun Yang and Rui Huang, Section
8 – *Multifarious Matter: Les Halles 2030* by Sihan Zhu, Lingyun Yang and Rui Huang, Plan

MULTIFARIOUS MATTER: LES HALLES 2030
Hao Zeng and Cai Zhang

Central Paris, and the site Les Halles in particular embody a strong atmosphere and practice of music. The project extends this into the new Les Halles transportation and retail centre as a soundscape. Landscape, retail, RER and Metro rail transit spaces are fused with a series of sound experiences, that encourage large, organized and small impromptu sound performances within the public realm. A series of spatial hybrids are proposed to support this including a auditorium/atrium/escalator entrance space that links the most public corner of the park to the underground. These diverse sound sources create a field of sound across the site that are open to visitor participation as audience or in performance. This field condition also integrates a rainwater water collection and distribution concept as integral to the spatial and formal articulation of the landscape, that incorporates a series of trees in locations that attract more water runoff, enabling passive watering.

9

10

11

9 – *Multifarious Matter: Les Halles 2030* by Hao Zeng and Cai Zhang, Render
10 – *Multifarious Matter: Les Halles 2030* by Hao Zeng and Cai Zhang, Plan
11 – *Multifarious Matter: Les Halles 2030* by Hao Zeng and Cai Zhang, Section Render

[ARCH 711] TOPICS IN ARCHITECTURE THEORY I
MODERN ARCHITECTURE IN JAPAN
Dr. Ariel Genadt

This seminar explores the diversity of forms and meanings that modern architecture took on in Japan since its industrialization in the 19th century. With this focus, it raises questions on the capacity of construction, materials and form to express and represent cultural, aesthetic, climatic, social and political concerns. Salient topics and milestones in Japan's architectural history are examined as a mirror of parallel practices in the world. The seminar begins with an introduction of canonical public buildings as these would reappear as references in the work of 20th century architects. Resistance to environmental forces and resilience are presented as two approaches to living within the environment. An overview of domestic architecture and *sukiya* teahouses, and a visit to *Shofuso House and Garden* demonstrate aspects of a locally, climatically-tuned practice. The socio-political context for the establishment of architecture as a profession in Tokyo is explained, with examples of the radical turn from carpentry to masonry in the Meiji Era. Wright, Raymond, Taut and Le Corbusier's Japanese disciples are presented as pioneers of Japanese modernism in the 1920s and 30s. Kenzo Tange's work elaborates the tensions between tradition and creation, in tectonic and technological expression. The work of the Metabolist architects in the 1960s is also examined from these aspects, as are their similarities to contemporary currents elsewhere. Then, questions of formal abstraction and symbolism are studied in the postmodern works of Arata Isozaki and Tadao Ando. In contrast, later works by Kengo Kuma exemplify the use of articulation and a reappraisal of tradition towards 'weak architecture,' reflecting a shift in the relation to the environment. Architects' reactions to the 2011 East Japan Earthquake open a discussion of the meaning of architectural resilience. The seminar concludes with works by Toyo Ito and SANAA and their respective versions of technology-enabled, visual dematerialization.

[ARCH 711] SYMMETRY: THE ONE AND THE MANY, OR,
TOWARD A SYMMETRICAL THEORY OF ARCHITECTURE
David Salomon

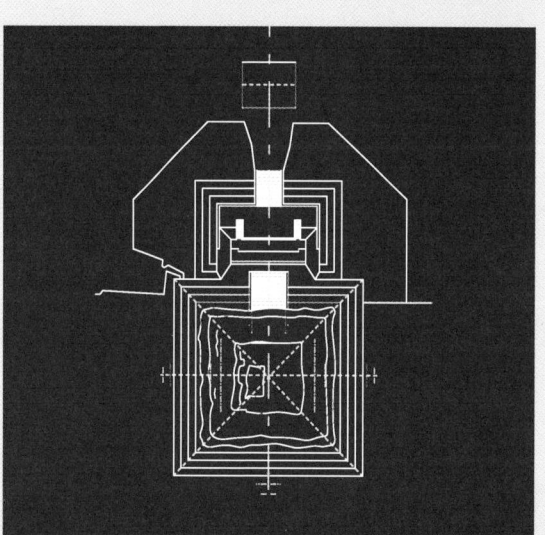

Why symmetry, why now? Is looking at it today a reactionary move, a backwards step towards insularity? Or, is it a device that serves to integrate architecture with other fields? Could it be both at once? In other words, might symmetry be a specifically architectural device that connects it to broader cultural issues, such as the tension between global and local identities? These were the questions at the core of the seminar.

The ubiquitous presence of symmetry in both the global history of architectural form and in contemporary architecture demanded that we look at texts and buildings from a wide variety of building types, traditions, eras, and geographical locations. Doing so had the advantage of allowing us to engage contemporary architectural history's attempt to place all modes of architectural production on an equal footing, and the cosmopolitan politics that comes along with this position. After an introductory set of lectures and discussions that located symmetry historically, and within contemporary architectural and intellectual thought, the seminar was structured as a series of hands one workshops and discussions in which students identified, researched and analyzed the presence of symmetry in ancient and contemporary projects, culminating in a graphic and written analysis of them.

Ultimately, it was the surprising ambiguity, elasticity and productivity of symmetry that was discovered in the seminar. Far from establishing seemingly superficial connections between disparate things, or being deployed as a universal, transcendent, and eternal structure that underlies the appearance of all things, it was recognized that symmetry functioned in architecture as it does in other intellectual arenas. That is, it serves as both a neutral analytical framework for recognizing equivalences and discrepancies, while simultaneously acting as a heuristic device for generating non-hierarchical and strangely familiar observations and objects. In other words, far from autonomous, obsolete or closed, the seminar found symmetry to be engaged, relevant and promiscuous.

[ARCH 737] SEMI-FICTITIOUS REALMS
Jeff Anderson

The pursuit of immersive digital experiences has long been a goal of the computing industry. Early wearable displays designed in the 1960s depicted simple three-dimensional graphics in ways that had never been seen before. Through trial and error, digital pioneers reframed the relationship between user and machine, and over the last five decades, have made strides that advanced both the input and output mechanisms we are so comfortable with today. As a field, architecture has been reliant on these advancements to design and document buildings, but these tools still leave the architect removed from the physicality of the design, with their work depicted as 2D lines or 3D planes alone. This course will study the evolutionary advancements made that now allow us to fully inhabit digital worlds through Virtual Reality. Using the HTC Vive and the Unity video game engine, students will generate immersive, photo-realistic models of unbuilt architectural works and explore digital/physical interactivity. From the terraces of Paul Rudolph's Lower Manhattan Expressway to Boullée's Cenotaph for Newton, the goal of this course is to breathe new life into places and spaces that have, until this time, never been built or occupied.

Through a series of lectures, this course explores the foundations and advancement of virtual reality as a mechanism of architectural representation. Alongside representation, the course also investigates the ability for contemporary VR tools to serve as a creation platform. In doing so, the course expects each project team to rigorously research and document a notable unbuilt work of architecture. Students are expected to seek out new and optimized processes of data management for utilizing Unity as a platform for visualization. Students will also be pushed to develop new storytelling and interaction techniques for architectural representation in VR.

Guest Critics Michele Gorman, Chris McAdams, Paul Ruppert, and Michael Kipfer reviewed 11 student VR projects in paperless review with two simultaneous VR headset workstations on Monday, December 16th, 2019 in the Morgan Building White Room.

[ARCH 749] INDETERMINATE DELINEATIONS
Maya Alam

Architecture has always been closely entangled with modes of vision. Devices ranging from Dürer's perspective machine to the photographic eye have strongly shaped the way we think and design the built environment of our cities. A strange loop is in place here: our world-views provide the development of specific modes of representation, of engagement with the world, and in turn they begin to have an impact in that same world, becoming an active element in the way we understand it. Put more simply, it is the technologies through which we see and experience the built environment that define the way we construct it.

In her essay "In Free-Fall" Hito Steyerl describes our current state of ubiquitous visual stimuli as a state of groundlessness for subjects and objects alike and while this is destabilizing at best, it can also be seen as an opportunity to question centralized optics like the renaissance's single-point linear perspective. While we accepted this mode of vision as an objective representation of space, it was the product of a Western worldview placing the individual at the center of its ideological construct. Today, we are faced with the challenge of developing alternative strategies to deal with the complex entanglement of images, politics and representation alike. This course asks students to look closely at the world we are constructing via new media in order to not simply accept but to find ways to become an active contributor as well as resister.

We focus on visual and physical points as anchors to tie modes of vision with modes of construction. Points play an important role in the history of visuality: if during Impressionism and Pointillism they were devised to delineate the contrast and alignments between what we see and how we see it in an attempt to investigate the mechanics of vision, it was during the post war period that Max Wertheimer's work at the Berlin School of Gestalt Psychology leveraged them as graphic elements to understand part to whole relationships central to Bauhaus' design pedagogy. They also played a central role during the seventies and eighties when the first generative artists started to use them as the smallest units to visualize design interactions between human and machine.

Today, imaging technologies are once again placing points as central elements in the construction of our contemporary visual language, transforming ever-growing datasets of partial images in three-dimensional machine-readable survey models: it is with points and aggregated clouds that we are constructing the figure of our cities. As such, they become a necessary site of design investigation to move beyond monolithic views of the world.

This class leverages the bi-product of scanning technologies—point clouds and image making—to explore inclusive modes of delineations: a visual sensibility to engage with the multi-faceted nature of the built environment. Starting from a series of pedestrian Philadelphia street corners, students are asked to transform these through multiple animations of point clouds and particles. The final deliverable is a student curated installation of monitor sculptures, that overlap digital work environments with environmental experimentation.

[ARCH 732] MATTER, MAKING & TESTING: DESIGNING WITH NEXT GENERATION PRECAST CONCRETE
Richard Garber

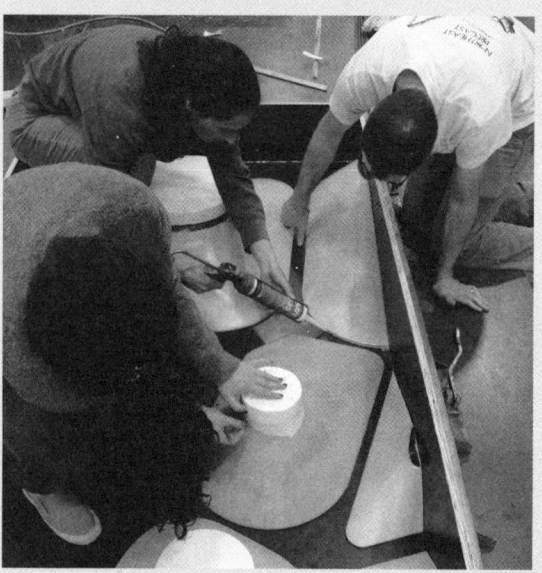

This seminar focuses on precast concrete and specifically its materiality—how it is manufactured and the logistics of its assembly—and its cultural affects through both traditional uses within the urban environment as well as new approaches to building typologies such as housing. Through a strategic partnership with Northeast Precast (NEP), based in Millville, NJ, students enrolled in the seminar will gain access to places where precast concrete is made, formed, and put into action. In addition to readings and case studies via traditional seminar delivery, students will have access to Northeast Precast's state-of-the-art facility where they will learn about the precast concrete manufacturing process and produce panel prototypes for wall assemblies that respond to structural, thermal, and water proofing performance. Students will develop a delivery workflow utilizing digital tools to communicate with and transmit panel, assembly and formwork concepts to NEP staff, fostering a collaboration opportunity for students that is not regularly experienced in architecture school.

[ARCH 732] MATTER AND ENERGY
Franca Trubiano

This seminar/workshop is focused on the basic principle of designing and constructing shelter in a time of climate crisis. When faced with the most extreme of conditions, how might we might develop smart, informed, and critical strategies for re-building the most primal of structures—that is, the home? This is not a question for the future, but one for our immediate present. There is really no more time to plan, wait, and hope. Architects must participate in developing innovative solutions, building products, and construction strategies for solving the problem of shelter in a time of environmental crisis. According to the UNHCR (UN Refugee Agency), millions of people are already on the move because of climate dangers. And every time a family is forced to move because of climate trauma, shelter is needed. And every time shelter is made, we contribute to the climate crisis. How do you end this cycle? What is our role and responsibility in addressing both the causes and the immediate housing needs of this crisis? And how do we address this through the lens of social justice?

[ARCH 771] PROFESSIONAL PRACTICE II
Philip Ryan

This is the second of a two-course sequence that discusses the issues and processes involved in running a professional architectural practice and designing buildings in the contemporary construction environment. Arch 771 will build on the knowledge of the Project process gained in ARCH 672 to examine the way in which an office is "designed" to facilitate the execution of design and construction. Issues of finance, liability, ethics, and the codes that overlay atop the design and construction industry will be discussed. The lectures will draw connections between the student's studio design knowledge to date and the instructor's experience in practice including local building examples and guest lectures by relevant professionals. Guests from within the field of architecture andconstruction (and outside frequently) will supplement the semester lectures.

[ARCH 710] CONTEMPORARY THEORY 1989-PRESENT
Alexandra Quantrill

A chronological overview of the approaches and attitudes adopted by architects, theorists and inter-disciplinary writers from 1993-today that have helped shape the current discourse of architecture. This course will introduce and contextualize key projects, and polemics over the last 25 years. Central themes in this course include the impact of digital technologies and methods of design, production and materiality. These are explored through texts, movements, projects and buildings that help form an overview that has shaped the contemporary condition that we live in.

[ARCH 711] ARCHITECTURE/COLLECTIVE: IMAGINATION, RESISTANCE, MEMORY
Sophie Hochhäusl

This course engages the themes of how architects imagine and build together, how they articulate collective forms of resistance as pedagogy and performance, and how they contribute to making public monuments and memory. The course will rely heavily on discussions of theoretical texts from Hannah Arendt and Maurice Halbwachs, to Paolo Freire, Fanon Frantz, Angela Davis, June Jordan, James Young, and Alaida Assmann. Throughout the seminar we will conduct research dedicated to groups of architects who collectively developed ideas on housing and the design of social institutions, pedagogy and public memory. Most of the practices we will analyze also practiced collectively. Some of them include, but are not exclusive to, the Regional Panning Association (USA), the Brigade May (Germany-Soviet Union), BBPR (Italy), Energoprojekt (Yugolavia-Nigeria), AUCA (Chile), Beijing Jianzhu Sheji Shiwusuo (China).

[ARCH 711] BUILDING THEORIES
Franca Trubiano

For decades, architectural theory has been remiss to recognize the contribution which building and its materials practices have made to how we 'think' about architecture. Redressing this condition is the goal of this seminar. Dedicated to the critical examination of ideas fundamental to the art of building, in a text-based review of seminal architectural writings in modern architecture, the seminar develops the first outlines of a nascent field that is the Theory of Building.

[ARCH 711] APPROACHES TO CONTEMPORARY THEORY
Joan Ockman

Architectural theory is back. After falling out of favor for a couple decades, theory has returned to the forefront of architectural discourse, but in new, different, and interesting ways. In previous eras theory offered architects a doctrine, a set of justifications for their work, and a canon of essential texts and authors. Today the very idea of a canon, and indeed the disciplinary definition of architecture itself, is being challenged and expanded. Theory now functions more as a mode of thought, a platform for debate, and an array of intellectual and critical strategies. At the same time, after the profound transformations that have taken place in the world over the last three decades—geo-political, technological, environmental—the necessity for theory has never been greater.

[ARCH 719] ARCHIGRAM AND ITS LEGACY: LONDON, A TECHNOTOPIA
Annette Fierro

Acknowledging the ubiquitous proliferation of "Hi-Tech" architecture in contemporary London, this research seminar examines the scope of technology as it emerges and re-emerges in the work of various architects currently dominating the city. This scope includes the last strains of post-war urbanism which spawned a legacy of radical architecture directly contributing to the Hi-Tech; a particular focus of the course will be the contributing and contrasting influence provided by the counter-cultural groups of the 60s—Archigram, Superstudio, the Metabolists and others. Using the premise of Archigram's idea of infrastructure, both literal and of event, the course will attempt to discover relational networks between works of the present day (Rogers, Foster, Grimshaw, etc.).

[ARCH 721] DESIGNING SMART OBJECTS FOR PLAY AND LEARNING
Assaf Eshet

Smart Objects of Play is a one-semester design course that integrates major aspects of classic product development process with an emphasis on designing smart tangible objects and playful experiences. The class will begin as a dialog of hands-on playful explorations, ideation, storytelling and a structured physical-computing workshops. A series of short projects and a set of lectures will allow the students to learn about the core values of a good playing object and receive an overview on the toy industry through its history and development culture. Students will be challenged to work in teams to explore concepts, share research and build prototypes of their experiences in the form of objects that may have accompanying electronic devices or software.

[ARCH 724] IMMERSIVE KINEMATICS/PHYSICAL COMPUTING: BODY AS SITE
Simon Kim and Mark Yim

The aim of this course is to understand the new medium of architecture within the format of a research seminar. The subject matter of new media is to be examined and placed in a disciplinary trajectory of building designed and construction technology that adapts to material and digital discoveries. We will also build prototype with the new media, and establish a disciplinary knowledge for ourselves. The seminar is interested in testing the architecture-machine relationship, moving away from architecture that looks like machines into architecture that behaves like machines: An intelligence (based on the conceptual premise of a project and in the design of a system), as part of a process (related to the generative real of architecture) and as the object itself and its embedded intelligence.

[ARCH 725] DESIGN THINKING
Sarah Rottenberg

Creating new product concepts was once a specialized pursuit exclusively performed by design professionals in isolation from the rest of an organization. Today's products are developed in a holistic process involving a collaboration amont many disciplines. Design thinking—incorporating processes, approaches, and working methods from traditional designers' toolkits—has become a way of generating innovative ideas to challenging problems and refining those ideas. Rapid prototyping techniques, affordable and accessible prototyping platforms, and an iterative mindset have enabled people to more reliably translate those ideas into implementable solutions. In this course, students will be exposed to these techniques and learn how to engage in a human-centered design process.

[ARCH 731] EXPERIMENTS IN STRUCTURE
Mohamad Al Khayer

This course studies the relationships between geometric space and those structural systems that amplify tension. Experiments using the hand (touch and force) in coordination with the eye (sight and geometry) will be done during the construction and observation of physical models. Verbal, mathematical and computer models are secondary to the reality of the physical model. However these models will be used to give dimension and document the experiments. Team reports will serve as interim and final examinations. In typology, masonry structures in compression (e.g., vault and dome) correlate with "Classical" space, and steel or reinforced concrete structures in flexure (e.g., frame, slab and column) with "Modernist" space.

[ARCH 732] DAYLIGHTING
Jessica Zofchak

This course aims to introduce fundamental daylighting concepts and tools to analyze daylighting design. The wide range of topics to be studied includes site planning, building envelope and shading optimization, passive solar design, daylight delivery methods, daylight analysis structure and results interpretation, and a brief daylighting and lighting design integration.

[ARCH 732] MATERIAL AND STRUCTURAL INTELLIGENCE
Sameer Kumar

The semester long project will involve a gradual development of architectural ideas that are intimately informed by and centered on knowledge of Structure and Materiality. Employing both physical and digital simulations, the students will synthesize knowledge acquired in previous courses in structures, materials, and construction methods to develop architectural solutions within a carefully selected set of determinants.

[ARCH 732] GEOMETRIC STRUCTURAL DESIGN
Masoud Akbarzadeh

Geometric structural design provides a comprehensive introduction to novel geometric methods of structural design based on 2D and 3D graphical statics. The primary emphasis of the course will be on developing a general understanding of the relationship between structural forms in equilibrium and the geometric representation of their internal and external forces. This link is the main apparatus for designing provocative structural forms using only geometric techniques rather than complicated algebraic/numerical methods. Moreover, special consideration will be given to materialization of the structural geometry and the proper fabrication techniques to construct the complex geometry of the structure.

[ARCH 739] NEW APPROACHES TO AN ARCHITECTURE OF HEALTH
Mike Avery

In order to frame our present day understanding of the role of architecture (and design) in fostering health for individuals and within communities, this seminar will begin with an exploration of the historical and contemporary perspectives on the role of the architect and built environment on health. Parallels between design and our ever-changing understanding of the biological, social, and environmental causes of sickness and disease will also be explored.

[ARCH 741] ARCHITECTURE DESIGN INNOVATION
Ali Rahim

The mastery of techniques, whether in design, production or both, does not necessarily yield great architecture. As we all know, the most advanced techniques can still yield average designs. Architects are becoming increasingly adept at producing complexity & integrating digital design and fabrication techniques into their design process—yet there are few truly elegant projects. Only certain projects that are sophisticated at the level of technique achieve elegance. This seminar explores some of the instances in which designers are able to move beyond technique, by commanding them to such a degree as to achieve elegant aesthetics within the formal development of projects.

[ARCH 743] FORM AND ALGORITHM
Ezio Blasetti

The critical parameter will be to develop the potential beyond finite forms of explicit and parametric modeling towards non-linear algorithmic processes. We will seek novel patterns of organization, structure, and articulation as architectural expressions within the emergent properties of feedback loops and rule-based systems. This seminar will accommodate both introductory and advanced levels. No previous scripting experience is necessary. It will consist of a series of introductory sessions, obligatory intensive workshops, lectures followed by suggested readings, and will gradually focus on individual projects. Students will be encouraged to investigate the limits of algorithmic design both theoretically and in practice through a scripting environment.

[ARCH 751] ECOLOGY, TECHNOLOGY, AND DESIGN
Dr. William W. Braham

This course will examine the ecological nature of design at a range of scales, from the most intimate aspects of product design to the largest infrastructures, from the use of water in bathroom to the flow of traffic on the highway. It is a first principle of ecological design that everything is connected, and that activities at one scale can have quite different effects at other scales, so the immediate goal of the course will be to identify useful and characteristic modes of analyzing the systematic, ecological nature of design work, from the concept of the ecological footprint to market share. The course will also draw on the history and philosophy of technology to understand the particular intensity of contemporary society, which is now characterized by the powerful concept of the complex, self-regulating system. The system has become both the dominant mode of explanation and the first principle of design and organization.

[ARCH 765] PROJECT MANAGEMENT
Charles Capaldi

This course is an introduction to construction management, project management and various construction project delivery systems. In the study of construction delivery systems, we will examine the players, relationships and the advantages and disadvantages of different contractual and practical relationships, both on the construction site and at the tops of the various "paper piles". Exercises and lectures will focus on developing perspectives into the various roles, needs and expectations of the many parties involved in a construction project and the management skills and techniques which help to bring a project to a successful conclusion.

[ARCH 768] REAL ESTATE DEVELOPMENT
Alan Feldman

This course evaluates "ground-up" development as well as re-hab, re-development, and acquisition investments. We examine raw and developed land and the similarities and differences of traditional real estate product types including office, R & D, retail, warehouses, single family and multi-family residential, mixed use, and land as well as "specialty" uses like golf courses, assisted living, and fractional share ownership. Emphasis is on concise analysis and decision making. We discuss the development process with topics including market analysis, site acquisition, due diligence, zoning, entitlements, approvals, site planning, building design, construction, financing, leasing, and ongoing management and disposition.

[ARCH 811] ARCHITECTURE'S CULTURAL PERFORMANCE: THE FACADE
David Leatherbarrow

The purpose of this course is to provide to students who are embarking on career in teaching and scholarship in architecture a re-introduction to some of the principal issues and writings of the tradition. In addition to introducing themes and texts, this course aims to increase and ease the student's familiarity with the practices that are typical of scholarship, the forms and habits of scholarly inquiry.

Palimpsest by Rentian Liu and Frank Xuefeng Li
Critic: **Wolf Prix** [p.299]

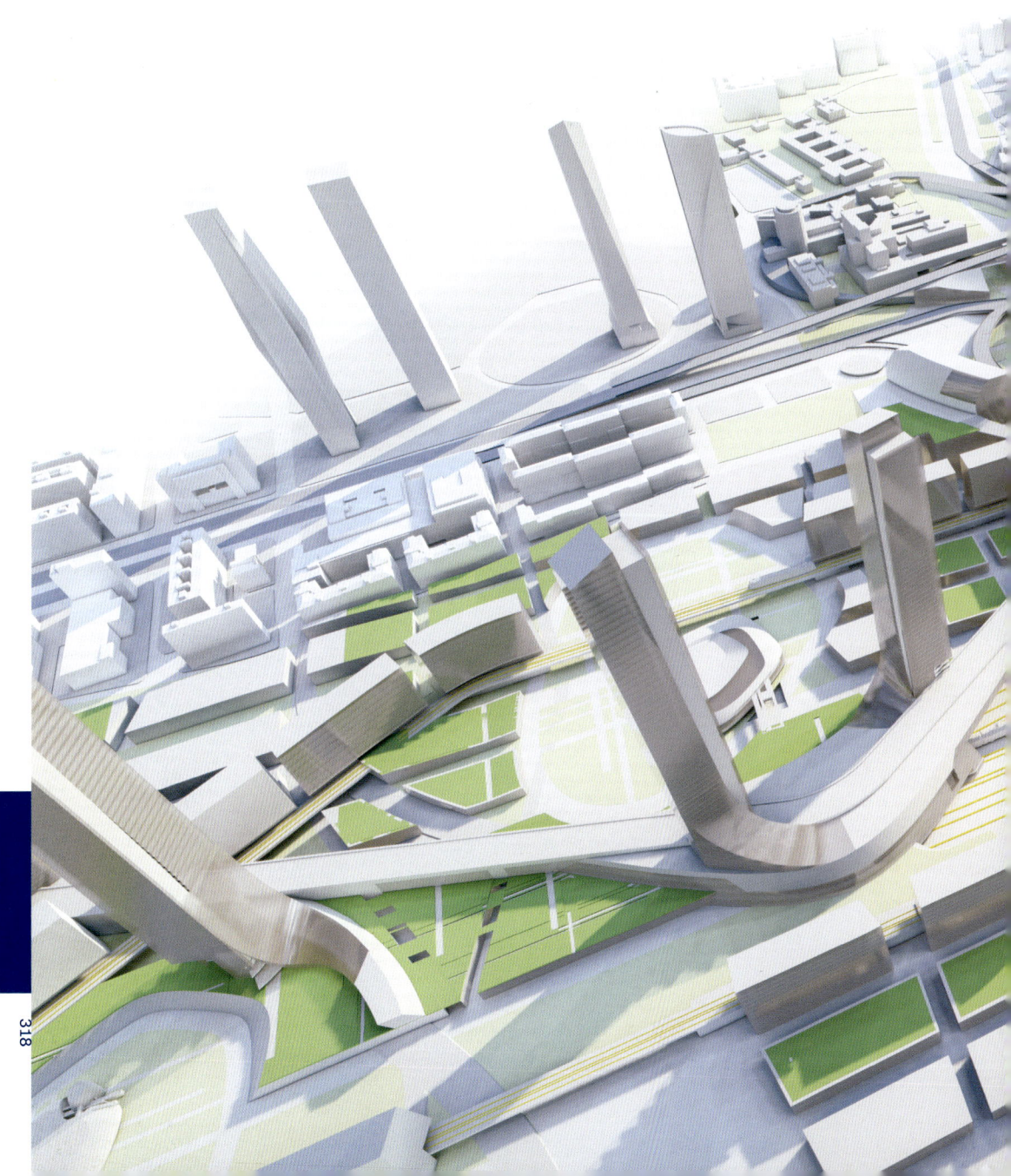

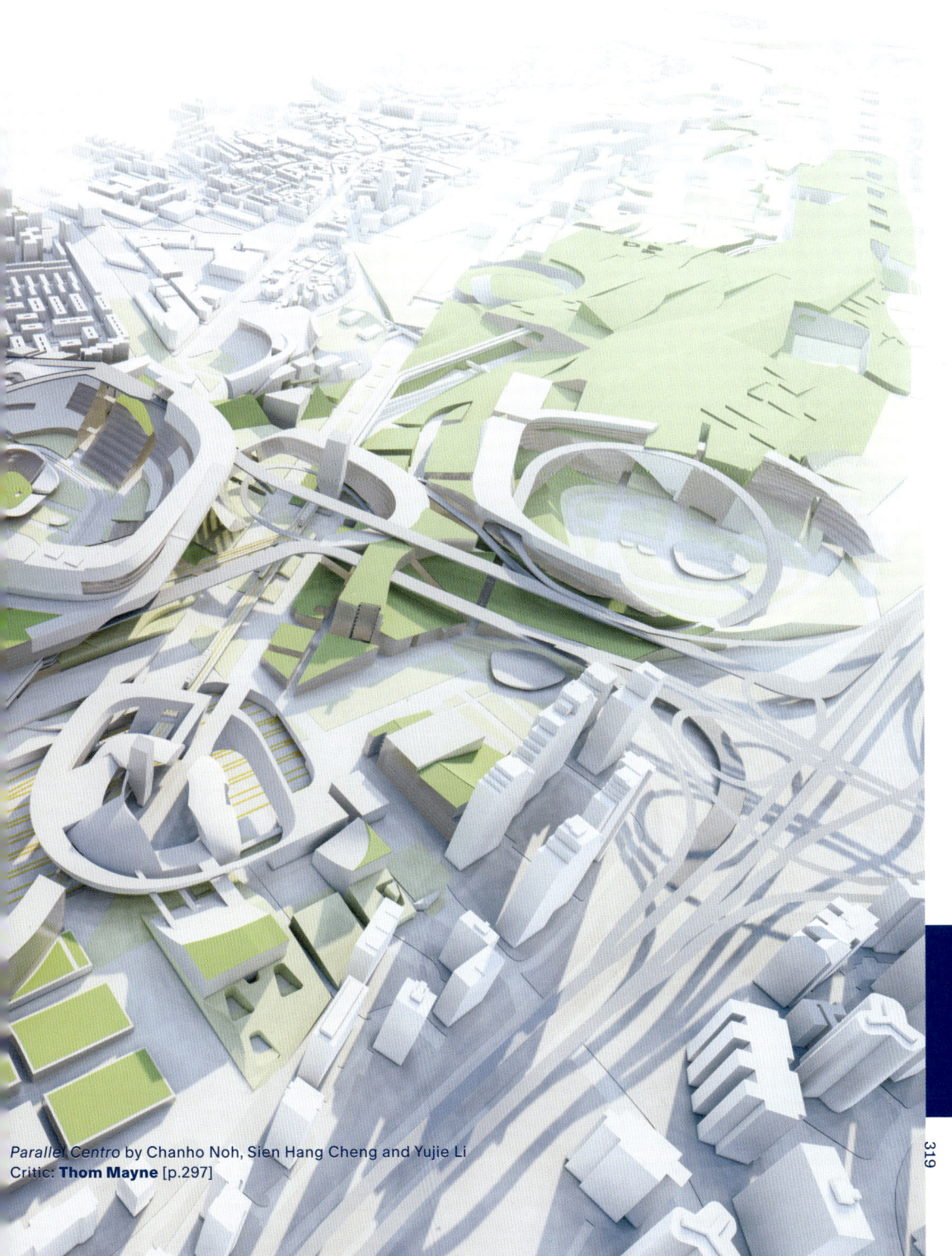

Parallel Centro by Chanho Noh, Sien Hang Cheng and Yujie Li
Critic: **Thom Mayne** [p.297]

Palimpsest by Tae Hyung Lee and Ryan Henriksen
Critic: **Ferda Kolatan** (p.285)

Urban stage by Yutian Tang and Bella Ding
Critic: **Matthias Hollwich** [p.264]

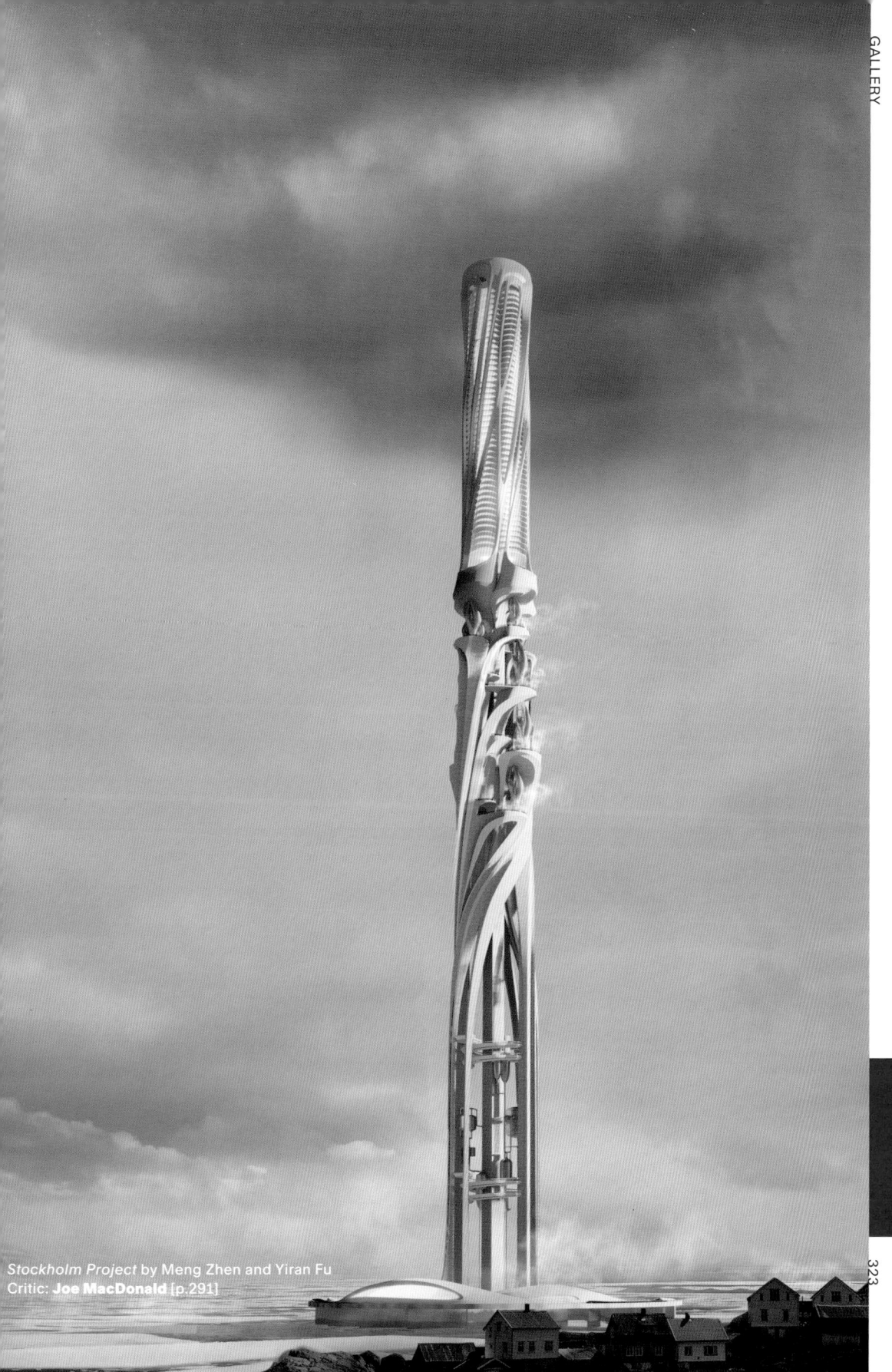

Stockholm Project by Meng Zhen and Yiran Fu
Critic: **Joe MacDonald** [p.291]

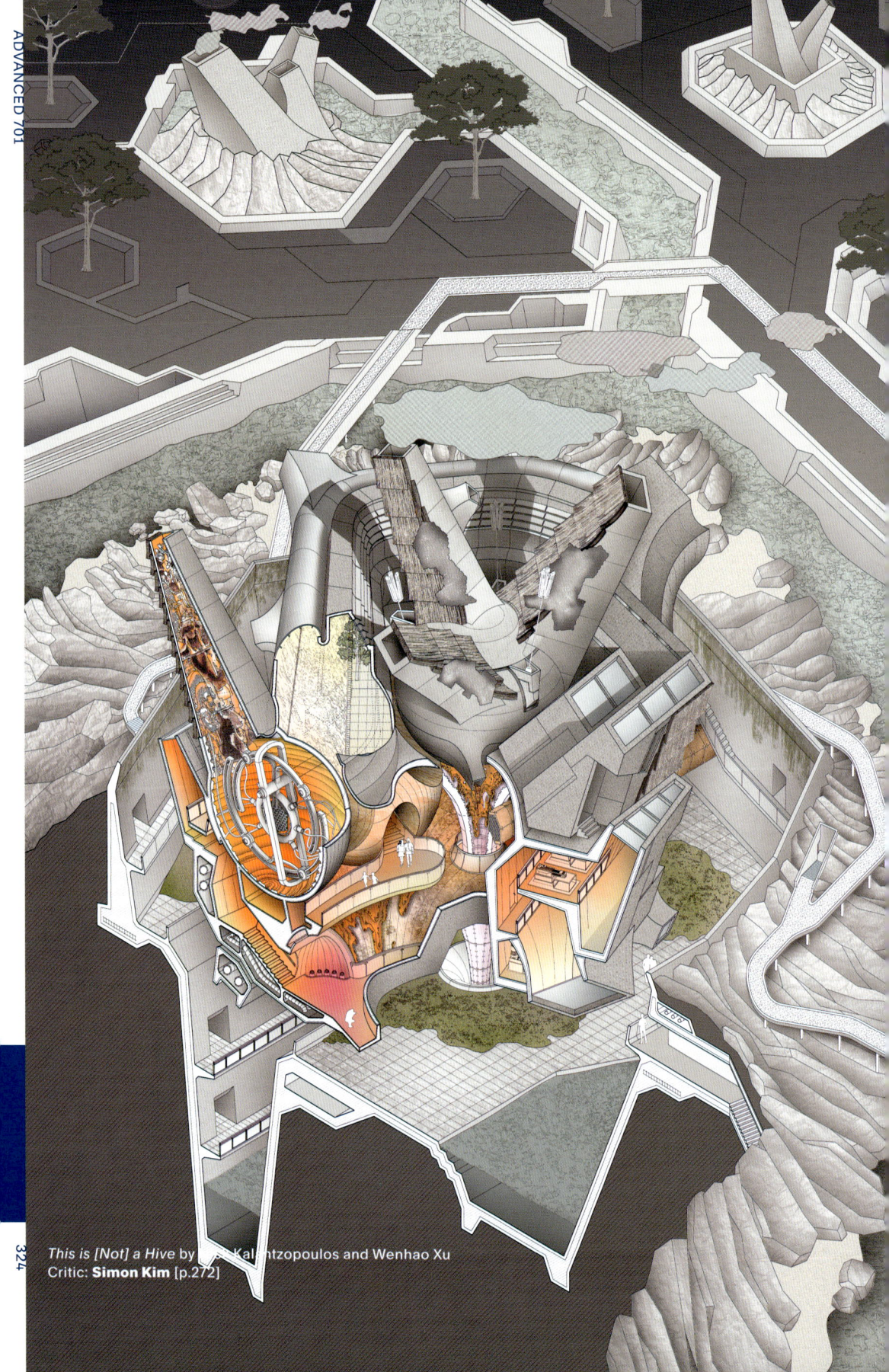

This is [Not] a Hive by Jose Kalantzopoulos and Wenhao Xu
Critic: **Simon Kim** [p.272]

COVID-19
FACE SHIELD PRODUCTION

In March, the University of Pennsylvania quickly shifted to virtual instruction in response to COVID-19. Students, faculty, and staff joined forces to produce clear-plastic protective face shields for hospital workers at Penn Medicine.

Production was led by the Penn Health Tech COVID-19 Rapid Response Team, and coordinated by Mark Yim, Asa Whitney Professor of Mechanical Engineering and director of the General Robotics, Automation, Sensing and Perception (GRASP) Laboratory. Yim is also faculty director in the Integrated Product Design program at Weitzman, a collaboration with Penn Engineering and Wharton. Associate Professor Franca Trubiano served as Weitzman's faculty advisor and coordinator in the effort. The Rapid Response Team is expecting a shipment of 10,000 face mask parts that an army of student volunteers will assemble for the hospitals next week.

With Penn's campus closed to all but those involved in life-sustaining activities, four Weitzman staff members received authorization to return to Meyerson Hall to operate three laser cutters in the Fabrication Lab to manufacture the straps used for the shields.

In addition to manufacturing new face shields, four employees in the Office of Operations and Planning collected personal protective equipment from around the school and delivered it to the Hospital of the University of Pennsylvania on March 23. The materials included 248 pairs of goggles, 181 masks, 100 shoe covers, 32 pairs of nitrile gloves, and three face shields provided by the Fabrication Lab, the Robotics Lab, and the Graduate Program in Historic Preservation.

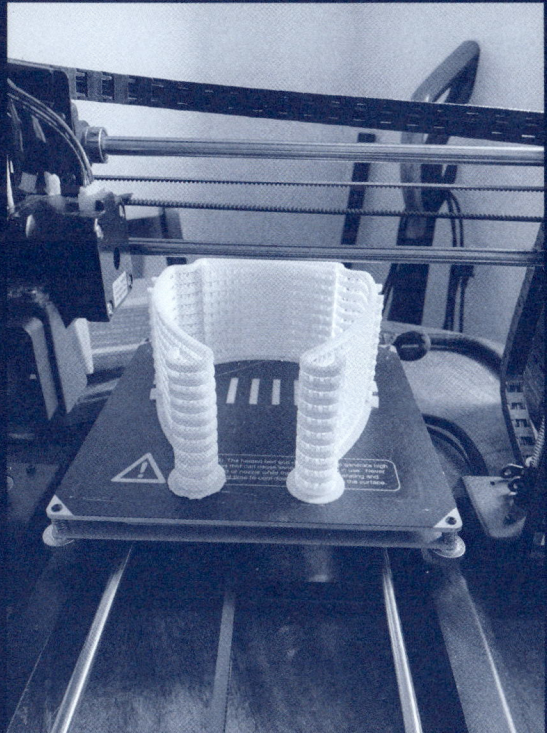 

MArch students Tynx Taneja and Megan McGaffigan help produce face shields from home using their own 3D printers.

ADVANCED 704

Ferda Kolatan, Coordinator
Associate Professor of Practice

The 704 Design Research Studios are an in-depth examination and exploration of critical architectural topics through rigorous conceptual thinking and advanced design methodologies. These elective studios are taught by a selection of leading professionals in the field who share and develop their research expertise with the students over the course of the semester. All studio topics and project briefs are devised in ways to support the various objectives of each specific research subject.

The primary goal of this final studio of the Master of Architecture program is to equip the outgoing students with a multi-facetted and robust knowledge base—encompassing design, theory, and technical skills—necessary to participate in the field of architecture at the highest level. The ability to formulate, develop, and conclude a design project based on a larger set of research parameters is a crucial experience toward achieving this goal.

The boundaries for design research have expanded with the increasingly diverse trajectories that define architecture's territories today. From the effects of global economic markets on cities to the ecological realities of the Anthropocene, we find ourselves entangled in forces seemingly elusive and yet profoundly impactful on our profession. The role of the research studio is to examine such forces in more depth and devise detailed architectural responses, which reflect sensibly on the cultural and environmental circumstances of our day.

Additionally, in recent years, new media and advanced technologies have provided us with uniquely powerful tools that require the integration of unprecedented technical skills and logistical expertise into the practice of design. However, in order to take full advantage of these tools, and to speculate productively on their vast potential to positively influence our world, we need to engage these new technologies in terms of their cultural, societal, and aesthetic ramifications as well. Several design research studios operate within this realm.

Architecture's unique ability to express physically and conceptually the circumstances of its own environment, to analyze and synthesize, to evoke and provoke, to learn from the past and to imagine the future, is contingent on our ability to integrate research-oriented thinking into our everyday practices. Only through this integration can we assure that design—and architecture at large—can maintain its disciplinary rigor while simultaneously engaging with the most pressing challenges of our contemporary times.

In this spirit, the 704 Design Research Studios are taught with a progressive and explorative mindset and without a default reliance on prior modes of design thinking and making. Each of these studios, in various ways, articulates a unique vision of what it means to practice architecture in the 21st century. The ever-diversifying context and complexity of our world can only be satisfactorily met with an equally dynamic approach to architectural design.

HYBRIDS AND MATERIAL ECOLOGIES

Winka Dubbeldam (MILLER PROFESSOR AND CHAIR)
Richard Garber (LECTURER)
Drew Busmire (TA)

Winka Dubbeldam (Miller Professor, Chair): Winka Dubbeldam is the founder and partner of the WBE certified New York firm Archi-Tectonics NYC, LLC. Dubbeldam is widely known for her award-winning work, recognized as much for its design excellence as for its use of smart building systems, sustainable materials, and innovative structures. Archi-Tectonics' work is found in the USA, Europe, and Asia. Archi-Tectonics recently won the *Asian Games 2022* Design Competition in Hangzhou China [2018], with a 16 acre park 5 buildings, and 2 stadiums, that is under construction to open in 2022.

Hybrids & Material Ecologies is a studio that looks at the bifold design-research of the future model of the Architecture school & Archive and its relationship with the indepth research in material ecologies. The cross pollination [a sharing or interchange of knowledge, ideas, etc., as for mutual enrichment; cross-fertilization] and coevolution between the two hybrids will lead to the final building proposal in Tel Aviv.

Political dynamics, climate change and demographic changes are contemporary global challenges. In our research-design Studio, we rely on a design methodology that integrates an interculturally engaged design network to bring about future-oriented architectural answers to worldwide issues.

Future Of Education

The Architecture school here is seen as a self-sufficient entity; the hybrid of shops, an archive, a gallery and then an architecture school will be an innovative model for a collaborative system of programs that will morph & adapt into each other. The building is supposed to serve about 400 students and about 60 administrative and academic staff, daily. About two years ago, the Xnet Architecture Channel reported the decision to build a new building for the David Azrieli School of Architecture. Imagine the visit to this building; it will open on the entrance floor, which faces both the street and campus. This floor will actually be stores and café's like an oriental market. One way or the other, after buying a shirt or coffee machine, you progress into the building via the gallery located between the commercial areas on the ground floor. The gallery is also a transition, it morphs into the Azrieli architecture archive, an independent entity, which does not belong to the school, nor to the university. The archive will function as a museum entity, but will likely be shared with the school as an academic institution. Above the gallery, on the second floor of the building, the archive itself will be located. The school will begin on the third floor, and will span

1   FUSION AND CONFLICT
         Yufei Wang and Zhihui Li

We initiate the project from the social condition of Israel, in which there is a duality of fusion and conflict, and intend to interpret it into spatial language. Given this and inspired by Peter Eisenman's idea of "voyeurism," we mix the programs of public and private, and organize them with two circulation loops, which stagger and twine without intersection. Prevented from physical disturbance, school members and visitors enjoy the visual connection when they move through the building. Researching on how to present this circulation relations in a real architectural space, we create a chunk including various ramps in the relationship of "voyeurism," which is set as entrances in two corners of the proposed building. Furthurly, some certain surfaces are extracted from the chunk as spatIal prototypes to connect the two chunks and develop atriums, associating with the other circulating and programmatic spaces. With the system of loops and atriums, integrated with public programs, the whole building is created as a vessel to contain diverse urban events and situations rather than just an education space, which can be regarded as a city fragment in contemporary architectural narration.

2

Richard Garber: AIA, is a founding partner at GRO Architects. Bachelor of Architecture from Rensselaer Polytechnic Institute and a Master of Science in Advanced Architectural Design from Columbia University.
Sponsor: John Ruga & Team from northeast Precast NJ

1 – *Fusion and Conflict* by Yufei Wang and Zhihui Li, Project Description
2 – *Fusion and Conflict* by Yufei Wang and Zhihui Li, Prototype

the top five floors, with a total built-up area of 5,000 square feet. It will include 24 studio rooms, offices, library, labs, classrooms and workshops, as well as spacious outdoor areas. A set of cinemas will be located in the basement, where two movie theaters (260 seats in total) will be operated. In total the project will include a gross 8,475 square meters.

The highlights in the building design to focus on are:

CAMPUS IDENTITY
Considering the height of existing construction in the area, with reference to the entrance floor.

DESIGN FLEXIBILITY
priority for modular design and possibility for changes, for example two-story addition in the future.

SUSTAINABILITY CONCEPT
energy and resource saving infrastructure systems and "green" building materials.

NATURAL CONSTITUENTS
utilizing natural lighting and ventilation.

INFRASTRUCTURE
a service yard will concentrate on the garbage disposal. The electrical systems will be concentrated in the basement.

TECHNOLOGY AND INNOVATION
the use of advanced technologies, especially in the archive. The coevolutionary transformative approach will also be instrumental in analyzing the self-sufficient relationship between the building and its site, not unlike how the orchid and the tree collaborate, or the orchid and the bee co-evolve.

Material Ecologies

The Material Ecologies Research will focus on precast concrete and specifically it's materiality—how it is manufactured and the logistics of its assembly —and cultural affects through both its traditional uses within the urban environment as well as new approaches to building typologies such as housing. Through a strategic partnership with Northeast Precast (NEP), based in Millville, NJ, students will gain access to places where precast concrete is made, formed, and put into action. In addition to readings and case studies via traditional seminar delivery, students will have access to Northeast Precast's state-of-the-art facility where they will:

1. Over two weekends, attend two six hour sessions to learn about the precast concrete manufacturing process. Students will be exposed to the fabrication process from material selection, to formwork production, to pour, and disassembly [in lieu of four (4) class periods].

2. Work in NEP's facilities and with their workforce—students will work in teams to produce panel prototypes for wall assemblies that respond to structural, thermal, and water proofing performance.

3. Receive feedback from NEP's expert staff on the construction feasibility and applicability of student-proposed prototypes.

3

3 – Students at Northeast Precast

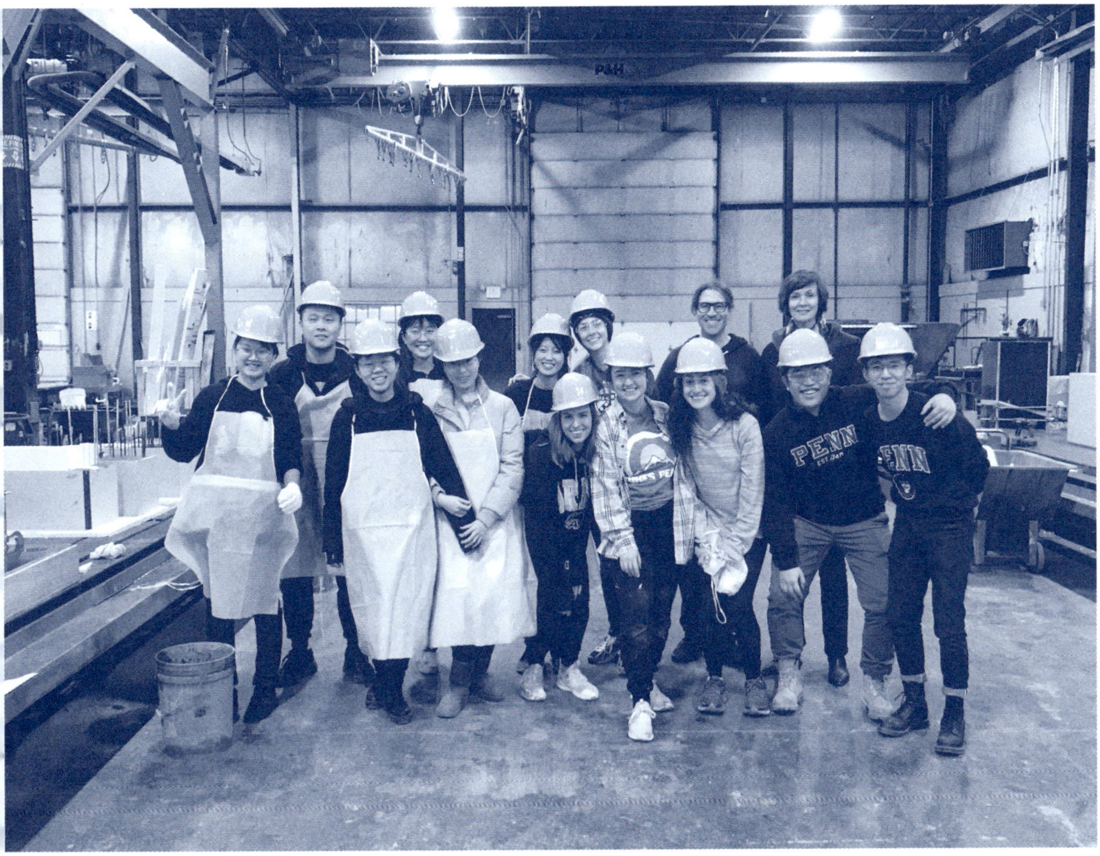

4

5

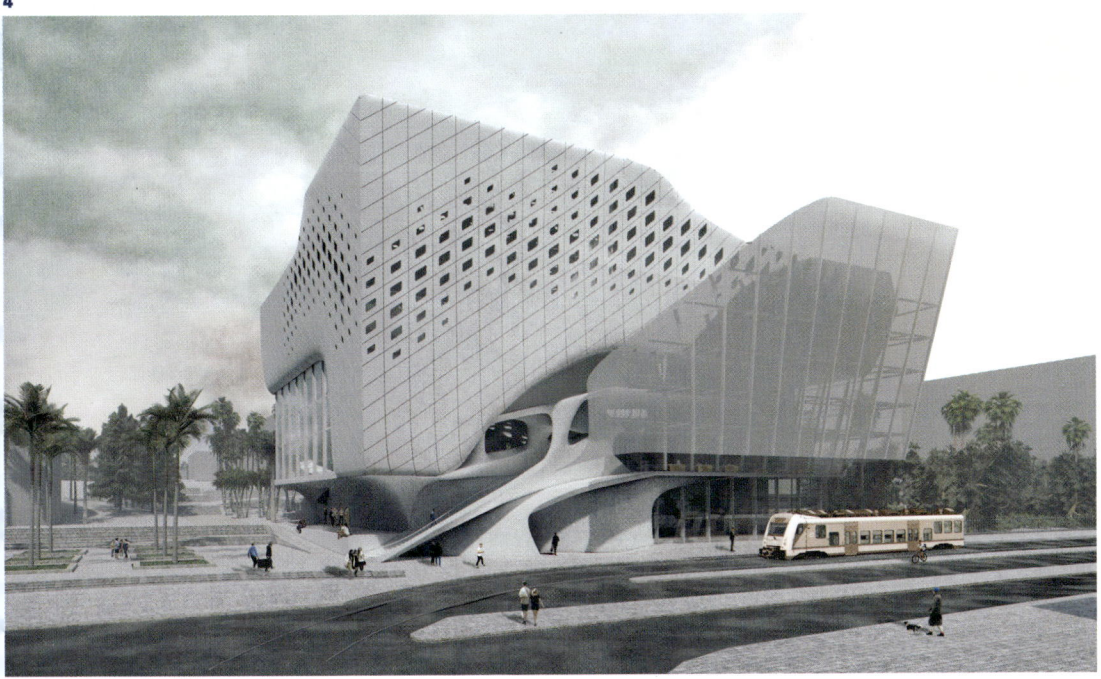

4 – Students at Northeast Precast
5 – *Fusion and Conflict* by Yufei Wang and Zhihui Li, Rendering

HYBRID MONOLITH
Eliana Weiner and Alexa Sternberg

Hybrid Monolith explores materiality and solidity, the duality of public and private, and the intersection of user and program. It challenges the standards of architecture pedagogy by hybridizing private spaces, the school, with public ones. This cohabitation creates a shifting of spaces, moments of architecture that do not formally fit together, but enable a unique overlap of use.

Through both an additive and subtractive process of the existing ground condition, a series of networks are created, tying together the future of the architecture school with the history of the site. The composition of pieces and layering of interiority allows for the intersection of programs and experiences which might not otherwise coexist or interact. Hybrid Monolith challenges the future of architectural education and its current existence beyond its own isolated industry, pushing the boundaries of interconnection while grappling with the notions of security and scale.

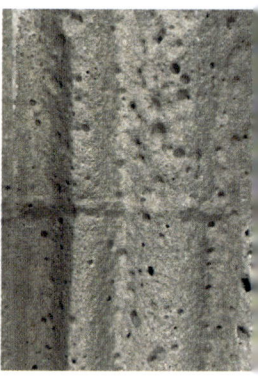

6

7   8

9

6 – *Hybrid Monolith* by Eliana Weiner and Alexa Sternberg, Preliminary Prototypes
7 – *Hybrid Monolith* by Eliana Weiner and Alexa Sternberg, Ground Student Entry East
8 – *Hybrid Monolith* by Eliana Weiner and Alexa Sternberg, Close Up Elevation
9 – *Hybrid Monolith* by Eliana Weiner and Alexa Sternberg, Rendering – Street Perspective

ARCH
Yifan Zhuang and Sifan Yang

The 21st-century architecture school, also, should be reconsidered with new understandings. The students are not only the recipients who incorporates the knowledge from the school, they are also producers of the brand-new architecture culture. The turning of the identity also need the public's participation, these groups need some space in the school building to meet together and have mutual feedback. The students and the public visitors enter the school form the two different entrances. Accordingly, there are two major staircases which invite the two people flow to meet together in the third floor, where the archive area locates. The merged functions encourage the visitors to participate in the interactions of the student works without disturbing the school's life. When public are inviting to admire the progress of the studio works, they will get to known better of the school's architecture education and culture and make some critics or suggestions in the communication board. At the mean time, students could get mutual feedback from the public and learn from another perspective. The staircase from the campus's side doesn't stop in the third floor, it could go up to the top studios and labs. The staircases connect the different levels of the school.

Arch, as a symbol that is defamiliarized into various new spatial sequences. The use of arch is three-dimensional, arch is not only reflected in the building facade, and in its internal space plane can also form arch enclosed space, become different closed rooms, some arch can also extend out of the facade to form high and low scattered balconies, making the space more flow and changeable. The arch symbol is hidden in the space geometry, some of them are not evident but display in a new formation. We try to spatialize the new understanding of narrative of the archs.

10

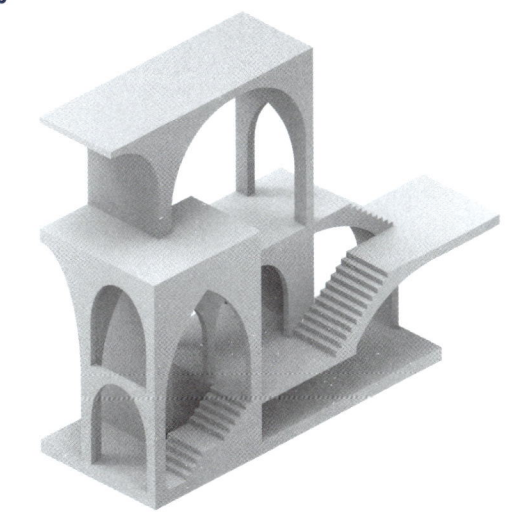

11

12

10 – *Arch* by Yifan Zhuang and Sifan Yang, Rendering
11 – *Arch* by Yifan Zhuang and Sifan Yang, Rendering
12 – *Arch* by Yifan Zhuang and Sifan Yang, Rendering

SITE / NON SIGHT

Homa Farjadi (PROFESSOR OF PRACTICE)
Chang Yuan Max Hsu (TA)
Anna Ishii (TA)

Homa Farjadi (Professor of Practice at Weitzman): Principal of Farjadi Architects (1987) — Received a Graduate Diploma from the AA School of Architecture in London and an MArch with distinction from Tehran University — The work of her office has been exhibited and published internationally.

LAND ART: WRITINGS OF ROBERT SMITHSON
REM KOOLHAAS: ELEMENTS OF ARCHITECTURE

Methodology

The two texts offered in this studio both in works and in words, are seen as two instances of reformulations of architecture's parameters. One in Art and one in Architecture the two were brought together side by side to engage in a dialogic encounter to frame the design parameters for a new contemporary project.

Topic

Land Art works—When discourses of Land Art movement were being developed during the 1960-70s the issue of 'site' along with what was termed by Robert Smithson as "non-site" challenged art in taking it outside of the institutional curated setting of museums and galleries. In parallel, radically different set of parameters and scales entered the work of art positioned in faraway natural sites. Unbound by human development these we may call "found" sites that foregrounded natural environmental processes with exchange with man-made works bracketing the limits and role of authorial control. They also brought forth the super scale of natural to challenge the boundaries of objecthood of the work of art designed in its relation to human body. In their displacement these works also took the accent from seeing to an experience of territorial environment where seeing was put in new brackets as *non-sight*.

Koolhaas's *Elements of Architecture* divides up architecture in its elements, door, window, floor, wall, ceiling etc. a work of analysis of parts, discussion of conventions, regulations, technology are offered as prompters of their historical development. This work's focus on elements can be read as an attempt to dislodge the contemporary emphasis on the work of the image foregrounded by digital processes of design. Hence *non- sight* in our project has also challenged the primary drivers of design to engage with elements of architecture and their processes of production and performance in a building/ design with a bias on elemental accumulation rather than authorial composition of the image.

1   ACCUMULATION AS SITE
Samia Kayyali

The project utilizes the processes of snow mitigation and snow fall as well as control in order to interpret Smithson's ideas on form and architecture and site/non-site. Site becomes the outside space where events as falling of snow/ avalanche occurs. The structure or the building that allows the change occurring outside to influence or be displaced within the building becomes both a site and non-site simultaneously. In its organization, influences and overall form, the building utilizes and pushes the element of the corridor.

2

1 – *Accumulation as Site* by Samia Kayyali, Project Description
2 – *Accumulation as Site* by Samia Kayyali, Structure with and Without Water

The Project

The initial set of exercises each student engaged one of the analytic chapters in the two texts, study its development, its technology and its contemporary potentials. Since our work as designers, by definition needs to synthesize, the key concepts derived from the two text were examined in their discursive conjunction and synthetic potential. The project was about the way we might make a building which is about itself and its placement/displacement relative to the site. It did not address program in the beginning. It looked for new economies in functional propriety of the lay-out. It did not presume an ecology, a system, a technology but came to it via a performative process which test the scales and the technologies of accumulation of elemental reorientation of discourse of site and *Non-sight* which we believe was a welcome conceptual displacement.

MESA
Maoqiang Li and Akarsh Sabhaney

The project seeks to encompass the intricacies found in Robert Smithson's aerial art accompanied by rem Koolhaas's deciphering of the roof structure. The idea lies in the duality of the finite and infinite, the logical conception and the illogical perception, and the artificiality of time with regard to space. Though the space is finite the conceptual reading of it or perceptional conditions is infinite.

Repetition, serial ordering and a play on perspective invite a sense of infinity within the system of a series of datums.

Playing with different scales and thresholds to create a multifarious experience in terms of apertures and internal voids that become habitable building spaces, the design subtly shifts from one quality to another by utilizing holistic spatial stretching as a tool.

The relationships between interior space and the effects of manipulating scale is crucial to this project. Shifts in topology and scale dictate breaks in the seriality of the space. The special stacking will conversely act as a cohesive element bringing a sense of stability and wonder in different pockets of the project. The site has an element of Mesa or in other words an isolated flat-topped hill with steep sides, found in landscapes with horizontal strata.

The design envisions to blur the distinction between the building design and normal objects such as rocks which are generally not considered as art. The roof plays multiple roles in the project. Invisible in some places, thick vertical structure in others and the level of intricacy varies depending on the scale of each space. Art today is no long an architectural afterthought, or an object to attach a building after it is finished, but rather a total engagement with the building process from the ground up and from the sky down.

3 – *Mesa* by Maoqiang Li and Akarsh Sabhaney, Project Description
4 – *Mesa* by Maoqiang Li and Akarsh Sabhaney, Diagram
5 – *Mesa* by Maoqiang Li and Akarsh Sabhaney, Render

6-8 – Studio Travel

PIERS OF TOMORROW: A NEW TOPOGRAPHY
Quan Hao Huynh and Shangzi Tu

Drawing inspiration from Robert Smithson's work and Rem Koolhaas's Elements of Architecture, our work seeks to explore and challenge the plane of oblique. Our project proposes an infrastructure to reimagine abandoned coastal front in this case we choose Olde Richmond's abandoned industrial port our site. As climate change, and unpredictable floods, the chosen site witness the ever rapid change in term of coastal soil and existing landscape, which plays a potential role in testing Smithson's notion about the relationship of the built work and its surrounding elements of nature. As stand, our proposal is a structural slab with perforations and voids that allow the extension from inside to outside, hence blurring the physical boundary that allow interior spatial continuity to connect and open to the light, air, and weathering. Furthermore, this extension from inside to outside allows the documentation of time through the changing of light, vegetation, and tidal. Projecting one hundred year from the present, our creation could become the new topography, which invites new interventions to emerge, whether artificial or results of natural phenomenal.

9

10

11

12

9 – *Piers of Tomorrow: a New Topography* by Quan Hao Huynh and Shangzi Tu, Atrium Cave
10 – *Piers of Tomorrow: a New Topography* by Quan Hao Huynh and Shangzi Tu, Entrance
11 – *Piers of Tomorrow: a New Topography* by Quan Hao Huynh and Shangzi Tu, Axon Diagram
12 – *Piers of Tomorrow: a New Topography* by Quan Hao Huynh and Shangzi Tu, Bird View

AIR-SCAPE
Xintong Zhao and Pengkun Wang

The project proposes an infrastructure of new public space at +300m above ground connected by public elevators placed at found sites along NS & EW axis.

Our inspirations come from two main areas, the limitation of a centralized network and the idea of nonsite by Robert Smithson. The historic incident that pushed us to build a decentralized proposal took place on Feb. 18, 1935 when NYC declared a state of emergency because of a citywide elevator operator strike. It really put a halt on most of the city operations since no one can get to their office without elevators. The idea of nonsite, on the other hand, builds connections in between places regardless of time and space.

The new infrastructure is to frame a new nature for New York. Learning from current and past health crisis, we are proposing the new layer to function as a health farm. From the middle of the 19th century, until the latter half of the 20th century, patients of tuberculosis (TB) were confined in specialized hospitals located at the outskirts of city for access to fresh air. With fresher air that comes with higher altitude, our proposal can be a place for people to cleanse themselves both physically and mentally.

The curvature of our form recollects the geological profile of New York City hundreds of years ago when the entire Manhattan Island was untouched by any modern developments. There are three parts to the design. The top layer is perforated for natural lighting and shelters people from extreme weather conditions. It would be coated with insulating paint for thermal protection and photovoltaic paint which are essentially Nanosolar Panels in order to be energy sustainable. The middle part is the main floor area for people to interact with the environment and with each other. The spaces shaped by glass cylinders project down from the perforations of the top layer. There will be public spaces for group therapy as well as rooms for rent for individuals and families as a respite from the city. Available to all, these are public amenities that offer democratic oxygen for citizens.

13

14

15

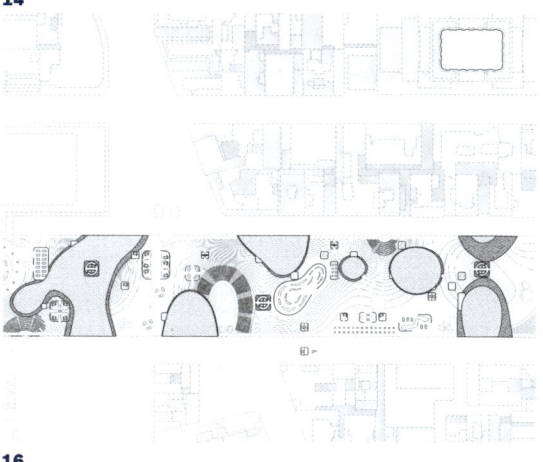

16

13 – *Air-Scape* by Xintong Zhao and Pengkun Wang, Render
14 – *Air-Scape* by Xintong Zhao and Pengkun Wang, Render Interior

13 – *Air-Scape* by Xintong Zhao and Pengkun Wang, Render
16 – *Air-Scape* by Xintong Zhao and Pengkun Wang, Plan Detail

15 MINUTES AND COUNTING:
A NEW ANDY WARHOL MUSEUM FOR TOKYO

Hina Jamelle (SENIOR LECTURER)
Caleb White (TA)

Hina Jamelle (Senior Lecturer): Director of the Urban Housing Studios at the Weitzman School of Design – Architect and Director, Contemporary Architecture Practice, New York and Shanghai – Awarded Fifty Under Fifty: Innovators of the 21st Century [2015] – Awarded 10 x 10_2 Phaidon Press 2005 – Awarded Architectural Record Design Vanguard Award [2004] – Author: Elegance. Architectural Design, John Wiley and Sons Inc., London.

> "THE IDEA IS NOT TO LIVE FOREVER;
> IT IS TO CREATE SOMETHING THAT WILL."
> – Andy Warhol

Pop Art in the West emerged in the post-war period as an ironic, self-examining, but enthusiastic look at the mass imagery of our consumerist society. Pop Art stood firmly at the crossroads of the elite avant-garde of the art world and the broader interests of popular culture and society at large. Andy Warhol, one of the leaders of the Pop Art movement also became a cult icon and a cultural symbol.

The Andy Warhol Foundation is the global keeper of Andy Warhol's legacy. One of the foundation's goals is to increase its influence and visibility and a new museum in the international city of Tokyo is a strategic one. Tokyo is one of the world's most vibrant cities and is also a confluence of art, fashion, architecture, and other contemporary cultural media. A new Warhol Museum would have an excellent opportunity to expose the work of Andy Warhol to new audiences but also to merge contemporary pop art with the long lineage of the genre.

The goal for each student is to evaluate the potentials of artistic techniques and to apply these to a range of familiar architectural issues. Using machine learning tools, the students were tasked with isolating techniques for color and light from their selected artworks. The final proposal of each student emerged out of an inter-related working method between artistic techniques, machine learning tools, program, space, atmosphere, and materials that combine to develop an innovative new museum proposal.

1

2

[2007]. IMPACT Architectural Design, John Wiley and Sons Inc., London. [2020]. – UNDER PRESSURE. Innovation in Urban Housing. Routledge. London [2021].

1 – Yusuke Obichi explains a Tadao Ando project
2 – Virtual Studio Review

SUPERFLAT CHROMATICS
Suwan Park and Xiaoyi Peng

Through our study of Japanese artist Takashi Murakami's piece, "First Love", we developed a specific interest in the role of color and figuration in contemporary Japanese pop art. Using machine learning style transfer as a tool, we selectively developed color fields from Murakami's painting into a taxonomy of colorful parts. We have used these colorful parts to populate the facade of our building, these figurations are nested into and carved out of an otherwise blank concrete box. These pieces are bundled into what appears to be a series of informal clusters or bundles. These bundles represent small galleries and shops that showcase individual artists. In this way, the formation of these figures has inspired a different way to view the contemporary museum—rather than a monolithic institution, the new Andy Warhol museum of Tokyo would be a vibrant collection of independent artists. The colorful windows will provide dynamic lighting effects within the interior spaces. The colorful figurations have also shaped the interior walls, circulation paths, and floor patterns. The users experience would be diverse and vibrant as they move from one intimate artistic experience to the next. Users can shape their own experiences by choosing their own way of moving through the building.

3

4

5

3 – *Superflat Chromatics* by Suwan Park and Xiaoyi Peng, Night Render

4 – *Superflat Chromatics* by Suwan Park and Xiaoyi Peng, Interior Render

5 – *Superflat Chromatics* by Suwan Park and Xiaoyi Peng, Render

BLURRED CHIAROSCURO
Fang Cheng and Tianxiao Wang

In the process of screen-printing, the multi layered printing process produces a misalignment of the color figures, which creates a unique "blurred" visual experience. Through careful analysis of Andy Warhol's "Butterfly", we quantify these offsets into an analysis diagram with a unique pattern. Based on the geometric elements of the diagram, we developed the 2D pattern into a 3D spatial technique. In the 3D space, the geometric shifting produces novel spatial conditions. Utilizing these variable spatial conditions, we formulated a spatial strategy for the Pop Art Museum. The "blurring" of one gallery space into another produces a novel museum experience.

On the facade of the building, the misalignment between facade layers produces a similar blurring effect, this is exemplified by different materials and color changes. The different scales of facade components are strategically blurred together to deny the unit and bring the facade together as a cohesive whole.

It is worth mentioning that through the combination of components of different sizes and depths outside the building, the different functional requirements of the indoor space are also met, such as the different requirements for natural lighting, the privacy of each function, and the ventilation requirements of the indoor building.

In short, the goal of this design process has been to capture the immaterial and phenomenological moments of the techniques of artwork and use this to further architectural design research.

6

7

8

6 – *Blurred Chiaroscuro* by Fang Cheng and Tianxiao Wang, Night Render
7 – *Blurred Chiaroscuro* by Fang Cheng and Tianxiao Wang, Interior Render

8 – *Blurred Chiaroscuro* by Fang Cheng and Tianxiao Wang, Render

CYBORG PAREIDOLIA

Karel Klein (LECTURER)
Ryan Barnette (TA)

Karel Klein (Lecturer): Partner, RuyKlein – Faculty, Southern California Institute of Architecture – Visiting faculty, University of Pennsylvania, Weitzman School of Design Visiting faculty, Pratt Institute, GAUD

Though some are panicking that AI is eventually going to replace human judgment, the more likely scenario is that human judgment will simply be altered and modified by the presence of AI "partners." Partners, perhaps, because the technology currently classified as AI does not comfortably fit our ideas of what a tool is. Because AI technologies seek to simulate our own capabilities, to say that AI is nothing but a tool would imply that we are also nothing but a tool. So, counter to this idea of AI being merely a new kind of tool would have to be the premise that AI is like us. Therefore, potential collaborators. This studio will be continuing an ongoing investigation into this potentiality. Using one or more networks from a new class of AI software, style transfer algorithms, cycleGANs (generative adversarial networks), etc., our studio will experiment with how this new automated process of "seeing" might begin to suggest both new architectural forms and expressions as well as new grounds upon which these new architectures would occupy.

2 MEMS (MICRO-LECTROMECHANICAL SYSTEM) TRAINING CHAMBER
Nahye Shin and Chengyang Wang

The Sensorium releases one's self from the expectations of perception; to widen the senses beyond what we experience in the everyday. Visitors wander in between and throughout worlds within worlds to experience a multitude of sensorial abstractions. The building aims to explore, question, and alter the nature of perception as one's senses are enhanced, blended, or manipulated through a variety of architectural strategies. Each character contained within the larger "big box" structure of the Sensorium both performs and contains qualities of its interior function via its posture and interaction with human occupants. Orientations and relationships between characters is important to an evocation of their highly specific interior world. The homunculus explores temporal qualities of growth, decay, absorption, discoloration and movement as ink and fungi transform the object throughout its life. As figural and biological representations of the Sensorium, the homunculi demonstrate qualities displayed by and contained within the characters throughout the building and provide a glimpse into the sensory qualities of the project.

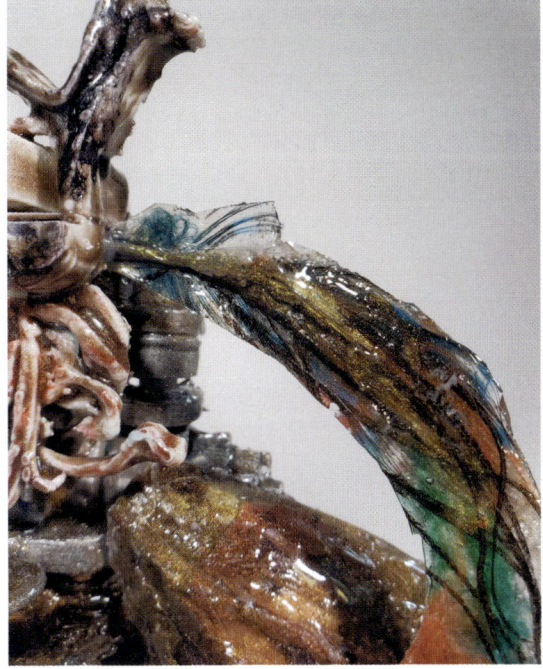

1
3

1 – Studio Photo
2 – *MEMS (micro-lectromechanical system) Training Chamber* by Nahye Shin and Chengyang Wang, Project Description

3 – *MEMS (micro-lectromechanical system) Training Chamber* by Nahye Shin and Chengyang Wang, Model Photo

4

Because these AI networks must be trained with images in order to learn how to "see," they can be introduced to architecture much in the same way that we study architecture, that is through images, drawings, photographs, etc. In other words, precedents. But, because machine vision appears to misalign or misinterpret precedents in an entirely novel way —one might say absurd, or uncanny— strange and exciting questions about the role of historical influence on the production of new objects begin to emerge. We will exploit these new potentials of precedent in our studio.

With regard to this mechanized misinterpretation, this studio continues the ambition to extend theories of artistic estrangement via these new technological regimes. The recent renewal of interest in Viktor Shklovsky and Harold Bloom suggests the ongoing relevance of the premise that creative expression is the result of a process of defamiliarization. In Art as Technique, Viktor Shklovsky argues that great works of art do their work by defamiliarizing normal reality and slowing down habits of perception in the beholder. Similarly, but with regard to difficulty of authoring great works, Harold Bloom asserts in The Anxiety of Influence that masterpieces are nothing more than creative misinterpretations of previous masterpieces—or precedents. The new question, however, is how these theories of estrangement are to be understood when it is not the human author doing the reading or the writing, or the seeing or the imaging, but the machine? Or even more convoluted is the same question relative to a hybrid human-machine author. The weird question of the studio is, how might a cyborg design architecture? This question should not be taken as a preposterous scenario of becoming a bionic designer as kitsch science fiction might like to imagine. As Donna Haraway points out, we are all already cyborgs. The studio will only ask you to recognize this and actively collaborate with our machines.

4 – MEMS (micro-lectromechanical system) Training Chamber by Nahye Shin and Chengyang Wang, Site Feature

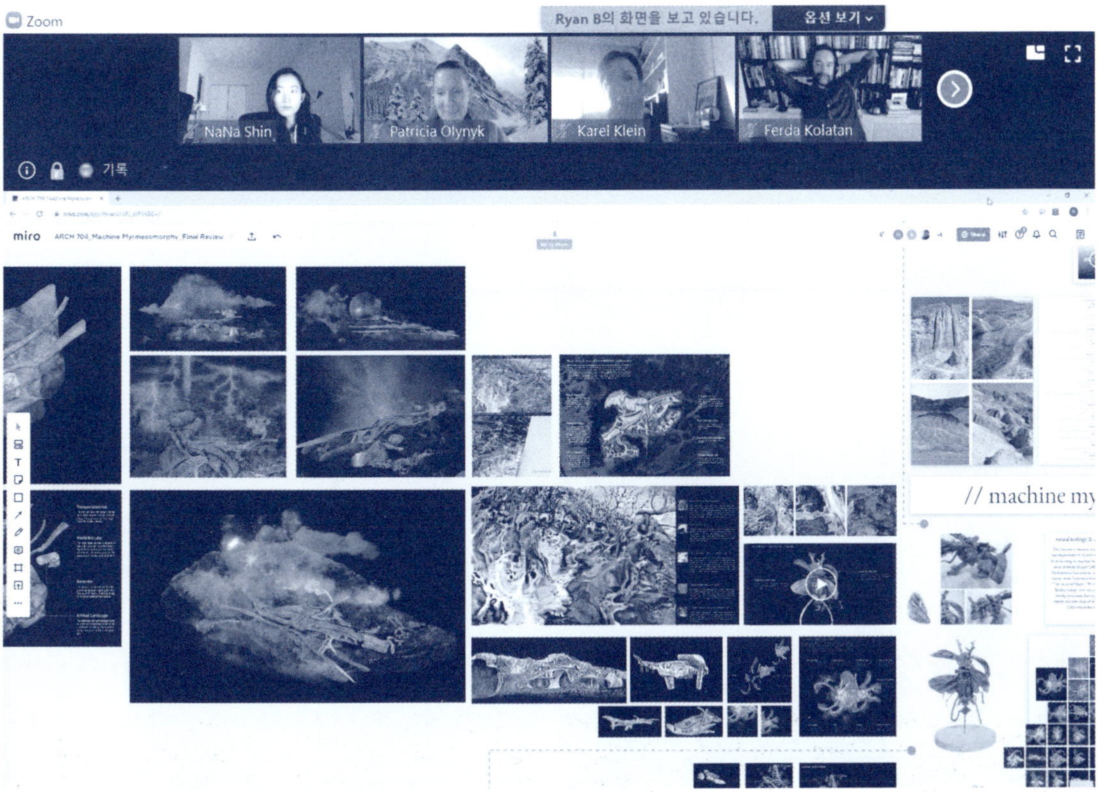

5

6

7

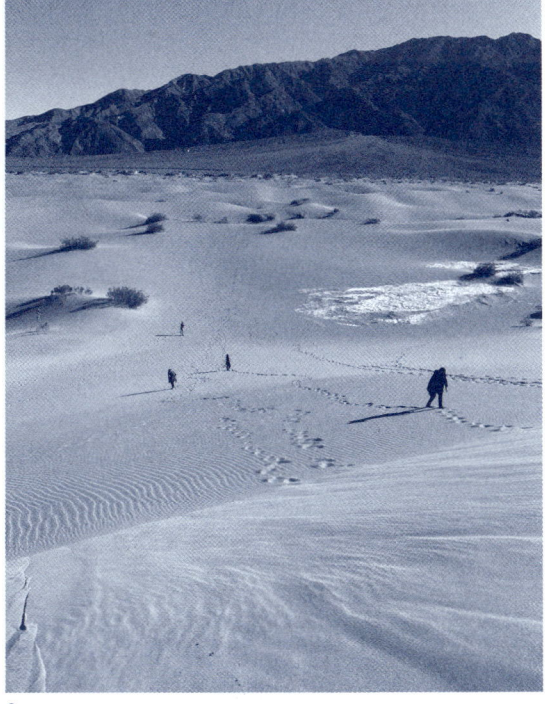

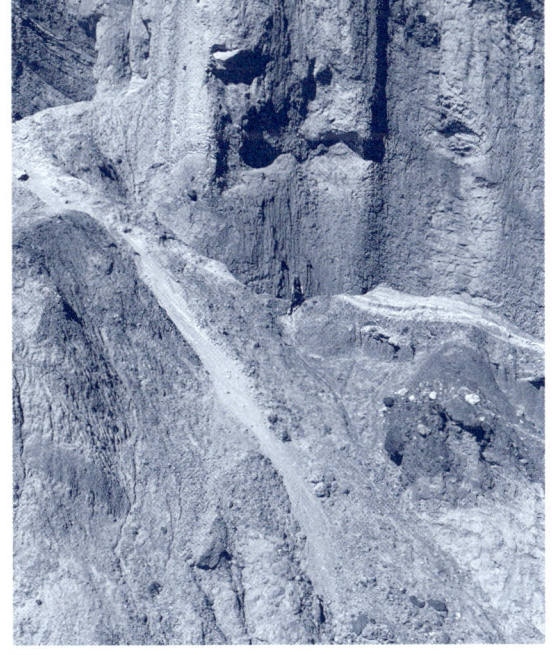

5 – Virtual Studio Review
6 – Travel Week LA—Death Valley, Mesquite Flat Sand Dunes

7 – Travel Week LA—Death Valley, Mesquite Flat Sand Dunes

DEATH VALLEY GEOLOGICAL RESEARCH CENTER
Heyan Xu and In Pun

Through the utilization of AI (artificial intelligence) and style-transfer networks, a new specimen—"Retiform Water Strider"—was developed with strange artificial features, hybrids of the biological and tectonic kinds, considered to be aspects of a specimen found in humid, water-side, and altogether synthetic environments. These generated features were then deployed across the project site of Death Valley, creating a sublime artificial nature. The project was further developed by engaging the artificial nature and artificial features with the program of a geological research center in the mountain range of Death Valley. The artificial features engaged the different scales of the project in various ways. They are recognizable in the webbing shape structure of the specimen, were further translated into the carbon fiber structures across Death Valley, and finally became the infrastructure of the architecture. The shared appearances of features across specimen and landscape translate into different functions in various scales and sometimes retain comparable functions similar to the translucent shell to protect the specimen's soft tissue, which became the environmental shelter exterior layer of the architecture protecting the laboratories underneath from the harsh weather. This machine-human collaboration facilitates new thinking of artificial nature and its synthesis with architectural design.

8

9

10

11

8 – *Death Valley Geological Research Center* by Heyan Xu and In Pun, Atmospheric Site Model Perspective
9 – *Death Valley Geological Research Center* by Heyan Xu and In Pun, Site Model Elevation 1
10 – *Death Valley Geological Research Center* by Heyan Xu and In Pun, Site Model Elevation 2
11 – *Death Valley Geological Research Center* by Heyan Xu and In Pun, Site Model Perspective

BADWATER BASIN TERRAFORMATION CENTER
Mo Shen and Tian Zhang

For our project, using AI (artificial intelligence) and style transfer as tools, we propose a Salt Basin Research Center in Death Valley to explore the machine-human collaboration and its production of the architecture and the surrounding environments. Analyzing the existing geological features on the site and introducing a curated set of new, synthetic features, we began to speculate on how AI would alter the salt terrain visually and programmatically. The creation of a strange new topography, which we refer to as the artificial nature, blends seamlessly with the research facilities and the infrastructures we are proposing. Utilizing AI in this way would reshape the tectonic features of the proposed vast ground as it constantly intermingles with the geology of the existing site. The project then develops a series of formal strategies for blending the artificial nature with the architecture. The artificial nature would wrap around, nest inside, and invade through the structures of the research center so they are inseparable. Besides the private research facilities, the project also aims to open this machine-human collaboration to the public. Therefore, the research center has its own educational programs and exhibition space open to the visitors.

12

13

12 – *Badwater Basin Terraformation Center* by Mo Shen and Tian Zhang, Small Chunk Detail

13 – *Badwater Basin Terraformation Center* by Mo Shen and Tian Zhang, Chunk Model Aerial

SALINE DREAMS 3: AN(OTHER) ALBUM OF FLUID MOTION
OWENS LAKE NATIONAL MONUMENT

Jason Payne (LECTURER)
Michael Zimmerman (TA)

Jason Payne (Lecturer)**:** Associate Professor, UCLA – Principal of Hirsuta – Co-partenered the award-winning office Gnuform. – Worked as Project Designer for Reiser + Umemoto RUR architects and Daniel Libeskind Studio. – Payne holds a Masters of Advanced Architectural Design Degree from Colombia University.

This project involves the engineered ecology and resultant aesthetic implications of the Los Angeles Department of Water and Power's Dust Mitigation Project at Owens Lake, a large site in eastern California of major environmental, historical, political, and infrastructural significance. Until very recently the largest single source of dust pollution in the U.S., the studio examines control methods developed by LADWP to manage this difficult landscape: a complex synthesis of fields, pools, plants, animals, microorganisms, chemicals, minerals, roads, berms, dams, plumbing, power lines, grading, gravel, roads, sensors, and salt that is only partially visible to the human eye. The effects of these reworkings of the landscape are striking, inevitably aesthetic in their expression. Our work imagines a near-future evolution of this infrastructure toward strange new landscapes, turning radically empirical environmental engineering techniques toward a more expansive, aesthetic dimension. The design problem imagines arguments, in the form of visual albums and design projections for the creation of a new national monument for this gigantic anthropocene landscape.

1

SALINE DREAMS
Yujie Li and Yi Rachel Lu

The juxtaposition of human and the hypersaline condition in Owens Lake poses us to reflect on a new ecology between human and extreme environment condition. Brine as the most intense and dynamic form of BACM, its striking color and texture pattern distinguish it from other BACM polygons immediately, leaving a strong impression of unreal and danger. Based on a didactic position, this project proposes to unpack the comprehensive ecology, by displaying all the color swatches though the highly organized and structured salt production process, and on the other hand estrange the experience of brine on the site by creating new painterly effects.

The tension between on ground experience and drone powered remote visiting are addressed throughout the design. They promote different levels and perspectives of close-reading to brine, thus unpack this land of compound differently. From the north brine reservoir, to the painterly mystifying brine field, to the south gridded performative salt pan, visitor and scientists could across diverse landscape transition caused by salinity.

Architecture together with infrastructures are designed to support various brine twining conditions (ecological life). They are also meant to house professionals, scientist, researchers, that are specifically to do with brine (human life). By displaying visual effects of double vision and ambiguity, the interfaces between architecture and landscape become equivocal.

2

External collaboration with two environmental specialists with LADWP: Los Angeles Department of Water and Power, Owens Lake Dust Mitigation Project – Jeffrey Nordin, Watershed Resources Supervisor Owens Lake, LADWP – Ray Ramirez, Environmental Specialist Owens Lake, LADWP

1 – *Saline Dreams* by Yujie Li and Yi Rachel Lu, Project Description
2 – *Saline Dreams* by Yujie Li and Yi Rachel Lu, Site

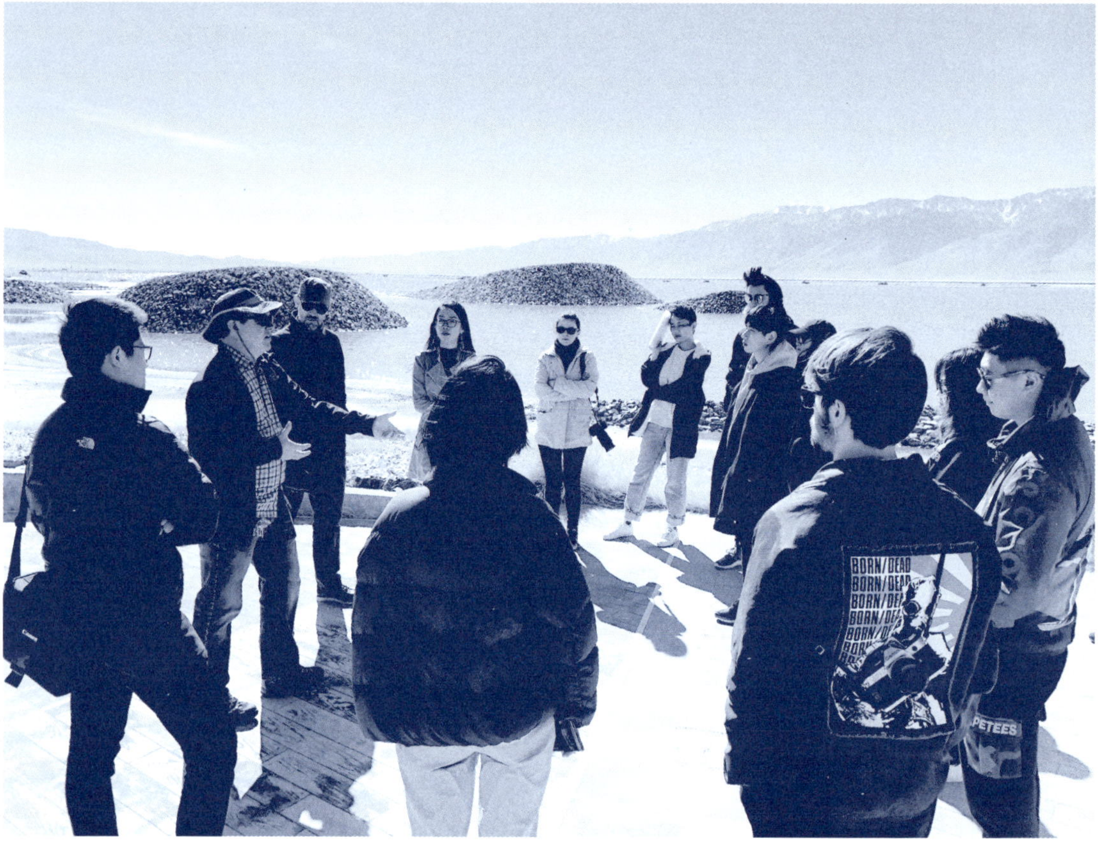

3

4

5

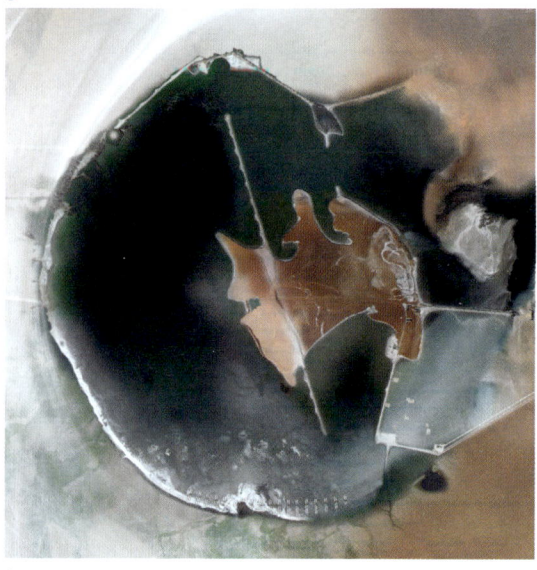

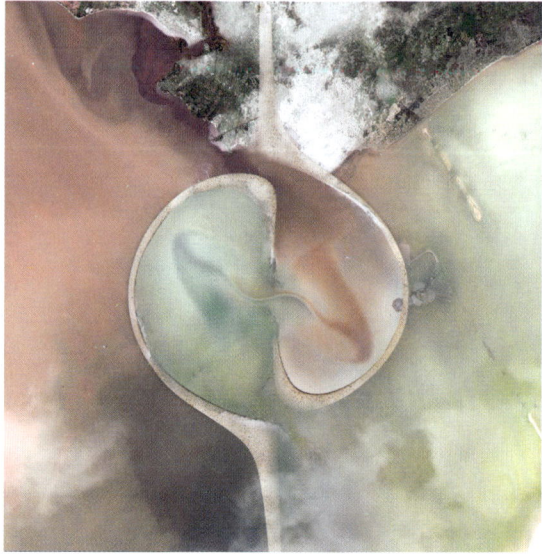

3 – Studio Photo
4 – *Saline Dreams* by Yujie Li and Yi Rachel Lu, Twin 1
5 – *Saline Dreams* by Yujie Li and Yi Rachel Lu, Twin 2

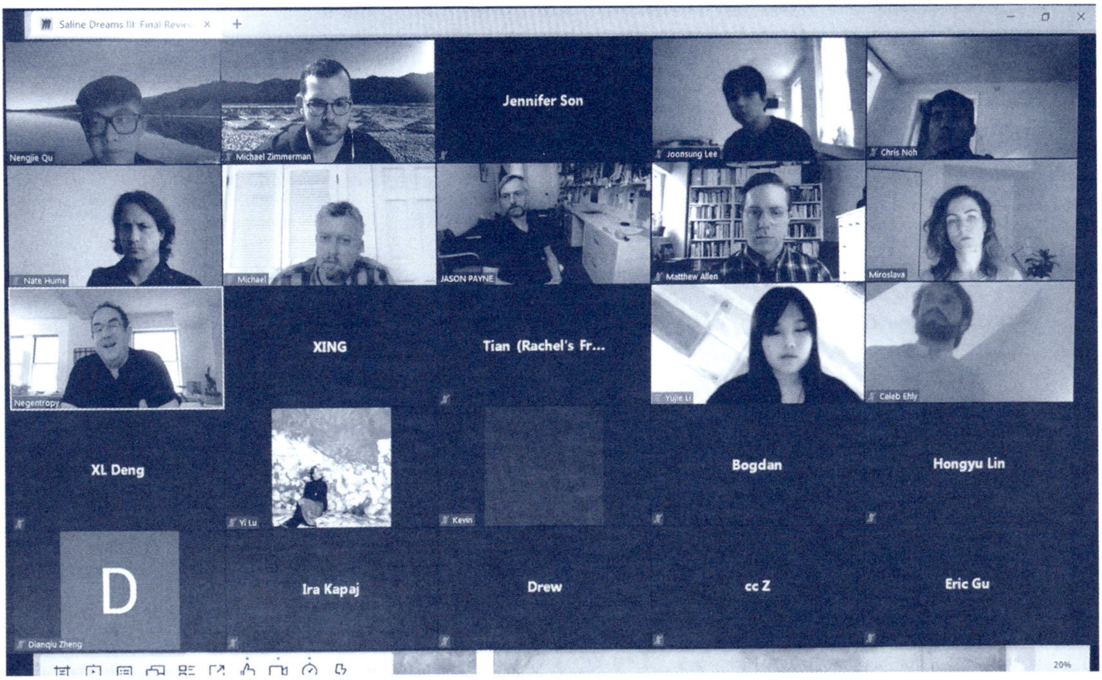

6

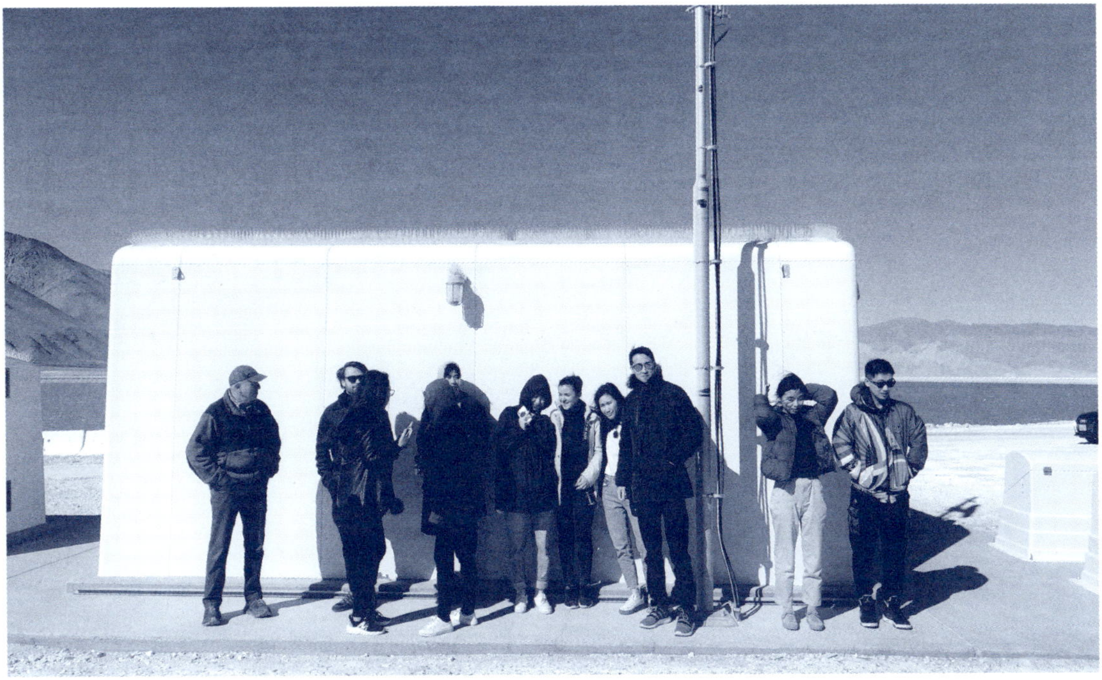

7

6 – Virtual Studio Review
7 – Studio Travel

SALINE DREAMS T1 2A
Caleb Birch Ehly and Joonsung Lee

Through the habitual use of frames, close readings between modes of representation, notions of non-body experience and the use of architectural infrastructural elements to build up a thickened aesthetic effect, we hope to challenge adjust how one registers notions of "architecture" and "landscape." These principles allow this projects to generate conditions that take advantage of our new reality of a mixed bag of experience and representation, those being the common use of Aerial photography found within Google maps and other such interfaces, and in effect produce non-place experience and ambiance. Building and infrastructural systems presents themselves both through the normative usage of elements familiar to the site of Owens lake, and the slightly new, through a refolding of the common place to sometimes normalize the existing that is nothing but "normal," while other times to curate and generate/force esoteric conditions.

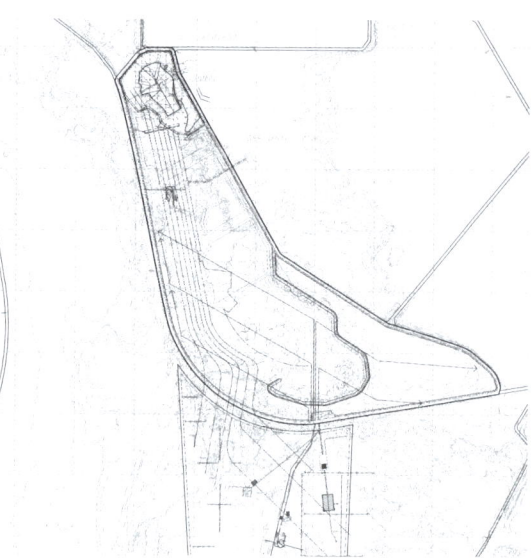

8

9

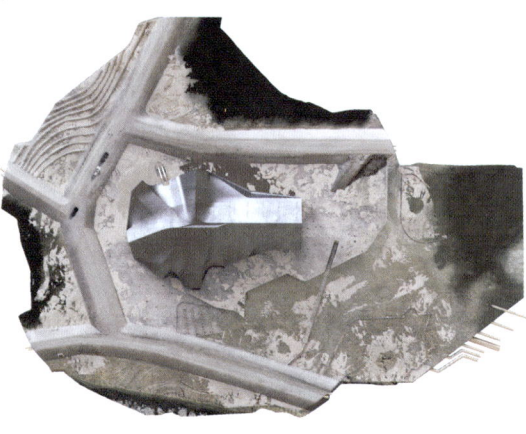

10

11

8 – *Saline Dreams t1 2a* by Caleb Birch Ehly and Joonsung Lee, Large Drawing
9 – *Saline Dreams t1 2a* by Caleb Birch Ehly and Joonsung Lee, Render

10 – *Saline Dreams t1 2a* by Caleb Birch Ehly and Joonsung Lee, PLan View
11 – *Saline Dreams t1 2a* by Caleb Birch Ehly and Joonsung Lee, Full Map Render

ANOTHER ALBUM OF FLUID MOTION
Ira Kapaj and Jennifer Son

The landscape of Owens Lake is distinguishable from the landscape we have perceived with a lens of Romanticism. It is highly specific due to the purpose of dust control, which is shaping the lake to be clearly unnatural in form.

Yet, at a closer look, this engineered landscape is still falling into the trap of deploying "natural" materials in a manner which tries to camouflage this enormous project into the existing lake bed, not at the scale of the playa, but at the scale of the single polygon we are assigned to work with. What is more important, the people involved with this new landscape everyday still seek to go back to an idea of "lakeness", different in geometry, but the same in what a lake means to its human and nonhuman "users."

As designers, we imagine ourselves tasked with changing these romantic notions of perceiving this landscape, and find opportunity in exploring what it means now and what it will mean in the future to design with such projects.

Inspired by the strong winds that characterize Owen's Lake and how the existing flooded areas behave under such force, we turned to the Album of Fluid Motion (Milton Van Dyke, 1982) and studied the fluid dynamics of liquids and obstacles create. Infrastructure and architecture here exist as an agency to create these secondary effects, and because of that the landscape is perceived in a radically different way. Through their highly specific and controlled design, they create the fantastical effects of flows that could not have been visible otherwise. This architecture is merely a machine that creates enormous numbers of variations in the landscape, and eventually in how we perceive this landscape.

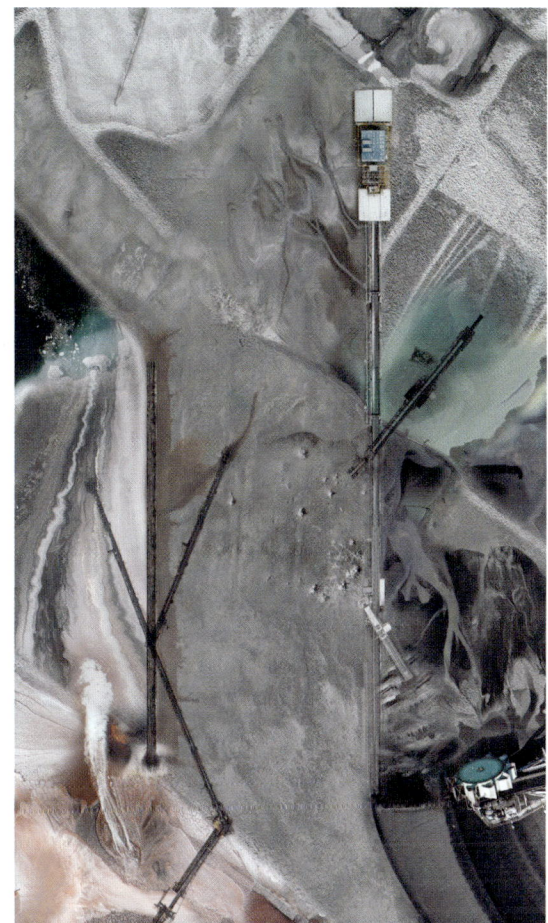

12

13

12 – *Another Album Of Fluid Motion* by Ira Kapaj and Jennifer Son, Middle Zoom
13 – *Another Album Of Fluid Motion* by Ira Kapaj and Jennifer Son, Zoom 1

PLAYHOUSE

Florencia Pita (LECTURER)
Caroline Morgan (TA)

Florencia Pita (Lecturer): Prinicpal of FPmod. – She graduated in 1998 from the National University of Rosario, Argentina, School of Architecture. – Her work has been widely published and received many awards. – Her work has been exhibited in numerous museums, galleries and biennals.

In her novels, Jane Austen (1775-1817) examined the elements of language and the expected social behaviors and class standards that confined the limits existing within the chatter of the daily rituals of her time. In opposition to the restrained structures of speech, her style of writing was loosen and playful, with words such as itty, sprawly and tittupy. These words give texture to the mundane elements of the every day, heightening the oddly normal details of her context, resulting in the conversion of the ordinary into the extraordinary. Austen's maneuver in weaving the qualities of language, threading elements of domesticity to those of amusement, presents an environment of playfulness and an acute speculation on the conflicting mandates that society presents. Her whimsical use of childish words warp through structures and compositions, exposing character and allure. Enter architecture, and architectural language. In an aim to "learn from Jane Austen" we might find design well suited to engage the whimsical and the odd, because design is the makeup of ideas, and ideas can be played up. Like a child's game, the fabric of play is formed by the intermingling of structures and oddities, realities and parodies, representations, and misrepresentations.

2   KALEIDO'SCOPE
Rentian Liu and Lichao Liu

The dramatic turns and rises of urban reformations and development taking place in the areas of the Bunker Hill since 1924, completely eliminated the old neighborhood including many Victorian Houses and transformed the land into today's core cultural districts in Downtown Los Angeles. The gradual establishments of skyscrapers, along with well-known artistic cultural institutions such as the Broad and Walt Disney Concert Hall, bring opportunities and successes of public attention that flourish the area with creativity and inspirations. On the other hand, the removal and disappearance of Victorian Houses from public eyesight, especially its Victorian Ornaments, intricate spaces and unique color palettes, are considered for us, a great loss of cultural and architectural identity that are worth bringing back. All those factors combined, lead to the proposal of creating a Playhouse, adopting itself on the steep slopes that integrates a Victorian House, programs of performances and practices together, with the location adjacent to the art district.

Taking advantage of the existing slope, various segments of public terraces are created in-between fragments of the building volumes, not only to break the continuous grounds into pocket spaces for activating small-group gatherings, but also to offer the better accessibilities into various interior spaces. Therefore, the boundary between inside and outside is blurred by such rhythmic joints of flexible elements, while certain degrees of visual transparencies are purposely embraced along the way. Being able to see through, listen to or get a glimpse of what the others are practicing or performing, potential motivations and inspirations could virtuously be stimulated during the process, which is an important learning atmosphere formulated in this built environment.

1

1 – *Kaleido'scope* by Rentian Liu and Lichao Liu, Research   2 – *Kaleido'scope* by Rentian Liu and Lichao Liu, Research

Project Site

This studio will focus on ideas of 'play' as an entry into architectural language. We will develop a vocabulary of forms and materials that will unravel living spaces and landscapes embedded with color, texture and ornament. For all that is odd and mundane, there is an architecture full of stuff, and an aesthetic of familiarity and cuteness.

In Sianne Ngai book 'Our Aesthetic Categories: Zany, Cute, Interesting' she presents the notion of 'cuteness' as one of 'mute poetics', were language detaches from experience and propels a 'deverbalizing effect':

We have seen how cuteness cutifies the language of the aesthetic response it compels, a verbal mimesis underscoring the judging subject's empathetic desire to reduce the distance between herself and the object.

That short distance suggest an aesthetic experience as an act of submission, an access to the enchantment of form and material.

The project for the studio will be the design of the Colburn School Campus Expansion, a multi-venue building with a 1,100-seat concert hall, a 700-seat studio theater, and a 100-seat cabaret-style space as well as classroom spaces, rehearsal and student housing. This program goes from the domestic scale of housing to the public sphere of music and theater venues. Because it is private and it is also exuberantly public, it is small and also large, it is the realm were the familiar and the extraordinary cohere.

The project site and program aims at connecting to the cultural corridor of Bunker Hill that includes Walt Disney Concert Hall, The Music Center, MoCA and The Broad, making Grand Avenue a unique example of the concentration in the world of performing and visual arts organizations.

The site for this project is Bunker Hill in Downtown Los Angeles. This site that until WWI was a residential suburb populated by grand Victorian mansions and an exclusive character. The fast urban growth of Los Angeles and the construction of the Pasadena Freeway permitted the mobility of the residents of this area to move to other suburbs such as Pasadena and Beverly Hills, making Bunker Hill home to poor tenements. The allure of the Victorian buildings began to fade and a new reputation was given to the area from bling to noir. In 1959 with the Bunker Hill Urban Renewal Project the area was razed and everything was demolished to give place to modern plazas and tall buildings, as an image of the modern world. In 2000 the Los Angeles City Council passed an adaptive reuse ordinance, giving new life to Downtown Los Angeles as old building could be converted for new living units. At the same time the resurgence of Bunker Hill was brought with new projects on Grand Avenue, such as the Disney Concert Hall, The Broad Museum and more ongoing projects.

3

3 – *Kaleido'scope* by Rentian Liu and Lichao Liu, Interior

4

The project site and program aims at connecting to the cultural corridor of Bunker Hill that includes Walt Disney Concert Hall, The Music Center, MoCA and The Broad, making Grand Avenue a unique example of the concentration in the world of performing-and visual arts organizations.

During the mid-XX century Bunker Hill was razed in order to open ground for modernization. All except two Victorian mansions were demolished, these two houses (the Castle and The Salt Box) were raised and moved to Heritage Square in Montecito Hights, just a few miles north. This studio will work with the premise that the houses return to Bunker Hill and are reused for a new life as Playhouse. We will aim at connecting the narrative of the site as a collage of history, with its past and future overlapping in a haphazard manner. As a stand in for the two Victorian houses, we will purchase

5

Victorian Doll houses in one-inch scale, these houses will be assembled and will become 1/3 of the project, the rest of the design will derive from a highly pictorial exercise, were paint becomes building mass as well as decorative ornament.

The design process will be done by a recursive feedback between analog mediums and digital ones. We will begin by creating fresh paint brushes that will be digitally reproduced by a sequence of steps: paint, photo, scan, mesh & print. The last step will be to print the images on fabric and 3D print the brush strokes. An array of softwares will drive this process, such as Maya, ZBrush & Adobe Substance Painter.

4 – Travel Photo

5 – Studio Travel with Florencia Pita

PLAYTIME
Ryan Henriksen and Nick Kalantzopoulos

As a means of further delving into the project and understanding paint at the scale of the user we developed a series of vignettes that highlight specific applications of paint within moments of the project. Through this series, accompanied by isolated ghosted details, we see paint in a variety of applications. At times, these applied brushes envelop underlying objects and become physicalized within spaces of the building. At other points, paint delineates threshold and begins to blur the reading of the underlying architectural language. In this light and through these series of images, the paint becomes an intermediary capturing the residue of the Victorian and augmenting its architectural qualities.

6

7

8

9

6 – *Playtime* by Ryan Henriksen and Nick Kalantzopoulos, Model Axo
7 – *Playtime* by Ryan Henriksen and Nick Kalantzopoulos, Close Up
8 – *Playtime* by Ryan Henriksen and Nick Kalantzopoulos, Entry Hall Vignette
9 – *Playtime* by Ryan Henriksen and Nick Kalantzopoulos, Painted Desk

PLAY HOME
Sierra Summers and Tynx Taneja

The intertwining of paint and architecture allows for a complex reassessment of two seemingly separate mediums. Paint informs architecture and architecture informs paint. The paint strokes transform architectural objects by defamiliarizing them from their classical forms. The proposal of paint as an architectural element also introduces scalar shifts that add complexity and new implications on the spatial experience. This is explored through the reintroduction and reappropriation of Victorian profile curves; a moulding contour becomes a balcony, a glob of paint becomes furniture, and a doorknob detail becomes a roof scape.

10

11

12

13

10 – *Play Home* by Sierra Summers and Tynx Taneja, Chair Table
11 – *Play Home* by Sierra Summers and Tynx Taneja, Doll House
12 – *Play Home* by Sierra Summers and Tynx Taneja, Facade
13 – *Play Home* by Sierra Summers and Tynx Taneja, Chunk Section

CULTURAL OBJECT:
CONTEMPORARY DETAIL TO AESTHETICS

Ali Rahim (PROFESSOR OF ARCHITECTURE)
Hanning Liun (TA)
Siyang Xiao (TA)

Ali Rahim: Professor of Architecture, Director Advanced Architecture Design. – Director, Contemporary Architecture Practice, New York and Shanghai – Awarded Fifty Under Fifty: Innovators of the 21st Century [2015] – Awarded 10 x 10_2 Phaidon Press 2005 – Awarded Architectural Record Design Vanguard Award [2004] – Author: IMPACT Architectural Design, John Wiley and Sons Inc., London. [2020].Future Airports. OROS Editions.

Design Research: Disjunctive Continuity

Within this studio, we will look at new design research techniques using style transfer to manipulate, blend, weave, splice different aesthetics from cultural objects. Japan is the perfect place to look for these cultural objects. Japan's cultural landscape has often been described as homogeneous but with extreme subcultures. This more fragmented and hybridized cultural reality requires a redefinition of space suitable for the new urban youth to thrive, allowing them to perform, to create and to drift away from preconceived ideas of normalcy and success. Architecturally, Japanese disjunctive society can be echoed as disjunctive continuity, where different qualities at times collide, overlap or merge in order to create an unexpected whole. Contrasting geometries can be woven into one another, in order to create visual sensation. Design techniques derive from visual cues of these various cultures, generating formal, spatial, structural and material innovation. In essence, Disjunctive Continuity can be defined as any blending of dissonant elements which creates an original, inexhaustible beauty.

1

DATA MUSEUM
Donghan Yan and Ming Jiang

In our project, we are trying to express what we find interesting in architecture's seaming. We started from the seams from Japanese automobile culture. Japan is not famous only for its automobile merchandise output, but also for its automobile culture output. The Japanese car racing culture shocked us when we watched a relative Japanese Anime or TV show.

When we were in Tokyo this February, we went to the Nissan store at Ginza, and could not move our eyes off this super car. There are different seams in architecture: one kind happens when a surface turns around and becomes an edge, one happens when different objects come together, while another happens when it reveals what happens inside.

Starting from these seams, we studied different space relationships that create these seams, such as layering, nesting, and revealing.

To apply these space relationships into our building, we use machine learning to combine seams and surface qualities. The result provides with us three major typologies: volumetric surfaces layered over each other, flat surfaces nested together, and poked out surfaces that reveal inner space.

Go back to our museum. The data museum would need a lot of space for servers, and the most part of them are on the ground. Its inhabitable space makes it a mechanical floor. The second floor is a broad corridor. That is the "way to the digital world".

After the visitors walk through the corridor and go up, they enter the galleries on the top part of the building, where people watch a video or enter a VR experience.

The building facade corresponds to the inner function.

2

Los Angeles.(2020). Catalytic Formations. China Building Press. Beijing. (2012). Elegance. Architectural Design, John Wiley and Sons Inc., London. [2007]. Catalytic Formations. Routlegde. London. (2007)

1 – *Data Museum* by Donghan Yan and Ming Jiang, Project Description
2 – *Data Museum* by Donghan Yan and Ming Jiang, Wall Section

3

Technique: Machine Learning Imagery and Style Transfer

Novelty and innovation in aesthetics is directly tied to technique and technology. To be influential and impactful in culture, Architects must understand what technologies are at the forefront in their day, develop techniques that utilize these technologies for novel aesthetics, and find a way to make them architecturally useful and relevant. Maybe the most talked about and misunderstood contemporary technological advancement is that of Artificial Intelligence. Many believe that this could be the most influential technological advancement since the computer itself and that it is poised to change everything about our way of life. Many point to self-driving cars, robotic automation, or cybernetics as future innovations of the AI era. However, one of the most important innovations that could transform architecture, art, and aesthetics is style transfer. Style transfer is a machine-learning based method of transferring aesthetic qualities from one image to another. It can be used as a design research tool to develop new techniques—producing new aesthetics.

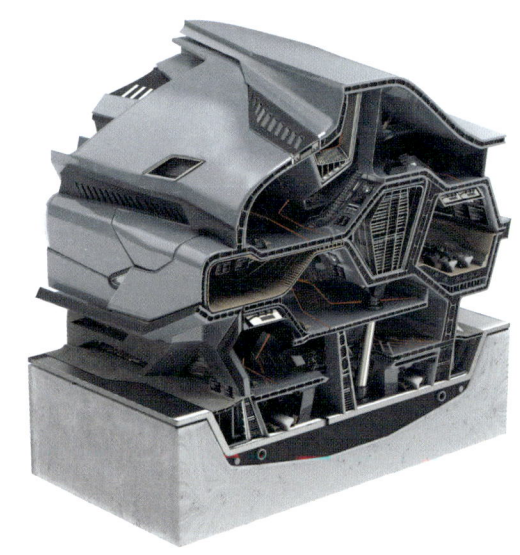

4

3 – *Data Museum* by Donghan Yan and Ming Jiang, Render   4 – *Data Museum* by Donghan Yan and Ming Jiang, Cross Section

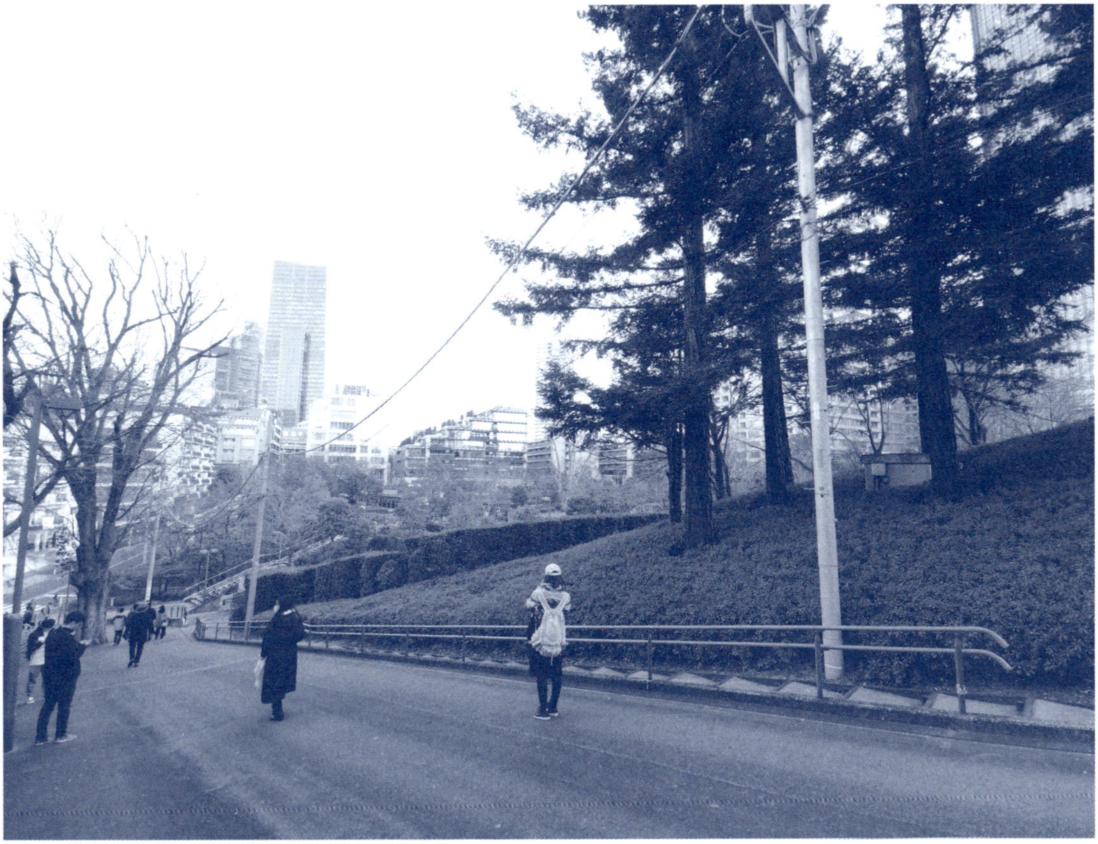

5

6

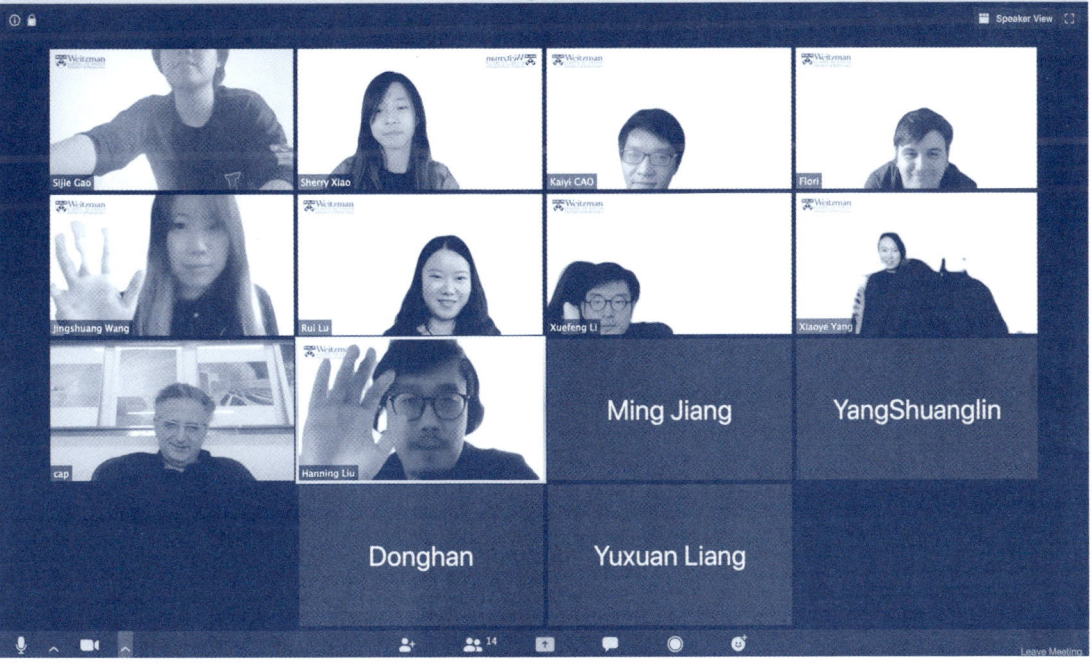

5 – Studio Travel
6 – Ali Rahim in Virtual Studio Review

ELEMENTAL DISCONTINUITY
Sijie Gao and Yuxuan Liang

Our project is focusing on disjunctive continuity, which is derived from Japanese aesthetics.

From our previous research, we studied animation and fashion both in studio and during our field trip. We learned that in these design, the continuous moments or components are broken in the context of Japanese aesthetics, like soft ruffles breaking down the continuous connection of body to arms. You can see here, the skylight window, or we call it cylinder space. Not only the form, it also breaks down the seam meant to cross it. That's exactly what we learned from fashion.

And these seams in different direction—vertical, horizontal, linear, and curvature—come together to break down the continuity of each other. Elements inserted in different scale on the surface and cross the seams. These are derived from science fiction or robot animation. We created the sense that the elegant fashion design is nested in the robot or animation design.

Before we move on, we want to speak more about Tokyo based on what we discussed. During our field trip, we find that these features also appear in architecture and city. In those high-density building areas, roofs, windows and details which designed by different architects, are practicing the same rule. They are all different but what's most fancy and attracting are the broken parts that come together, regenerating a sense of disjunctive continuity. In conclusion, it affect not on the aesthetics, but within the program, circulation, and most of the architectural parts.

7

8

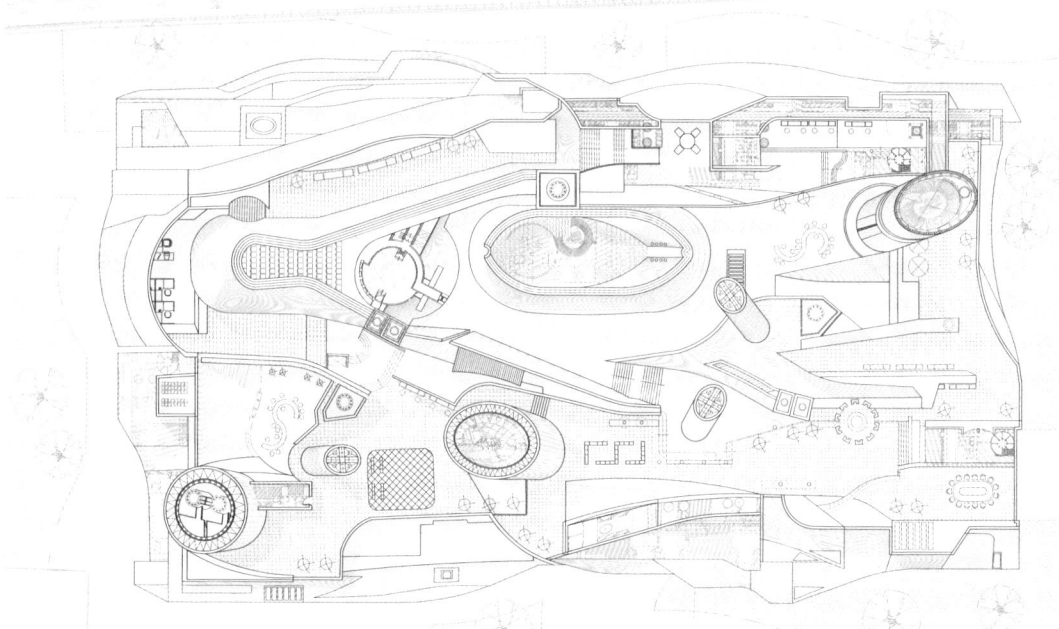

9

7 – *Elemental Discontinuity* by Sijie Gao and Yuxuan Liang, Top Down
8 – *Elemental Discontinuity* by Sijie Gao and Yuxuan Liang, Detail

9 – *Elemental Discontinuity* by Sijie Gao and Yuxuan Liang, Plan

LUSH CLOUDS
Xiaoye Yang and Ninghsin Chuang

Located at the heart of Roppongi, the project aims to redefine Japanese culture through synthesizing various cultural qualities. Focusing on the introvert characteristic of Japanese people, the project employs the concept of hiding and reveal to adapt with design research. Furthermore, the project explored the possibilities to bring nature into Tokyo's urban life within its cultural context. The exterior is defined by adopting the basic geometry of spheres through various methods of carving and colliding to form fine seams that emerge from a counter configuration. The project explores the zoning of different materials and texture to disguise the form and create a diverse surface definition to create continuity on disjunctive geometry. Extending the concept from exterior to interior, the project utilizing contrasting geometry, straight cylinder, to produce different effects but achieve the same goal of hiding and revealing.

10 – *Lush Clouds* by Xiaoye Yang and Ninghsin Chuang, Top View
11 – *Lush Clouds* by Xiaoye Yang and Ninghsin Chuang, Wall Section
12 – *Lush Clouds* by Xiaoye Yang and Ninghsin Chuang, Aerial

POLYVALENT MATTER:
AN ADDITIVE MANUFACTURED ARCHITECTURE

Robert Stuart-Smith (ASSISTANT PROFESSOR OF ARCHITECTURE)
Musab Badahdah (TA)

Robert Stuart-Smith: Assistant Professor of Architecture and Program Director, MSD Robotics and Autonomous Systems (MSD-RAS) – Assistant Professor of Architecture, University of Pennsylvania, Weitzman School of Design – Director of the Autonomous Manufacturing Lab | Penn Architecture & UCL Computer Science. – Director of Robert Stuart-Smith Design, Founding Partner of Kokkugia – Ma. Architecture & Urbanism, Architectural Association School of Architecture, London

Polyvalent Matter explores an additive manufactured industrial architecture that operates as a form of cultural production, while aiming to integrate material-scales of design-expression as an intrinsic property of formal, spatial and structural order.

Shapeways Factory-Showroom

Manufacturing companies are known and valued for their products but also for the quality and identity of the buildings in which these products are made. Factory-showrooms such as Vitra's Weil-am-Rhein campus operate as both industrial buildings and arenas for public visitation. Marco Zanuso's design for Olivetti's Buenos Aires Factory (1964) or Heatherwick's Bombay Safire Distillery directly relate each company's production ethos within the aesthetics and manufacture of architecture. The studio developed designs for a Shapeways factory yet unlike other manufacturing companies, shapeways does not sell a defined set of products but manufactures items on-demand that can be designed and sold by anyone. Since 2007, the 3D printing company has manufactured and sold more than ten million objects, all-the-while, only employing 22 people on its Long Island site. Economical and logistical benefits of this are self-evident, yet there is a socio-cultural impact from businesses that operate with reduced employment. How could Shapeways offset this through other activities that might provide a positive impact on the local community, and reduce the impact of automation on urban centers? Shapeways has already engaged NYC Government backed incubator activities to support the local community. The studio explores an extension of this: the addition of sponsored artist-in-residence studio spaces and a gallery-shop to provide local designers a means of access to facilities and the market, fostering greater community and human engagement.

1   SHAPEWAYS 4.0: BRIDGED & HYBRIDIZED
Jing Yuan, Youyu Zhang, Zhe Zhong

Shapeway's new 3D printing factory aims to re-brand the company both as an industry-leader by introducing new modes of manufacturing, and also as a community-builder by creating a new technological cultural district. The new factory site extends beyond the old factory through three bridges that connect to adjacent buildings to unite production with community activities, thereby creating a new-interconnected neighborhood. Inspired by Pierre Luigi Nervi's integrated approaches to columns and roof-spanning structures, the additively manufactured building is supported by multi-manifold branching columns that form the space of floors, mezzanines and valleys (lower-set floors). This novel spatial strategy enables safe co-habitation and co-working of people and machines undertaking Industry 4.0 manufacturing activities. The exterior of the building operates as a hybrid between building-scale continuous geometry and the discrete triply-periodic gyroid elements that operate as both a material lattice structure and as a louvre system while attempting to convey a similar variable aesthetic to the exterior as seen in additively manufactured metal component parts.

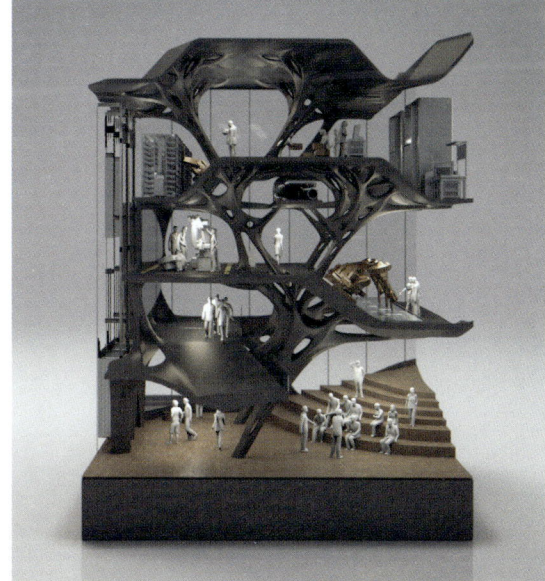

2

1 – *Bridged & Hybridized* by Jing Yuan, Youyu Zhang and Zhe Zhong, Project Description
2 – *Bridged & Hybridized* by Jing Yuan, Youyu Zhang and Zhe Zhong, Chunk

Additive Manufactured Architecture

Shapeways inhabits a "Ford-ist" (mass-produced) building whose serial repetition, and geometrical resolution are derived from an age prior to the advent of 3d printed mass-customized production. Additive manufactured buildings have already been constructed by Winsun, Apis Khor and others in concrete, while MX3D has 3D-printed a formally complex metal bridge. To date, 3D-printed buildings are relatively low-resolution compared to aerospace or industrial products, or historical buildings formed in plastic materials such as reinforced concrete. Piere Luigi Nervi's isostatic slabs seen in the Gatti Wool Factory (1951) and Manifattura Tabacchi (1952) served as precedents in the studio due to their embodiment of structural principles whilst operating as highly-articulated forms of design expression. The studio commenced with structural analysis of a structural bay from some of Nervi's projects, and development of design variations that were topologically, structurally optimized and analyzed to determine a relation between form, topology, structural force propagation and material grain-direction. These studies served as inspiration in projects that aimed to develop a material-order that operated in a polyvalent manner: as architectural space, form, structure and ornament, and as a wider range of aesthetic and scenario-driven properties, characteristics and affects. *Polyvalent Matter* investigates an Industrial architecture recast as an engaging, urban condition that incorporates both production and community activities, and articulates a mass-customized, high-resolution material-architectural order.

SHAPEWAYS 4.0: RAPID MEDICAL MANUFACTURING
Siyi Wang, Tsui-Lun Wang, Yuqing Ye

In parallel to 3D printing technology rapid development has been its infiltration and up-take within many different fields, including medicine. The international 3D print manufacturing company Shapeways sees the value and potential of utilizing its expertise and technology within the medical sector. Situated in a prime location on Long Island City, Shapeways new headquarters aims to become a major medical 3D print supplier for the numerous hospitals located across the East River near the Manhattan shore. The headquarters contains manufacturing and public spaces, with part of the building elevated above grade to allow access for commercial and emergency vehicles to cross the site at street level. Two types of product are manufactured in the building; medical prints (such as life-critical medical equipment and implants), and non-medical goods, necessitating a dual-speed manufacturing and circulatory system within the building. A medical-related circulation route connects a rooftop helipad and ground-floor loading area with a high-speed medical manufacturing zone while a second non-medical production and circulation series of spaces is located in an adjacent, independent area that also links into a public visitation set of spaces and circulatory routes. The building is constructed using additive manufacturing technology, allowing its structural system to vary in geometry and density. Columns and structural lattices vary in porosity and topology, and create a sense of openness with substantial top-light natural lighting. The building exterior negotiates the raised ground to support the medical deliveries at grade while also touching down to provide entry access points that double as primary structural supports.

4

3 – *Rapid Medical* by Siyi Wang, Tsui-Lun Wang and Yuqing Ye, Project Description
4 – *Rapid Medical* by Siyi Wang, Tsui-Lun Wang and Yuqing Ye, Atrium View

5

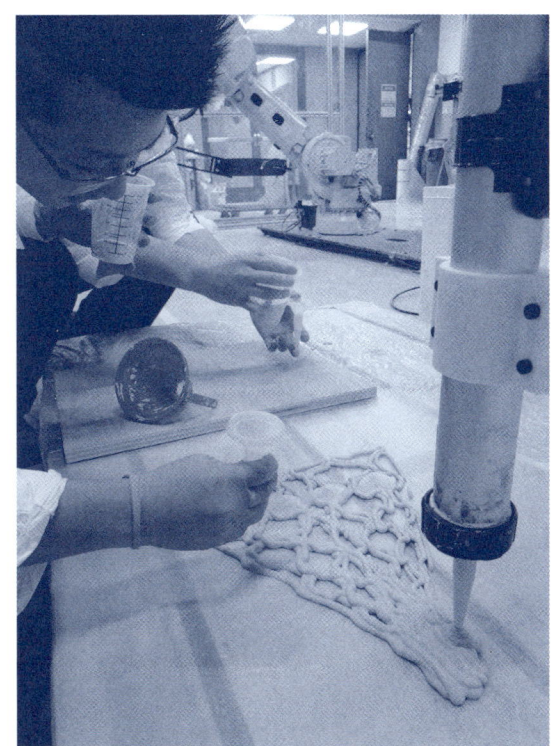

6

7

5 – *Rapid Medical* by Siyi Wang, Tsui-Lun Wang and Yuqing Ye, Render

6-7 – Studio Travel

MEKHOS
Yichao Jin, Zachary Jones, and Ian Hoi Yin Lai

Can a building be both an agent and a remedy, a producer and also a product? This project looks to Shapeways, a 3D Printing company, and the prospect of re-imaging their current factory. Electronic Waste (E-Waste) has become a global problem, exceeding current recycling capacity. The proximity of an E-Waste recycling facility to the Shapeway's site presents an opportunity for a reliable source for materials, and a means to combat this global problem. This new factory, *Mekhos*, aims to re-envision the factory not only as an iconographic new facility, but also as a mission-critical project, aiming to expand and demonstrate recycling and advanced fabrication working harmoniously. *Mekhos* is a fully 3D printed structure that is fabricated on its industrial site from neighboring recycled E-Waste material, and operates as a storage and material processing facility, factory, showroom and gallery.

8

9
10

11

8 – *Mekhos* by Yichao Jin, Zachary Jones and Ian Hoi Yin Lai, RCP
9 – *Mekhos* by Yichao Jin, Zachary Jones and Ian Hoi Yin Lai, Gallery Render Perspective
10 – *Mekhos* by Yichao Jin, Zachary Jones and Ian Hoi Yin Lai, Rendered Chunk
11 – *Mekhos* by Yichao Jin, Zachary Jones and Ian Hoi Yin Lai, Front Elevation

SHAPEWAYS AUTOMOTIVE FACTORY
David Forero, Ruxin Zheng, and Atharva Ranade

Shapeways, an international 3D printing company has recently partnered with DSM, a material science company to produce large scale industrial products. The project proposes that Shapeways-DSM will enter the automotive industry with their ability to fabricate at a large scale and utilize their vast resources of materials to offer the industry novel designs for 3d printed vehicles. The project proposes a renovation to the "Ford-ist" (mass produced) warehouse that they currently inhabit to create a connection between the manufacturing model that they operate within, and their working environment. The new factory will be built to introduce their new service of 3D automotive prototyping and manufacturing. They will also host an artist in residency program that focus on robotics and automation to propose speculative solutions for the automotive industry, with ideas that can be realized and tested on-site. The new factory will house two types of public gallery spaces; one dedicated to vehicles, and the other to showcase Shapeways existing product line of 3D-printed objects and their material library. The new Shapeways factory expresses the potentials of additive manufacturing at a building scale where complexity and variety is not a limiting factor in design or construction. The qualities of the fabrication process become expressive and excessive. The highly articulated 3D printed product is indexical of a process of extrusion and layering formed additively using dynamic formwork, placing material organization as an active agent in building element formation. The building in its entirety can be conceived of hybridized building parts that synthesize space and structure.

12

13

14

12 – *Shapeways Automotive Factory* by David Forero, Ruxin Zheng and Atharva Ranade, Interior
13 – *Shapeways Automotive Factory* by David Forero, Ruxin Zheng and Atharva Ranade, Rendering
14 – *Shapeways Automotive Factory* by David Forero, Ruxin Zheng and Atharva Ranade, Facade

THE CITY OF NEWARK, THE SOUTH WARD, AND THE AIRPORT
In Collaboration with the Department of City and Regional Planning

Marilyn Jordan Taylor
Robbie Romo (TA)

Marilyn Jordan Taylor (Professor of Architecture and Urban Design, Former Dean): FAIA – Professor of Architecture & Urban Design – Dean of Weitzman 2008 – 2016 – Former Partner and Chairman of Skidmore, Owings & Merrill

Collaborations: New Jersey Institute of Technology, Hillier School of Architecture, Darius Solluhub, Professor of Architecture – Regional Plan Association, Nat Bottigheimer – City of Newark, Chris Watson, Planning Director, City of Newark – Gensler, James Klauder, Architect

The brilliant new Headhouse at Newark Liberty International Airport will bring 21st century travel experiences to the millions of airline and train passengers sharing this iconic new air/intercity rail terminal. Its site, adjacent to and spanning over the Northeast Corridor rail line, situates the Headhouse squarely in Newark's "airport city" which blends historic industries and new ones in an array of livable, healthy neighborhoods. A continuous shared public realm winding through the terminal and the urban districts will connect the experiences of travelers with everyday Newark, which is becoming one of the region's thriving 21st century workplaces and neighborhoods. The City of Newark, through its equitable growth initiatives, will create a vibrant economy, sharing its identity and culture through local food, art, and music. The Headhouse will secure EWR's international reputation as one of the world's unique and enjoyable airports.

EWR AIRPORT HEADHOUSE AND TRAIN STATION 2050
Daniel Shin, Xiangyu Chen, Yiding Wang

The EWR headhouse and the train station proposal introduces a new concept for extending the public realm into spaces that are often considered private and secure. The design connects the headhouse to the South Ward neighborhood with an elevated bridge, seeking to improve neighborhood access to local trains and regional and international air travel. The residents of the community and visitors can walk on the bridge to access the extensive collection of public amenities conveniently located in the headhouse's interior and exterior, including restaurants, shopping center, performance venue, and public plaza. In addition to serving as a connection to the headhouse, the elevated bridge serves as a train station that will service both regional and inter-regional train, including Amtrak, NJ Transit, and PATH. The new design takes the unprecedented step of giving right of access to public at the center of domestic and international travel.

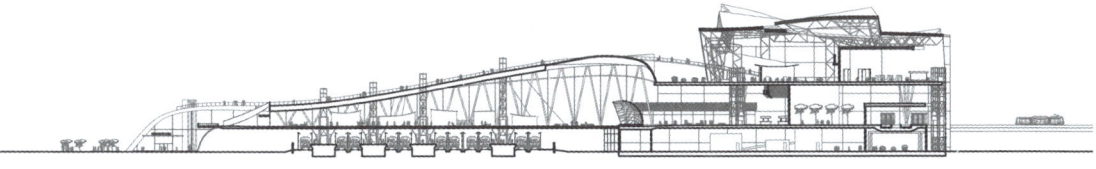

1 – *EWR Airport Headhouse and Train Station 2050* by Daniel Shin, Xiangyu Chen and Yiding Wang, Project Description
2 – *EWR Airport Headhouse and Train Station 2050* by Daniel Shin, Xiangyu Chen and Yiding Wang, Section
3 – *EWR Airport Headhouse and Train Station 2050* by Daniel Shin, Xiangyu Chen and Yiding Wang, Train Station and Platforms

FUTURE SYMMETRIES:
LA BREA TAR PITS ON THE MIRACLE MILE

Marion Weiss (GRAHAM PROFESSOR OF PRACTICE)
Michael A. Manfredi (GUEST CRITIC)
Nicole Bronola (TA)

Marion Weiss (Graham Professor of Practice): Marion Weiss is cofounder of WEISS/MANFREDI Architecture/Landscape/Urbanism based in New York City and the Graham Chair Professor of Architecture at the University of Pennsylvania. Her multidisciplinary firm operates at the nexus of architecture, art, landscape, and urban design. Her firm's Olympic Sculpture Park exemplifies this cross disciplinary design approach and the project has been

Los Angeles is a city of paradoxes, nurturing both real and fictional histories while inventing yet to be imagined futures. La Brea Tar Pits, the largest urban paleontological research site in the world, is located on Wilshire Boulevard, the city's "Miracle Mile" and embodies these diametrically oppositional identities.

The discovery of the La Brea Tar Pits, a sticky petri dish for research, emerged from the Los Angeles oil industry that excavated oil and tar for the thousands of miles of roadway that pave the expanse of Los Angeles Valley. Since 1923, more than 3.5 million exceptionally well-preserved prehistoric specimens, from the very large mastodon skeletons to the smallest paleo-botanical pollens, have been discovered. Acting as a time capsule of the Pleistocene past, the research from this site has revealed insights about the evolution of life on the planet and increasingly relevant information about the science of climate change.

Now focused on 13 acres, the Tar Pits and the nearly 50-year-old Page Museum reflect the impact of constant active on-site excavation and research and visitation that continues to grow as it serves both metropolitan and international communities.

which makes visible the interconnected matrices and wider relevance of the tar pits through scientific engagement, research, play and discovery. The new campus creates an infrastructural framework for temporal, immersive pavilions that increase the visibility of the work as more excavations are uncovered in time. The proposal creates an immersive environment, one that allows the work to be brought to the surface and invites the public to see the tar from different perspectives and scales.

2

3

The Research

The studio was initiated with a three-week research project on Hybrid Prototypes, with case studies that ranged from historic infrastructural projects to iconic museum and research centers. From these studies, new prototypical hybrids, with distinctly different architectural DNA, were produced and recast to address new programmatic and site-specific challenges. To understand the evolving cultural identities of museums and research centers, the studio travelled to Los Angeles and met with cultural and

1

LA BREA RESEARCH CAMPUS
Perry Ashenfelter, Marta Llor, Catherine Shih

As much as LA is known for its stunning views, skyline, and sunsets, it's also a city where oil and the automobile have threatened the diverse ecological populations present, not unlike the tar pits thousands of year ago. Our proposal reinvigorates one of the few large urban green spaces in the area and connects a series of cultural icons through a gridded organizational framework to create a cohesive cultural district. Through our understanding of La Brea's rich history, our mission was to create a community-oriented campus,

recognized internationally through museum exhibitions and design awards. Time Magazine identified the park as one of the top 10 projects in the world, Barcelona's World Architecture Festival selected the project as winner in the Nature Category, I.D. Magazine awarded it the highest Environment Design Award, and it was the first project in North America to win Harvard University's Veronica Rudge Green Prize in Urban Design.

scientific leaders at the Los Angeles Museum of Natural History as well as other Los Angeles Institutions that are actively shaping the city's cultural imagination.

4   UNFOLDING HORIZON
Jungwen Luo and Regina Wei

Creating a backbone that connects Wilshire Boulevard and Mchael Heizer's Levitated Mass, this project aims to establish an urban pathway that responds to adjacent cultural landmarks and subway line. The design elevates ground circulation to roof level, which unfolds the horizon of Museum Row. It also unfolds the story of the sity by creating various viewing platforms and pathways that engage visitors with the process of finding, excavatng, and preserving fossils.

New Symmetries
the collection, the community, and the center for research:

This studio proposed the creation of a place to convene scientists, museum visitors and scholars to leverage this site of science and paleontological research. The research raised a series of questions: what new symmetries between these prehistoric artifacts and contemporary science can be discovered? What architectural "DNA" can be extracted and abstracted from a series of infrastructural and cultural hybrids? How can the specificity of this place of science, located in the heart of Wilshire Boulevard's "Miracle Mile," be leveraged to tell a globally pressing story? How can a series of projective strategies recast symmetries between architecture and landscape, culture and science, the paleontological past and projective future?

5

6

1 – *La Brea Research Campus* by Perry Ashenfelter, Marta Llor, Catherine Shih, Project Description
2 – *La Brea Research Campus* by Perry Ashenfelter, Marta Llor, Catherine Shih, Perspective Cage
3 – *La Brea Research Campus* by Perry Ashenfelter, Marta Llor, Catherine Shih, Site Plan
4 – *Unfolding Horizon* by Jungwen Luo and Regina Wei, Project Description

7

8

5 – *Unfolding Horizon* by Jungwen Luo and Regina Wei, Stair Case Day
6 – *Unfolding Horizon* by Jungwen Luo and Regina Wei, Excavation

7-8 – Studio Travel with Marion Weiss

MUSEUM OF THE UNPREDICABLE
Gordon Cheng, Xuechen Chen and Xiaotong Jiang

Museum of the Unpredictable is located at the La Brea Tar Pits in Los Angeles, where uncertainty lies underneath the thick tar, and such uncertainty is what makes the Tar Pit captivating. The history of the tar pit demonstrates how the process of excavation, discovery, and preservation play huge roles in the site. We want to focus on these three elements in our design and capture the uncertainty of the Tar Pits.

Entering from Wilshire Boulevard, people will first experience the journey of being submerged underneath tar and will arrive at the gathering and exhibition space underneath page museum's canopy. When we enter into the building, we will see the exhibition of fossils from both storage and hallway. In the research building, each excavation site is connected with each other to create a maze-like circulation, while people see the process of excavation at the ground. In our institution building, people are able to learn from lectures, while gazing through the vast excavation sites across.

The uncertainty within excavation triggers the excitement of discovery, while searching through these uncertainties, we need to read and uncover the stories behind them. So we can discover and re-tell these majestic stories in the future.

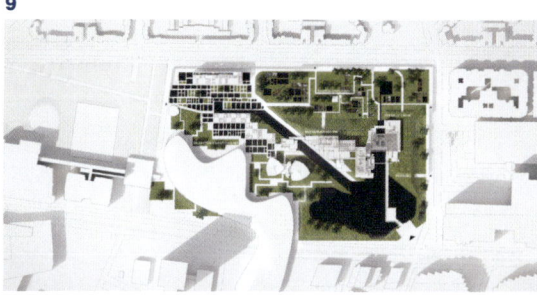

9 – *Museum of The Unpredicable* by Gordon Cheng, Xuechen Chen and Xiaotong Jiang, Excavation
10 – *Museum of The Unpredicable* by Gordon Cheng, Xuechen Chen and Xiaotong Jiang, Plan Program
11 – *Museum of The Unpredicable* by Gordon Cheng, Xuechen Chen and Xiaotong Jiang, Canal
12 – *Museum of The Unpredicable* by Gordon Cheng, Xuechen Chen and Xiaotong Jiang, Section

WORLD WITHIN A WORLD
Cheng Sien Hang (Carl) and Deng Xianlong (Dominic)

The project explores the past and present of La Brea Tar Pits in Los Angles relative to its context and the artifacts embedded in the site. The mission of the project is to unravel the magnificence of the unique geological site and open up the museum to showcase the history that is buried. Our vision for the project is to create a journey that carries people from the present to the past.

The design frames the existing Page Museum with new light-filled exhibition spaces and a parametric canopy that extends over the new museum. The new museum interacts with the landscape through a pathway that leads the visitors across the site. Alongside the pathway, visitors can access the tar pits research field and enjoy the pre-historic landscape. The new canopy also provide shade to the much needed Los Angeles climate. People can enjoy the refreshing breeze in the semi-outdoor atrium surrounded by exhibition halls that showcases fossils illuminated by the natural light.

The design aims to create a dialogue between the new building and the existing museum, the materiality of the new building and the texture of the fossil, the pattern of the canopy and the tectonic of the fossil bones.... these dialogues bring people from the present to the past.

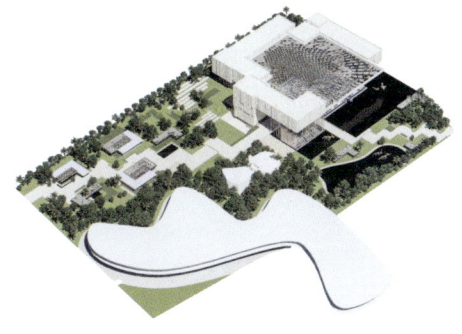

13 – *World Within A World* By Cheng Sien Hang (Carl) and Deng Xianlong (Dominic), Diagrams
14 – *World Within A World* By Cheng Sien Hang (Carl) and Deng Xianlong (Dominic), Site
15 – *World Within A World* By Cheng Sien Hang (Carl) and Deng Xianlong (Dominic), Exterior
16 – *World Within A World* By Cheng Sien Hang (Carl) and Deng Xianlong (Dominic), Long Section

[ARCH 712] VISUAL RESEARCH: ARCHITECTURE AND MEDIA AFTER WWII
Taryn Mudge

This seminar questioned how architects have engaged in visual research of the built environment within the process of architectural design. In particular, we considered the media and methods architects have used to observe and to record building sites and how visual information has influenced design thinking and informed architectural proposals in the postwar period. The visual material under investigation in this course included photography (aerial, documentary, street, etc.), film, sketches, painting, collage, mapping as well as magazines and advertisements.

Additionally, we considered the physical distance and relationship between the observer and the observed. We asked, does the architect observe the site from the air, as a pedestrian, or through a windshield? Do they barrow images or make their own? Are they in search of precise information or are they hoping to uncover the mood or local character? Are they preparing for a commissioned project or are they dreaming of a utopian future?

The course was organized into three parts: Part I concentrated on approaches to visual research and observation in Europe immediately following the Second World War, Part II focused on the American context and images of postwar consumer culture, and Part III discussed the rapid evolution of media and architecture in the late 20th century and question the trajectory of the "post" periods – post-modern, post-post-modern, post-documentary, post-digital and beyond.

In addition to studying historical and theoretical content, the students were asked to implement a method of visual research discussed in the seminar. This was a creative exercise that took on the form of a visual essay and many students chose to focus on sites under investigation in their design studios. The outcomes ranged in media from collage, montage, photography, 3d modeling, mapping, and video.

[ARCH 712] ARCHITECTURAL ENVELOPES: TECHNOLOGY AND EXPRESSION
Dr. Ariel Genadt

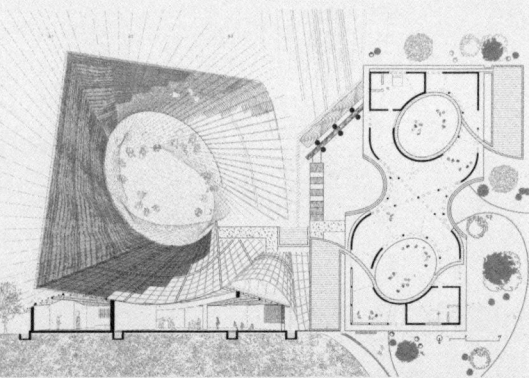

Since the commercialization of steel and glass technologies in the mid 19th century, building envelopes have become the prime architectural subject of experimentations and investments, as well as physical failures and theoretical conflicts. This seminar takes that technological revolution as a point of departure to examines the relationship between construction technologies and architectural expression in the 20th and 21st centuries. It unfolds the reciprocal nourishment between theory and practice in salient case studies from around the world, built in different cultures and climates, and in a wide range of techniques.

The seminar's premise is that technological and quantifiable parameters, such as the exchanges of energy, air, light and water, and also structure and mechanical services, so often over-determinant in the appreciation of architectural performance, ought to be coupled with their expressive or cultural function. Technology can be used intentionally as a design component, rather than merely exposed or concealed.

The seminar's lectures are organized thematically, looking at the various aspects of the relationship between technology and expression, including structure, tectonics, material properties, fabrication, climate control, sensorial aspects, dressing and image-making, symbolism and atmosphere. These topics prepare students to architectural thinking and contemporary practice, where the globalization of technology in conjunction with large capital often hinders the creation of culturally meaningful architecture. Understanding the reciprocities between construction technology and expression is crucial for architects who seek to overcome that predicament and creatively sustain architecture's civic agency.

[ARCH 712] BAROQUE PARAMETERS
Andrew Saunders

Baroque Parameters provides an overview of the debate surrounding the term Baroque and its contemporary implications. The term Baroque is the subject of many discussions ranging from its etymological origin, to disputes on the emergence of an aesthetic "style" post Council of Trent in the seventeenth century by historians such as Heinrich Wölfflin, and the more current and most broad application of the term as a recursive philosophical concept suggested by Gilles Deleuze to "fold" through time. Although illusive and as dynamic as the work itself, students become familiar with how the term Baroque has been associated with specific characteristics, attitudes and effects or more specifically the architectural consequences it has produced.

BAROQUE GEOMETRY

Deep plasticity and dynamism of form, space and light are explicit signatures of the Baroque Architecture; less obvious are the disciplined mathematical principles that generate these effects. This course examines how geometry and mathematics were integral to 17th-century science, philosophy, art, architecture and religion. The geometric and political influences on such innovation link Baroque architects Francesco Borromini and Guarino Guarini to other great thinkers of the period including René Descartes, Galileo Galilei, Johannes Kepler, Girard Desargues and Isaac Newton.

FORMAL ANALYSIS

Formal analysis originated as an attempt by art historian Heinrich Wölfflin in 1886 to develop an objective method to assess how and what the art and architecture that degenerated from the clear and rational Renaissance style in Rome, Italy expressed. This empirical approach suspended unseen aspects of the work including cultural and historical context, subject matter, emotional impact and even the persona of the artist or architect, in favor of a rigorous examination of the "expressive elements of architecture." Ultimately, continuing this lineage, students develop innovative computational techniques to reassess the Baroque through the lens of contemporary discourse.

[ARCH 726] FURNITURE DESIGN AS A STRATEGIC PROCESS
Mikael Avery, Brad Ascalon

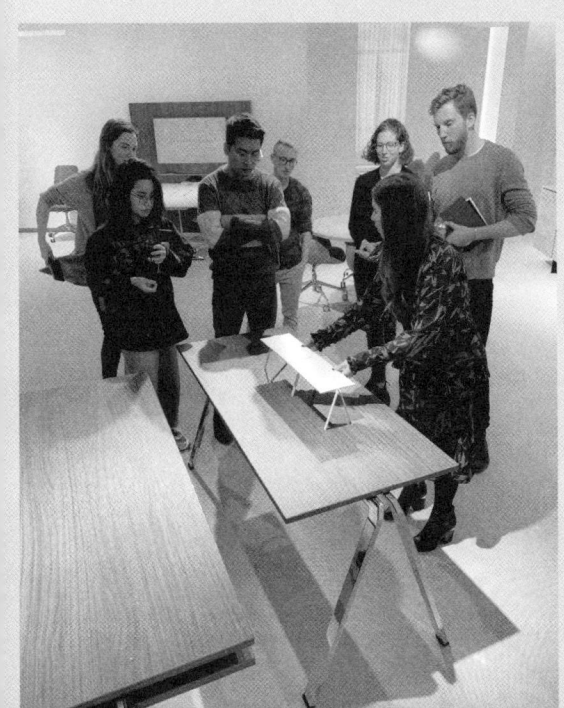

A special thank you to Bluescape and Haworth for their support throughout the semester and for providing the Bluescape platform in order to make the transition to online course deliver seamless.

Like architecture, furniture exists at the intersection of idea and physical form. Due to the specific scale that furniture occupies, however, this physical form relates not only to the environment in which the furniture is set, but also intimately to the physical bodies that interact with and around it. Additionally, as a manufactured product, often specified in large quantities, furniture must also address not only poetic considerations, but practical and economic ones as well. Instead of being seen as one-off objects, the furniture created in this seminar focuses on furniture development as a strategic design process where the designer's role is to understand the various responsibilities to each stakeholder (client/manufacturer, market/customer, environment) and the additional considerations (materials, processes, manufacturability, etc.), that ultimately translate these points into a potentially successful product.

In order to approach furniture in this manner, the course is structured around specific design briefs and clustered into two distinct but continuous stages. First, through research into stakeholder needs and potential market opportunities —as well as hearing from industry insiders—students craft tailored design proposals and develop concepts accordingly.

Next, students work towards realizing a concept (complete with sketches, mock-ups, scale-model prototypes, technical drawings, connections, and other pertinent details) in order to refine their proposals and secure a real world understanding of the manufacturing processes as well as the potential obstacles created by their decisions. From insights gained and feedback from these steps, students ultimately develop a final design proposal for a piece, collection, or system of furniture that successfully leverages their understanding of a thoughtful and deliberate design strategy.

[ARCH 732] DEPLOYABLE STRUCTURES
Dr. Mohamad Al Khayer

The objective of this course is to introduce the field of deployable and kinetic structures through hands on experiments conducted in workshop environment. Students develop skills necessary to understand these complex geometries and will acquire the necessary knowledge to compose deployment configuration based on, the fundamental geometries introduced during the semester. Additionally, students learn the necessary steps to fabricate, and automate working prototypes of fully deployable structures.

In this course the focus is concentrated on deployable geometric configurations, based on planner lattices, of regular and semi-regular tessellation, followed by the introduction to the polar deployment of Platonic and Archimedean polyhedrons. The Spatial studies develop into the arrangement of the deployable polyhedron into deployable space filling geometries.

The surface-based linkage is researched using negative curvature surfaces, namely the deployment of polygonal hyperboloids of revolutions. As the basic geometries, related to the development of this class of deployable structures are introduced, the students would build working prototypes and simulate the deployment, by fabricating and assembling the structures' components.

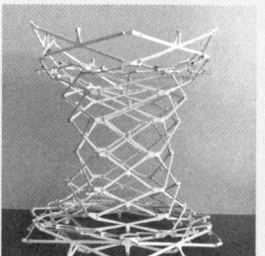
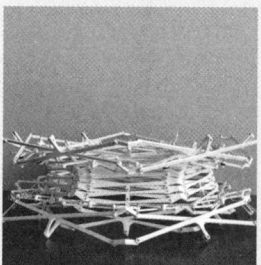

Due to the remote teaching environment, during the second half of the semester, and the lack of access to fabrication laboratories, the course shifted from the development of the physical prototypes, to digital simulation modeling. The work and deliverables focused on developing, computational models, using available modeling computer programs, and assortment of scripting software tools to model deployable germinal cells and input their interconnectivity, relations and arrangement using set of mathematical logics. This approach enabled us to simulate the movement caused by the structures that are designed to have single degree of freedom.

Areas of geometric studies explored in this course contains, geometric studies of Platonic and Archimedean solids and space filling geometries, topology, and morphological transformations, studies of different mechanical joints, and computational analysis of deployable structures structural behavior.

[ARCH 751] ECOLOGY, TECHNOLOGY, & DESIGN
Dr. William W. Braham

The course draws on systems ecology and the history and philosophy of technology to examine the complex task of environmental building design. Rethinking ecological design at the beginning of the twenty-first century means reconsidering the strong claims made about ecology and technology—utopian and dystopian—through the 20th century, as the impacts of technology on eco-systems were encountered.

Environmental building design is a process of discovery, of deciding what to work on, before it ever becomes a matter of design. The first half of the course will examine energy and resource flows in buildings, exploring the principles of systems ecology, developed by HT Odum. Considering the theories of self-organization, natural selection, maximum power, and energy transformation hierarchies will provide a scientific basis for the second half of the course, which will apply those concepts to different kinds and scales of practice, from the intimate aspects of product design to the largest infrastructures, from the use of water in bathroom to the flow of traffic on the highway.

Course work included weekly readings, in-class exercises, and a project developed in three stages. The first stage analyzed the value of a particular location in an urban site anywhere in the world, the second stage analyzed all the work, energy, and resource flows involved in a residence located on that site, and the third stage looked at the improvement of some component of the building.

[ARCH 685] ENVIRONMENTAL READINGS
Frederick Steiner

A long, deep green thread exists in American literature from Ralph Waldo Emerson and Walt Whitman through Herman Melville and William Carlos Williams on to Terry Tempest Williams and Wendell Berry. This literature has influenced how we perceive our environments and, in the process, many planners, designers, and conservationists such as Frederick Law Olmsted, Jane Addams, Aldo Leopold, Lewis Mumford, Ian McHarg, and Anne Whiston Spirn. In this seminar, we will explore this green thread and analyze its influence on how we shape our environments through design and planning.

[ARCH 712] ARCHITECTURES OF REFUSAL: THE BRONX V.2
Eduardo Rega

A neighborhood with a remarkable history of struggle against inept municipal governments neoliberalism and the forces behind the breeding of decay, the South Bronx is currently experiencing an aggressive wave of gentrification and policies that keep benefitting few elites and oppressing many longtime residents. Grassroots organizations are fighting back while practicing radical imaginations for a more just future. In its second installment, Architectures of Refusal: The Bronx aims to expand on last year's collective architecture research, using drawing and film, on visionary architectural and urban activist practices in the South Bronx. The course learns from social movements that refuse capitalist exploitation vis a vis New York City's economic transformation: from top-down public disinvestment and privatization to bottom-up self-provisioning and organizing.

[ARCH 714] MUSEUM AS SITE: CRITIQUE, INTERVENTION, AND PRODUCTION
Andrea Hornick

In this course, we will take the museum as a site for critique, invention, and production. As architecture, cultural institution, and site of performance, the museum offers many relevant opportunities. Students will visit, analyze, and discuss a number of local exhibitions and produce their own intervention in individual or group projects. Exhibition design, design of museum, the process of curating, producing artworks ranging from paintings to installation and performance, as well as attention to conservation, installation, museum education, and the logistics and economics of exhibitions will be discussed on site and in seminar.

[ARCH 718] HISTORY AND THEORY OF ARCHITECTURE AND CLIMATE
Dr. Daniel Barber

Climate change is upon us. This course discusses the history of thinking about climate in architecture, from long before climate instability was a civilizational threat. We confront the geographic and epistemic challenges of climate instability and other environmental threats, and reconsider the forces seen to condition the development of modern architecture. The course will explore the history of buildings as mechanisms of climate management, and the theoretical and conceptual frameworks that pertain.

[ARCH 732] ENCLOSURES: SELECTION, AFFINITIES & INTEGRATION
Charles Berman

This seminar seeks to establish a framework of understanding enclosures in this sense of the revelatory detail. We will seek to counterpoint the numerical (external) facts of what is accepted as facade design (criteria, codes, loads, forces and consumptions) with an understanding of the generative processes underlying these physical criteria. The aim of this seminar is to arm the student with a guided understanding of the materials and assemblies available to them to form enclosures.

[ARCH 732] COMPUTATIONAL COMPOSITE FORM
Ezio Blasetti

This seminar will research algorithmic generative methods and the use of carbon fiber in robotics for architectural design. The research will focus on the intersection of computation, form generation, simulation and robotic fabrication. The objective is to develop and document specific computational tools and material prototypes than span across design phases, from concept to fabrication.

[ARCH 732] HEAVY ARCHITECTURE
Philip Ryan

Heavy Architecture is a seminar that will examine buildings that, through their tectonics or formal expression, connote a feeling of weight, permanence, or "heaviness". Analysis of these buildings and methods of construction stand in relation to the proliferation of thin, formally exuberant, and, by virtue of their use or commodified nature, transient buildings. The course is not a rejection or formal critique of "thin" architecture, but instead an analysis of the benefits and drawbacks of the "heavy" building type in terms of a building's financial, environmental, symbolic or conceptual, and functional goals. The course will parse the alleged nostalgic or habitual reputation of "heavy" architecture within the context of architecture's ongoing struggle to be the vanguard of the built environment even while its relevancy and voice is challenged by economic, stylistic, and social forces.

[ARCH 732] PRINCIPLES OF DIGITAL FABRICATION
Mikael Avery

Through the almost seamless ability to output digital designs to physical objects, digital fabrication has transformed the way designers work. At this point, many of the tools and techniques of digital fabrication are well established and almost taken for granted within the design professions. To begin this course we will review these "traditional" digital fabrication techniques in order to establish a baseline skill set to work from. We will then explore hybrid approaches to digital fabrication in which multiple techniques are utilized within the same work. During all of these exercise we will discuss the development of 3D printing and its place in the digital fabrication dialogue.

[ARCH 732] EMBODIED CARBON AND ARCHITECTURE
Stephanie Carlisle

This course brings together an introduction to Life Cycle Assessment (LCA), the industry-standard method for evaluating the environmental impacts of a building over its whole life cycle, paired with discussion on broader industry trends and technologies aimed at radically decarbonizing the built environment. In the course, students will receive hands-on experience building comparative LCA models, while also exploring material life cycles, industrial processes, supply chain dynamics, and political and economic dimensions of environmental impact data. We will also discuss current innovations in materials manufacturing and policy changes that focus on embodied carbon, which will transform construction practices. The overall goal of the course is to increase carbon literacy and to empower students with a working understanding of climate change, life cycle assessment, and the many strategies by which designers can immediately reduce the carbon footprint of their projects.

[ARCH 734] ECOLOGICAL ARCHITECTURE, CONTEMPORARY PRACTICES
Todd Woodward

Architecture is an inherently exploitive act – we utilize resources from the earth and produce waste and pollution to create and occupy buildings. Green building design practices are seemingly becoming mainstream. This course will investigate these trends and the underlying theory with a critical eye. Is "mainstream green" really delivering the earth-saving architecture it claims? As green building practices become more widespread, there remains something unsatisfying about a design approach that focuses on limits, checklists, negative impacts and being "less bad." Can we aspire to something more? If so, what would that be? How can or should the act of design change to accommodate an ecological approach?

[ARCH 736] ARCHITECTURAL WORKFLOWS IN THE DESIGN AND DELIVERY OF BUILDINGS
Richard Garber

This seminar in design and technology will focus on the concept of the architectural workflow as it pertains to both contemporary operations in design practice as well as novel project delivery methods enabled by Building Information Modeling (BIM). The synthesis of these digital design platforms with simulation and increasing access to data in the form of natural phenomena, ecology, and building performance has allowed contemporary architects to engage the notion of workflows with others in design and construction practices.

[ARCH 736] BIM: BUILDING INFORMATION MODELING
Patrick Morgan

The production of an information rich BIM is the ground upon which all construction activities for advanced and complex buildings take place. BIM is also the origins of contemporary innovations in Integrated Design, the creation of collaborative platforms which aim to maximize the sustainable outcomes in the project delivery of buildings. Moreover, being able to collaboratively produce, share and query a BIM makes possible the global practice of design and construction. The course will familiarize students to this important field of architectural practice.

[ARCH 736] BUILDING ACOUSTICS
Joe Solway

This course investigates the relationship between sound and space and encourages students to think more about how their buildings sound. The course explores the effects of materials and shape on sound absorption, reflection and transmission, and demonstrates how modeling, visualization and auralization can be used to understand acoustic and aid the design process. The course includes a lecture on the history and future of performance space design, a visit to the Arup SoundLab in New York and two assignments, one practical (Boom Box) and one theoretical (Sound Space).

[ARCH 736] WATER SHAPING ARCHITECTURE
Stuart Mardeusz, Jonathan Weiss

While efforts in sustainable design have focused on energy use, carbon footprint, light and materials impact on human occupants, it could be argued that water is the ultimate test of sustainability. As our planet is ever more challenged to provide for increasing populations with finite resources, our approach to water will need to evolve to meet our new and future realities. The goals of this course are to recognize the significant history of designing water, and touch upon the social, cultural, ecologic, and economic impact that designed water has had and will play in the 21st century, and in addressing urgent global challenges linked to climate change.

[ARCH 742] THE FUNCTION OF FASHION IN ARCHITECTURE
Danielle Willems

This seminar will survey the history of fashion in parallel to architecture starting from Ancient Civilization to Present. The focus will be on the relevance of garment design, methods and techniques and their potential to redefine current architectural elements such as envelope, structure, seams, tectonics, and details. The functional, tectonic, and structural properties of garment design will be explored as generative platforms to conceptualize very specific architectural elements. One of the challenges in the course is the reinvention of a means of assessment, the development of notations and techniques that will document the forces and the production of difference in the spatial manifestations of the generative systems.

[ARCH 746] CINEMA AND ARCHITECTURE IN TRANSLATION
Nicholas Klein, Danielle Willems

This course surveys key cinematic moments and techniques within the history of film and finds new intersections between architecture and dramatic situational narratives. This course is organized into a series of thematic lectures that parallel the contemporary development of the two disciplines both in theory and technique. The focus will be on the analysis of mise-en-scène, the architecture of the film scene, and developing speculative architectural futures.

[ARCH 748] ARCHITECTURE AND THE NEW ELEGANCE
Hina Jamelle

The seminar will define and elaborate on the following topics for the digital discourse- the contemporary diagram, technique, structure, architectural systems and aesthetic projections. Technological innovations establish new status quos and updated platforms from which to operate and launch further innovations. Design research practices continually reinvent themselves and the techniques they use to stay ahead of such developments. Reinvention can come through techniques that have already been set in motion. Mastery of techniques remains important and underpins the use of digital technologies in the design and manufacturing of elegant buildings. But, ultimately, a highly sophisticated formal language propels aesthetics.

[ARCH 750] PARAFICTIONAL OBJECTS
Kutan Ayata

This representation/design seminar explores the aesthetics of estrangement in realism through various mediums. The reality of the discipline is that architecture is a post-medium effort. Drawings, Renderings, Models, Prototypes, Computations, Simulations, Texts, and Buildings are all put forward by architects as a speculative proposal for the reality of the future. Students will explore the reconfiguration of a "found object" in multiple mediums and represent parafictional scenarios in various techniques of realism. At a time when rendering engines enable the production of hyper-realistic images within the discipline without any critical representational agenda, it has become ever more imperative to rigorously speculate on realism.

[ARCH 762] DESIGN AND DEVELOPMENT
Alan Razak

This newly reconstituted course will introduce designers and planners to practical methods of design and development for major real estate product types. Topics will include product archetypes, site selection and obtaining entitlements, basic site planning, programming, and conceptual and basic design principles. Project types will include, among others; infill and suburban office parks, all retail forms, campus and institutional projects. Two-person teams of developers and architects will present and discuss actual development projects.

[ARCH 765] PROJECT MANAGEMENT
Charles Capaldi

This course is an introduction to techniques and tools of managing the design and construction of large, and small, construction projects. Topics include project delivery systems, management tools, cost-control and budgeting systems, professional roles. Case studies serve to illustrate applications. Cost and schedule control systems are described. Case studies illustrate the application of techniques in the field.

[ARCH 768] REAL ESTATE DEVELOPMENT
Asuka Nakahara

This course focuses on "ground-up" development as well as re- development, and acquisition investments. We will examine traditional real estate product types including office, R&D, retail, warehouses, lodging, single-family and multi-family residential, mixed use, and land. "Specialty" uses like golf courses, resorts, timeshares, and senior assisted living will be analyzed. You will learn the development process from market analysis, site acquisition, zoning, entitlements, approvals, site planning, building design, construction, financing, and leasing to ongoing management and disposition. Additional topics—workouts, leadership, and running an entrepreneurial company—will be discussed. Throughout, we will focus on risk management, as minimizing risk first results in maximizing long run profits and net worth accumulation.

[ARCH 812] METHODS IN ARCHITECTURAL FIELD RESEARCH
Franca Trubiano

The course will cover the full context of research methods in both the humanities and sciences attendant to architecture. Students will be tasked with identifying and naming a field of study, an initial research question to investigate, a methodology they will employ, and a value proposition for their work.

[ARCH 814] IDEA OF AN AVANT-GARDE IN ARCHITECTURE
Joan Ockman

The seminar undertakes a close reading of one of Tafuri's richest and most complexly conceived books, The Sphere and the Labyrinth: avant-gardes and Architecture from Piranesi to the 1970s. The concern is equally with history and historiography: with specific material and ideological contexts, and with the ways they have been written into architectural history. Our central aim is to explore the role and function of avant-gardes in the history of architecture. Does the concept of the avant-garde still have relevance today? Or should it be relegated to the dustbin of 20th-century ideas?

Elemental Discontinuity by Gao Sijie and Yuxuan Liang
Critic: **Ali Rahim** [p.366]

ADVANCED 704

Air-Scape by Xintong Zhao and Pengkun Wang
Critic: **Homa Farjadi** [p. 339]

Blurred Chiaroscuro by Fang Cheng and Tianxiao Wang
Critic: **Hina Jamelle** [p.343]

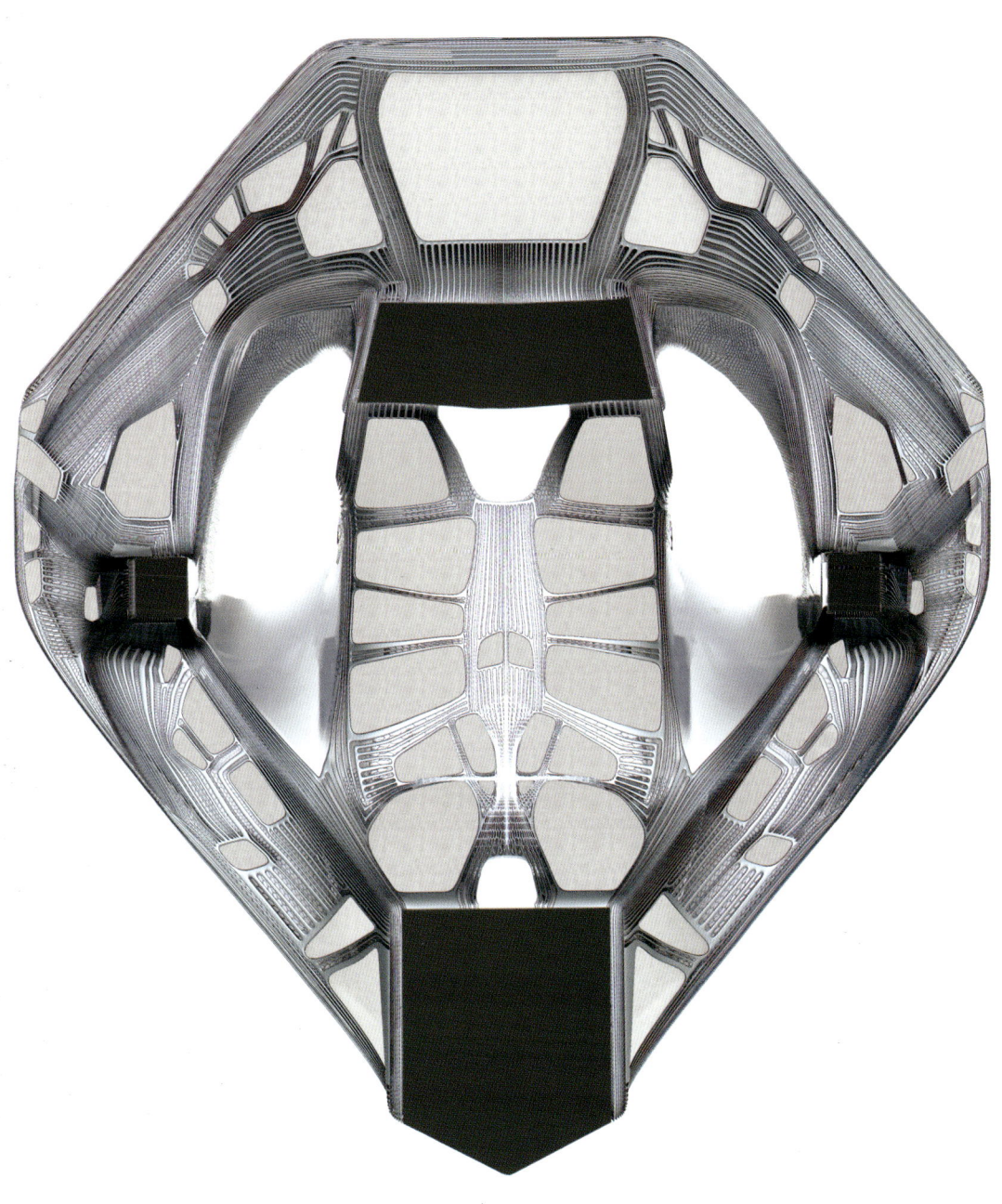

Rapid Medical by Siyi Wang, Tsui-Lun Wang and Yuqing Ye
Critic: **Robert Stuart-Smith** [p.370]

Museum of the Unpredicable by Gordon Cheng, Xuechen Chen, Xiaotong Jiang
Critic: **Marion Weiss** [p.380]

Arch by Yifan Zhuang and Sifan Yang
Critic: **Winka Dubbeldam and Richard Garber** [p.333]

2019 STUART WEITZMAN SCHOOL OF DESIGN AWARDS

At the second annual awards gala in New York, The Kanter Tritsch Prize in Energy and Architectural Innovation and the Kanter Tritsch Medal for Excellence in Architecture and Environmental Design were awarded to a current student and Weitzman alumnus.

The Kanter Tritsch Prize includes a $50,000 scholarship for a Master of Architecture student in their final year of study. The 2019 Prize was awarded to student Patrick Danahy (MArch'21). At Penn, he has worked as a research assistant in the Autonomous Manufacturing Lab, led by Assistant Professor Robert Stuart-Smith, and helped create an innovative prototype of a tiny house in the school's Robotics Lab. With the Autonomous Manufacturing Lab, he's working on a speculative redesign for the Notre Dame cathedral spire in Paris, which was destroyed by a fire in the spring.

A. Eugene Kohn (BArch'53, MArch'57) received with the Kanter Tritsch Medal, given in recognition of his years leading with the international architecture firm Kohn Pedersen Fox (KPF), which he co-founded in 1976.

Both awards were established through a generous gift from Weitzman alumna Lori Kanter Tritsch and Penn Trustee and Wharton alumnus William P. Lauder.

"It taught me something about ethics, and about moral leadership,"
Kohn said.

A. Eugene Kohn

Patrick Danahy with Chair Winka Dubbeldam

November 4th, 2019
CHARLES L. DAVIS II AND SOLMAZ SHARIF IN CONVERSATION

February 4th, 2020
DENICE FROHMAN

Denice Frohman

Panelists included Assistant Professor of Persian Literature Fatemeh Shams, Architecture PhD candidate Ali AlYousefi, and Planning Postdoc Fellow Matt Miller.

"A crisis of borders, a fold in time, a rupture in space. An assertion of gradience. [...] Visions of power and pride and grief and desire community and celebration and abandonment and a wandering itinerant solitude. I want to hold all of these things together in this synthetic moment; as intersectional and porous concepts of identity as expressed in art, architecture and language. A compound description of the world as vast and contingent."

With these words David Hartt, Assistant Professor of Fine Arts, at the Stuart Weitzman School of Design described the idea for the yearlong Lecture Series of the Synthetic, co-curated with architect and Visiting Lecturer Maya Alam and Assistant Professor of Architecture Sophie Hochhäusl. Speakers in the series included artist Liz Johnson Artur, architectural historian and Weitzman alum Charles L. Davis II (PhD'09), and poets Denice Frohman and Solmaz Sharif, who focused on questions of identity and radical utopian thought in visual culture and language as well as systems of knowledge deriving from diasporic thought.

The lecture series was sponsored by the Provost's Initiative and the Deans Office as well as the Departments of Fine Arts and Architecture. It was supported by La Casa Latina, the program in Gender, Sexuality, and Women's Studies, the LGBT Center, the Architectural Archives, and Kelly Writers House.

Charles L. Davis II

Solmaz Sharif

SUMMER SCHOOL AT PENN

In June, Winka Dubbeldam, Miller Professor and chair of the Department of Architecture, invited Weitzman students to respond to a brief for architectural and design solutions for a mobile medical testing unit for COVID-19. Over four weeks, 76 students gathered for a series of weekly online lectures by leading designers as well as doctors on the front lines of the pandemic. Students also took part in weekly tutorials to develop their analytical thinking, design strategies, and presentation techniques. Submissions were due on June 29, and a total of 35 individual and team-based submissions were received.

Along with Dubbeldam, the jury included: Manuel Colon Amador, co-founder, Intemperie Studio; Yves Béhar, founder, Fuseproject; Annette Fierro, associate professor of architecture at Weitzman; Mark Gardner (MArch'00), principal, Jaklitsch/Gardner Architects, professor of Architectural Practice & Society, School of Constructed Environments at Parsons the New School, and member of the Board of Overseers at Weitzman; Ferda Kolatan, founding director, su11, and associate professor of practice at Weitzman; Thom Mayne, founder and design director, Morphosis, Cret Chair Professor of Practice at Weitzman, and distinguished faculty Sci-Arc; Marc Miller, assistant professor, Stuckeman School of Architecture, Penn State University; and Joseph Scharzkopf, general manager, Uribe & Schwarzkopf.; Susan Sellers, founding partner and executive creative director, 2x4, and senior design critic, Yale School of Art; and Marion Weiss, Graham Professor of Practice at Weitzman and co-founder, WEISS/MANFREDI.

"Everyone loves a good playground for its vivid color palette, cute shapes, and the smooth [forms],"

Yao explains of her intention to help release the tension of those being tested for COVD-19.

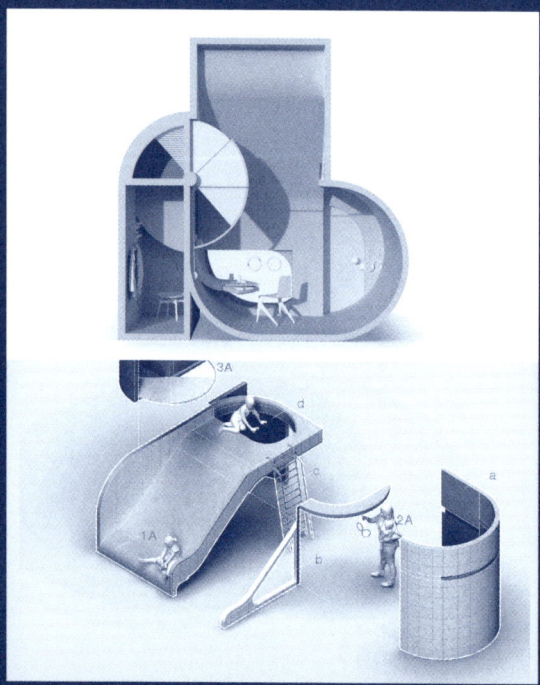

Hanqing Yao, First Place

Jiewei Li, Mrinalini Verma, Third Place

Hadi El Kebbi, Nicholas Houser, Anna Lim, Danny Ortega, Honorable Mentions

Speakers for the Summer School at Penn program included: Manuel Colon Amador and Fabiana Alvear Gilbert, co-founders, Intemperie Studio; Yves Béhar; Dror Benshetrit, founder, Dror; Joe Doucet, founder, Joe Doucet x Partners; Dr. Enrique Boloña Gilbert, director of the Intensive Care Unit, La Clinica Guayaquil; Ferda Kolatan; Thom Mayne; V. Mitch McEwen, assistant professor of architecture, Princeton University; Marc Miller; Michael Rock, founding partner and executive director, 2x4; Dr. Harvey Rubin, professor of medicine and infectious disease specialist, Penn Medicine; and Marion Weiss.

1st Place: Hanqing Yao, *FLIP IT*
2nd Place: Lauren Hunter and Valerie Pretto, *Community Cumuli*
3rd Place (tie): Jiewei Li and Mrinalini Verma, *UNFOLD*
3rd Place (tie): Hillary Morales and Molly Zmich, *Dimensioning Remembrance*

Honorable Mentions were awarded to:
Beikel Rivas, Miguel Matos, and Dario Sabidussi, *Personal Protective Pod*
Fang Cheng, Shifei Xu, and Chengzhe Zhu, *Breezing/Breathing Cloud*
Hadi El Kebbi, Nicholas Houser, Anna Lim, and Danny Ortega, *Matryoshka Kit*

Hanqing Yao's *FLIP IT* was inspired by the children's slides and trapeze rings found at public parks around the world. The design uses melon hues and simple, curvilinear forms to create both physical and mental comfort to those being tested by bringing a playful element to the experience while still maintaining medical and safety requirements.

MSD-AAD

Ali Rahim, Director
Professor of Architecture

The Master of Science in Design: Advanced Architectural Design is a three-semester post-graduate program that is focused on design innovation and material practice grounded in real-world application. The discipline of architecture is foregrounded, and issues including building assembly, structure, and organization are forefronted and combined with the latest technology and techniques to rethink architectural precedent.

Technology has matured within architecture over the last 25 years. Through the process of maturation, key issues of the discipline were neglected in favor of creativity-enhancing abstraction. Abstract experiments were fundamental to rethinking the design process, and material form was sidelined for virtual analogues. This was counterintuitive, as the centrality of buildings and their construction in the discipline was left behind.

The AAD program recenters the building in architectural pedagogy. Contemporary Theory studies theory since the digital turn in architecture in the early 1990s, considering a broad spectrum of conditions including labor, as, for instance, studied through the floor plan and section of Zaha Hadid's BMW factory and office building in Leipzig, Germany. Design Innovation explores the narrow use of Artificial Intelligence directed at material assembly and building facades. Visual Literacy makes a bridge between architecture and representation techniques within contemporary culture, foregrounding their usefulness in addressing disciplinary issues.

Reinvigoration through narrow applications of technology has the potential to continually open up the discipline to contemporary culture, allowing it to affect and inflect the techniques that we use in more critical ways. This enables a richer and more rigorous architecture engaged with intersectional cultural issues including climate change, racial justice, and the non-human.

The robust nature of the program empowers students to think creatively and gives them the tools and knowledge necessary to make incisive buildings with material impact.

MSD-AAD

Ali Rahim
Nate Hume
Brian De Luna
Caleb White, Zachary Kile, and Gary Polk (TAs)

Ali Rahim (Professor and Director MSD-AAD): Architect and Director. Contemporary – Architecture Practice. New York [2002-] and Shanghai [2014-]. – Awarded: Fifty Under Fifty: Innovators of the 21st Century. [2015] – Awarded: Architectural Record Design Vanguard Award [2004] – Author: Catalytic Formations, Routledge. [2012 and 2008]

This studio speculates that a new typology can help sustain New York City's financial global leadership in the world. New York cannot solely rely on import and export economies with the uncertainty of political pressures that affect the prices of goods and services. New York and other cities need to re-invent existing networks to be able to compete with trade barriers that are cumbersome and willfully destroying the growth of the economy. The future brings with it new opportunities that fuse technological innovation with growth in the US economy. The re-tooling of global manufacturing networks is underway with Vietnam, Taiwan and Malaysia becoming the recipients of global manufacturing needs. To add to a versatile and robust manufacturing agenda existing networks such as UPS, DHL, USPS, and FedEx can gain considerably by allowing for new opportunities that extend their networks into facilities that aid in the development of quick prototypes for each point on their network, reducing the cost of shipment internationally and hence making pricing cost effective with a quick turnaround. Price Water-house Coopers indicates that currently 90 percent of global trade flows through 39 airports and states, which pales around 28,000 points of distribution only for UPS along the networks that can enhance efficiency nationally. The city's that become the most important along these networks will thrive. US manufacturing will benefit with an efficient hub accessible directly from New York City establishing it as the leader of prototyping nationally. The new hub will increase the relevance of NYC as a business and logistics hub making a stronger connection to global centers due to the quick turnarounds of the prototypes and strengthening development locally.

1

FORD + LLOYDS
Qi Che, Chengzhe Zhu and Zhihui Li

The project is based on two systems: the mechanical envelope and the diagonal gaps.

The envelope works as the perimeter of the building and also as the storage facility that is a part of the whole logistics system. The gaps are infrastructure spaces that accommodate movements of parcels and people and integrates building service modules. Enclosed by the envelope and divided by the gaps, the interior inhabitable space is subdivided into a series of clusters that either function as additional storage and sorting areas for the logistics system or as office spaces and public spaces for human activity.

The depth and composition of the envelope are then affected by the cluster and gap behind each sector. This variation provided multiple dimensions for storage and circulation. By exposing the process of handling and storing parcels, the envelope creates a dynamic and theatrical image for observers around the block and users working in the clusters behind it. As users move through the gaps to reach their destinations inside the building, they are always traveling through layers of logistics and building service equipment, and thus have the chance of understanding how the different systems work inside the structure.

One of the central questions concerning the studio: what should the 21st-century office look like, moving beyond the free

1 – *Ford + Lloyds* by Qi Che, Chengzhe Zhu and Zhihui Li, Model

plan office of the modernist era? The typology of the office has transformed a great deal since its 18th century introduction. Initially offices were considered another form of factory, no different than an industrial manufacturing space —containing desks rather than machinery. This concept was re-evaluated with the German Burolandschaft or "office landscape", a concept which sought to diversify the office workspace and create a variety of semi-public spaces for work. The office was reinvented once again with the implementation of the "cubicle" and other modularized office furniture which brought a degree of affordable privacy to the office. The monotony of the "cubicle farm" created an image of the office which was isolated and sterile. This has led many companies to do away with the cubicle in favor of the open office. The open office concept, which persists to this day, relies on the modernist notion of the "free plan." Flexible, open, adaptable, the open office has many qualities which make it economically desirable for businesses. The open office has come under recent criticism for being loud, chaotic, and contributing to a lack of productivity. It has also been said that the open office plan does not offer enough diversity of workspace to satisfy employees with different needs in terms of noise level, environmental comfort, and social interaction. The contemporary questions surrounding the office are many: the shared workspace such as Wework and similar brands, the opportunity to work from home that information technology has brought us, and the implementation of work place amenities that we see implemented in startups and in the tech sector. The most important question however is what the future office will look like when we put aside the modernist notion of the open office plan?

From the long evolution of the office typology, students were asked to research and document some of the most important office buildings. Students were asked to examine not only the architecture of these buildings but also the underlying office models and organizations of these projects. The various models were then be hybridized with the logistics and light manufacturing functions of the UPS Hub to produce a new typological proposal for a UPS facility in West SoHo in New York City.

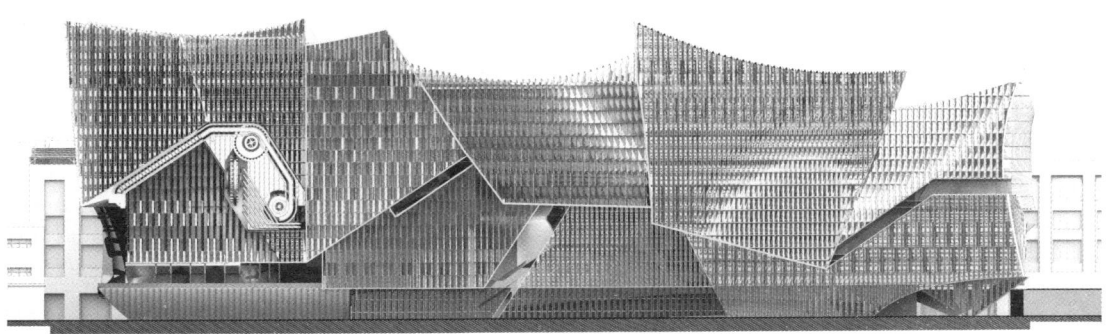

2

2 - *Ford + Lloyds* by Qi Che, Chengzhe Zhu and Zhihui Li, Elevation Line

RENN CENTER + SEAGRAMS
Bingkun Deng, Jiang Ming, Yang Yang

The idea of the project is to create a continuous surface that goes through the whole building to connect office spaces, mechanical spaces and logistic spaces. The surface, starting from one detailed column and growing to cover the whole site, is layered horizontally and supported by slender vertical columns. It also forms several atriums for natural light to come into the building. The facade of the building is the building system itself, revealed on the outside with mechanical systems, logistic systems, and storage spaces.

The soaring atrium connects the offices on higher floors, loading spaces on the ground floor, and conveying belts going through the floors. As a result, it brings the effect of the logistic systems penetrating human spaces. A lot of architectural moments took place at theses joints or nodes, such as interior balconies and bridges, providing unique experiences when people are moving through and watching the logistic system functioning. The building is also separated into several portions, and between them, creates several canyon-like spaces for public to go through and experience. Bridges and elevators could shoot into those annexes.

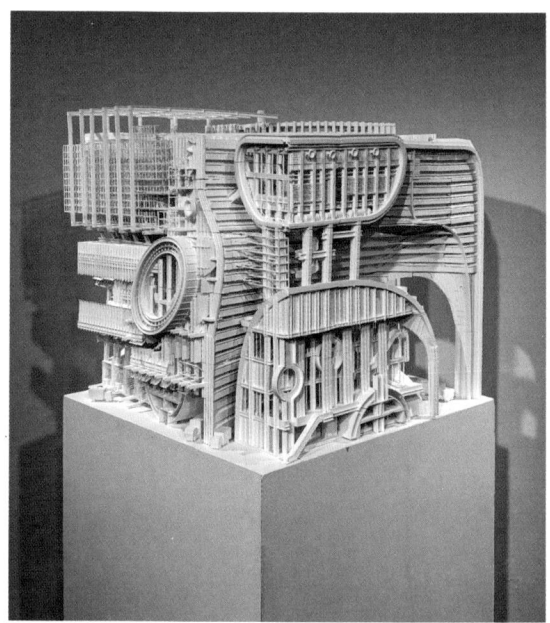

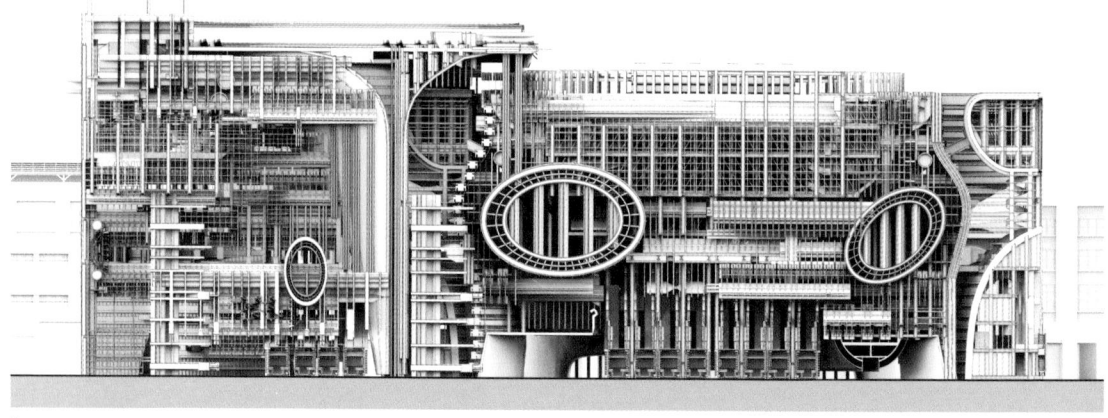

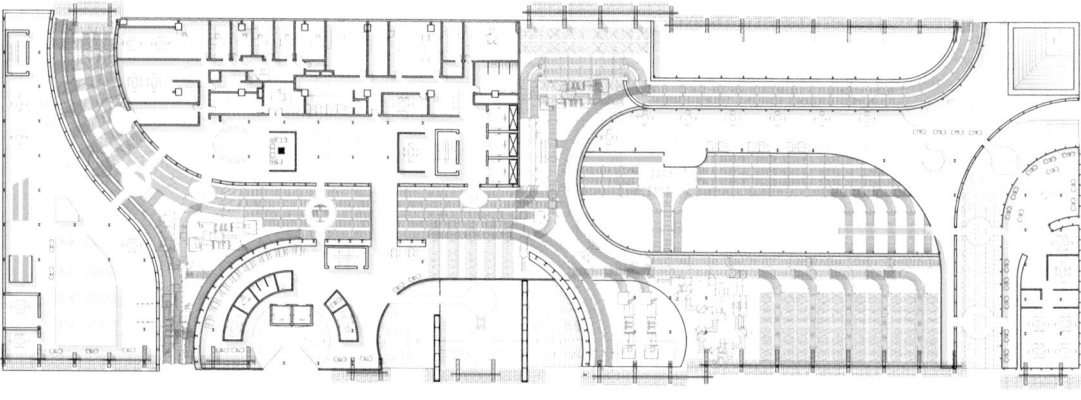

3 – *Renn Center + Seagrams* by Bingkun Deng, Jiang Ming, Yang Yang, model
4 – *Renn Center + Seagrams* by Bingkun Deng, Jiang Ming, Yang Yang, elevation
5 – *Renn Center + Seagrams* by Bingkun Deng, Jiang Ming, Yang Yang, floor plan

LIPPO + JOHNSON WAX
Huajie Ma, Chaoqiong Guo and Jingrong Ning

The main concept of this project is the studies of the interlocking space. It not only creates an interlocking space created by the floor plates but also interlocks in multi-directions. While the programs are mainly defined as logistic space and office, this form of space allow each program to have its own autonomous function. Several designed logistic pieces are nesting into the space to create connection in between the space. The facade is designed as a double layer glass system which allows different types of glass panel (transparent, translucent, opaque) to be installed. Glass type would be defined by the program type which allow the most efficient lighting and shading. In order to support the facade system, inhabitable trusses are installed as the main structure system.

For the site strategy, three similar interlocking chunks are connected by the truss system and the nesting logistic pieces. The human space and non-human space are evaluated equally in this UPS hub. The interaction between human and the logistic system has changed the way we perceive scale. Human interacting with automated system should be redefined in this project.

6

7

6 – *Lippo + Johnson Wax* by Huajie Ma, Chaoqiong Guo and Jingrong Ning, model
7 – *Lippo + Johnson Wax* by Huajie Ma, Chaoqiong Guo and Jingrong Ning, site axon

MSD-EBD

Dr. William W. Braham, Director
Professor of Architecture

The global pandemic has made clear that spatial arrangements and the cultural practices embedded in them are directly related to environmental impact. It has been clear for decades that to confront the pressing task of reducing carbon emissions, environmental building design must be integrated in the disciplinary practices of architecture. The MSD-EBD is a post-professional degree program created to teach architects to innovate in the field of energy and environmental design, training them for a low-carbon economy.

The program's pedagogy is based on theories of ecology and sustainability, building science and performance analysis, and their integration into design workflows. The challenges of low-carbon construction demand practices and/or practitioners that can reconcile the divide between design and engineering, recognizing that architecture has to directly address environmental problems and also make the results visible and intelligible to its occupants. Five guiding principles organize the program: 1) make visible the invisible, 2) many simple models, not one complex simulation, 3) design for comfort and specific climates, not energy, 4) find the architectural narrative, not the energy score, 5) innovate through modeling and prototyping.

The program has a two design studio sequence, the first on Bioclimatic Design and the second a Research Studio. The bioclimatic studio begins with passive strategies in multiple climates, but also seeks to explore the impact of the many novel techniques that are being deployed in progressive buildings, from thermal air movement and evaporative cooling to double glass walls, diurnal and season thermal storage, solar recharged desiccants, and radiant night-sky cooling. The Research studio continues that work with direct modeling and experimentation.

MSD-EBD 709

A BIOCLIMATIC KIT-OF-PARTS FOR MOBILE, MANUFACTURED HOMES

Dr. William W. Braham
Evan Oskierko-Jeznacki (TA)
Max Hakkarainen (COLLABORATORS)
MiaoMiao Hou (COLLABORATORS)

Dr. William W. Braham: Received an MArch and a PhD from the University of Pennsylvania and a BSE from Princeton University — Organized the Architecture and Energy symposium and published the books Rethinking Technology: A Reader in Architectural Theory (2006) and Modern Color/Modern Architecture: Amédée Ozenfant (2002)

Manufactured mobile homes developed in response to a catalog of ever-evolving socio-economic, technical, and cultural demands, becoming a fundamental component of the American vernacular landscape and its narratives. This studio explored the application of this ubiquitous American typology to the demands of a changing climate. They are a well-scaled platform for implementing climate adaptation strategies, renewable energy infrastructure, and for expanding access to affordable and sustainable energy to low-income populations.

1   FOUR SEASONS MOBILE
Chunyi Wang, Liang Zhang, Yunwen Zhu

In our project, an operable glazed-box on the south side performs as a buffer zone. It is used not only for higher performance in energy consumption and thermal performance, but also for more possibilities in architectural space and articulation. During the research, we focused on the Window to Wall Ratio (WWR) and used Computational Fluid Dynamic (CDD) simulation and physical models tests to find the optimum design parameters.

Housing Unit
(Bioclimatic Kit-of-Parts)

Studio teams developed new models of manufactured housing to reduce energy consumption and make the units net-zero capable. Teams built and tested scaled prototypes of new bioclimatic elements, such as a water walls, rechargeable desiccant units, buoyancy driven ventilation, and a water filtering roof. This kit-of-parts will propel the already space-efficient manufactured home typology into the climate-tuned, energy efficient housing "wave of the future" first dreamed of in the early 1950s.

Collections of Units
(Parks and Grids)

The studio simultaneously explored energy and environmental opportunities at the scale of the "mobile home park." With greater attention to energy use, climate effects, and environmental impacts, manufactured housing communities can be redeemed from their marginal status, becoming valuable components in the reduction of urban carbon emissions, sprawl, and the ability of cities to accommodate changing climates and shifting populations.

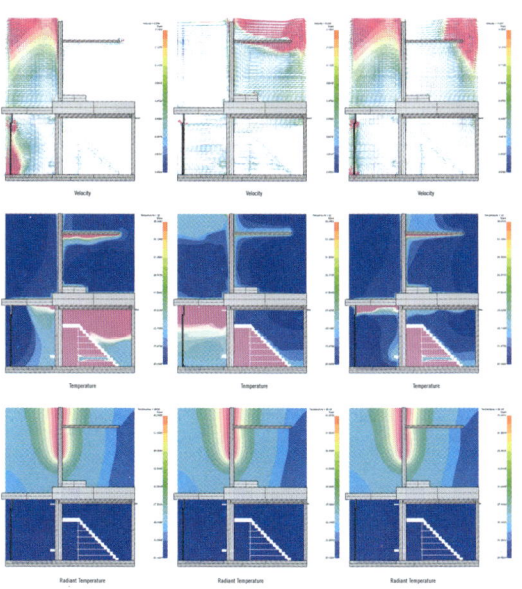

2

1 – *Four Seasons Mobile* by Chunyi Wang, Liang Zhang, Yunwen Zhu, project description
2 – *Four Seasons Mobile* by Chunyi Wang, Liang Zhang, Yunwen Zhu, model

3 – *Four Seasons Mobile* by Chunyi Wang, Liang Zhang, Yunwen Zhu, render

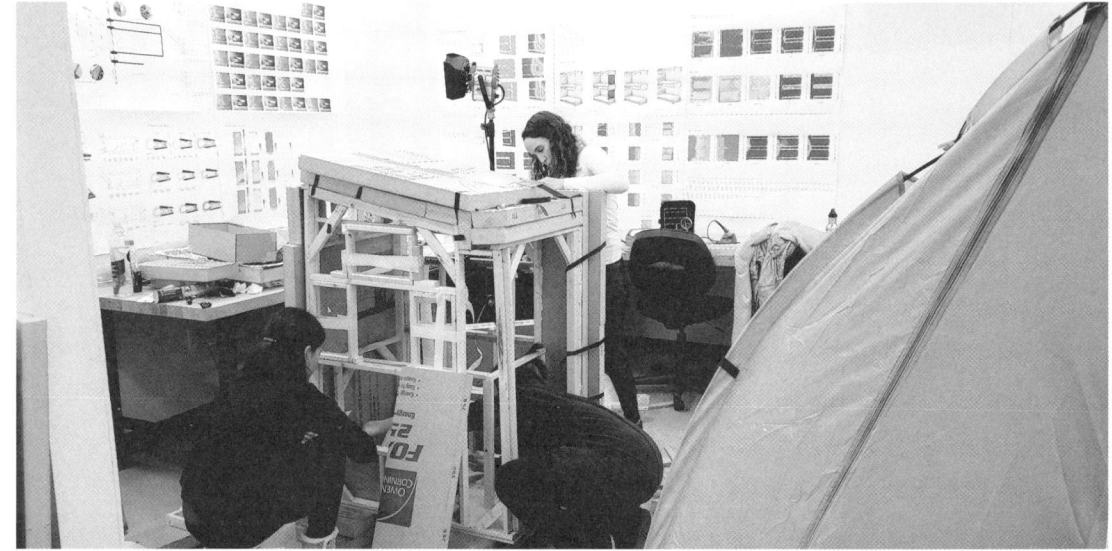

4

5

4-5 – Studio Review

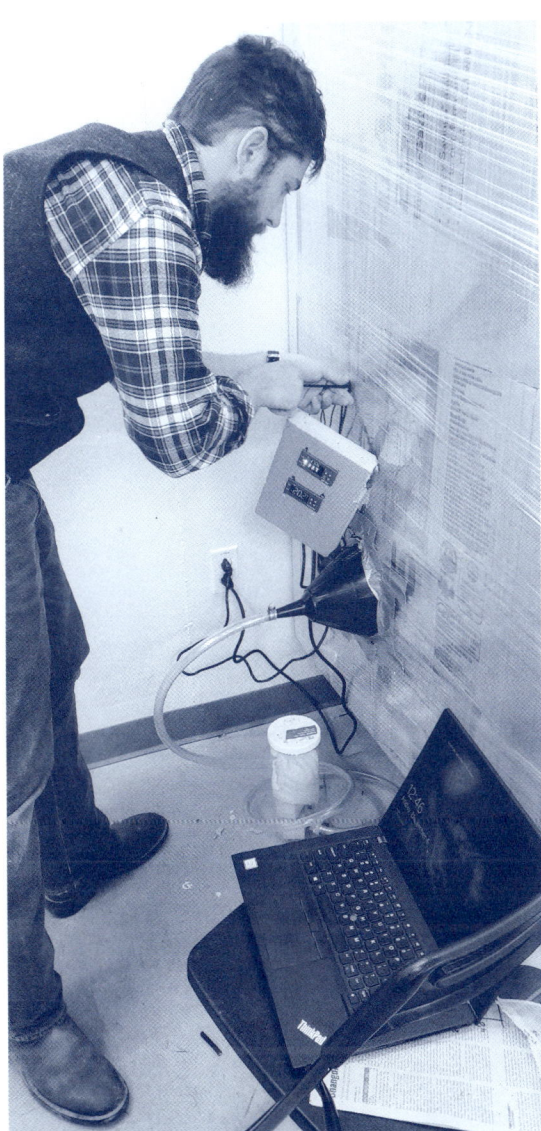

6

7

8

6 – Studio Review
7 – Dr. William W. Braham In Studio Review
8 – Studio Review

SUN PACKAGE
Lanyue Hu, Ce Liu, Uroosa Ijaz

Our manufactured housing is called the Sun Packages We pack the lifestyle you want, we pack the close relationship between people, and most importantly, we pack the sun for you.

We use water-walls to capture the heat of the sun, and we use a skylight designed to trap the sunlight. All the packages are standardized size and are very efficient when being shipped. These sun packages end up warm, bright and comfortable, they are the wisest choice for your home in Buffalo.

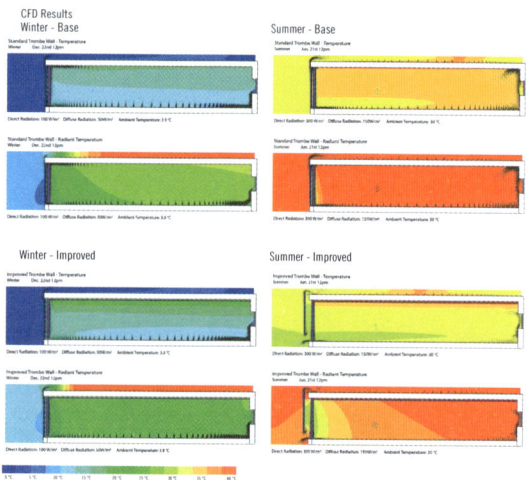

9

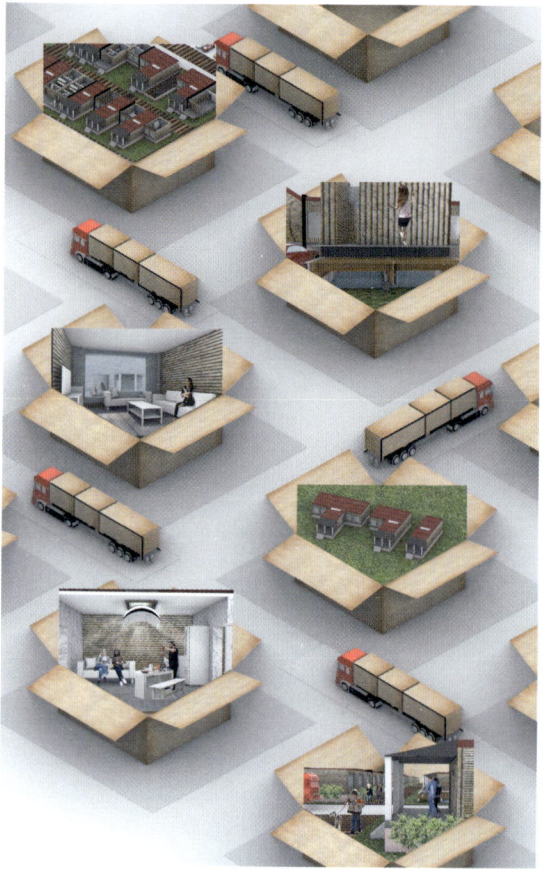

10

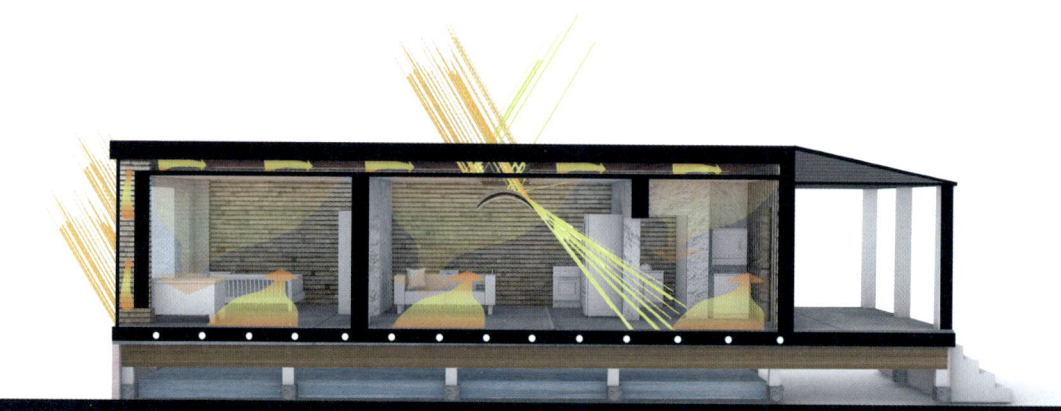

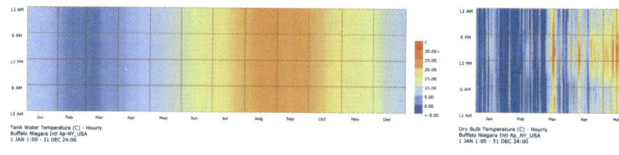
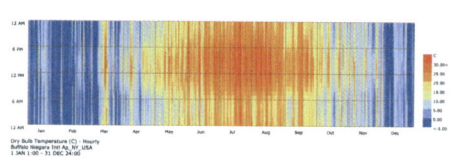

11

9 – *Sun Package* by Lanyue Hu, Ce Liu, Uroosa Ijaz
10 – *Sun Package* by Lanyue Hu, Ce Liu, Uroosa Ijaz
11 – *Sun Package* by Lanyue Hu, Ce Liu, Uroosa Ijaz

WATERSHED HOUSE
Shibei Huang, Michaela Angela Antonio Singson,
Maria Fernanda Trevino

The Watershed is a project that re-evaluates the conditions of current mobile homes in the United States. This project was designed with a focus on water quality and human comfort in a resilient setting. The formative question was "what if our infrastructure can no longer provide human needs?" What if tomorrow there was no water adequate water supply? How do design decisions affect the comfort and performance of the home? The Watershed re-evaluates the current conditions of the infrastructure of mobile parks and adapts to new design strategies that improve the quality of living of the mobile communities, natural ecosystems, water, energy and waste management, and climate refugees for present and future generations.

12

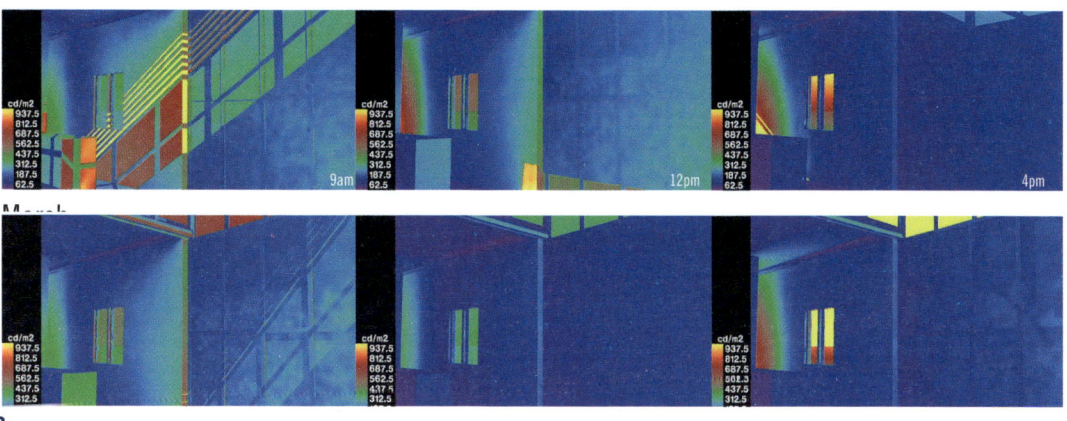

13

14

12 – *Watershed House,* by Shibei Huang, Michaela Angela Antonio Singson, Maria Fernanda Trevino
13 – *Watershed House,* by Shibei Huang, Michaela Angela Antonio Singson, Maria Fernanda Trevino
14 – *Watershed House,* by Shibei Huang, Michaela Angela Antonio Singson, Maria Fernanda Trevino

MSD-EBD 708

**COOLING THE CLOUD:
CLIMATE-ADAPTIVE DESIGN FOR
DATA CENTERS IN THE CONTEMPORARY CITY**

Dorit Aviv
Zherui Wang (TA)
Kit Elsworth (TECHNICAL ASSISTANTS)
Kian Wee Chen (TECHNICAL ASSISTANTS)

Dorit Aviv: Dorit is an Assistant Professor of Architecture and Director of the Thermal Architecture Lab, a cross-disciplinary laboratory at the intersection of thermodynamics, architectural design and material science. She is also part of the Center for Environmental Building & Design. Aviv holds a PhD in architectural technology from Princeton University, an M.Arch degree with a certificate in urban policy from Princeton University, and a B.Arch from The Cooper Union.
External partnerships and collaborations:
As part of the studio, we met for workshops with the data

The data center is an emerging building typology, proliferating in the 21st century to provide cloud computing services to a rapidly growing number of users worldwide. Data centers are the physical infrastructure of all Cloud Computing applications. These centers consume large amounts of energy, partially due to the servers' electricity load, but more significantly, 40 percent of the energy load is spent by the mechanical systems necessary to reject the heat produced by the servers. In order to minimize data centers' environmental footprint, we must conceive of architectural strategies to mitigate that enormous heat load. What would be a model for the design of the data center? How can we envision an architecture that provides the cloud infrastructure while managing its environmental impact?

WIND CUBE
Junjie Lu and Yaning Yuan

Our group designed a highly efficient data center in city environment and studied a synergetic program to maximize the reuse of waste heat from the servers for the heating needs of people. Based on the study and simulation of the Seattle climate, we have realized that it is the perfect city for data centers as we can directly use the outdoor air to cool down the servers in the majority of the year. We used two strategies to help improve the energy efficiency of the building. First, use of wind and stack effect to optimize the passive ventilation system. With the simulation of the wind direction and air pressure differences, we located the stacks and wind tunnels to bring in more fresh and cool air through the server rooms and the offices. The second strategy is to help recycle the waste heat. We located office spaces and a rooftop greenhouse and introduced a heat-distribution system through the building. Combined with the adjustment of the passive ventilation system, we were thus able to heat up the offices and vegetation areas with the heat from server rooms in winter. To conclude, our goal was to design a building that would benefit both the machines and people inside it.

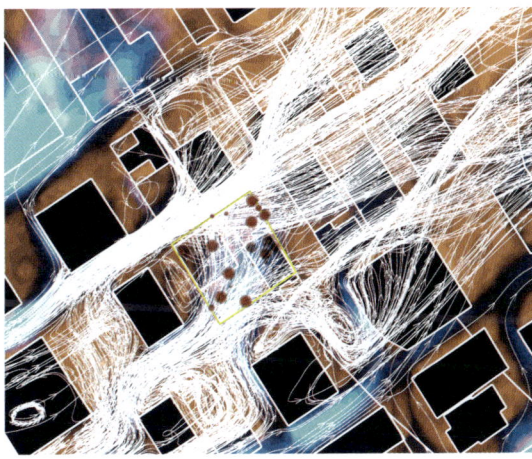

Our design studio explored the potential to create a climate-adaptive building model for data centers in each of the different climatic zones in the United States: temperate, cold, marine, hot-humid and hot-dry. During a studio trip to Seattle we were able to visit existing data centers alongside meetings with industry professionals from Microsoft and Google, to learn of the requirements and challenges involved in data center design.

Programmatically, the data center posits a fascinating building type for architects, because the majority of the building's volume is dedicated to sheltering and providing the thermal needs of machines rather than of human beings. As both inhabit the contemporary city,

center design teams of Microsoft and Google and with other faculty members at other universities, working on data center design research: Julie Kriegh from University of Washington, and Aletheia Ida, from University of Arizona.

1 – Studio Travel
2 – *Wind Cube* by Junjie Lu and Yaning Yuan, Project Descritpion
3 – *Wind Cube* by Junjie Lu and Yaning Yuan, Research

a synergy between servers and humans must be explored. Studying the potential thermodynamic cycles and heat transfer processes between human and machine spaces for energy efficiency has been part of the design research. Daylighting opportunities and the overall experience of inhabiting the data centers played a role in the design as well. As data centers are becoming more widespread in urban areas all over the planet, the studio projects investigated the emergent building typology for an urban, climate-responsive data center.

4
GEOSCAPE
Mrinalini Verma, Navaz Falee Bilimoria, and Tianshuo Wang

Geoscape is a data center designed to harness natural forces on-site and to create a harmony between duality of the urban and natural landscape. The landforms of the upper grasslands in the City Creek Valley inspired the form of the data center. Vigorous research on micro-climate, wind, solar radiation, soil, and vegetation at a regional scale, led to the site selection near the Capitol Hill facing the City Creek. We decided to embed our design into the ground as it would act as a natural heat sink. Our design strategies were dictated by the available natural resources, like wind, geothermal, natural lighting, and PCM. Due to its high efficiency, Geothermal became our core cooling strategy for server spaces. We aimed at creating a closed-loop system, using the waste heat from the server spaces to heat the offices. The windcatchers became our second design feature, capturing predominant wind, cooling it with natural cascade pools, and channeling the cooled air into the server spaces. The glulam timber form is covered with an undulating green roof planted with natives to sequester carbon, also serving as a public space.

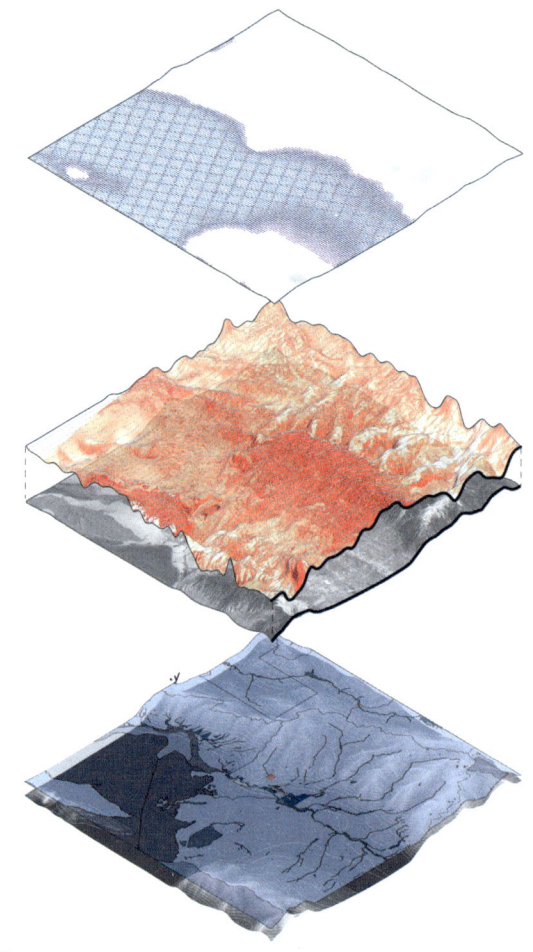

5

6

4 – *Geoscape* by Mrinalini Verma, Navaz Falee Bilimoria and Tianshuo Wang, Project Description
5 – *Geoscape* by Mrinalini Verma, Navaz Falee Bilimoria and Tianshuo Wang, Research
6 – *Geoscape* by Mrinalini Verma, Navaz Falee Bilimoria and Tianshuo Wang, Render

7

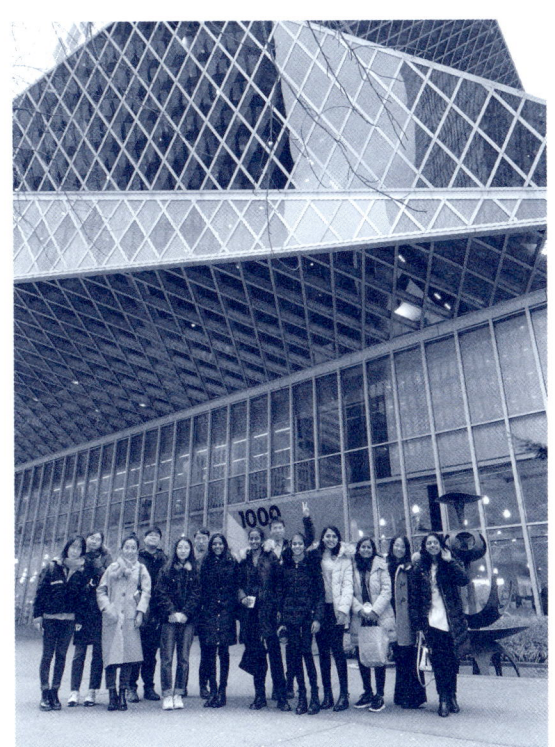

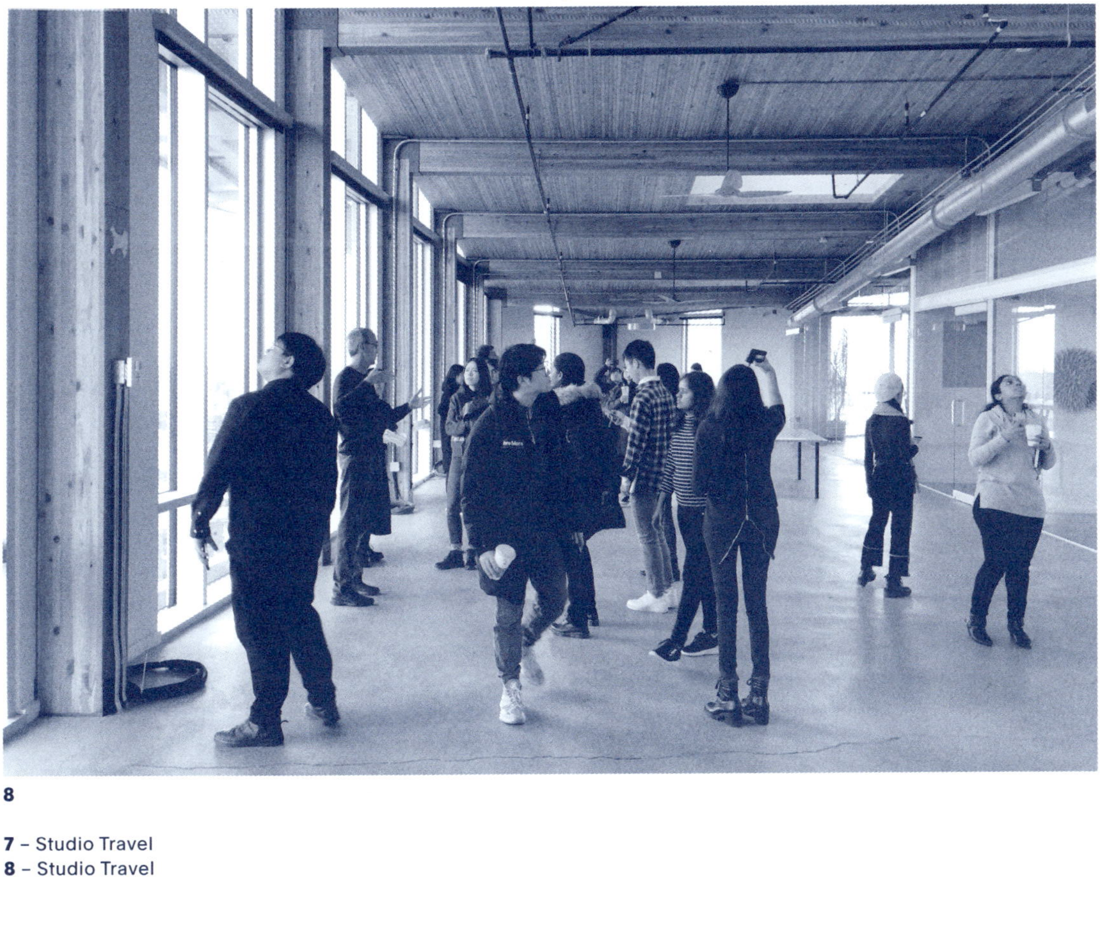

8

7 – Studio Travel
8 – Studio Travel

SHAPE OF THE "L"
Jiewei Li, Shiqi Liu, Zhan Shi

The climate in Houston is hot and humid, both of which are adverse conditions for a data center. Meanwhile, the south wind prevails in Houston, providing the potential of using wind to cool down the servers. As the site is in central Houston, wind tunnels are generated in the high-density area. We design a system with large-scale wind catchers to channel the wind and help cool the equipment in the building. The windward facade is designed to keep air intake into the server rooms constantly. A liquid-desiccant system is embedded in the facade to absorb the moisture from the incoming air. The desiccant can be regenerated in a high-temperature chamber heated passively by solar radiation. PV panels are arranged according to the radiation intensity. The building also includes a rainwater collection and a greywater recycling system. Taking advantage of local climatic conditions, the project proposes a cooling solution for server and office spaces in hot humid climate.

9

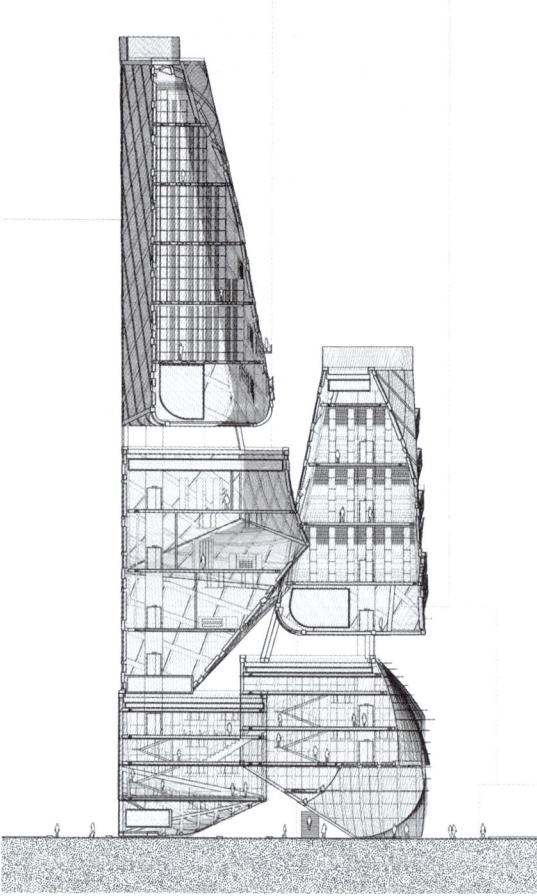

10

11

9 – *Shape Of The 'L'* by Jiewei Li, Shiqi Liu, Zhan Shi, Overall Render
10 – *Shape Of The 'L'* by Jiewei Li, Shiqi Liu, Zhan Shi, Section
11 – *Shape Of The 'L'* by Jiewei Li, Shiqi Liu, Zhan Shi, research

DATA MASS: A HEAT-EMITTING DATA CENTER IN A HOT-ARID CLIMATE
Abinayaa Perezhilan, Suryakiran Jathan Prabhakaran and Sung Di

We took references from vernacular desert architecture and used them as a baseline to iterate our form-finding module —maximizing internal volume and minimizing exposed area to solar radiation, while exploiting night cooling potential from earthen materials. The mass form is derived from optimized aggregation incorporating thermal mass, evaporative cooling potential, and data server on a floor-less, porous organic form. The conventionality is broken down to design "data trees" which maximize stack effect potential within the volume. A well-integrated analysis addresses the aesthetic qualities of the space within and without. While intricately weaving the geometry and systems creating a design language dominated by its materiality of adobe and glass blocks.

In our proposal, the envelope seeks to coalesce space, material and form with bioclimatic considerations. for server and office spaces in hot humid climate.

12

13

14

12 – *Data Mass: A Heat-Emitting Data center in a Hot-Arid Climate* by Abinayaa Perezhilan, Suryakiran Jathan Prabhakaran and Sung Di, Night Radiation
13 – *Data Mass: A Heat-Emitting Data center in a Hot-Arid Climate* by Abinayaa Perezhilan, Suryakiran Jathan Prabhakaran and Sung Di, Drawings
14 – *Data Mass: A Heat-Emitting Data center in a Hot-Arid Climate* by Abinayaa Perezhilan, Suryakiran Jathan Prabhakaran and Sung Di, Render

IPD
INTEGRATED PRODUCT DESIGN (IPD)

Sarah Rottenberg (ADJUNCT ASSISTANT PROFESSOR)
Executive Director, IPD Program

Sarah Rottenberg: Executive Director, IPD Program (Adjunct Assistant Professor) Faculty Director of the Executive Program for Social Innovation Design— Co-Founder of LIA Diagnostics

The Integrated Product Design Master's program brings the School of Design together with two other world class institutions, the School of Engineering and Applied Sciences and Wharton School of Business, to offer students an opportunity to develop a holistic understanding of the product design process. Students from design, engineering, and business backgrounds learn how to integrate the other disciplines into their process and design what's next. Our graduates go on to become product designers, design engineers, corporate innovation leaders, and entrepreneurs.

The Integrated Product Design program addresses many trends that are reshaping design. Businesses increasingly acknowledge the impact of design on their bottom lines, and bring designers into the product development process earlier and in strategic roles. Rapid prototyping capabilities like 3D printing have shrunk the resources required to prototype, test, and manufacture products. And the products, services, and experiences that attract both customers and capital are those that combine hardware and software to create a compelling user experiences. IPD draws upon the heritage and research strengths at Penn and teaches students how to implement fully formed product ideas.

In addition to skills in design, business and engineering, IPD students learn how to creatively solve problems, how to wade into ambiguity and create a path forward, and how to adapt and evolve their projects in response to new learnings and feedback. This creative agility became incredibly useful as teams transitioned from in-person to remote work and from physical to digital prototyping due to COVID-19. The students were able to successfully complete their projects while learning new tools

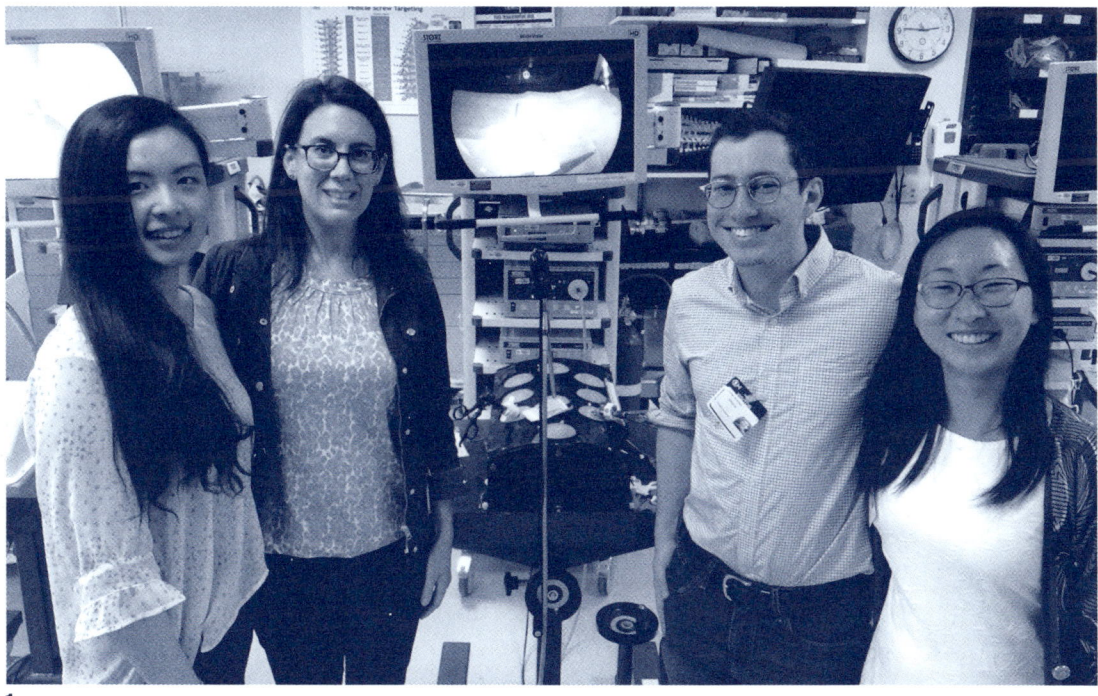

1

1 – Studio Travel

CATCH
Paige Kennedy, Brooke Rosenthal and John Sylvester

It's hard to be an athlete. It's even harder on your period. Tampons leak, pads chafe, and neither lasts more than a few hours. Menstrual cups are better period gear, but most cup designs are decades old and not optimized for the demands of an athlete's body. Catch is a brand that helps athletes play their best game through performance-driven menstrual cups and a period gear support network. Catch Cups are a line of six anatomically informed cups that account for variations in female anatomy and are built for athletes and active lifestyles. Our FitFinder quiz and Cup Coaches help people find the right cup and support them through their first cycles using a cup.

Catch Cups are designed to be comfortable and reliable in the most intense environments by utilizing anatomically informed profiles in three dimensions based on research on vaginal shape analysis in magnetic resonance imaging. Most competitors, by comparison, use a basic bullet shape that is not designed for the contours of the vaginal walls. By designing our cups around an elliptical rim and internal channels, we have created a cup that pops open and easily breaks the seal for removal like a stiff cup while using more comfortable low durometer silicone.

Cup Coaching begins with finding your fit. Most cup companies only design two sizes with often confusing advice on how to choose a cup. Catch is the only brand offering a range of six sizes to accommodate for variations in vaginal anatomy and create a more customized experience. The FitFinder quiz matches women with the two cups in our lineup most likely to work for them. Our Cup Coaches then proactively help athletes through first cycle challenges via text to provide the most comprehensive service offering of any company in the market.

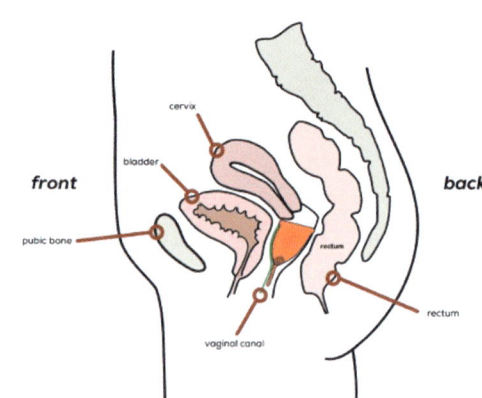

2 – *Catch* by Paige Kennedy, Brooke Rosenthal and John Sylvester, Packaging Render
3 – *Catch* by Paige Kennedy, Brooke Rosenthal and John Sylvester, Project Concept
4 – *Catch* by Paige Kennedy, Brooke Rosenthal and John Sylvester, Rendering

HEADWAY
Jonah Arnheim, Laura Ceccacci, Julia Lin and Alex Wan

Headway is a wearable device for the future of laparoscopic minimally invasive surgery (MIS), making communication among members of the surgical team safer, easier, and more efficient.

Communication difficulties are the most frequent cause of adverse outcomes in surgery, accounting for 22-32% of cases. Surgical teams that exhibit fewer teamwork behaviors put patients at higher risk for death and other serious complications. Inefficient communication occurs in minimally invasive surgery between the surgeon, who operates the surgical tools, and the assistant, who manipulates the camera.

Headway allows surgeons to precisely point to anatomical structures, gesture, and teach, without scrubbing out and without using their hands. The system has two components: a Headset worn by the surgeon throughout a full day of surgery, and a Hardware Box that processes infrared signals from the Headset and overlays an on-screen indicator.

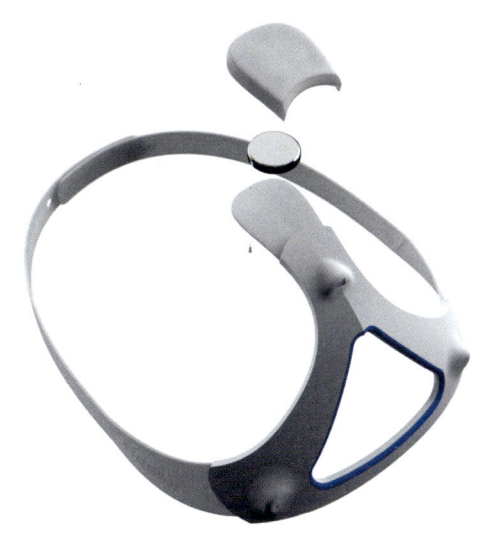

5

6

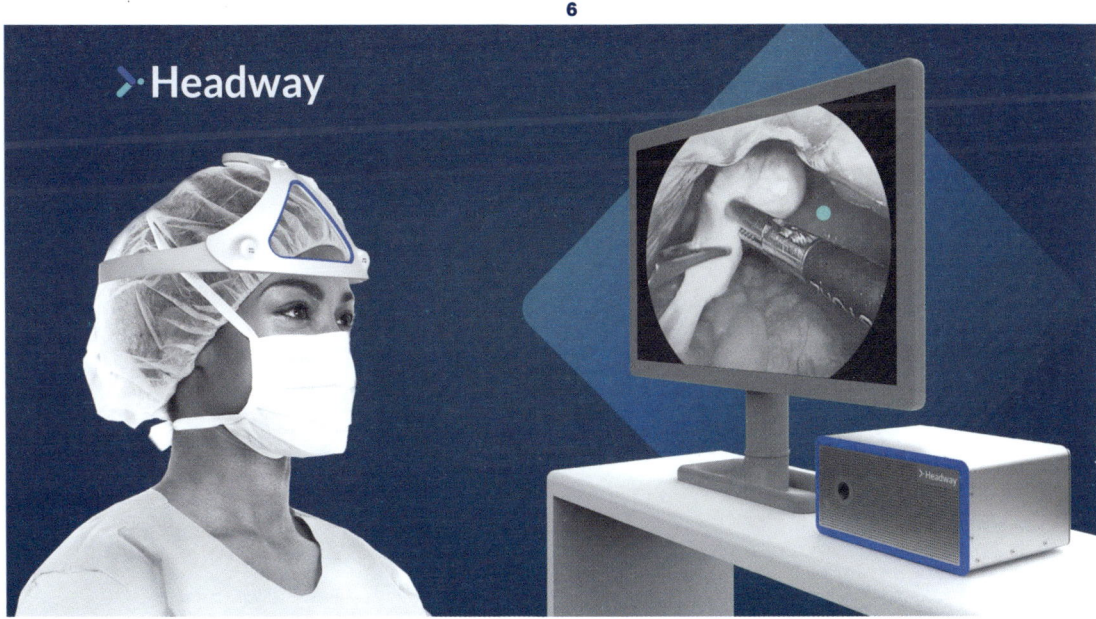

7

5 – *Headway* by Jonah Arnheim, Laura Ceccacci, Julia Lin and Alex Wan, Battery Explode
6 – *Headway* by Jonah Arnheim, Laura Ceccacci, Julia Lin and Alex Wan, Exploded
7 – *Headway* by Jonah Arnheim, Laura Ceccacci, Julia Lin and Alex Wan, Concept

DOCTORAL DEGREE

Dr. Daniel Barber, Associate Professor of Architecture
Chair of the Graduate Group in Architecture

Advanced research in architecture is of increasing importance to understanding and engaging the changing social, political, and technological context for architecture and allied disciplines. The Graduate Group in Architecture at the Weitzman School offers a PhD in Architecture focused on the production of knowledge in historical, theoretical, or technological realms of architecture, landscape architecture, and historic preservation. Operating within the context of a design school in a university setting, it is a fundamentally interdisciplinary program, and explores opportunities across Weitzman and in the wider university to reconsider the terms, methods, and futures of architectural knowledge.

Daniel Barber: Associate Professor of Architecture — Chair of the Graduate Group in Architecture — Topic Director of the Penn Program in the Environmental Humanities — Co-Director of the UPenn/Mellon Humanities + Urbanism + Design seminar on the Inclusive City – Author of Modern Architecture and Climate: Design before Air Conditioning (Princeton University Press 2020)

The Program is especially focused on interdisciplinary scholarship that explores and rescripts the boundaries of relevant disciplines. Projects in History/Theory often explore connections between architectural or landscape histories and theories; histories of technology and environment; of race, class, and gender; of politics, economics, and equity. Many are attuned to the role of media in producing and understanding architectural ideas. Technological research operates on structural and environmental knowledge, offering innovative methods and processes within a rich humanistic context.

The Graduate Group in Architecture is also a place for exploring equity and social justice in the architectural discourse, hosting lectures and events that encourage a relational, engaged understanding of how design interacts with wider social and ecological world. Recent visitors to the program's "PhD Talks" series include: Sigal Davidi on the legacy of female Israeli architects; Daniel Naegele on Le Corbusier's photography; Julio Bermudez on experiencing architecture; Jie Zhao on sensing and indoor environments; Penn faculty Sonja Dumpelmann (LARP) and Megan Ryerson (CPLN) presented their current research.

Research by advanced students in the PhD program is diverse and wide ranging, reflecting the multifaceted nature of the design fields. Recently completed projects are described below, projects in progress include:

Aminah Alkanderi's "AN ARCHITECTURE FOR THE ARAB WORLD TO CALL ITS OWN: SABA GEORGE SHIBER'S RETHINKING OF THE ARAB ENGINEER" highlights Shiber's concept of collaboration among design architects, landscape architects, planners, and engineers and its influence on urban architecture in the Arab World. Spavit Darnthamrongkul's "CHALLENGING MODERNISM: THE ARCHITECTURAL FACADE OF PHILADELPHIA SCHOOL" reconsiders the notion of architectural facade by examine the ideas and works of Louis Kahn and Robert Venturi.

Lori Gibbs' "CRAFTING EVIDENCE OF ARCHITECTURAL HERITAGE: SURVEYING METHODS AND HISTORICAL PROJECTS IN THE US AND CHINA, (1920S-1940S)" examines architect's survey drawing methods in France, the US, and China.

Sang Pil Lee's "EXPANDED ENVIRONMENTS: ARATA ISOZAKI AND HANS HOLLEIN AS ARCHITECTS OF MEDIA, 1955 – 1976" examines postwar architects' design endeavors to envision new living environments in association with electronic technology.

Miranda Mote's "READING AND WRITING A GARDEN, MATERIALS OF A GARDEN IN GERMANTOWN, PENNSYLVANIA (CA. 1683–1719)" describes a relationship between religious belief, reading, writing, and the art of gardening in colonial North America.

Taryn Mudge's "METHODS OF OBSERVATION IN ARCHITECTURE: DEFERRING JUDGEMENT FROM THE SMITHSONS TO VENTURI SCOTT BROWN TO REM KOOLHAAS" investigates architectural practices that claimed to 'defer judgement' in visual research, and illustrates the importance of street photography and sociology postwar architectural theory and practice.

Evan Oskierko-Jeznacki's "FORENSIC FEEDBACK MODELING IN ARCHITECTURE" models intransigent problems of increasing complexity that lie between the design of architecture and the preservation, maintenance, operation, and reuse of existing fabric.

German Pallares' "LIFE ON THE BORDER: CONSTRUCTING THE MÉXICO/U.S. BORDERLAND (1961 – 1971)" interprets urban projects in the México/U.S. borderland as projections of the political, socioeconomic and cultural policies.

Anna Weichsel's "ACTIVATING THE OBSERVER" explores Russian efforts to manipulate creativity and perception with architecture.

ARCHITECTURE, ENVIRONMENT, DEVELOPMENT: THE UNITED STATES
AND THE MAKING OF MODERN ARABIA, 1949-1961
Dalal Musaed Alsayer

ADVISOR:
Daniel Barber, Etienne S. Benson, and Pamela Karimi

This dissertation examines the ways in which the architectures of U.S. development programs sought to transform the social, environmental, and urban fabric of the Arab World in the mid twentieth century. The period between the establishment of President Truman's Point Four Program in 1949 and President Kennedy's U.S. Agency for International Development (USAID) in 1961 saw the genesis of a distinct global form of development, rooted in projects that divided regions into "rural" and "urban." By examining four different projects in four nations, this dissertation aims to document this critical discourse, placing environment and development within the field of architecture, and tracing within them the emergence of (and resistances to) rural and urban models of development.

This dissertation examines the confrontations between the U.S. one-size-fits-all aid-funded model of development, and the range of receptions it received when implemented. Four architectural case studies are explored. First, the oil company town of Dhahran, Saudi Arabia, provides evidence for how the American "good life" was transported to the Arabian desert for the benefit of U.S. workers, and what happened when locals demanded similar accommodation. Second, the U.S. Information Agency (USIA) Pavilions at the Syria International Fairs show how the U.S. curated its self-representation with a focus on domesticity, consumerism, and rurality in places where direct aid was rejected. Third, community development projects and model homes in the Hashemite Kingdom of Jordan funded by U.S. aid programs like Point Four are shown to have reinforced domesticity and gender roles, while concurrent local programs, such as Musa Alami's Arab Development Society (ADS), were targeted by anti-Western protesters when they received U.S. funding. Lastly, Nelson A. Rockefeller and Wallace K. Harrison's experiments in mechanized housing in Baghdad, Iraq through the International Basic Economy Corporation (IBEC) are examined, demonstrating how technological programs failed when they ignored local conditions.

Though the projects examined were not successful as models of development, their story bridges the gap between environmental and architectural histories by demonstrating how images of the environment shaped the architecture built, and how architecture was able to occlude social, spatial, and environmental differences.

© Photograph. Courtesy of National Archives and Records Administration (NARA), College Park, MD, USA.

URBANITY AND THE ARCHITECTURAL PROJECT: THE CASE OF SVERRE FEHN
Stephen M. Anderson

ADVISOR:
David Leatherbarrow

Sverre Fehn's work is instructive for better understanding the role of the architectural project in structuring the engagement, sustenance, and dynamism of urbanity. That aspect of Fehn's work has so far been substantially neglected. This dissertation explores select writings, project proposals, and constructed works in order to plumb Fehn's thinking in regard of the urban milieu and its relationship to building. The dissertation expands understanding of Fehn's architecture into the realm of the city, and considers what Fehn's approaches suggest more generally about the fit between, and the potential of, the architectural project and the essence of urban settings.

Image of Sverre Fehn's proposal for the Royal Danish Theater, Copenhagen, 1996.

JAN. NEWS

MASOUD AKBARZADEH RECEIVES NATIONAL SCIENCE FOUNDATION CAREER AWARD

Assistant Professor of Architecture Masoud Akbarzadeh has received a Faculty Early Career Development (CAREER) grant from the National Science Foundation. The grant will support the development of a robust computational framework for the use, development, and integration of geometry-based structural design methods in three dimensions.

The CAREER grant is the NSF's most prestigious award for junior faculty members who exemplify the role of teacher-scholar through outstanding research, excellence in teaching, and the integration of education and research within the context of the mission of their organizations.

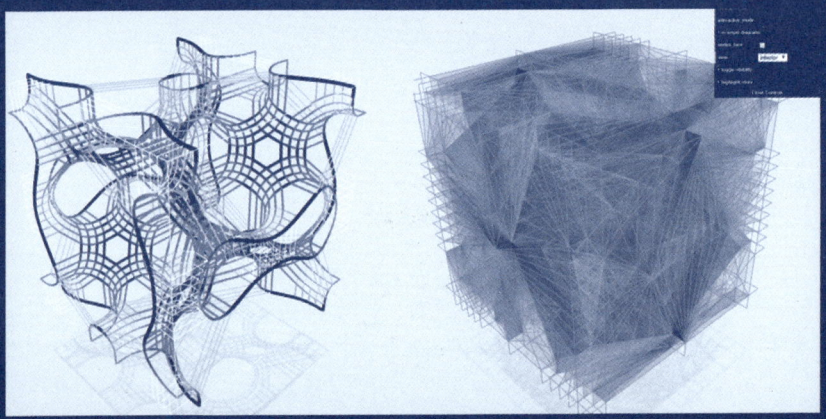

As director of the Polyhedral Structures Lab at the Weitzman School, Akbarzadeh is charting the unexplored realm of efficient spatial structural designs. Straddling design and engineering, his work is rooted in 2D graphic statics (GS), powerful geometric techniques that have been used to determine the forms of many iconic bridges and long-span structures over the past 150 years. But he intends to build on that legacy by establishing the mathematical foundations of 3D graphic statics. The project's goals include the development of open-source software, a web-based, interactive educational platform and library, and activities through which students, designers, and practitioners can learn, share, explore, and design innovative, high-performance, lightweight spatial structural solutions.

Akbarzadeh holds a PhD from the Institute of Technology in Architecture, ETH Zurich, where he was a research assistant in the Block Research Group. He holds two degrees from MIT: a Master of Science in Architecture Studies (Computation) and an MArch, the thesis for which earned him the renowned SOM award. He also has a degree in Earthquake Engineering and Dynamics of Structures from the Iran University of Science and Technology and a BS in Civil and Environmental Engineering.

FEB. NEWS

STUDENTS FROM THE WEITZMAN SCHOOL OF DESIGN WERE AMONG THE TOP THREE FINALISTS IN THE 2020 HOK FUTURES DESIGN CHALLENGE

Master of Architecture students from the Weitzman School of Design were among the top three finalists in the 2020 HOK Futures Design Challenge. They were recognized at an award ceremony on February 18 in HOK's Philadelphia studio. "Thoroughfare Towers" by Eric Anderson (MArch'21) and Megan York (MArch'21) earned Second Place and "800 Market Street—A New Common Asset" by Matthew Alan Kohman (MArch'21) and Paul Germaine McCoy (MArch'21) earned Third Place. This is McCoy's second year placing in the competition. The challenge asked architecture students from seven Philadelphia-area universities to propose a new development along Market Street in Center City with multifamily housing, commercial, community, and retail space. In HOK's 2018 and 2019 competitions, Weitzman students were awarded all three of the finalist spots.

APR. NEWS

JAMES ANDREW BILLINGSLEY AWARDED SECOND PRIZE IN THE AVERY REVIEW'S ANNUAL ESSAY COMPETITION

James Andrew Billingsley (MArch'20, MLA'20) was awarded Second Prize in *The Avery Review*'s annual essay competition. *The Avery Review* is a monthly journal of critical essays on architecture published by Columbia University's Graduate School of Architecture, Planning and Preservation. Published in the April 2020 issue, Billingsley's essay, "An Arboretum at the End of an Epoch," explores an alternative portrait of Greenland that is layered, complex, diverse, and rogue. *The Review* recognizes the winning pieces as "evidence of a commitment to deepening our collective understanding of the objects of architectural thought, and we are proud to present them here." The essay stemmed from independent research Billingsley conducted in Greenland, which was funded by the Susan Cromwell Coslett Traveling Fellowship.Established in memory of former Assistant Dean, Susan Coslett, the fellowship is awarded to a School of Design student for summer travel to visit gardens and landscapes.

MARION WEISS AWARDED THOMAS JEFFERSON FOUNDATION MEDAL IN ARCHITECTURE

Graham Professor of Practice in Architecture Marion Weiss and Michael Manfredi of WEISS/MANFREDI have been awarded the 2020 Thomas Jefferson Foundation Medal in Architecture. It is the highest honor given by the University of Virginia and the Thomas Jefferson Foundation at Monticello.

"Marion Weiss and Michael Manfredi have been critically redefining the relationship between landscape, architecture and urbanism," said University of Virginia School of Architecture Dean Ila Berman.

"Their transformation of coastal brownfields in Seattle and New York has breathed new life back into these cities, while generating truly public spaces that support inclusiveness and social equity. Innovative, thoughtful and carefully crafted, their works are both powerful and beautiful—urban social condensers and light-filled landscapes that express the profound cultural significance and transformative potential of architecture."

Previous recipients include Ludwig Mies van der Rohe, I.M. Pei, Frank Gehry, Zaha Hadid, Toyo Ito, and Sir David Adjaye.

MAY. NEWS

MASOUD AKBARZADEH RECEIVED THE SILVER A' DESIGN AWARD IN FURNITURE, DECORATIVE ITEMS AND HOMEWARE DESIGN CATEGORY BY THE INTERNATIONAL DESIGN ACADEMY

Assistant Professor of Architecture Masoud Akbarzadeh received the Silver A' Design Award in Furniture, Decorative Items and Homeware Design Category by the International Design Academy. The A'Design Award and Competition attracts submissions from designers, innovators, and companies to showcase their work for media, publishers, and buyers.

In describing his submission, Saltatur Furniture, Akbarzadeh writes:
> The Saltator is a long-span structure, which is an ensemble of form, function, and aesthetics inspired by the ground-breaking works of Gaudi. The furniture extends Gaudi's designs and other conventional funicular forms, by exhibiting a unique balance of tension and compression forces in 3D space. The structure shows how to minimize the volume of construction materials and reduce the carbon footprint of a structure while preserving the necessary mass for structural performance. The Greco-Roman wrestling technique, Salto, has inspired the structural form.

The grand jury panel consisted of influential press members, established designers, leading academics, and prominent entrepreneurs worldwide.

SOPHIE HOCHHÄUSL, AN ASSISTANT PROFESSOR OF ARCHITECTURAL HISTORY AND THEORY IN THE DEPARTMENT OF ARCHITECTURE, RECEIVED A G. HOLMES PERKINS TEACHING AWARD FOR DISTINGUISHED UNDERGRADUATE TEACHING

The awards are given annually in honor of G. Holmes Perkins, an architect and longtime faculty member who was dean of the School of Design from 1951-1971, and based on nominations by students.

Hochhäusl's scholarly work centers on modern architecture and urban culture in Austria, Germany, and the United States, with a focus on the history of social movements, environmental history, and women's and gender studies. Her work has been published in Architectural Histories, Landscapes of Housing, and Reading the Architecture of the Underprivileged Classes and she is coauthor of the forthcoming volume Architecture, Environment, Territory: Essential Writings since 1850.

JULY. NEWS

FRANCA TRUBIANO NAMED SENIOR FELLOW AT PERRY WORLD HOUSE

Associate Professor of Architecture Franca Trubiano was named Senior Fellow at the University of Pennsylvania's Perry World House and awarded a Perry World House Penn Faculty Workshop Grant for her proposal "Forced Labor, Urban Migration, and the Built Environment: Global Policies for Eradicating Supply Chain Slavery in the Building Industry." The workshop, scheduled for Spring 2021, will convene an international panel of building industry researchers and global policy engagement experts working to address both challenges and opportunities associated with eradicating forced labor in the globalized supply chain of buildings. The project was also awarded a Humanities, Urbanism, and Design (H+U+D) Initiative grant where Franca is a HUD Fellow from 2018 to 2022.

SOPHIE HOCHHÄUSL APPOINTED PRINCETON MELLON FELLOW

Assistant Professor for Architectural History and Theory Sophie Hochhäusl was appointed the Princeton Mellon Fellow in Architecture, Urbanism, and the Humanities for the 2020-2021 academic year. She will also be a Visting Assistant Professor at Princeton's School of Architecture (SoA) in 2021. During the fellowship, Hochhäusl will be completing her book *Memories of the Resistance: Margarete Schütte-Lihotzky and the Architecture of Collective Dissidence, 1918-1989*. She is also working on a forthcoming monograph titled *Housing Cooperative: Politics, Architecture, and Urban Imagination in Vienna, 1904–1934*.

VIRTUAL COMMENCEMENT AND GRADUATION CELEBRATION

Dean Steiner invited graduates, their guests, and friends of the school to join him, the department chairs and program directors, and guest speakers James Corner (MLA'86) and Dr. Kellie Jones in celebrating the Weitzman Class of 2020 with a virtual webcast.

Immediately following, the Department of Architecture hosted a graduation celebration for students, faculty, and their guests. Award winners for graduating students were also announced. "If we are to truly recover from the pandemic, we need to think about our future with courage and vision as well as creativity and wisdom," said Dean Steiner. "As we move forward, the voices of Jim Corner and Kellie Jones will be more important than ever in our work."

The webcast included a preview of the Year End Show, an extensive online gallery featuring work by the Class of 2020. The webcast was recorded for those unable to watch live and students received a printed program commemorating their achievements by mail.

Like the University, the Weitzman School is also planning to host an on-campus celebration of the Class of 2020 in the 2020-2021 Academic Year.

DEPARTMENT OF ARCHITECTURE AWARD WINNERS

American Institute of Architects Henry Adams Medal
Perry Ashenfelter

Arthur Spayd Brooke Memorial Prize Gold Medal
Ryan Henriksen

Arthur Spayd Brooke Memorial Prize Silver Medal
Patrick Danahy

Paul Philippe Cret Medal
Katarina Marjanovic

Alpha Rho Chi Medal
Ryan Henriksen

Faculty Prize
Eliana Weiner

MSD-AAD Prize in Design Excellence
Hanning Liu
Yihao Zhang